lolololol

So Cute It Hurts!!

(>_<)

Story and Art by
Go Ikeyamada

1

So Cute It Hurts!! ····· 2
So Cute! X Suzuki-kun:
The Miraculous Collab
Manga!!! ·········· 182
Glossary ·········· 190

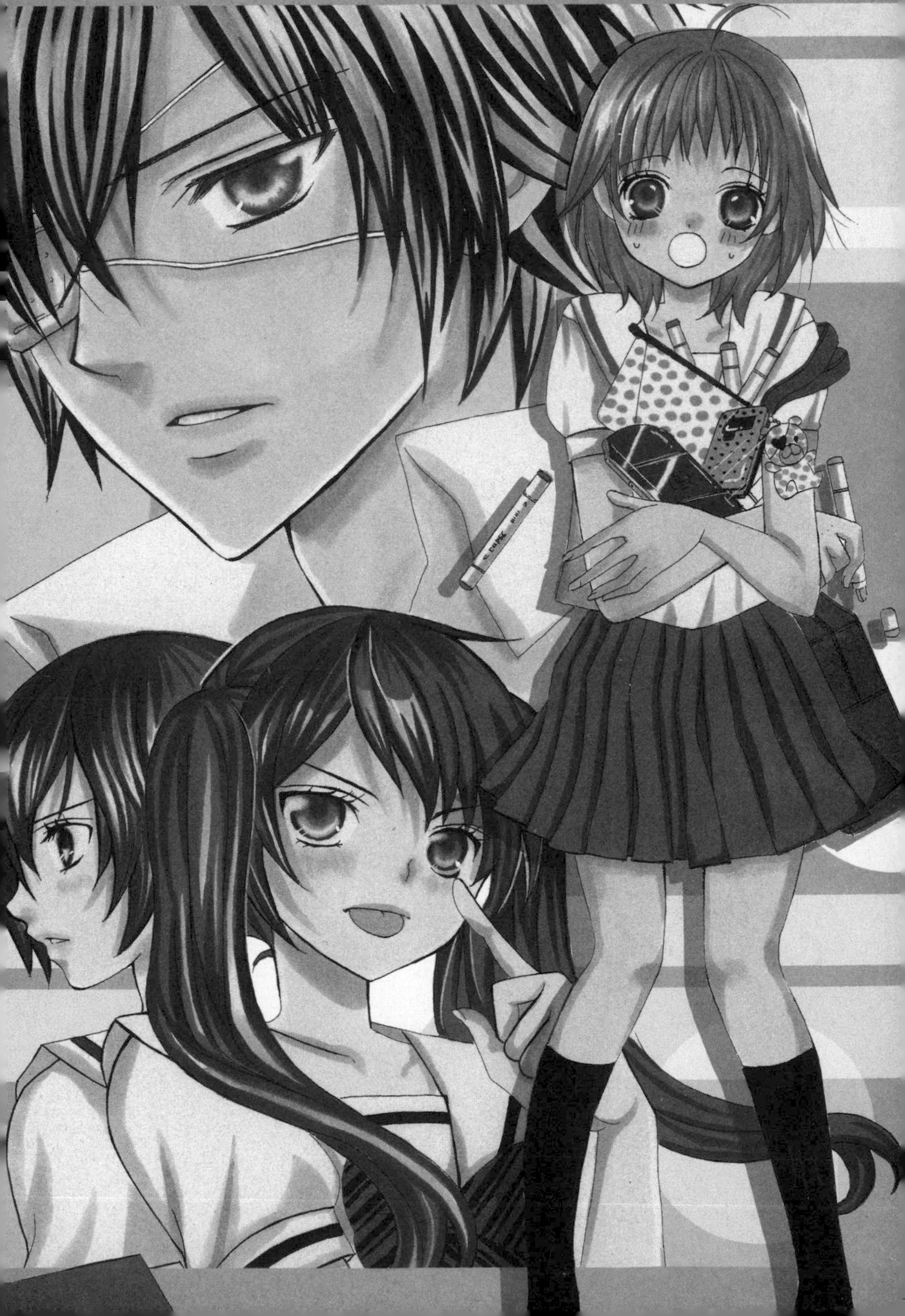

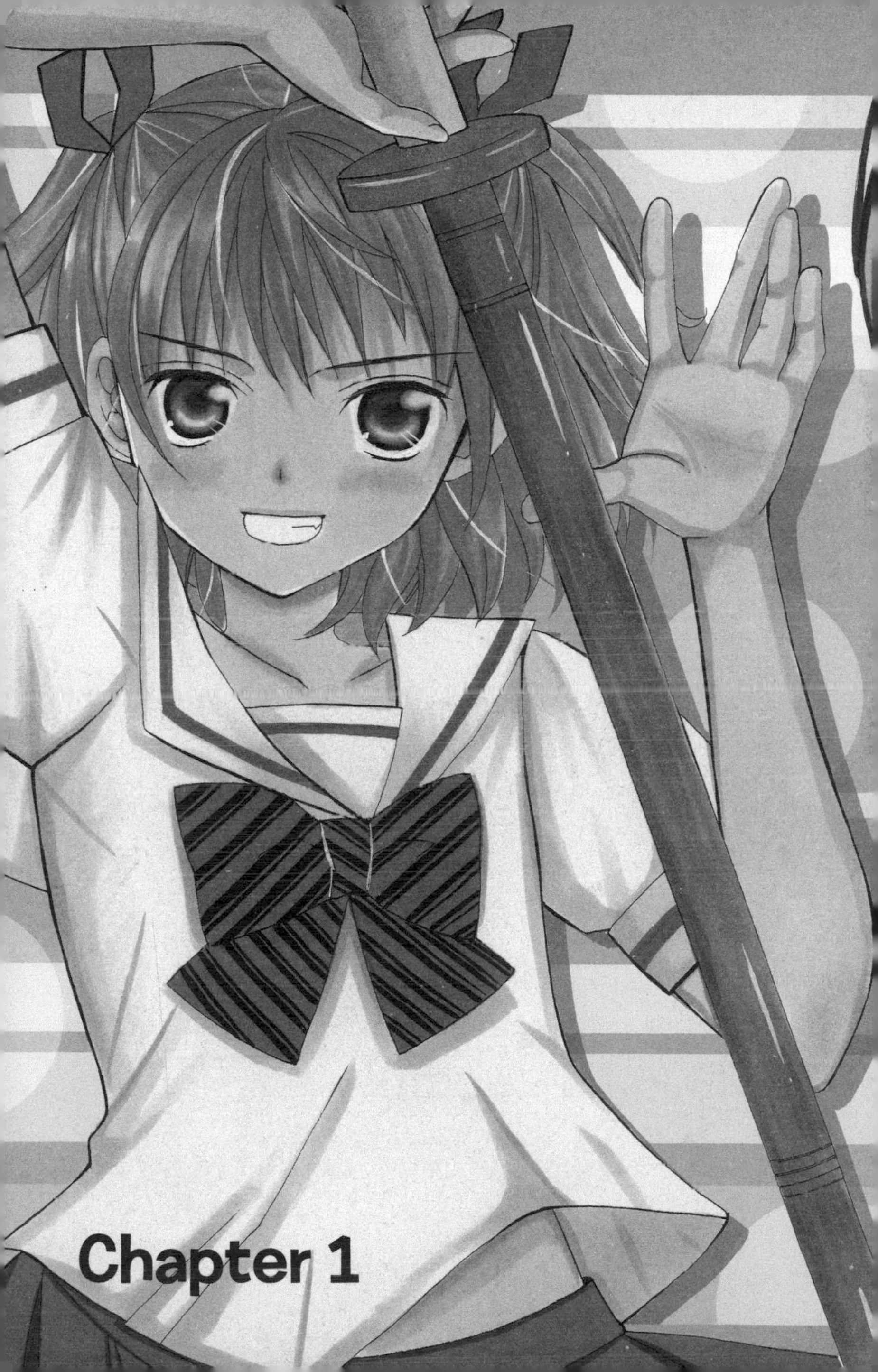
Chapter 1

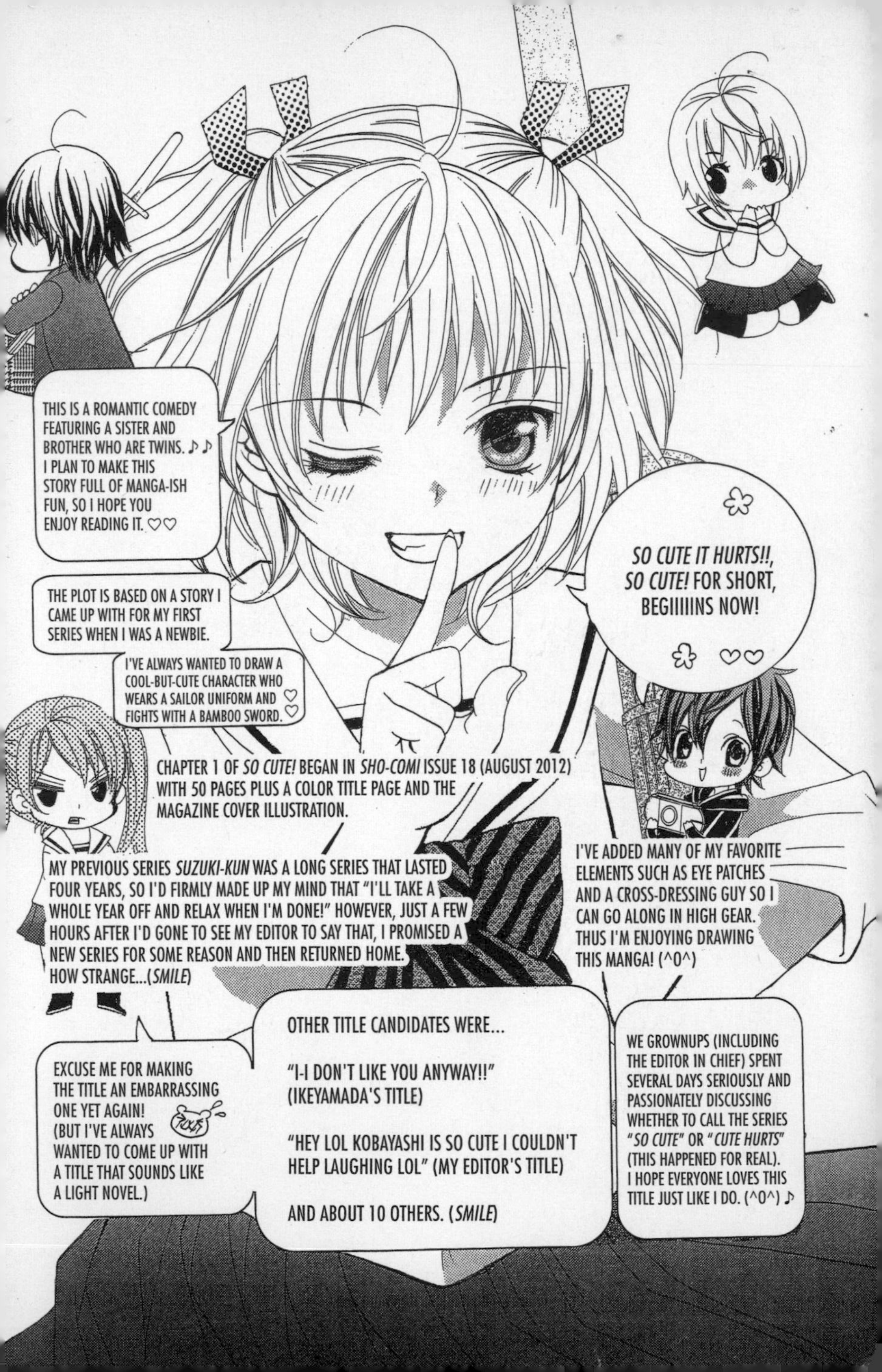
SO CUTE IT HURTS!!, *SO CUTE!* FOR SHORT, BEGIIIIINS NOW!
THIS IS A ROMANTIC COMEDY FEATURING A SISTER AND BROTHER WHO ARE TWINS. ♪♪ I PLAN TO MAKE THIS STORY FULL OF MANGA-ISH FUN, SO I HOPE YOU ENJOY READING IT. ♡♡
THE PLOT IS BASED ON A STORY I CAME UP WITH FOR MY FIRST SERIES WHEN I WAS A NEWBIE.
I'VE ALWAYS WANTED TO DRAW A COOL-BUT-CUTE CHARACTER WHO WEARS A SAILOR UNIFORM AND FIGHTS WITH A BAMBOO SWORD. ♡♡
CHAPTER 1 OF *SO CUTE!* BEGAN IN *SHO-COMI* ISSUE 18 (AUGUST 2012) WITH 50 PAGES PLUS A COLOR TITLE PAGE AND THE MAGAZINE COVER ILLUSTRATION.
I'VE ADDED MANY OF MY FAVORITE ELEMENTS SUCH AS EYE PATCHES AND A CROSS-DRESSING GUY SO I CAN GO ALONG IN HIGH GEAR. THUS I'M ENJOYING DRAWING THIS MANGA! (^0^)
MY PREVIOUS SERIES *SUZUKI-KUN* WAS A LONG SERIES THAT LASTED FOUR YEARS, SO I'D FIRMLY MADE UP MY MIND THAT "I'LL TAKE A WHOLE YEAR OFF AND RELAX WHEN I'M DONE!" HOWEVER, JUST A FEW HOURS AFTER I'D GONE TO SEE MY EDITOR TO SAY THAT, I PROMISED A NEW SERIES FOR SOME REASON AND THEN RETURNED HOME. HOW STRANGE...(*SMILE*)
WE GROWNUPS (INCLUDING THE EDITOR IN CHIEF) SPENT SEVERAL DAYS SERIOUSLY AND PASSIONATELY DISCUSSING WHETHER TO CALL THE SERIES "*SO CUTE*" OR "*CUTE HURTS*" (THIS HAPPENED FOR REAL). I HOPE EVERYONE LOVES THIS TITLE JUST LIKE I DO. (^0^) ♪
OTHER TITLE CANDIDATES WERE... "I-I DON'T LIKE YOU ANYWAY!!" (IKEYAMADA'S TITLE) "HEY LOL KOBAYASHI IS SO CUTE I COULDN'T HELP LAUGHING LOL" (MY EDITOR'S TITLE) AND ABOUT 10 OTHERS. (*SMILE*)
EXCUSE ME FOR MAKING THE TITLE AN EMBARRASSING ONE YET AGAIN! (BUT I'VE ALWAYS WANTED TO COME UP WITH A TITLE THAT SOUNDS LIKE A LIGHT NOVEL.)

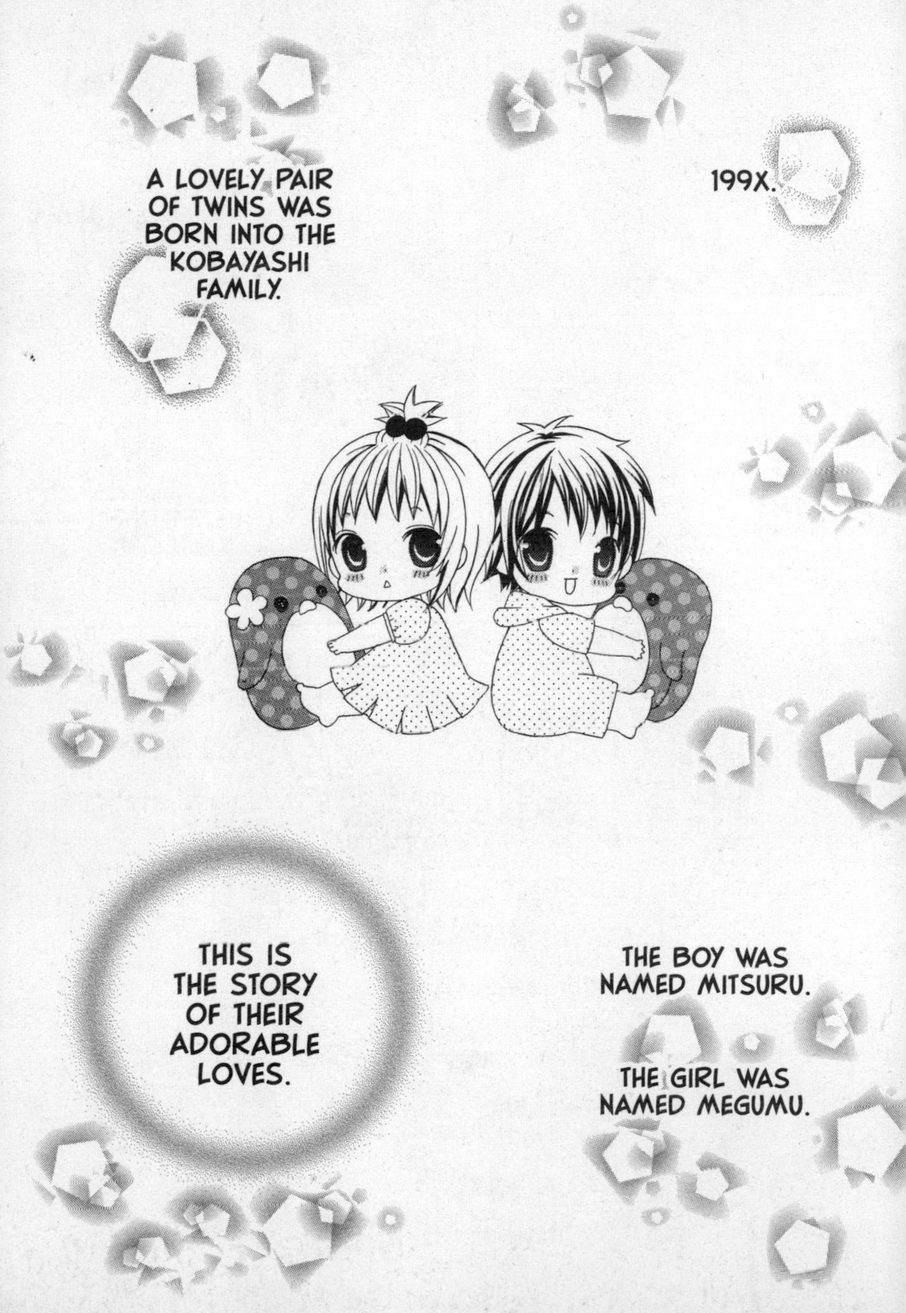
199X.
A LOVELY PAIR OF TWINS WAS BORN INTO THE KOBAYASHI FAMILY.
THE BOY WAS NAMED MITSURU.
THE GIRL WAS NAMED MEGUMU.
THIS IS THE STORY OF THEIR ADORABLE LOVES.

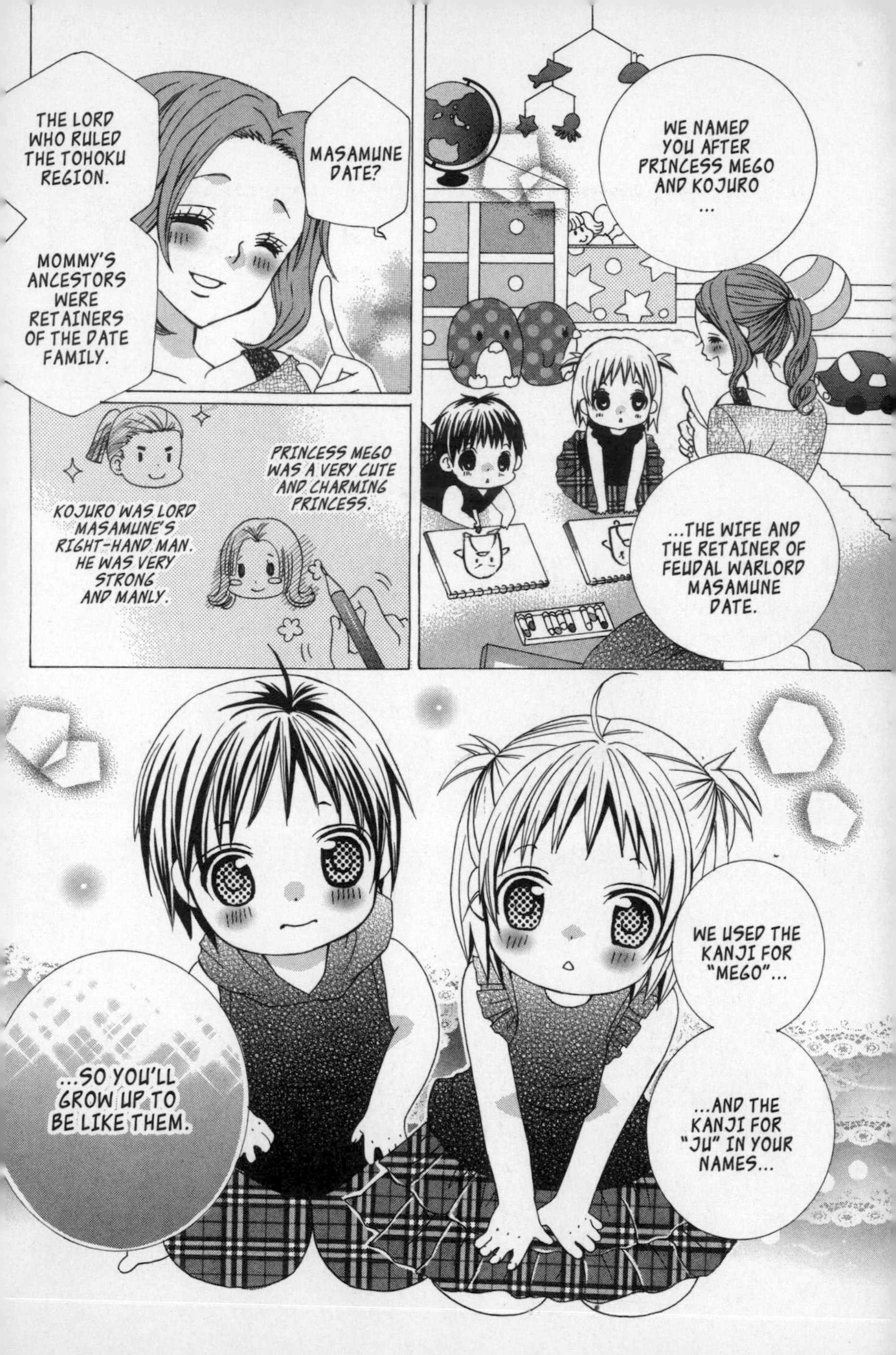
WE NAMED YOU AFTER PRINCESS MEGO AND KOJURO ...
...THE WIFE AND THE RETAINER OF FEUDAL WARLORD MASAMUNE DATE.
MASAMUNE DATE?
THE LORD WHO RULED THE TOHOKU REGION.
MOMMY'S ANCESTORS WERE RETAINERS OF THE DATE FAMILY.
PRINCESS MEGO WAS A VERY CUTE AND CHARMING PRINCESS.
KOJURO WAS LORD MASAMUNE'S RIGHT-HAND MAN. HE WAS VERY STRONG AND MANLY.
WE USED THE KANJI FOR "MEGO"...
...AND THE KANJI FOR "JU" IN YOUR NAMES...
...SO YOU'LL GROW UP TO BE LIKE THEM.

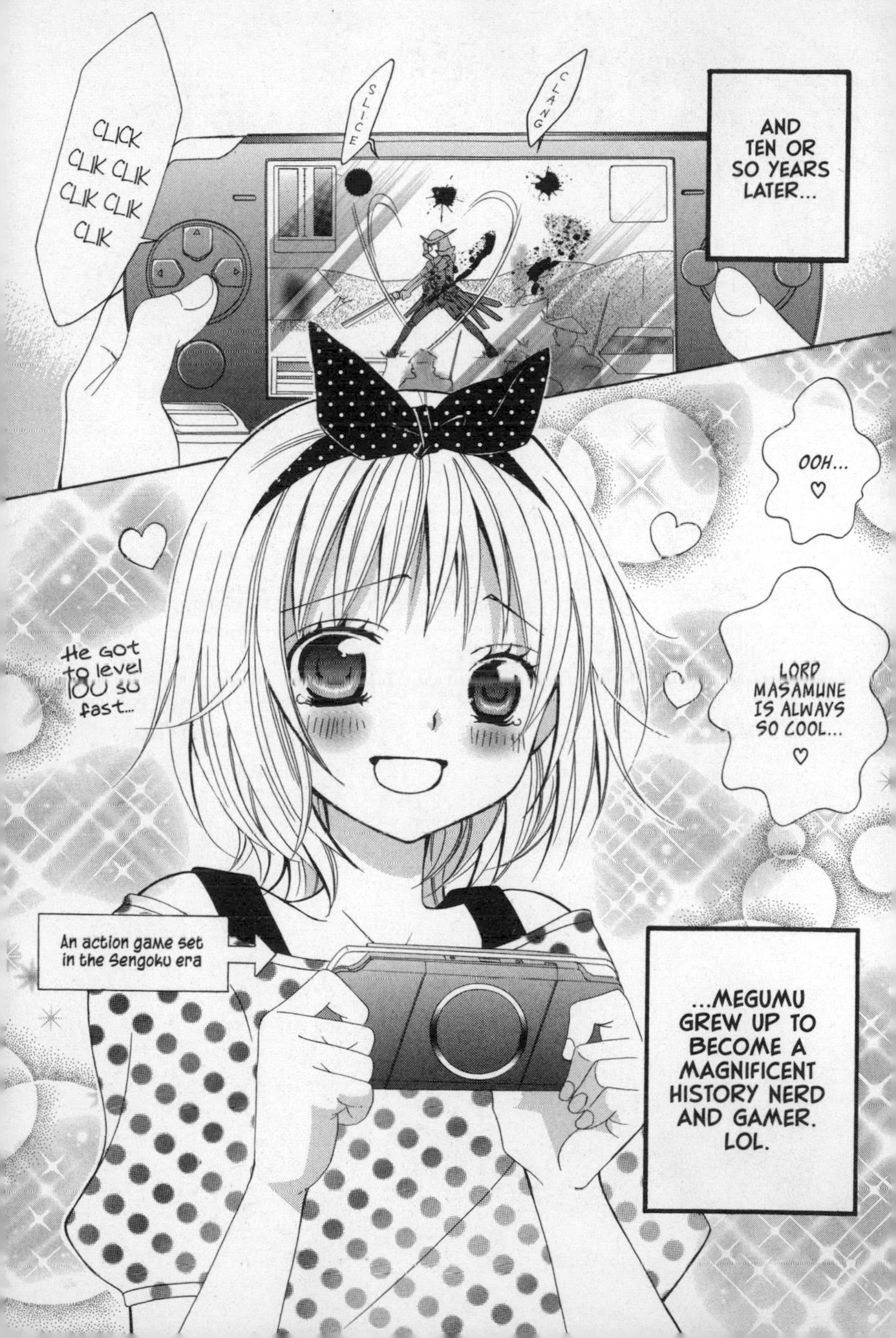
AND TEN OR SO YEARS LATER...
CLANG
SLICE
CLICK CLIK CLIK CLIK CLIK CLIK
OOH...
LORD MASAMUNE IS ALWAYS SO COOL...
He got to level 100 so fast...
...MEGUMU GREW UP TO BECOME A MAGNIFICENT HISTORY NERD AND GAMER. LOL.
An action game set in the Sengoku era

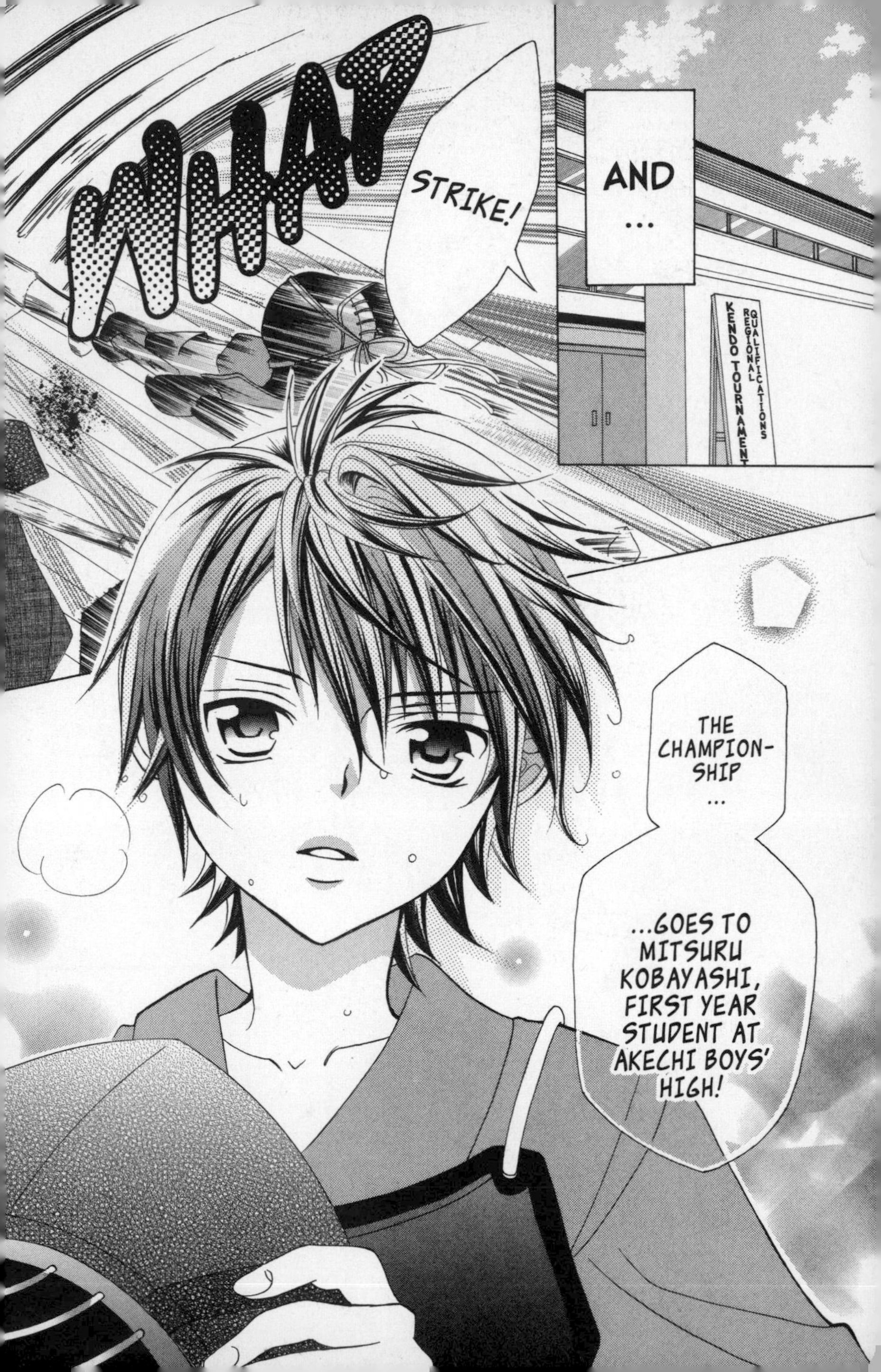
AND ...
KENDO TOURNAMENT
REGIONAL QUALIFICATIONS
STRIKE!
WHAP
THE CHAMPIONSHIP ...
...GOES TO MITSURU KOBAYASHI, FIRST YEAR STUDENT AT AKECHI BOYS' HIGH!

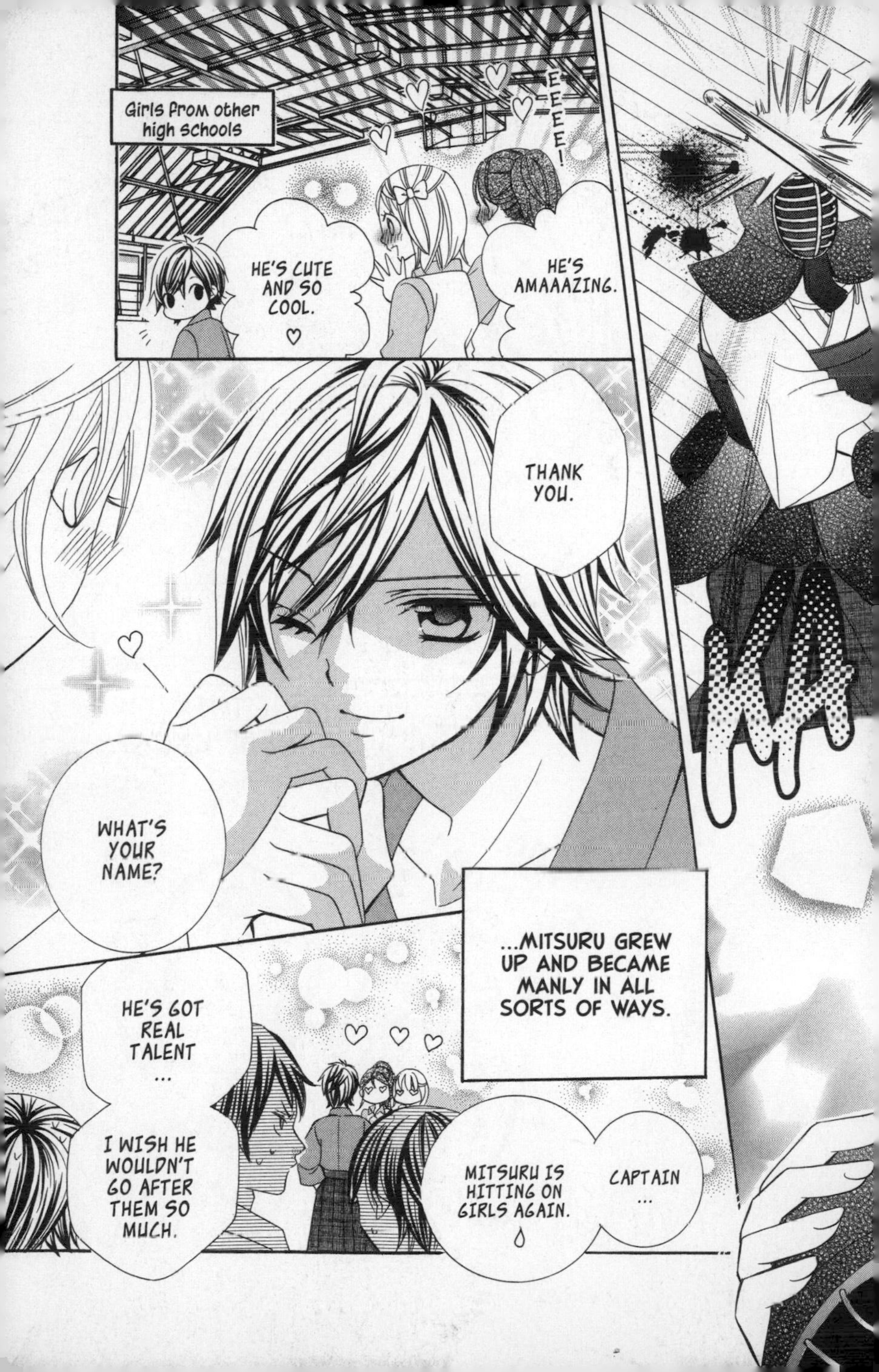
EEEEE!
Girls from other high schools
HE'S AMAAAZING.
HE'S CUTE AND SO COOL.
THANK YOU.
WHAT'S YOUR NAME?
...MITSURU GREW UP AND BECAME MANLY IN ALL SORTS OF WAYS.
CAPTAIN ...
MITSURU IS HITTING ON GIRLS AGAIN.
HE'S GOT REAL TALENT ...
I WISH HE WOULDN'T GO AFTER THEM SO MUCH.

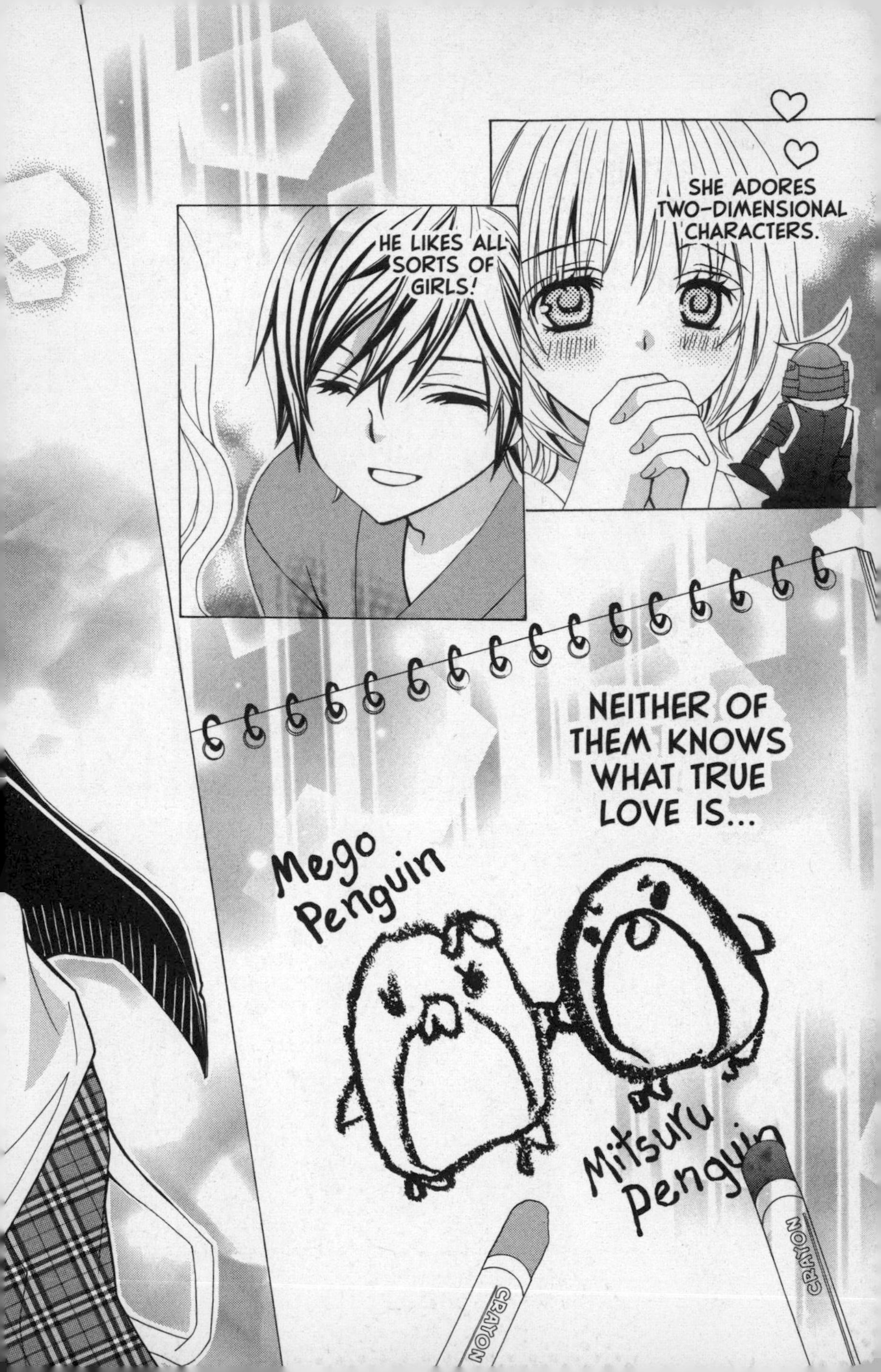
SHE ADORES TWO-DIMENSIONAL CHARACTERS.
HE LIKES ALL SORTS OF GIRLS!
NEITHER OF THEM KNOWS WHAT TRUE LOVE IS...
Mego Penguin
Mitsuru Penguin
CRAYON
CRAYON

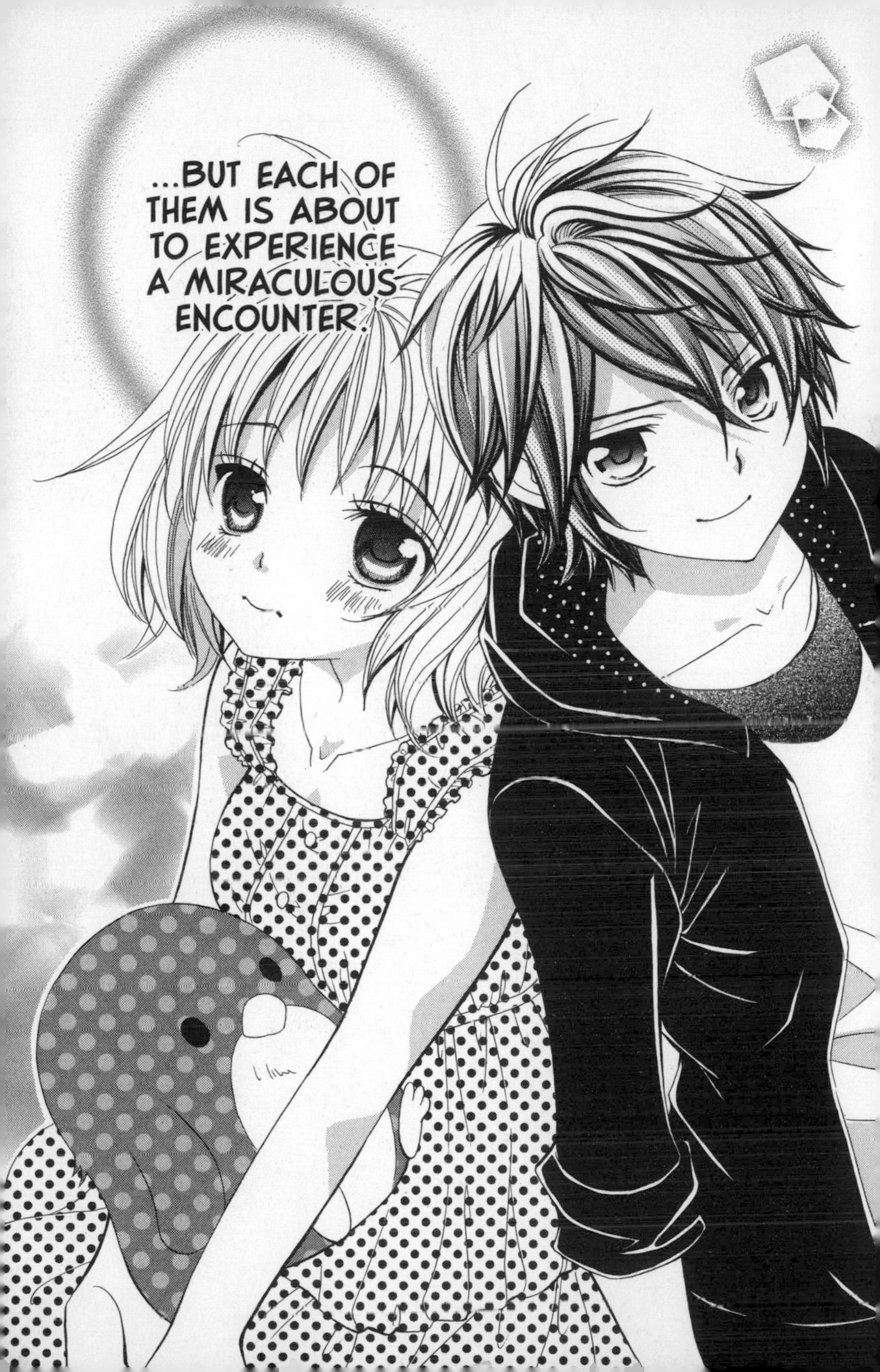
...BUT EACH OF THEM IS ABOUT TO EXPERIENCE A MIRACULOUS ENCOUNTER.

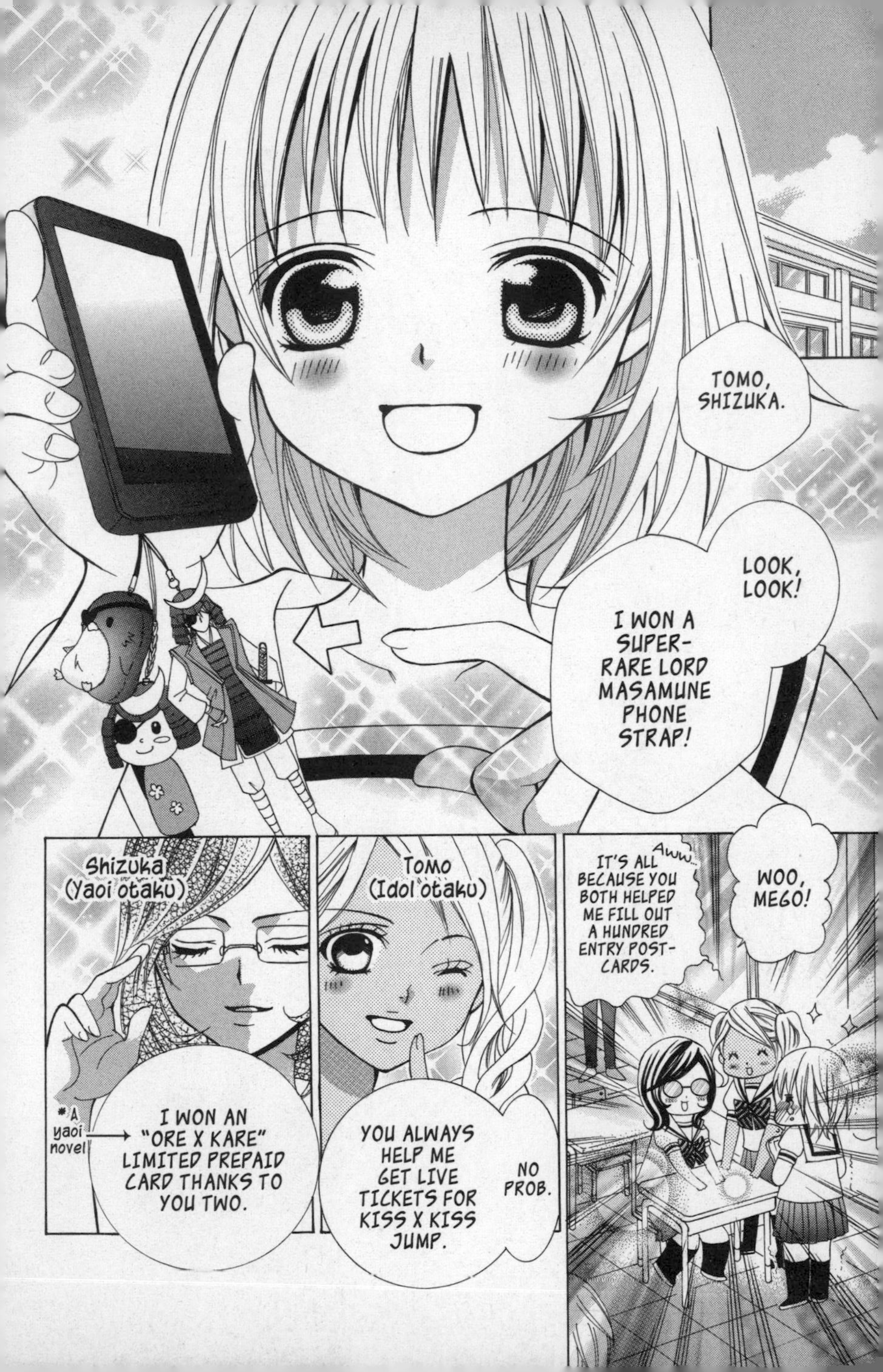
TOMO, SHIZUKA.
LOOK, LOOK!
I WON A SUPER-RARE LORD MASAMUNE PHONE STRAP!
WOO, MEGO!
Aww...
IT'S ALL BECAUSE YOU BOTH HELPED ME FILL OUT A HUNDRED ENTRY POST-CARDS.
Tomo (Idol otaku)
YOU ALWAYS HELP ME GET LIVE TICKETS FOR KISS X KISS JUMP.
NO PROB.
Shizuka (Yaoi otaku)
I WON AN "ORE X KARE" LIMITED PREPAID CARD THANKS TO YOU TWO.
* A yaoi novel

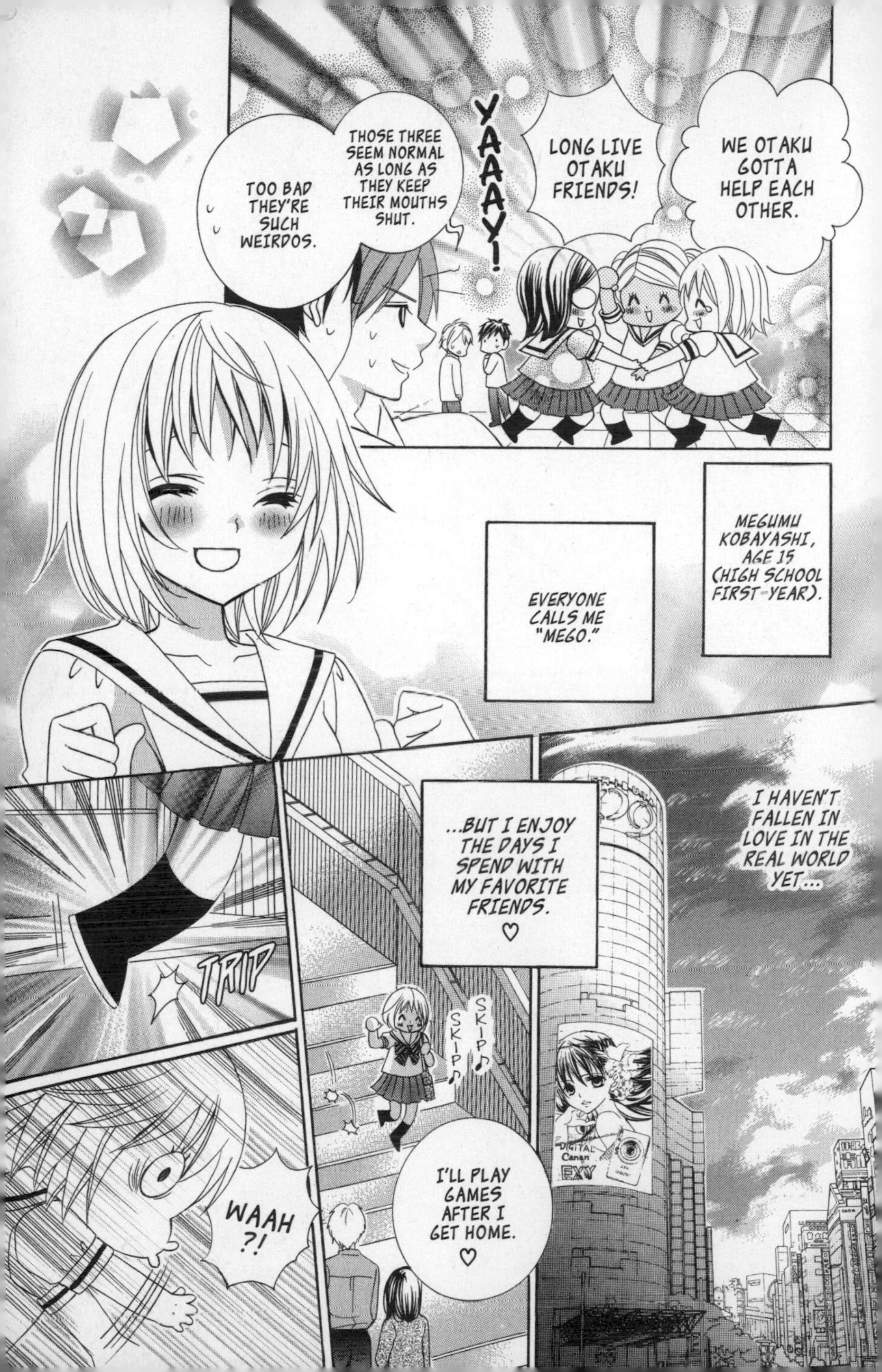
WE OTAKU GOTTA HELP EACH OTHER.
LONG LIVE OTAKU FRIENDS!
YAAAY!
THOSE THREE SEEM NORMAL AS LONG AS THEY KEEP THEIR MOUTHS SHUT.
TOO BAD THEY'RE SUCH WEIRDOS.
MEGUMU KOBAYASHI, AGE 15 (HIGH SCHOOL FIRST-YEAR).
EVERYONE CALLS ME "MEGO."
I HAVEN'T FALLEN IN LOVE IN THE REAL WORLD YET...
DIGITAL Canan
EXY
...BUT I ENJOY THE DAYS I SPEND WITH MY FAVORITE FRIENDS. ♡
SKIP SKIP♪
I'LL PLAY GAMES AFTER I GET HOME. ♡
TRIP
WAAH ?!

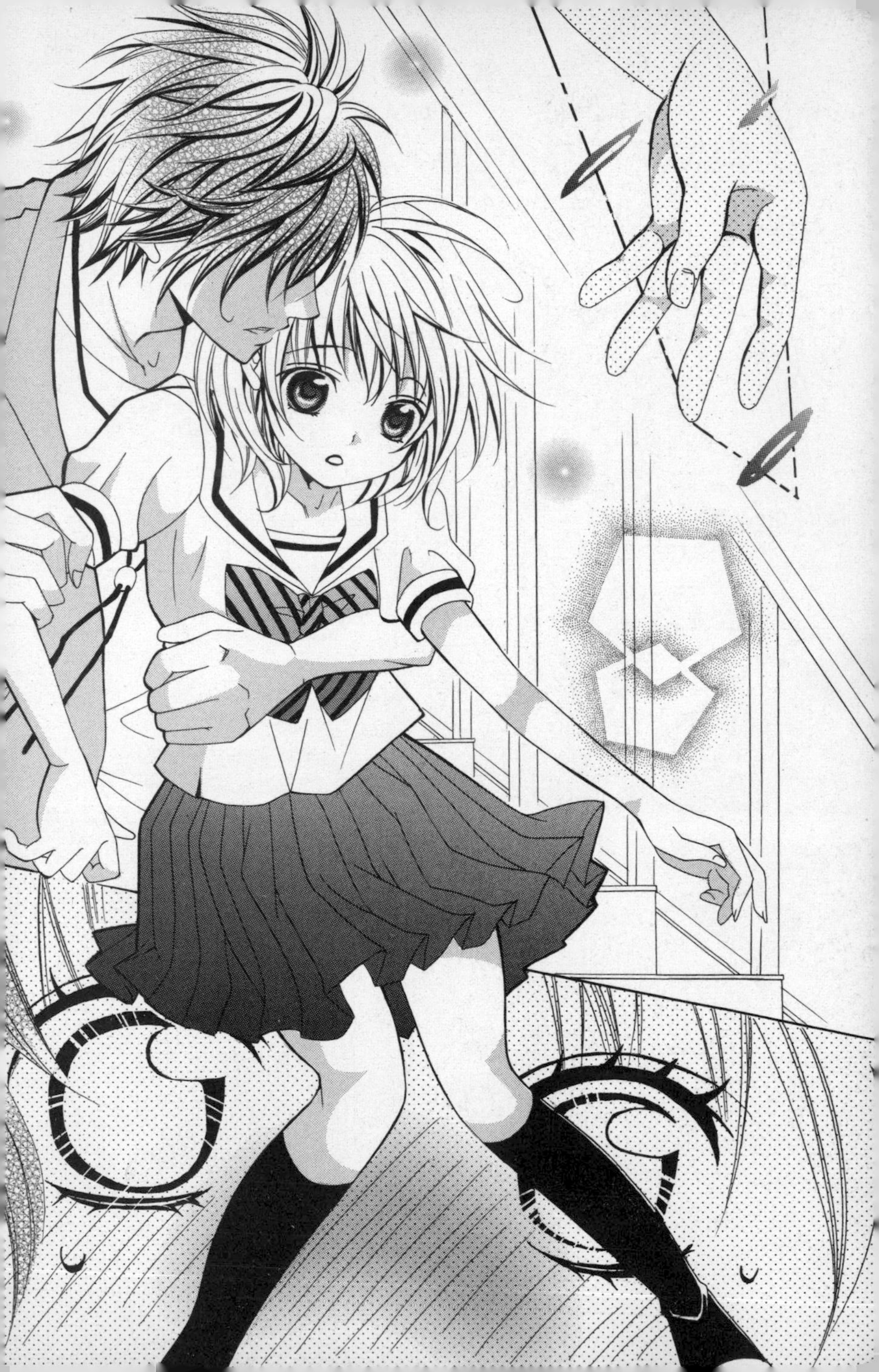

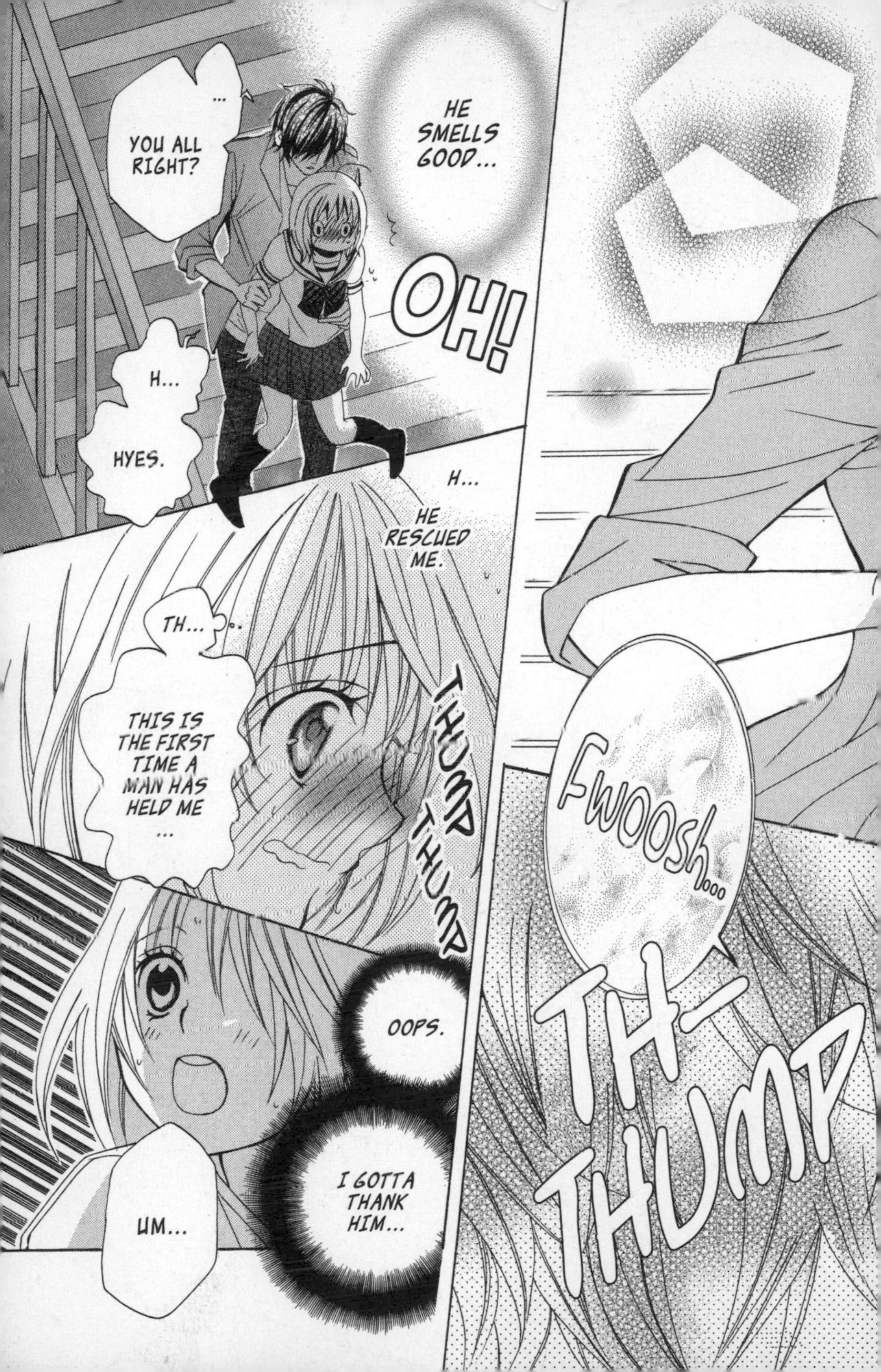
Fwoosh...
TH-THUMP
HE SMELLS GOOD...
OH!
... YOU ALL RIGHT?
H... HYES.
H... HE RESCUED ME.
THUMP THUMP
TH...
THIS IS THE FIRST TIME A MAN HAS HELD ME ...
OOPS.
I GOTTA THANK HIM...
UM...

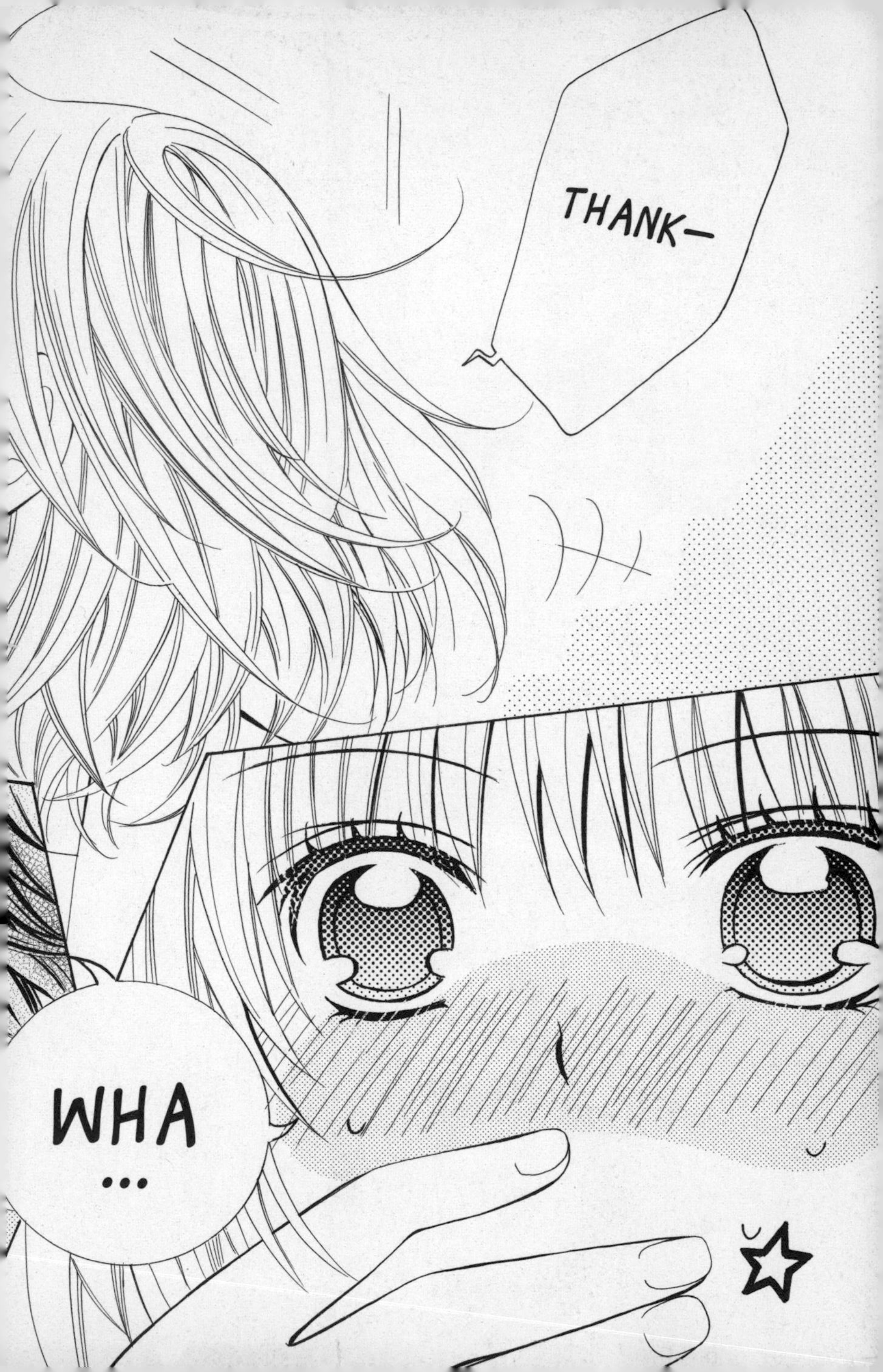
THANK—
WHA
...

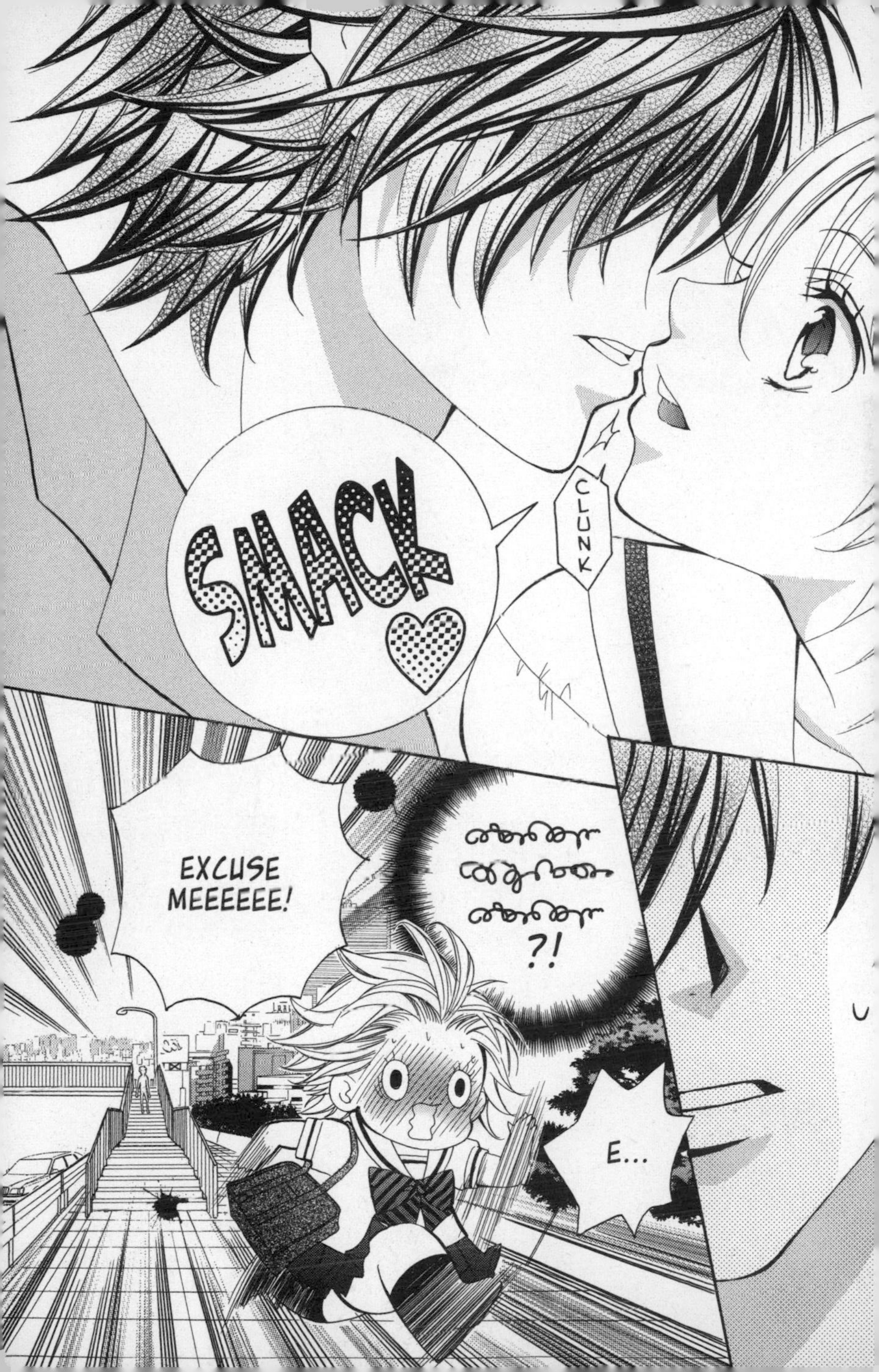
CLUNK
SMACK ♥
U
E...
?!
EXCUSE MEEEEEEE!

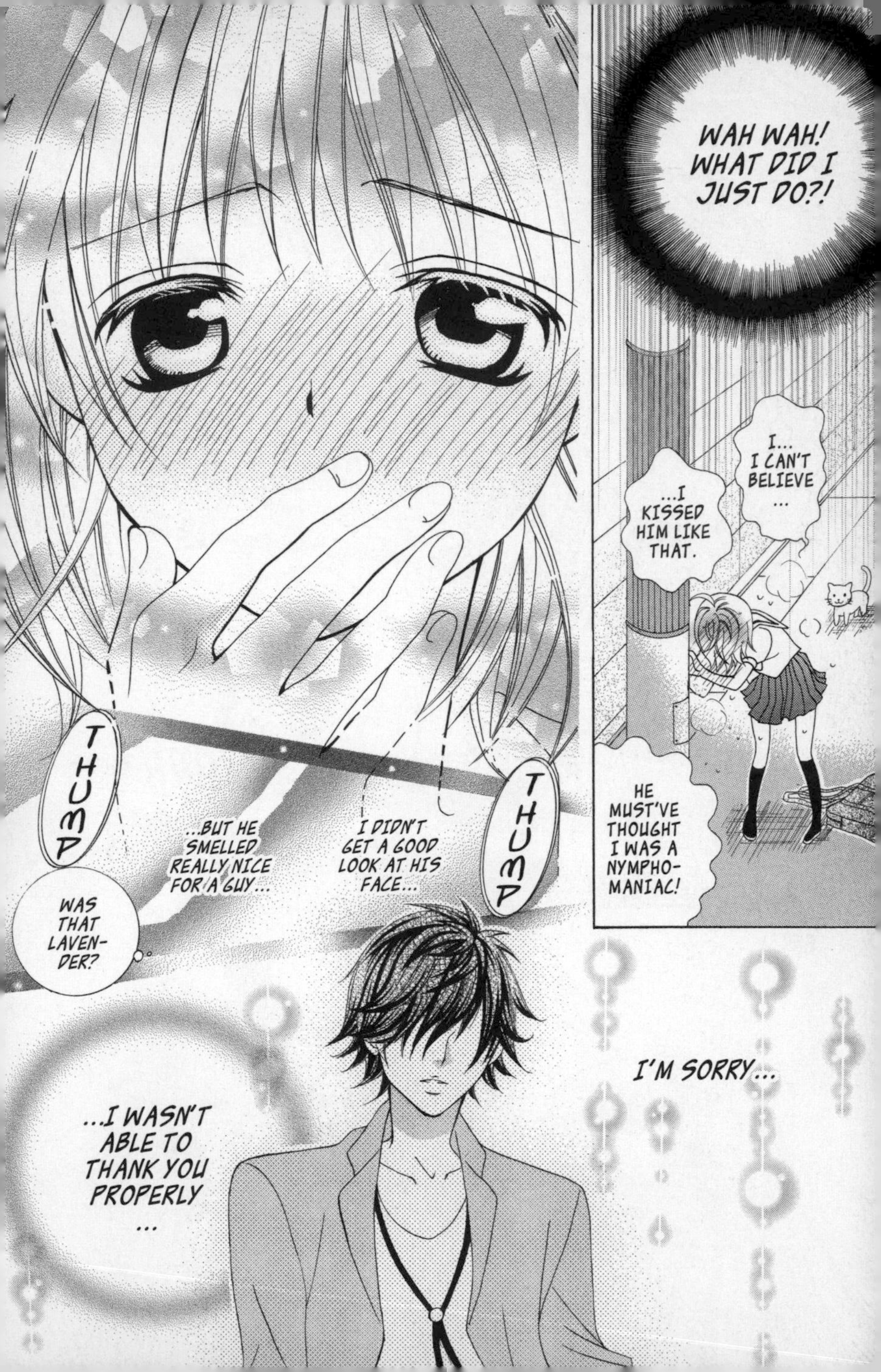
WAH WAH! WHAT DID I JUST DO?!
I... I CAN'T BELIEVE...
...I KISSED HIM LIKE THAT.
HE MUST'VE THOUGHT I WAS A NYMPHO-MANIAC!
THUMP
I DIDN'T GET A GOOD LOOK AT HIS FACE...
...BUT HE SMELLED REALLY NICE FOR A GUY...
THUMP
WAS THAT LAVEN-DER?
I'M SORRY...
...I WASN'T ABLE TO THANK YOU PROPERLY...

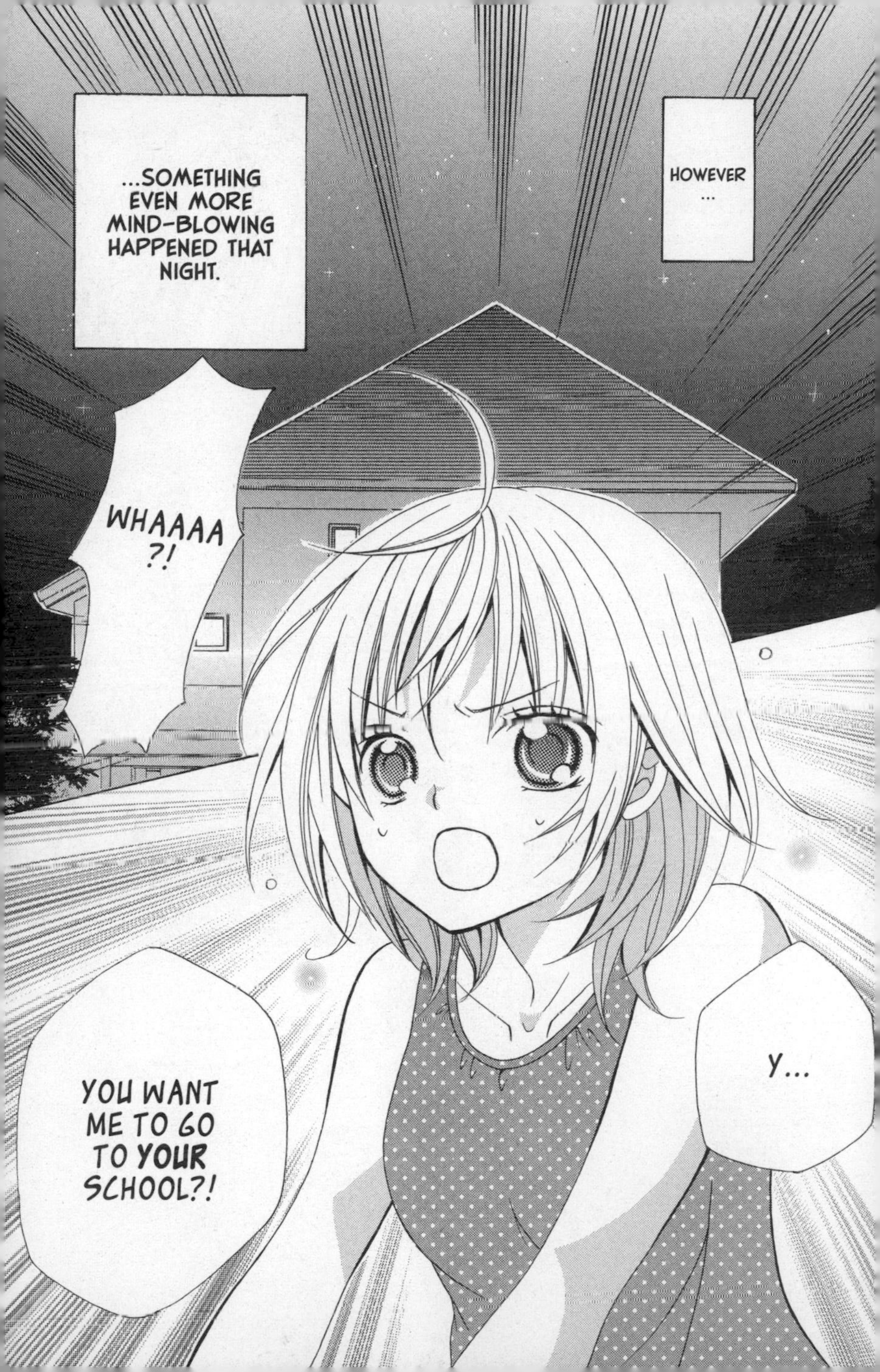
HOWEVER ...
...SOMETHING EVEN MORE MIND-BLOWING HAPPENED THAT NIGHT.
WHAAAA ?!
Y...
YOU WANT ME TO GO TO **YOUR** SCHOOL?!

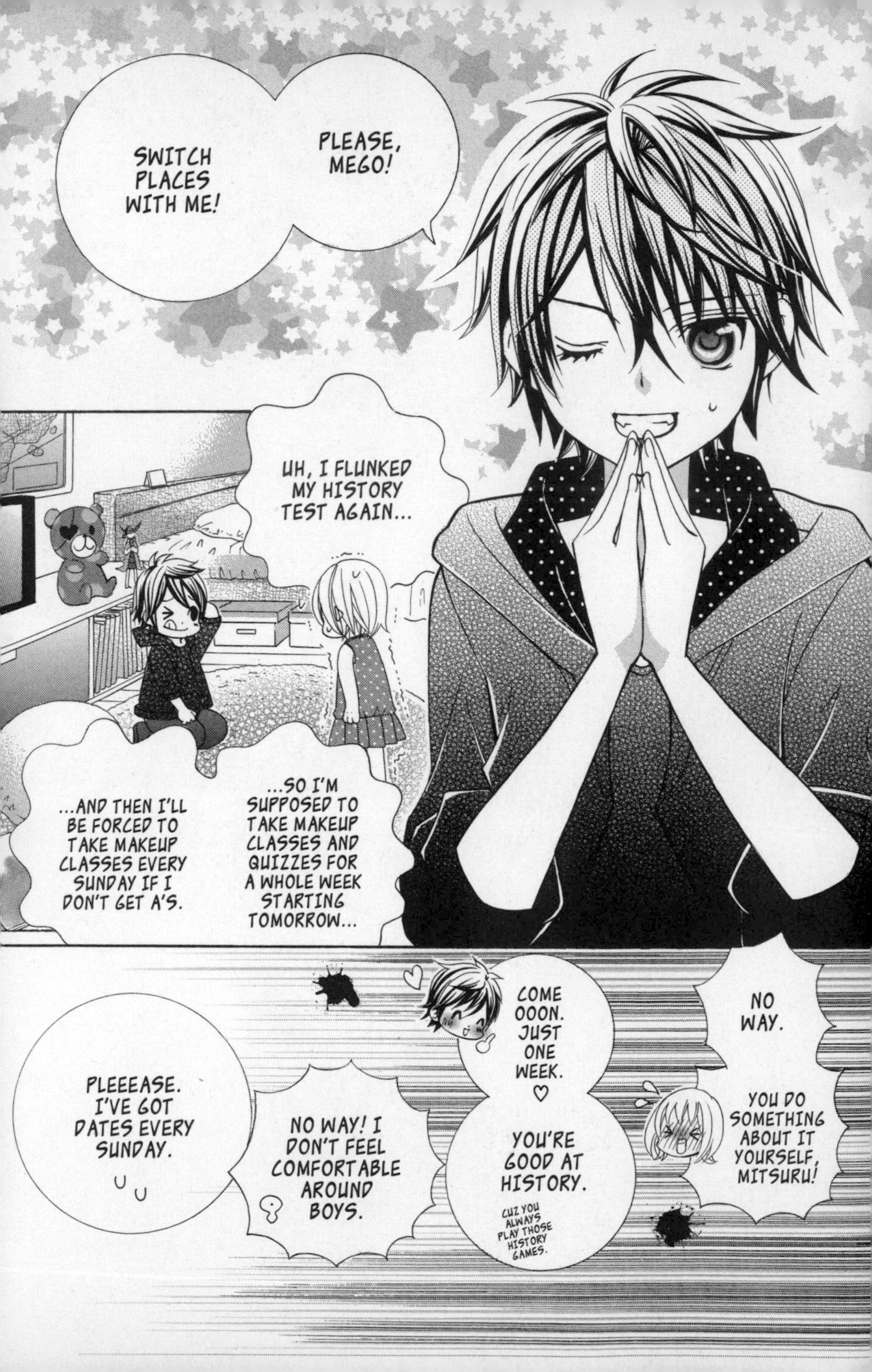
PLEASE, MEGO!
SWITCH PLACES WITH ME!
UH, I FLUNKED MY HISTORY TEST AGAIN...
...SO I'M SUPPOSED TO TAKE MAKEUP CLASSES AND QUIZZES FOR A WHOLE WEEK STARTING TOMORROW...
...AND THEN I'LL BE FORCED TO TAKE MAKEUP CLASSES EVERY SUNDAY IF I DON'T GET A'S.
NO WAY.
YOU DO SOMETHING ABOUT IT YOURSELF, MITSURU!
COME OOON. JUST ONE WEEK. ♡
YOU'RE GOOD AT HISTORY.
CUZ YOU ALWAYS PLAY THOSE HISTORY GAMES.
NO WAY! I DON'T FEEL COMFORTABLE AROUND BOYS.
PLEEEASE. I'VE GOT DATES EVERY SUNDAY.

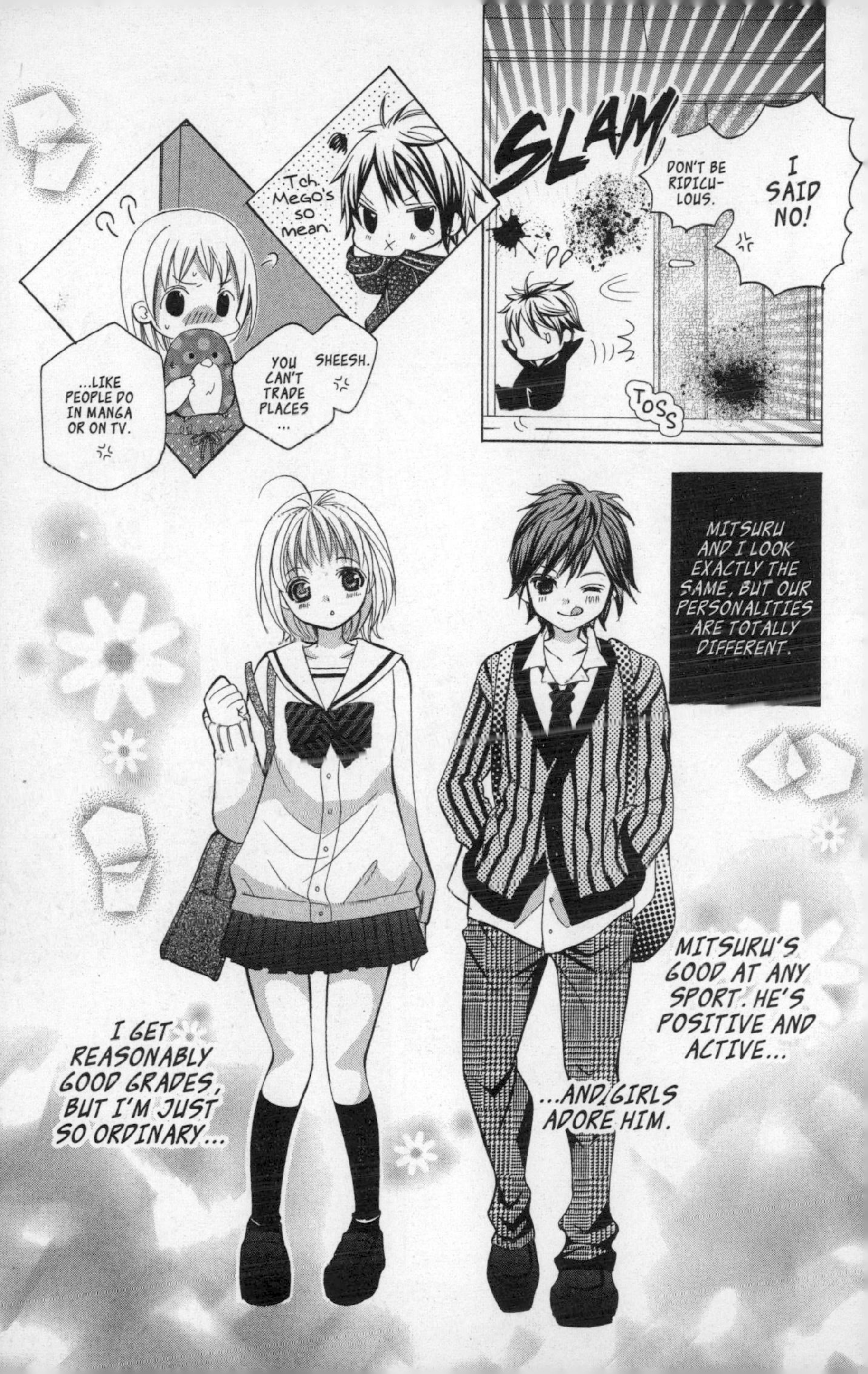
I SAID NO!
DON'T BE RIDICULOUS.
SLAM
TOSS
Tch. Mego's so mean.
SHEESH.
YOU CAN'T TRADE PLACES...
...LIKE PEOPLE DO IN MANGA OR ON TV.
MITSURU AND I LOOK EXACTLY THE SAME, BUT OUR PERSONALITIES ARE TOTALLY DIFFERENT.
MITSURU'S GOOD AT ANY SPORT. HE'S POSITIVE AND ACTIVE...
...AND GIRLS ADORE HIM.
I GET REASONABLY GOOD GRADES, BUT I'M JUST SO ORDINARY...

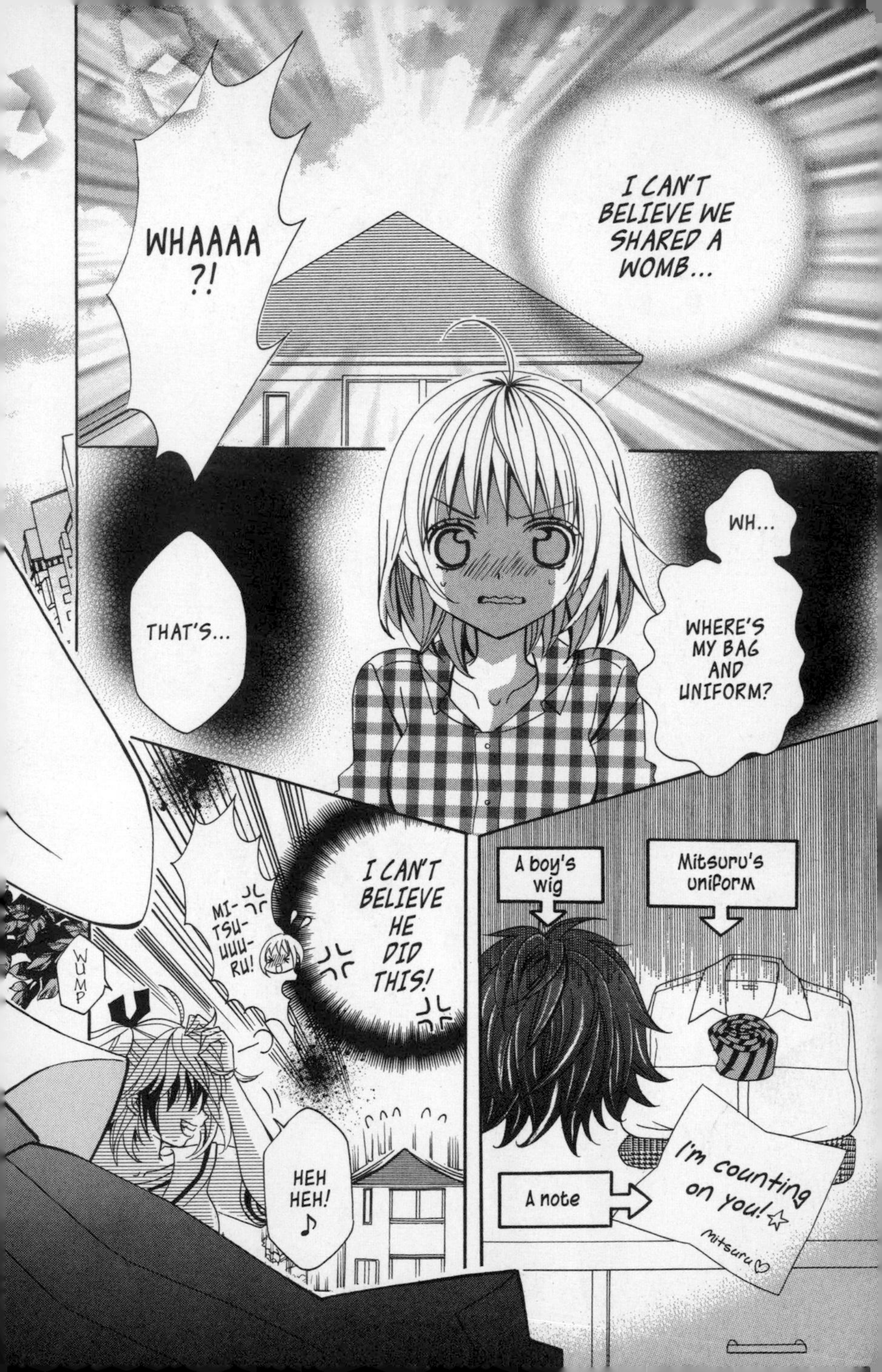

I CAN'T BELIEVE WE SHARED A WOMB...
WHAAAA ?!
WH...
WHERE'S MY BAG AND UNIFORM?
THAT'S...
Mitsuru's uniform
A boy's wig
A note
I'm counting on you! ☆
Mitsuru ♡
I CAN'T BELIEVE HE DID THIS!
MI-TSU-UUU-RU!
WUMP
HEH HEH! ♪

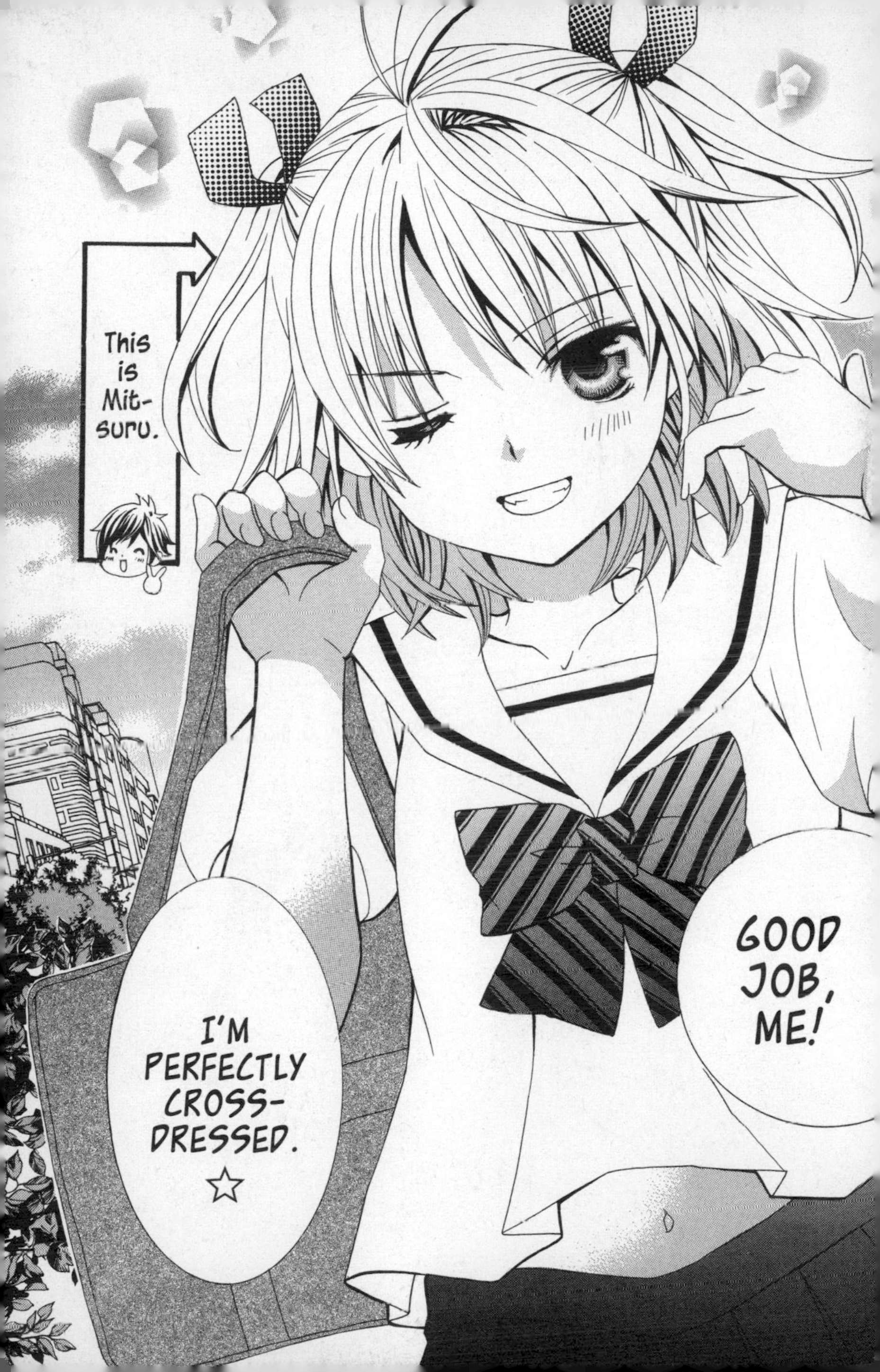
This is Mitsuru.
GOOD JOB, ME!
I'M PERFECTLY CROSS-DRESSED. ☆

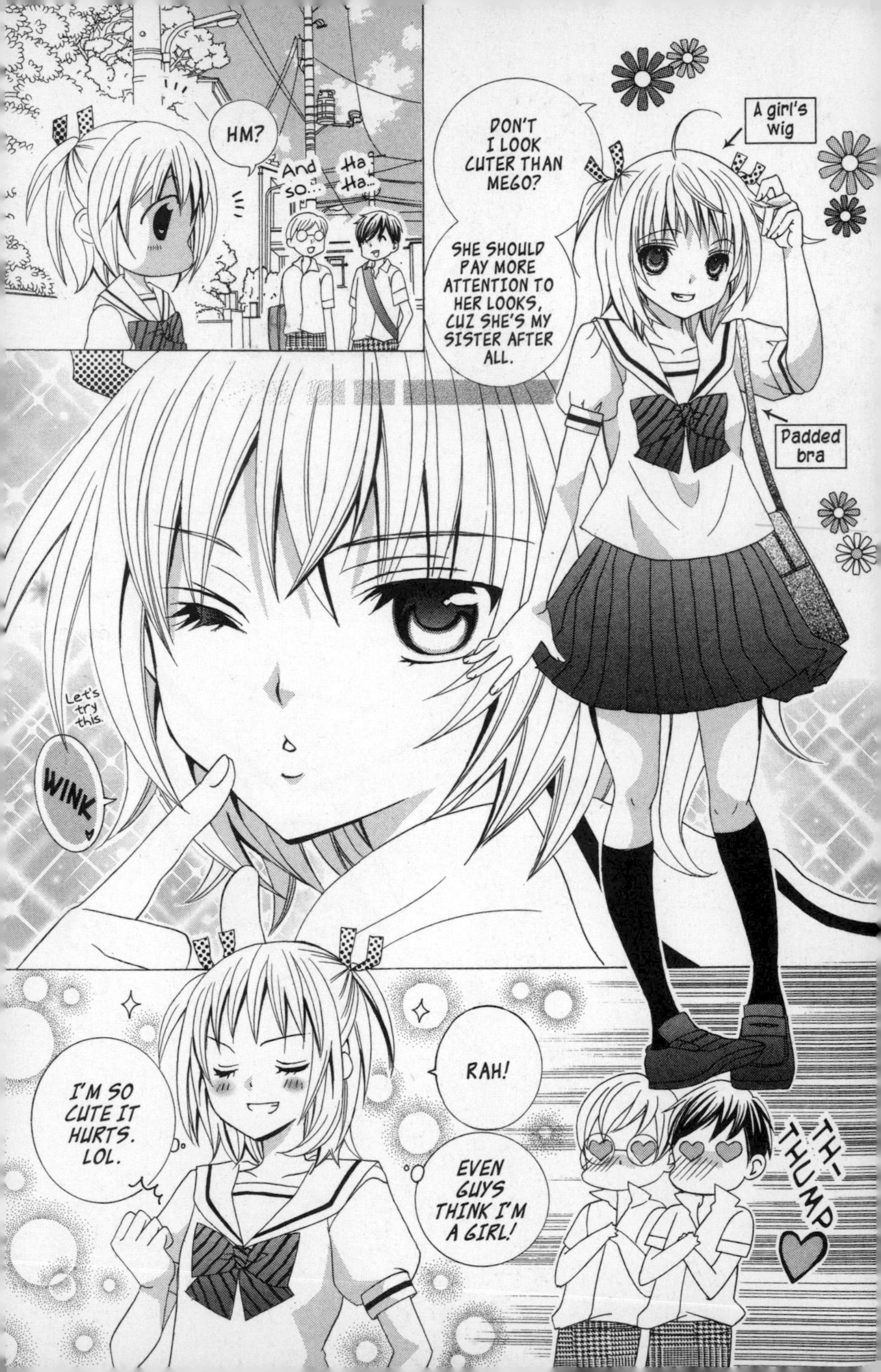
DON'T I LOOK CUTER THAN MEGO?
SHE SHOULD PAY MORE ATTENTION TO HER LOOKS, CUZ SHE'S MY SISTER AFTER ALL.
A girl's wig
Padded bra
HM?
Ha Ha...
And so...
Let's try this.
WINK
TH-THUMP
RAH!
EVEN GUYS THINK I'M A GIRL!
I'M SO CUTE IT HURTS. LOL.

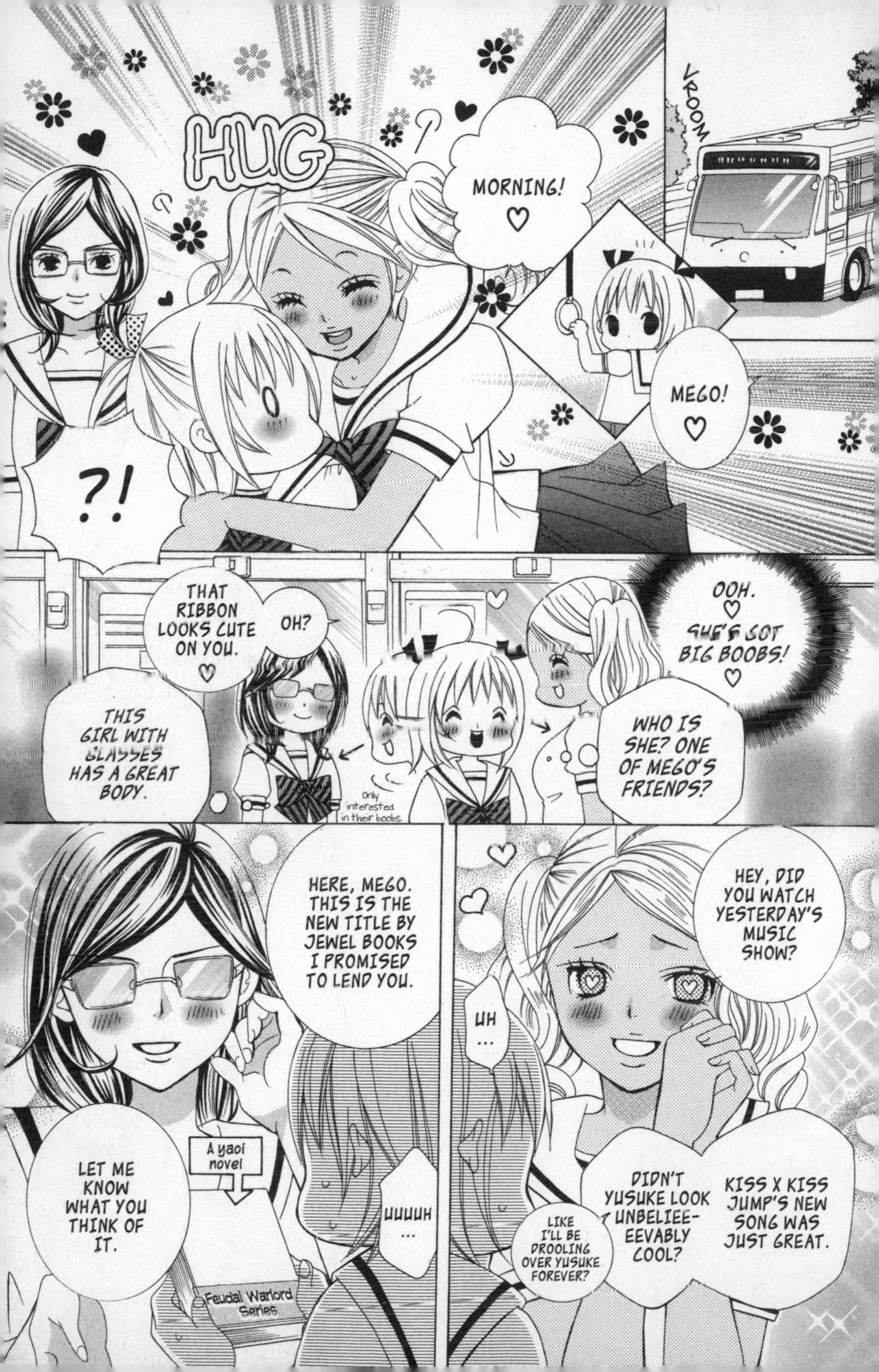
VROOM
MEGO! ♡
MORNING! ♡
HUG
?!
OOH. ♡ SHE'S GOT BIG BOOBS! ♡
WHO IS SHE? ONE OF MEGO'S FRIENDS?
OH?
THAT RIBBON LOOKS CUTE ON YOU. ♡
THIS GIRL WITH GLASSES HAS A GREAT BODY.
Only interested in their boobs.
HEY, DID YOU WATCH YESTERDAY'S MUSIC SHOW?
UH ...
KISS X KISS JUMP'S NEW SONG WAS JUST GREAT.
DIDN'T YUSUKE LOOK UNBELIEE-EEVABLY COOL?
LIKE I'LL BE DROOLING OVER YUSUKE FOREVER?
HERE, MEGO. THIS IS THE NEW TITLE BY JEWEL BOOKS I PROMISED TO LEND YOU.
UUUUH ...
A yaoi novel
LET ME KNOW WHAT YOU THINK OF IT.
Feudal Warlord Series

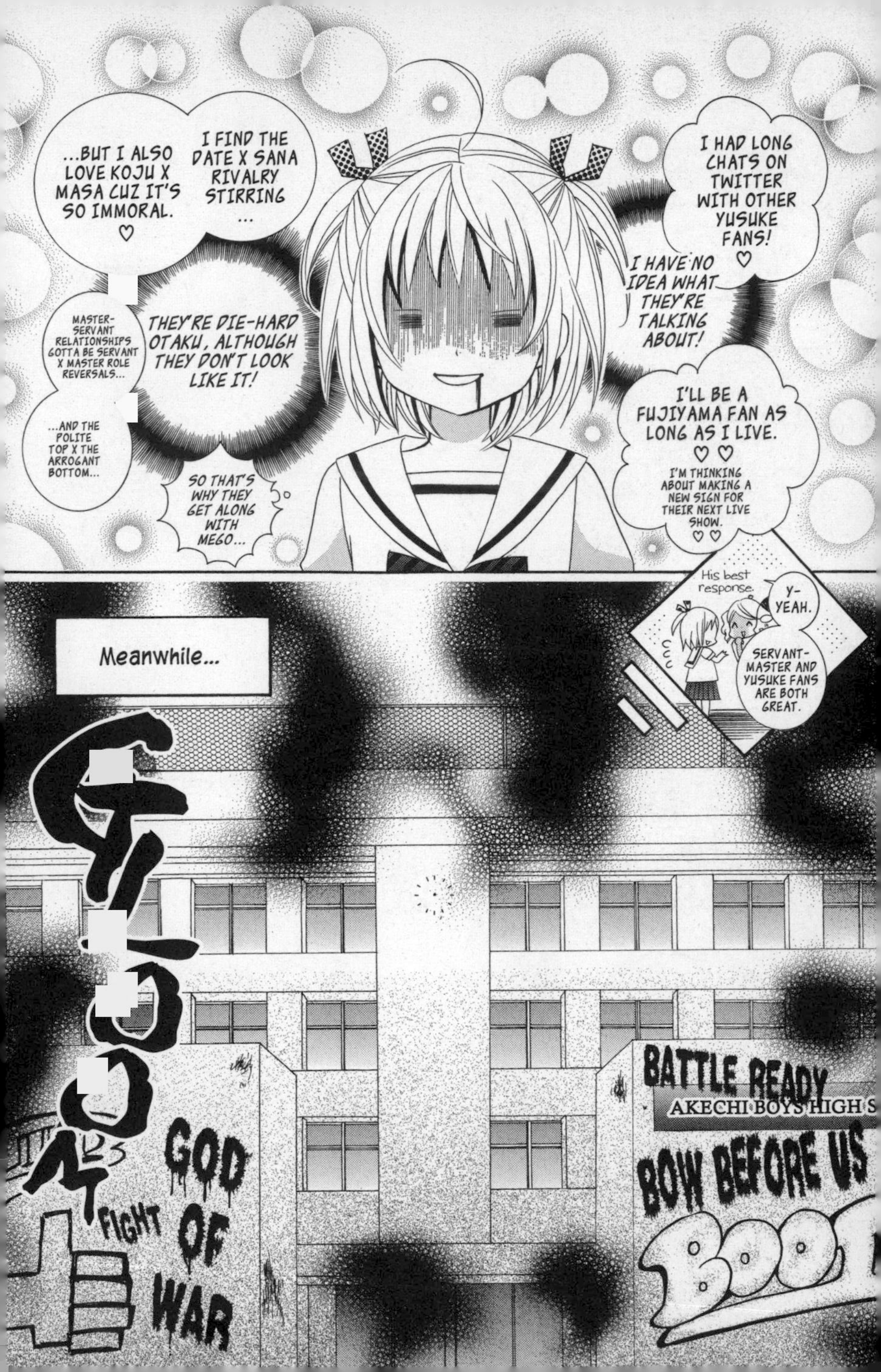
I HAD LONG CHATS ON TWITTER WITH OTHER YUSUKE FANS! ♡
I'LL BE A FUJIYAMA FAN AS LONG AS I LIVE. ♡ ♡
I'M THINKING ABOUT MAKING A NEW SIGN FOR THEIR NEXT LIVE SHOW. ♡ ♡
I HAVE NO IDEA WHAT THEY'RE TALKING ABOUT!
I FIND THE DATE X SANA RIVALRY STIRRING ...
...BUT I ALSO LOVE KOJU X MASA CUZ IT'S SO IMMORAL. ♡
THEY'RE DIE-HARD OTAKU, ALTHOUGH THEY DON'T LOOK LIKE IT!
MASTER-SERVANT RELATIONSHIPS GOTTA BE SERVANT X MASTER ROLE REVERSALS...
...AND THE POLITE TOP X THE ARROGANT BOTTOM...
SO THAT'S WHY THEY GET ALONG WITH MEGO...
His best response.
Y-YEAH.
SERVANT-MASTER AND YUSUKE FANS ARE BOTH GREAT.
Meanwhile...
BATTLE READY
AKECHI BOYS HIGH S
BOW BEFORE US
BOO
GOD OF WAR
FIGHT

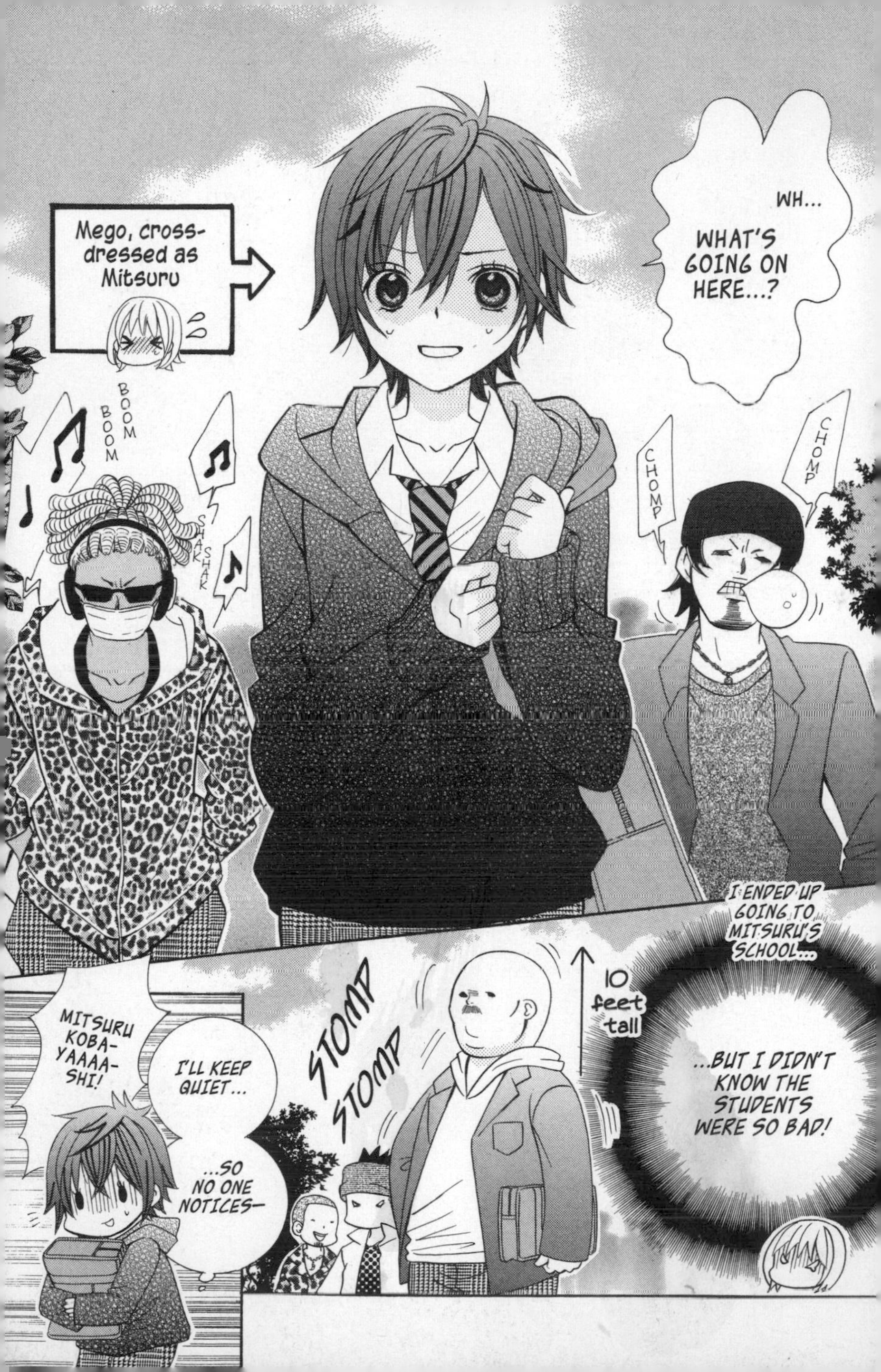
WH...
WHAT'S GOING ON HERE...?
CHOMP
CHOMP
Mego, cross-dressed as Mitsuru
BOOM BOOM BOOM
SHAK SHAK
I ENDED UP GOING TO MITSURU'S SCHOOL...
...BUT I DIDN'T KNOW THE STUDENTS WERE SO BAD!
10 feet tall
STOMP STOMP
MITSURU KOBA-YAAAA-SHI!
I'LL KEEP QUIET...
...SO NO ONE NOTICES—

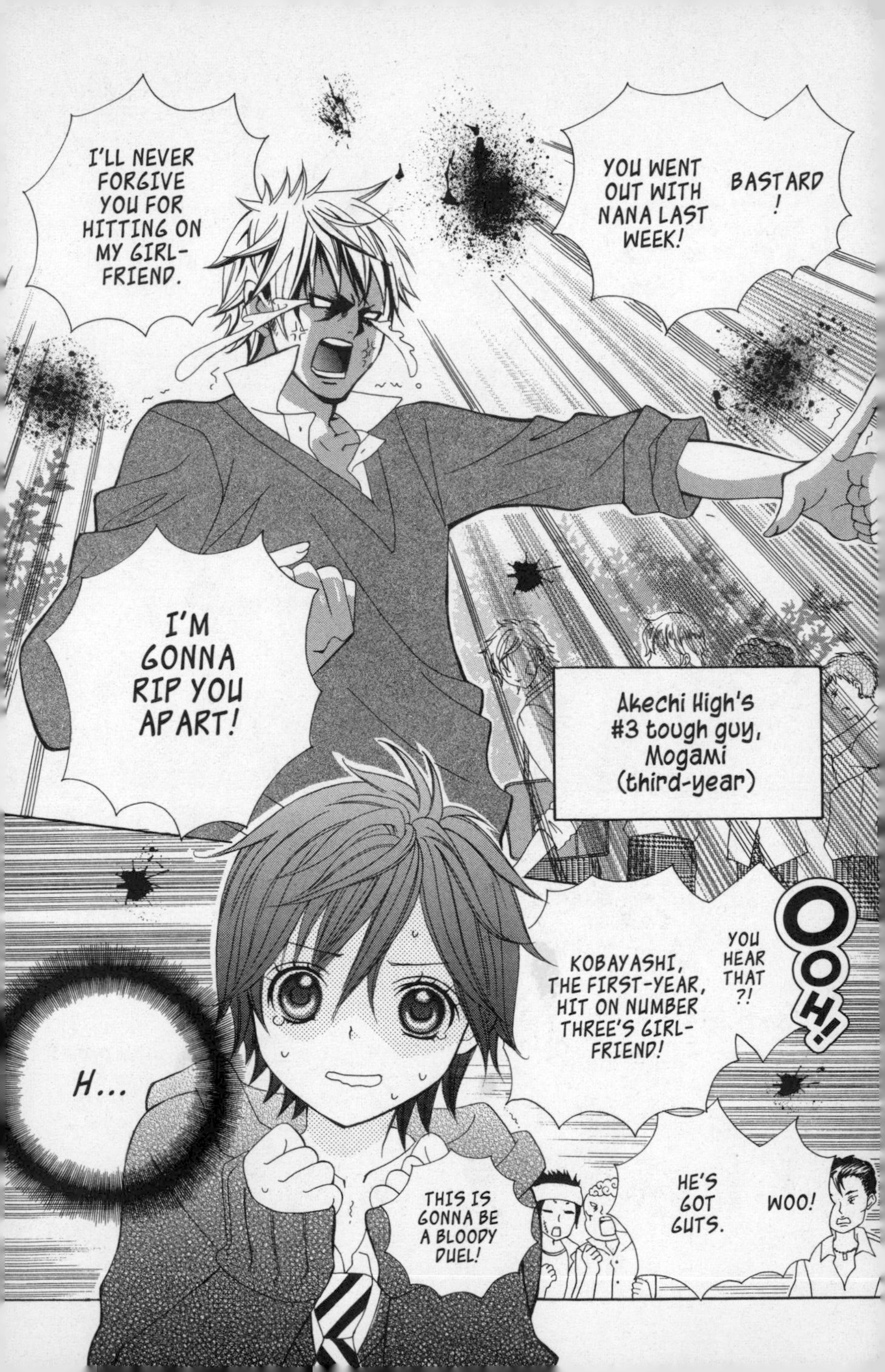
BASTARD!
YOU WENT OUT WITH NANA LAST WEEK!
I'LL NEVER FORGIVE YOU FOR HITTING ON MY GIRLFRIEND.
I'M GONNA RIP YOU APART!
Akechi High's #3 tough guy, Mogami (third-year)
OOH!
YOU HEAR THAT?!
KOBAYASHI, THE FIRST-YEAR, HIT ON NUMBER THREE'S GIRLFRIEND!
WOO!
HE'S GOT GUTS.
THIS IS GONNA BE A BLOODY DUEL!
H...

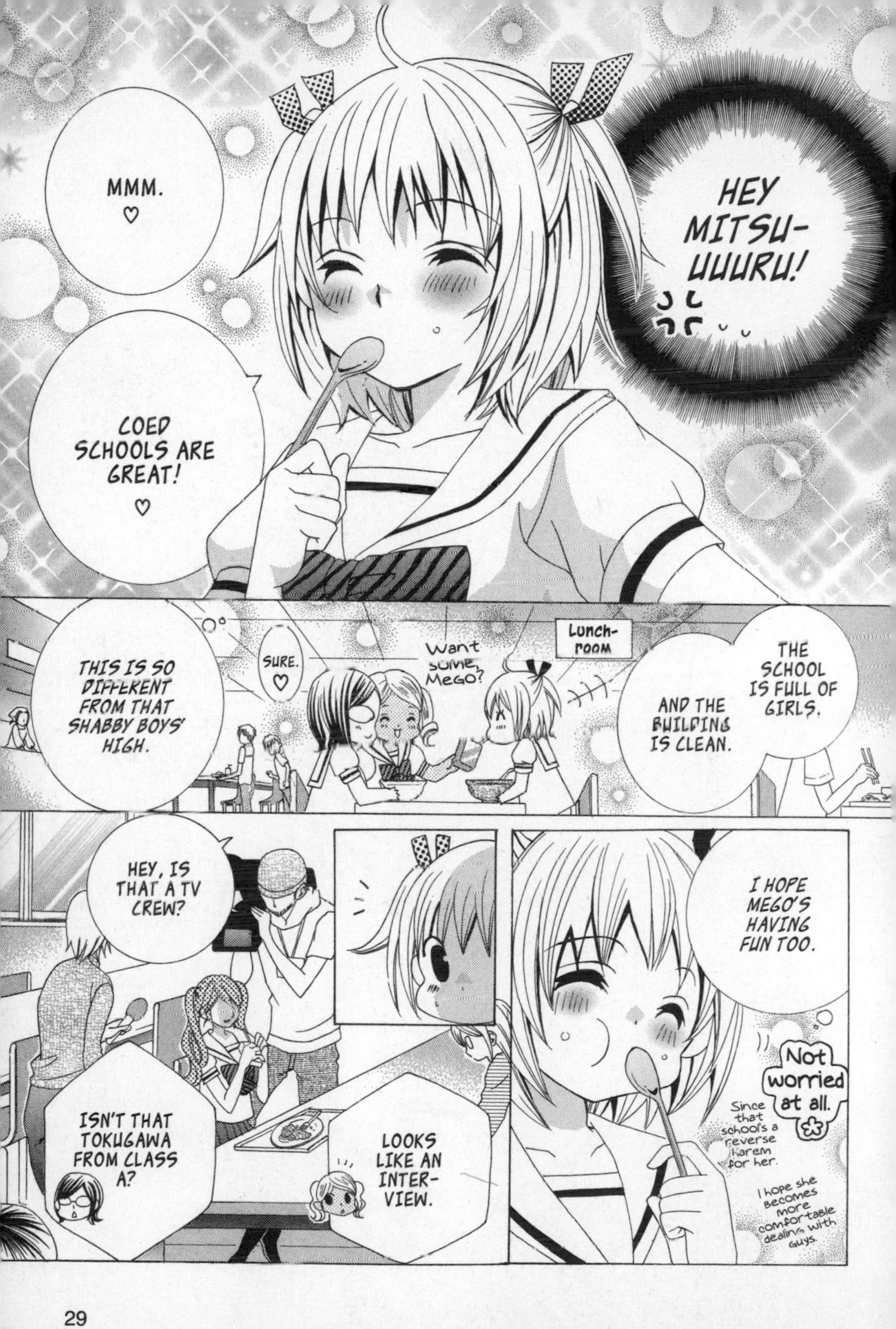
HEY MITSU-UUURU!
MMM. ♡
COED SCHOOLS ARE GREAT! ♡
THE SCHOOL IS FULL OF GIRLS.
AND THE BUILDING IS CLEAN.
Lunch-room
Want some, Mego?
SURE. ♡
THIS IS SO DIFFERENT FROM THAT SHABBY BOYS' HIGH.
I HOPE MEGO'S HAVING FUN TOO.
Not worried at all.
Since that school's a reverse harem for her.
I hope she becomes more comfortable dealing with guys.
HEY, IS THAT A TV CREW?
LOOKS LIKE AN INTER-VIEW.
ISN'T THAT TOKUGAWA FROM CLASS A?

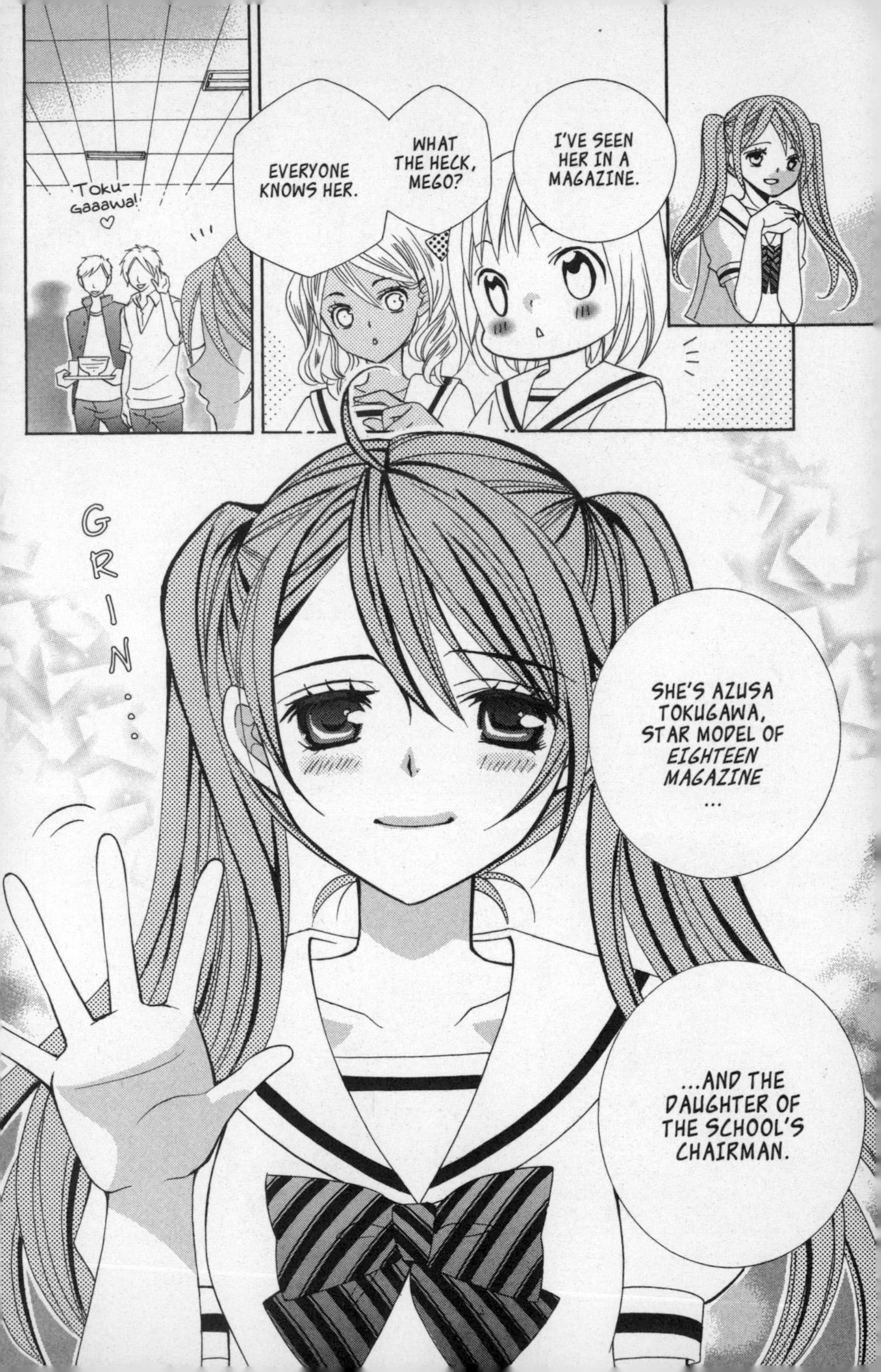
I'VE SEEN HER IN A MAGAZINE.
WHAT THE HECK, MEGO?
EVERYONE KNOWS HER.
Toku-Gaaawa!
GRIN...
SHE'S AZUSA TOKUGAWA, STAR MODEL OF EIGHTEEN MAGAZINE ...
...AND THE DAUGHTER OF THE SCHOOL'S CHAIRMAN.

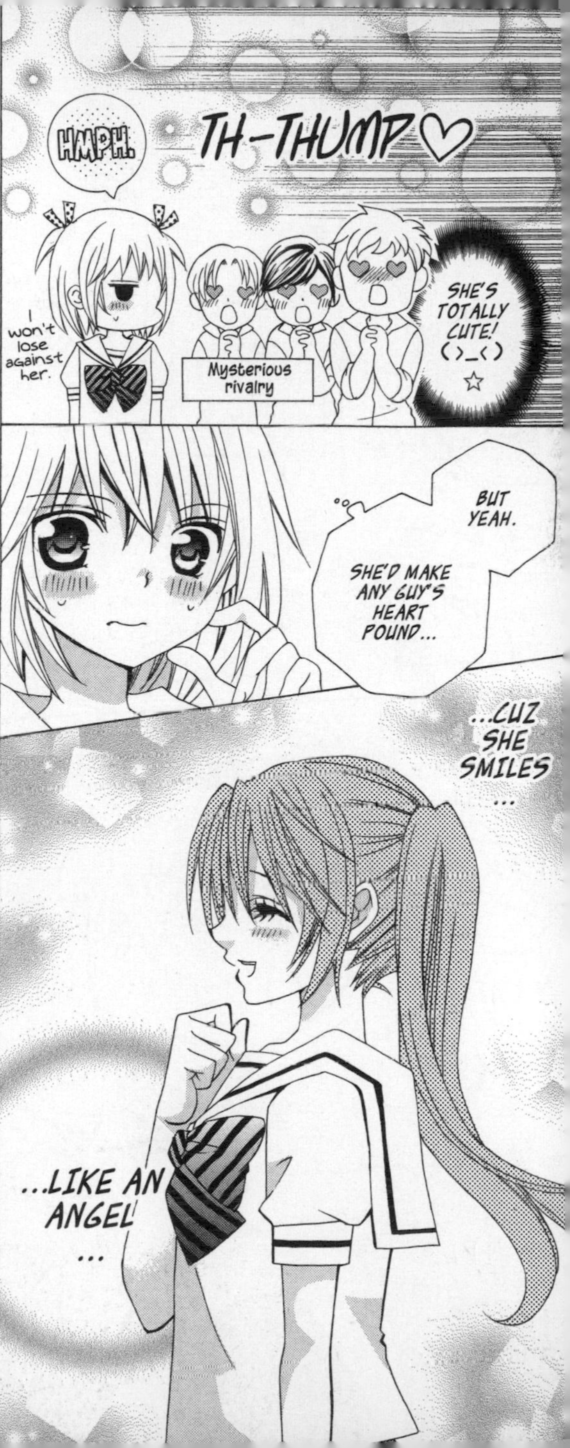
TH-THUMP ♡
SHE'S TOTALLY CUTE! (>_<) ☆
HMPH.
Mysterious rivalry
I won't lose against her.
BUT YEAH.
SHE'D MAKE ANY GUY'S HEART POUND...
...CUZ SHE SMILES ...
...LIKE AN ANGEL ...

SPECIAL THANKS

Yuka Ito-sama,
Rieko Hirai-sama,
Kayoko Takahashi-sama,
Kawasaki-sama,
Nagisa Sato Sensei.

Rei Nanase Sensei,
Arisu Fujishiro Sensei,
Mumi Mimura Sensei,
Masayo Nagata-sama,
Naochan-sama,
Asuka Sakura Sensei,
and many others.

Bookstore Dan Kinshicho Branch, Kinokuniya Shinjuku Branch, LIBRO Ikebukuro Branch, Kinokuniya Hankyu 32-Bangai Branch.

Sendai Hachimonjiya Bookstore, BOOKS HOSHINO Kintetsu Pass'e Branch, Asahiya Tennoji MiO Branch, Kurashiki Kikuya Bookstore.

Salesperson:
Mizusawa-sama

Previous salesperson:
Honma-sama

Previous editor:
Nakata-sama

Current editor:
Shoji-sama

I also sincerely express my gratitude to everyone who picked up this volume. ♡♡

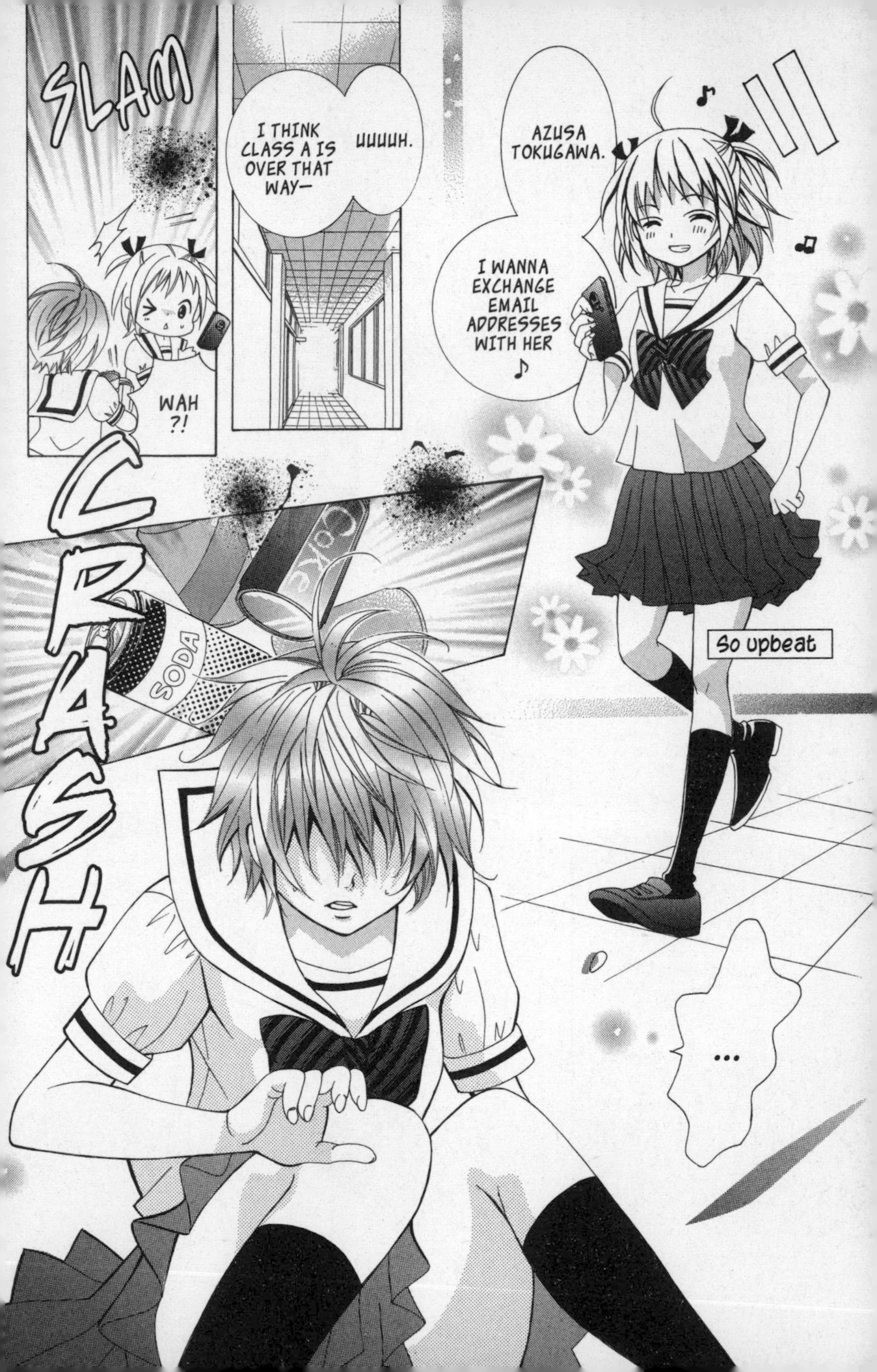
AZUSA TOKUGAWA.
I WANNA EXCHANGE EMAIL ADDRESSES WITH HER ♪
UUUUH.
I THINK CLASS A IS OVER THAT WAY—
SLAM
WAH ?!
So upbeat
CRASH
COKE
SODA
...

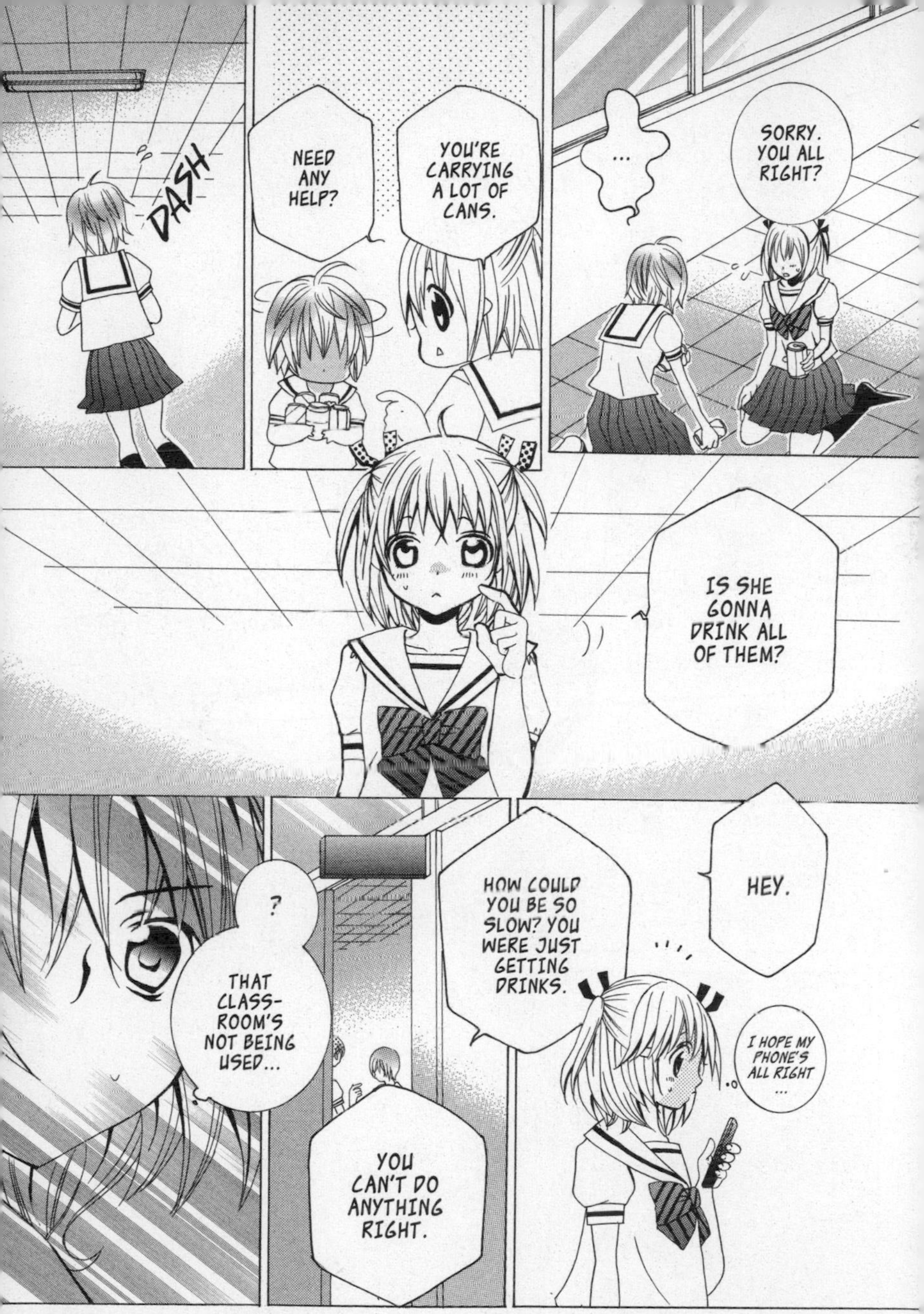
SORRY. YOU ALL RIGHT?
...
YOU'RE CARRYING A LOT OF CANS.
NEED ANY HELP?
DASH
IS SHE GONNA DRINK ALL OF THEM?
HEY.
I HOPE MY PHONE'S ALL RIGHT ...
HOW COULD YOU BE SO SLOW? YOU WERE JUST GETTING DRINKS.
YOU CAN'T DO ANYTHING RIGHT.
?
THAT CLASS-ROOM'S NOT BEING USED...

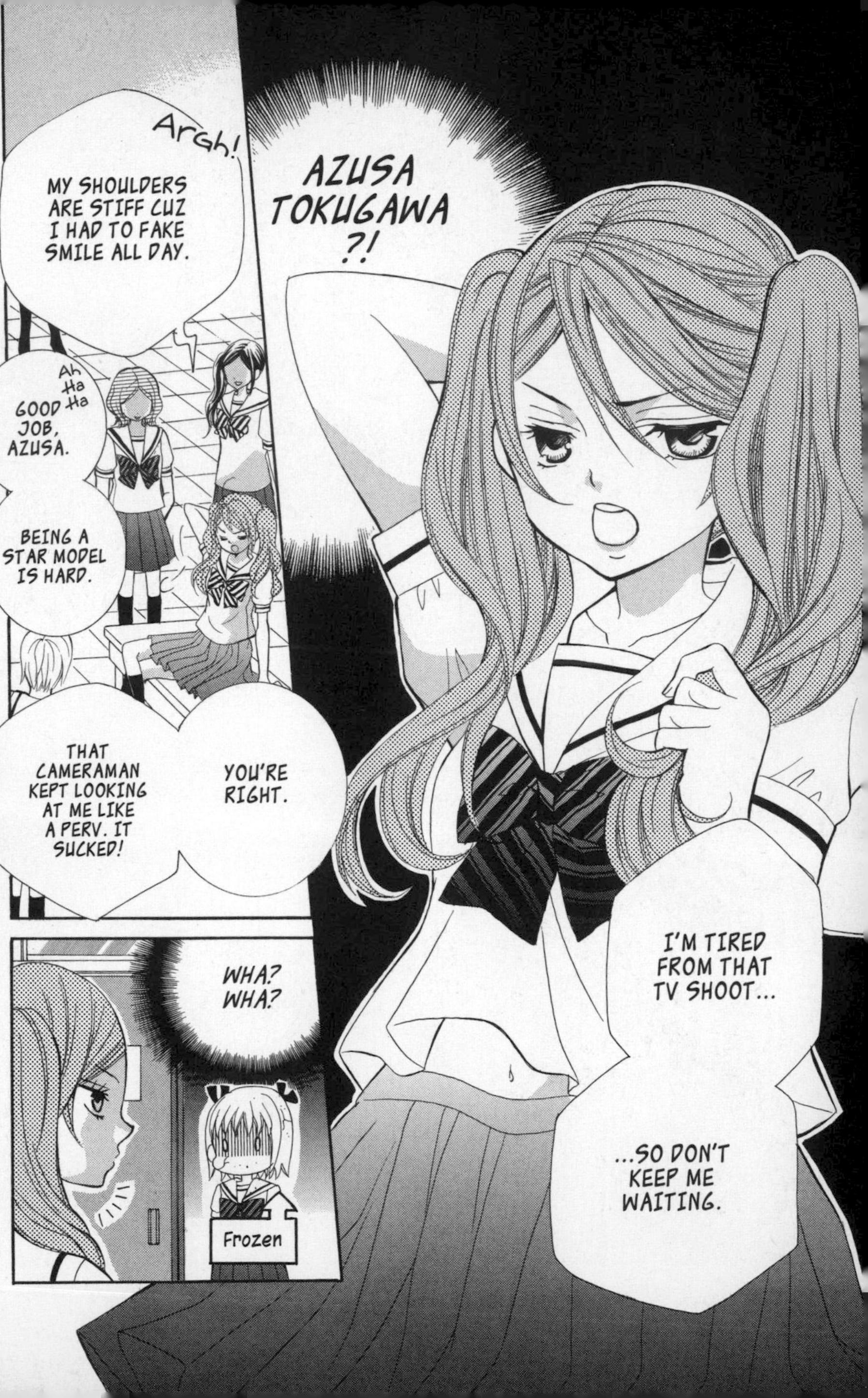
AZUSA TOKUGAWA ?!
I'M TIRED FROM THAT TV SHOOT...
...SO DON'T KEEP ME WAITING.
Argh!
MY SHOULDERS ARE STIFF CUZ I HAD TO FAKE SMILE ALL DAY.
Ah Ha Ha
GOOD JOB, AZUSA.
BEING A STAR MODEL IS HARD.
YOU'RE RIGHT.
THAT CAMERAMAN KEPT LOOKING AT ME LIKE A PERV. IT SUCKED!
WHA? WHA?
Frozen

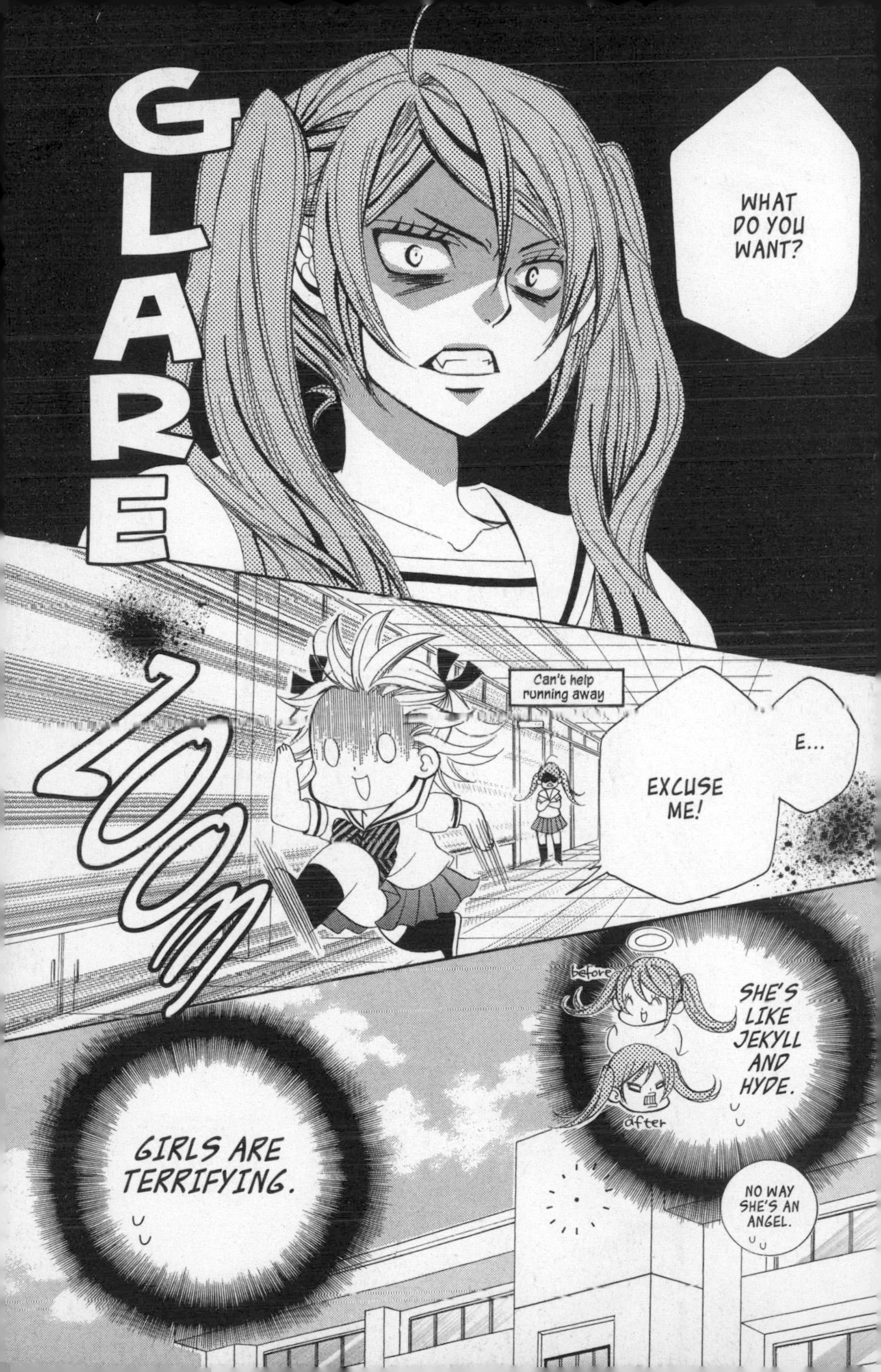
WHAT DO YOU WANT?
GLARE
E... EXCUSE ME!
Can't help running away
ZOOM
before
after
SHE'S LIKE JEKYLL AND HYDE.
NO WAY SHE'S AN ANGEL.
GIRLS ARE TERRIFYING.

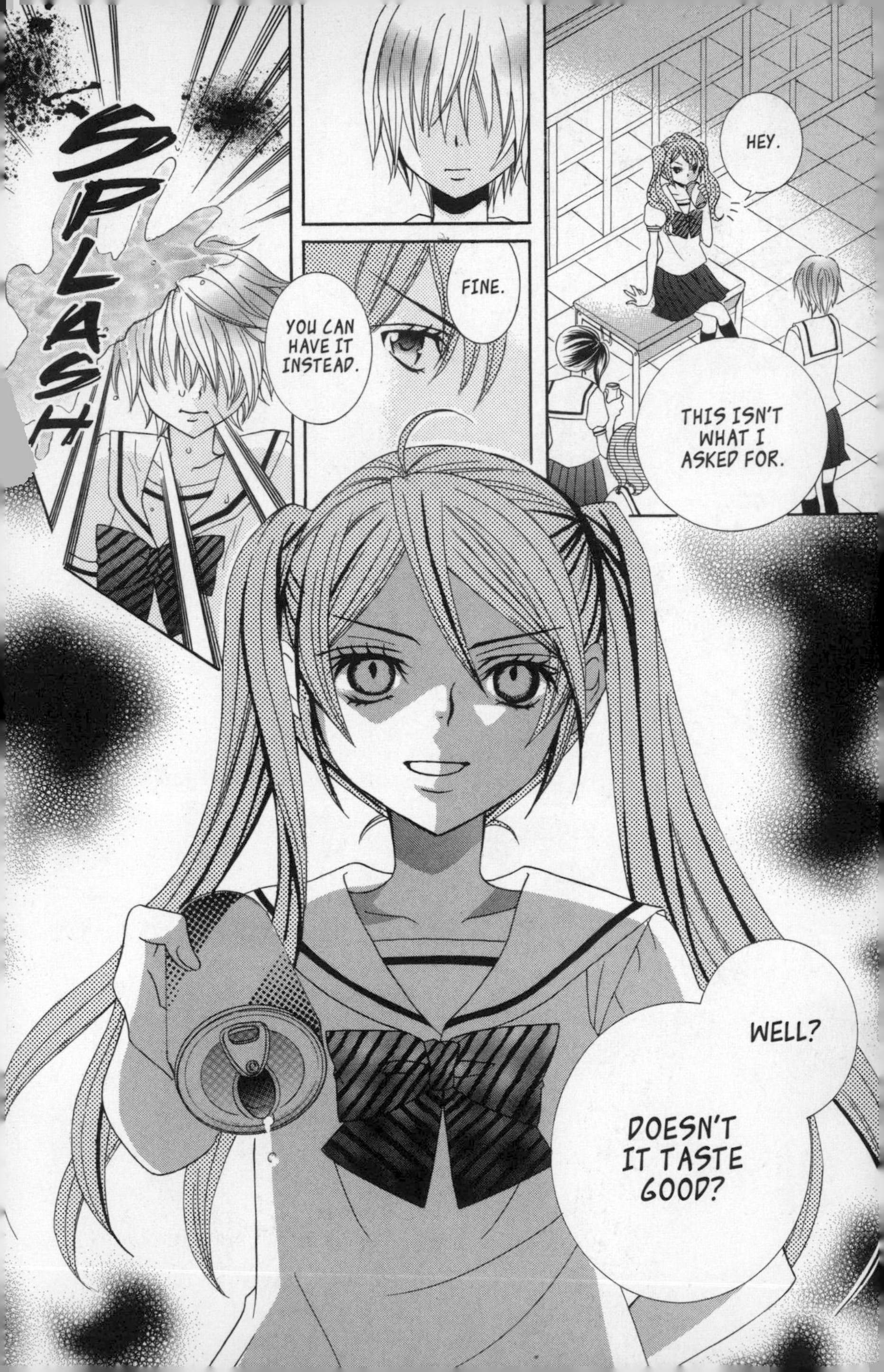
HEY.
THIS ISN'T WHAT I ASKED FOR.
FINE.
YOU CAN HAVE IT INSTEAD.
SPLASH
WELL?
DOESN'T IT TASTE GOOD?

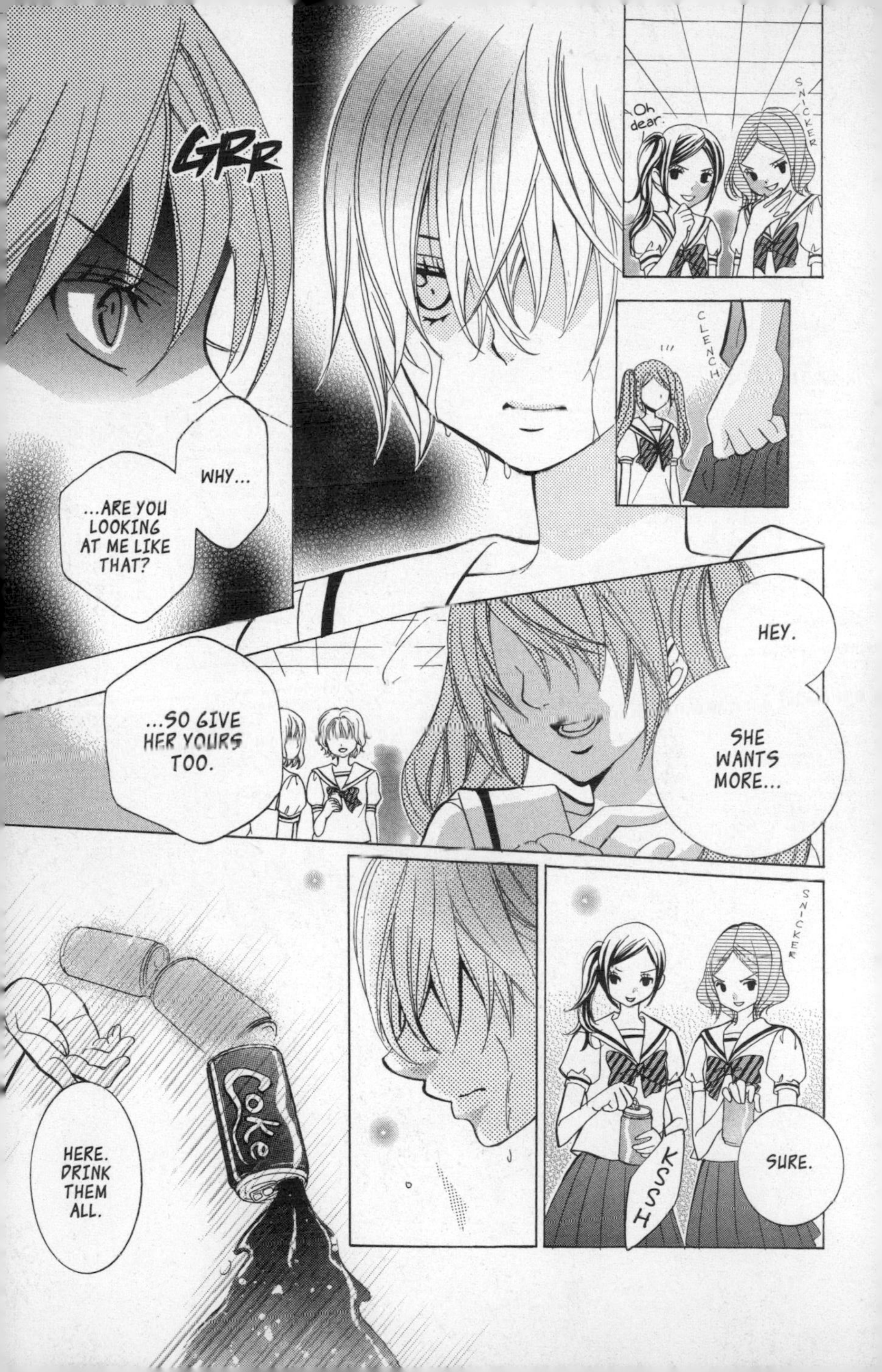
Oh dear.
SNICKER
!!!
CLENCH
GRR
WHY...
...ARE YOU LOOKING AT ME LIKE THAT?
HEY.
SHE WANTS MORE...
...SO GIVE HER YOURS TOO.
SNICKER
SURE.
KSSH
HERE. DRINK THEM ALL.
Coke

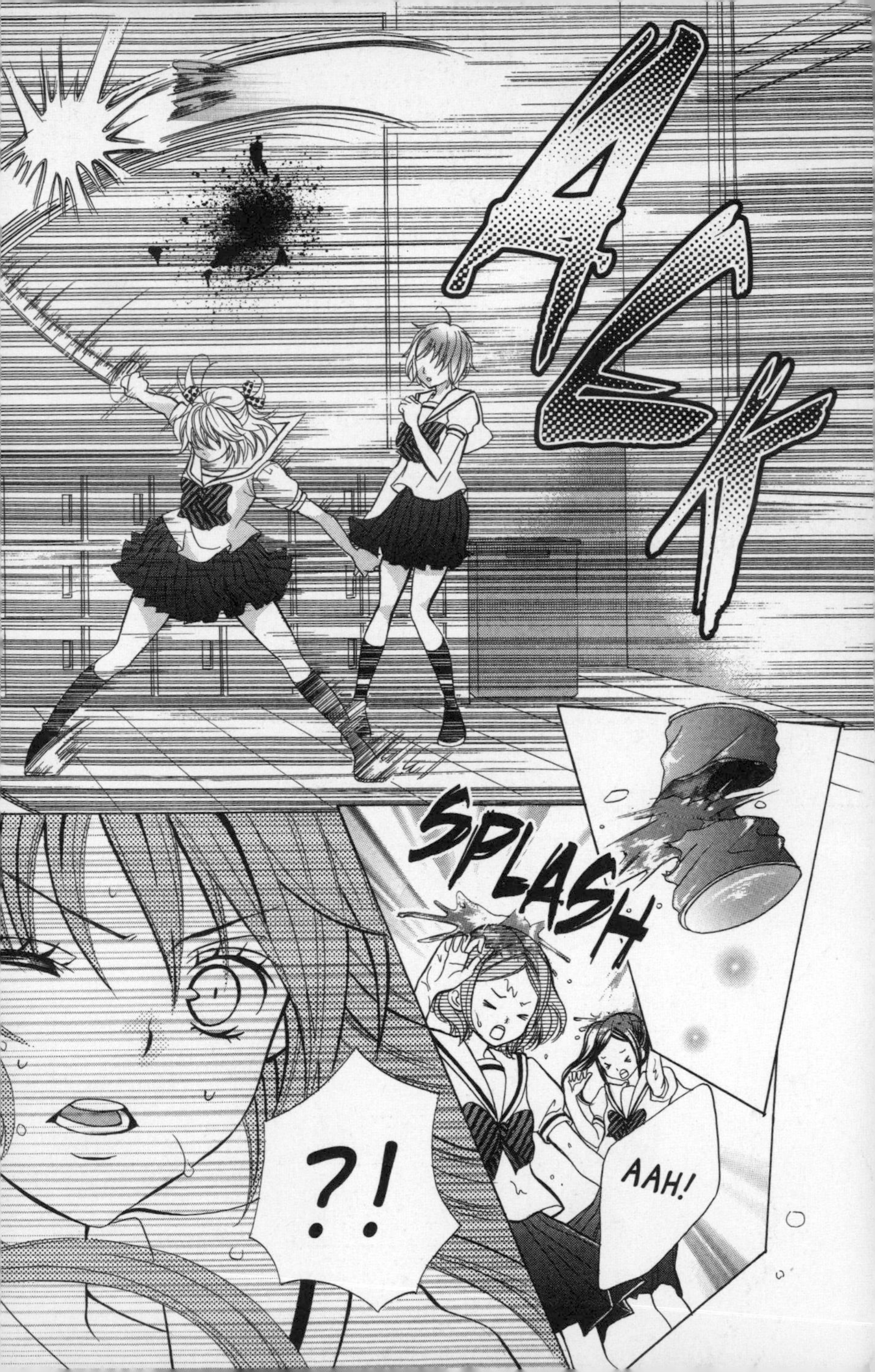
ACK
SPLASH
AAH!
?!

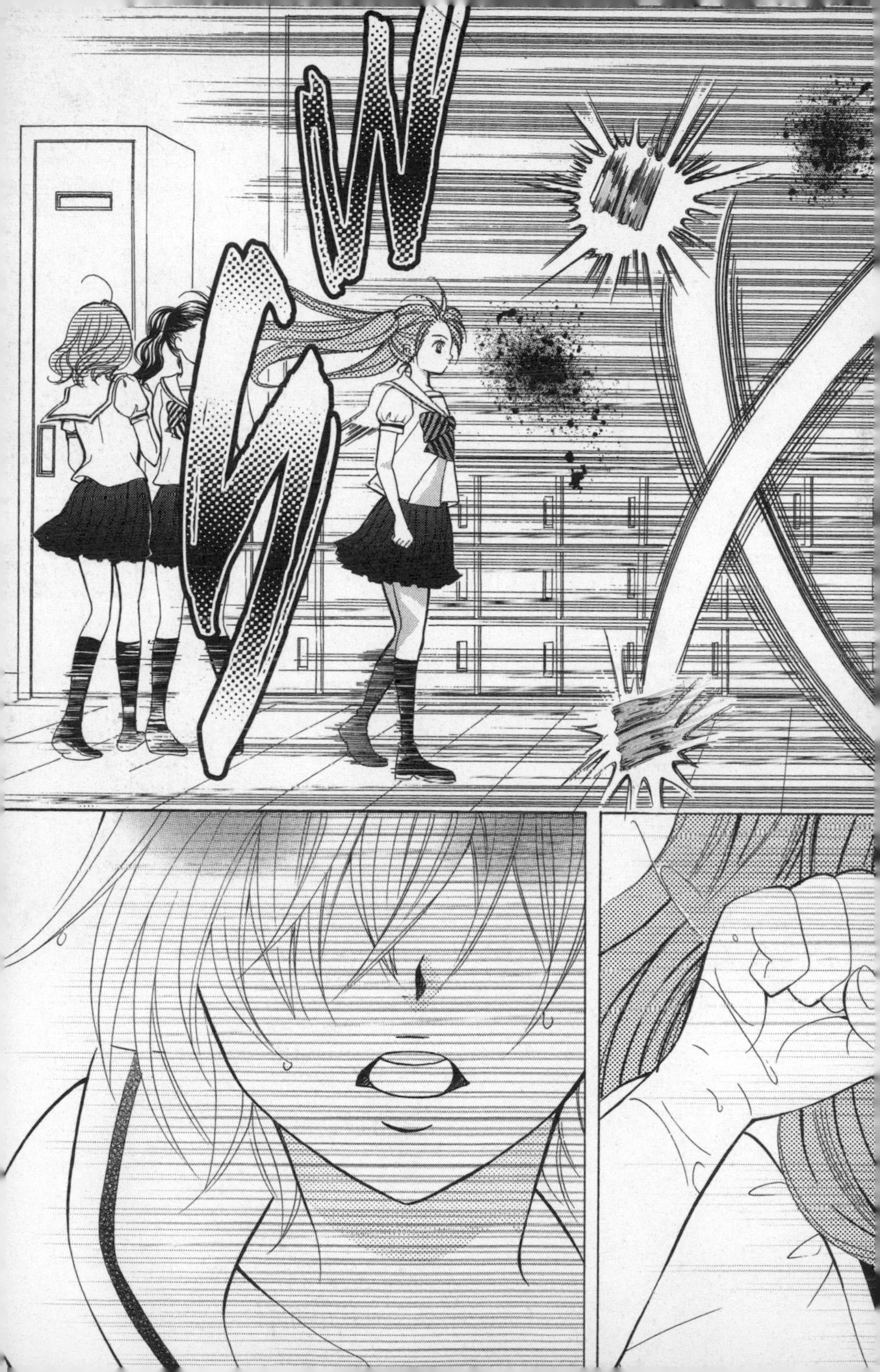

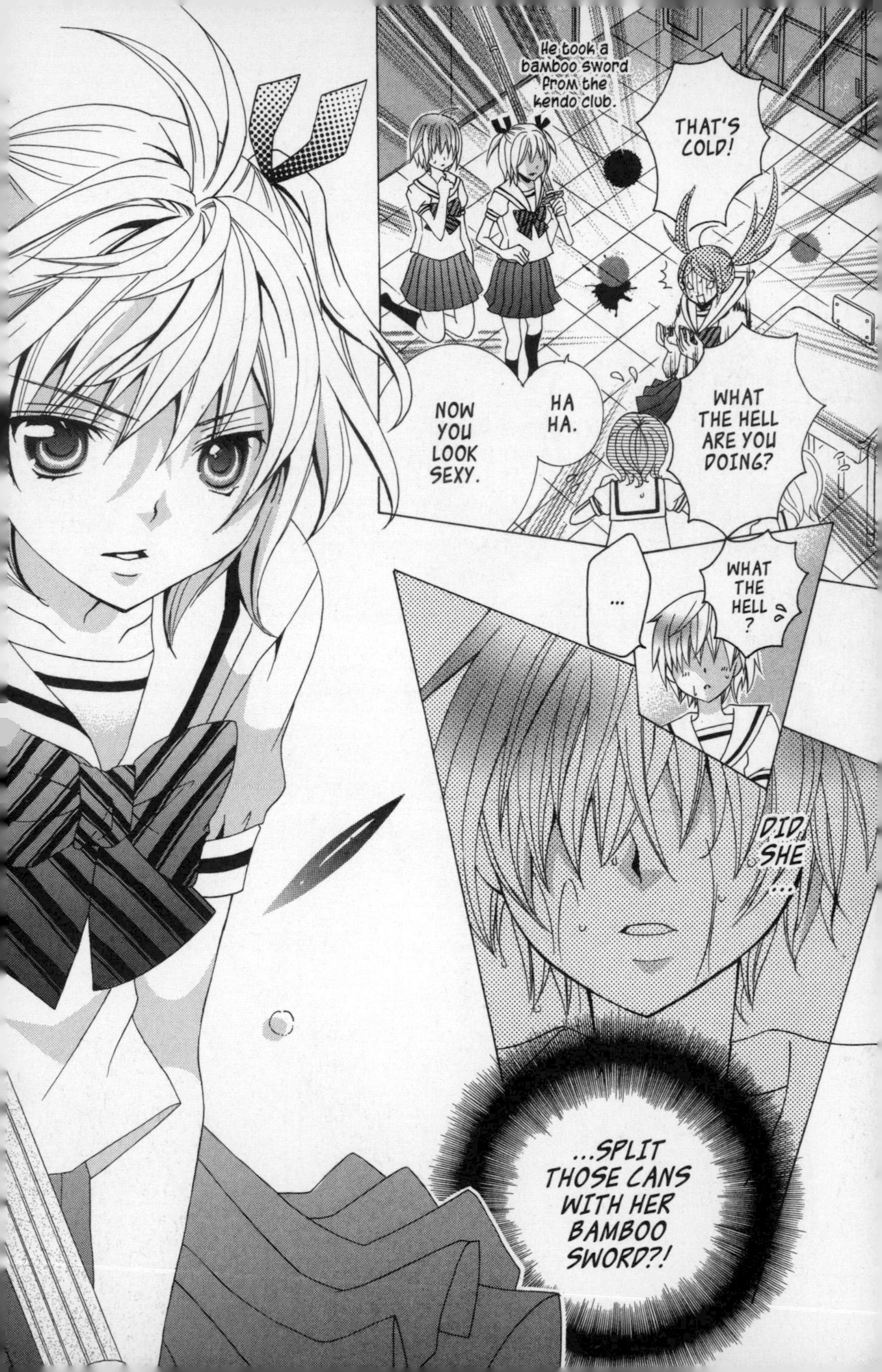
He took a bamboo sword from the kendo club.
THAT'S COLD!
WHAT THE HELL ARE YOU DOING?
HA HA.
NOW YOU LOOK SEXY.
WHAT THE HELL?
...
DID SHE...
...SPLIT THOSE CANS WITH HER BAMBOO SWORD?!

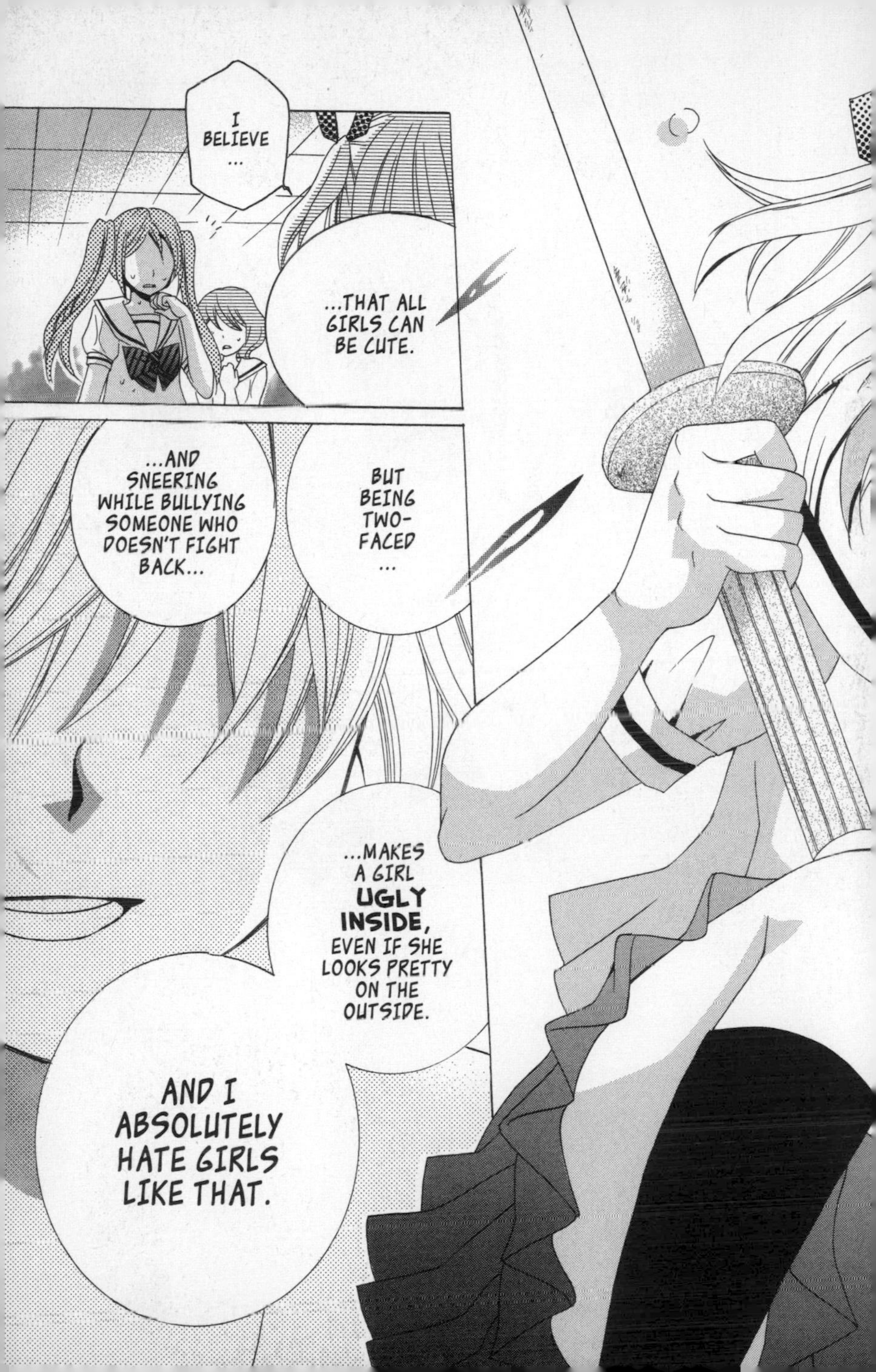
I BELIEVE ...
...THAT ALL GIRLS CAN BE CUTE.
BUT BEING TWO-FACED ...
...AND SNEERING WHILE BULLYING SOMEONE WHO DOESN'T FIGHT BACK...
...MAKES A GIRL **UGLY INSIDE**, EVEN IF SHE LOOKS PRETTY ON THE OUTSIDE.
AND I ABSOLUTELY HATE GIRLS LIKE THAT.

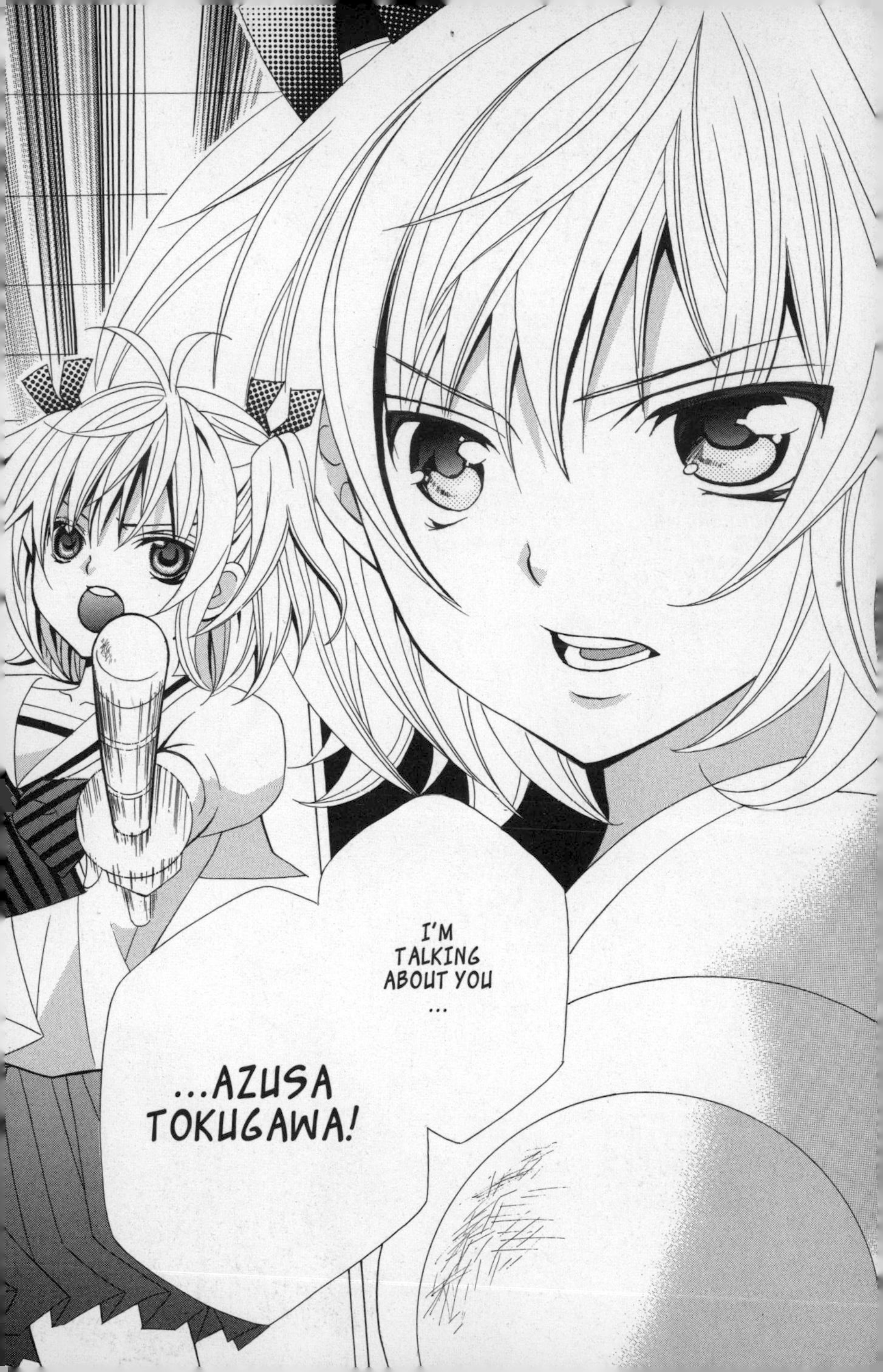
I'M TALKING ABOUT YOU ...
...AZUSA TOKUGAWA!

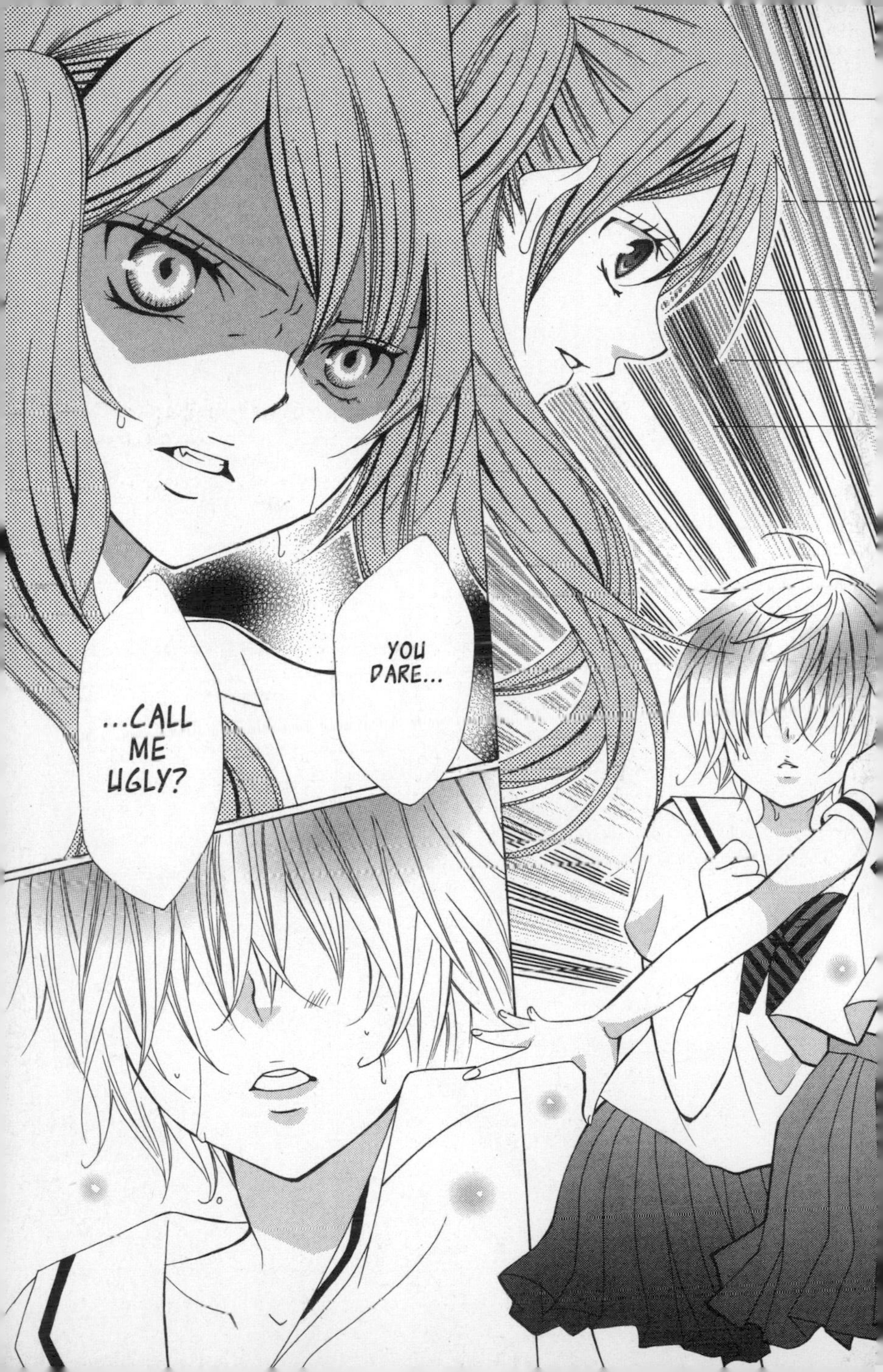
YOU DARE...
...CALL ME UGLY?

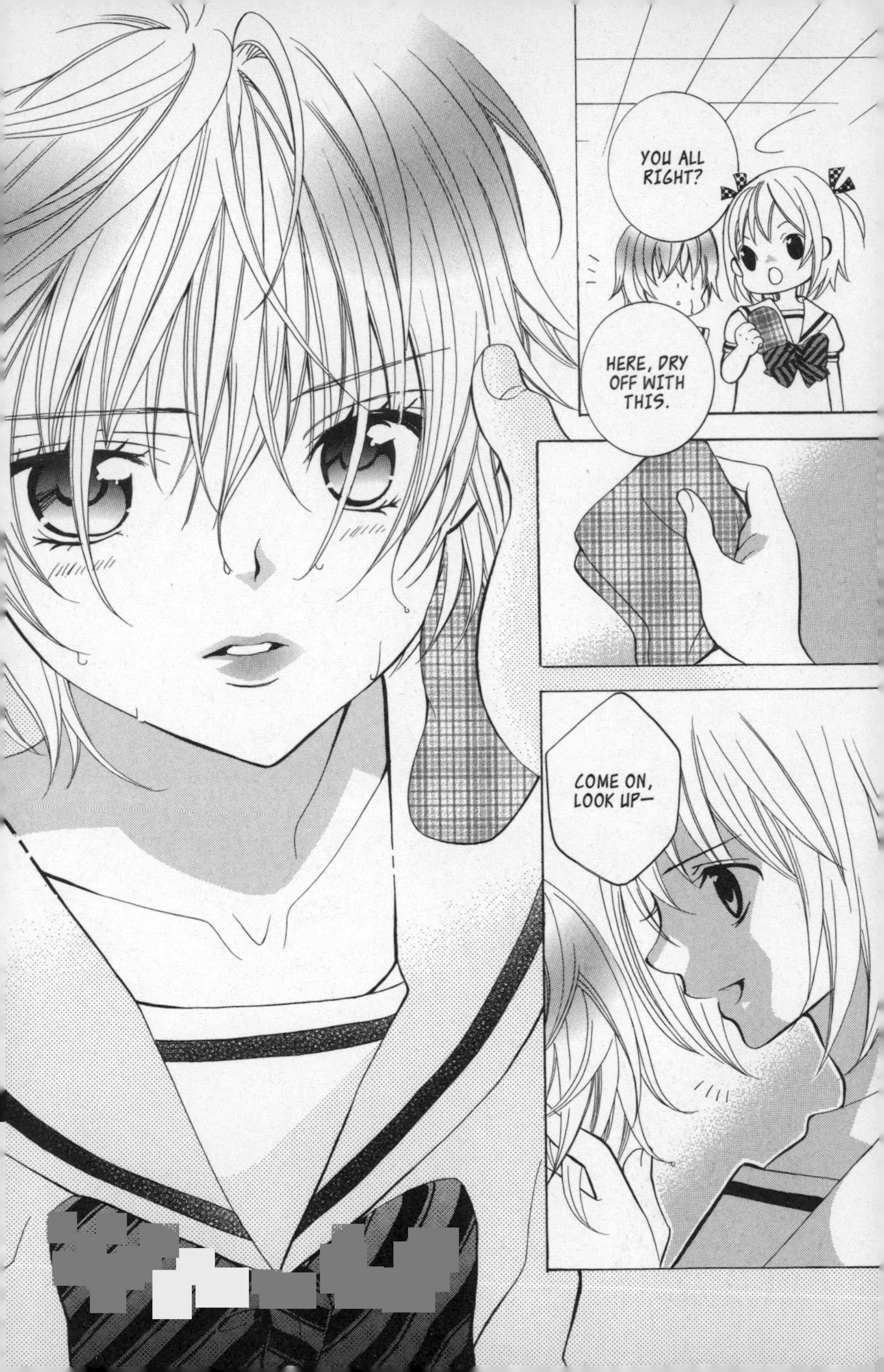
YOU ALL RIGHT?
HERE, DRY OFF WITH THIS.
COME ON, LOOK UP—

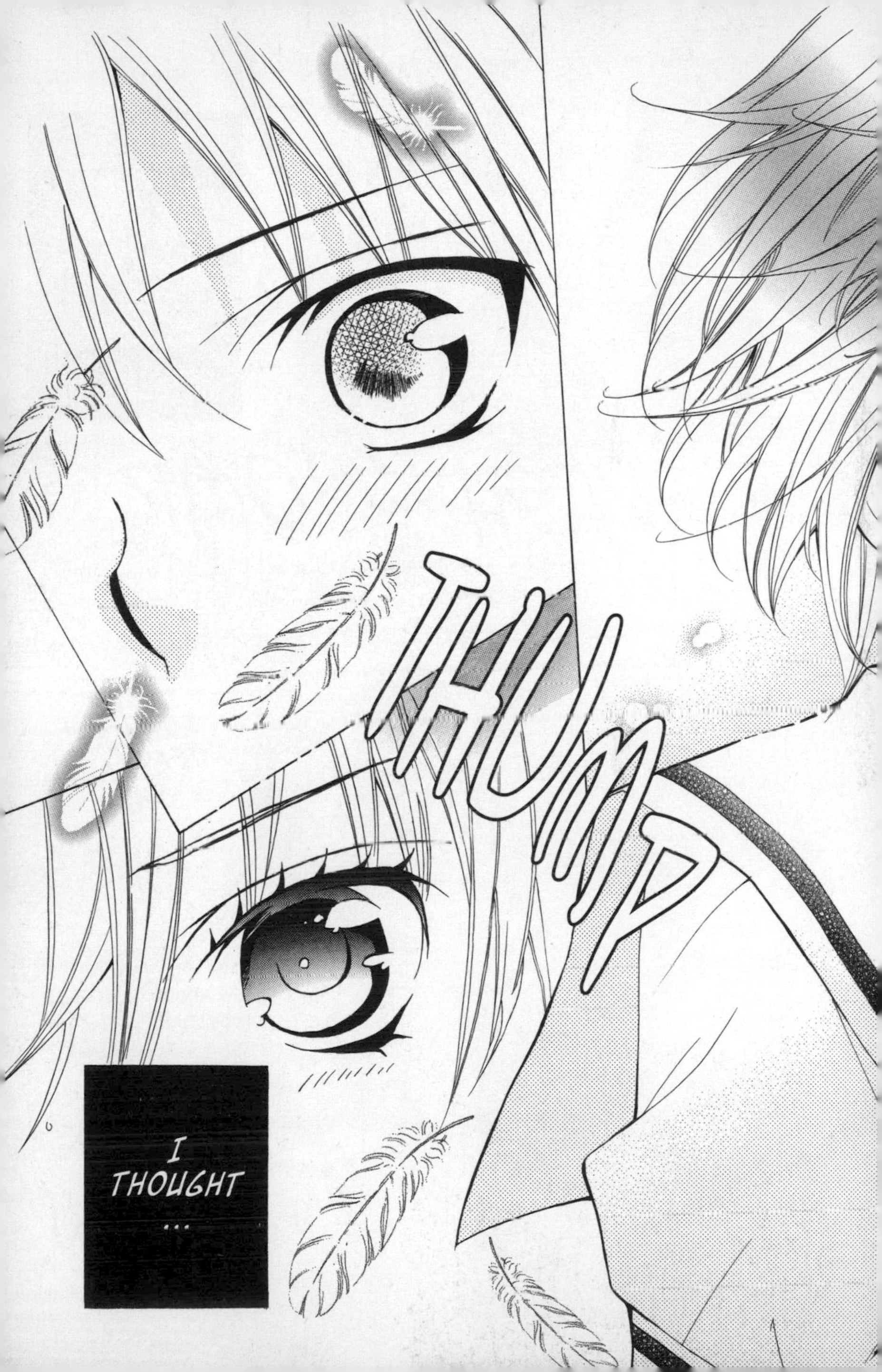
THUMP
I THOUGHT ...

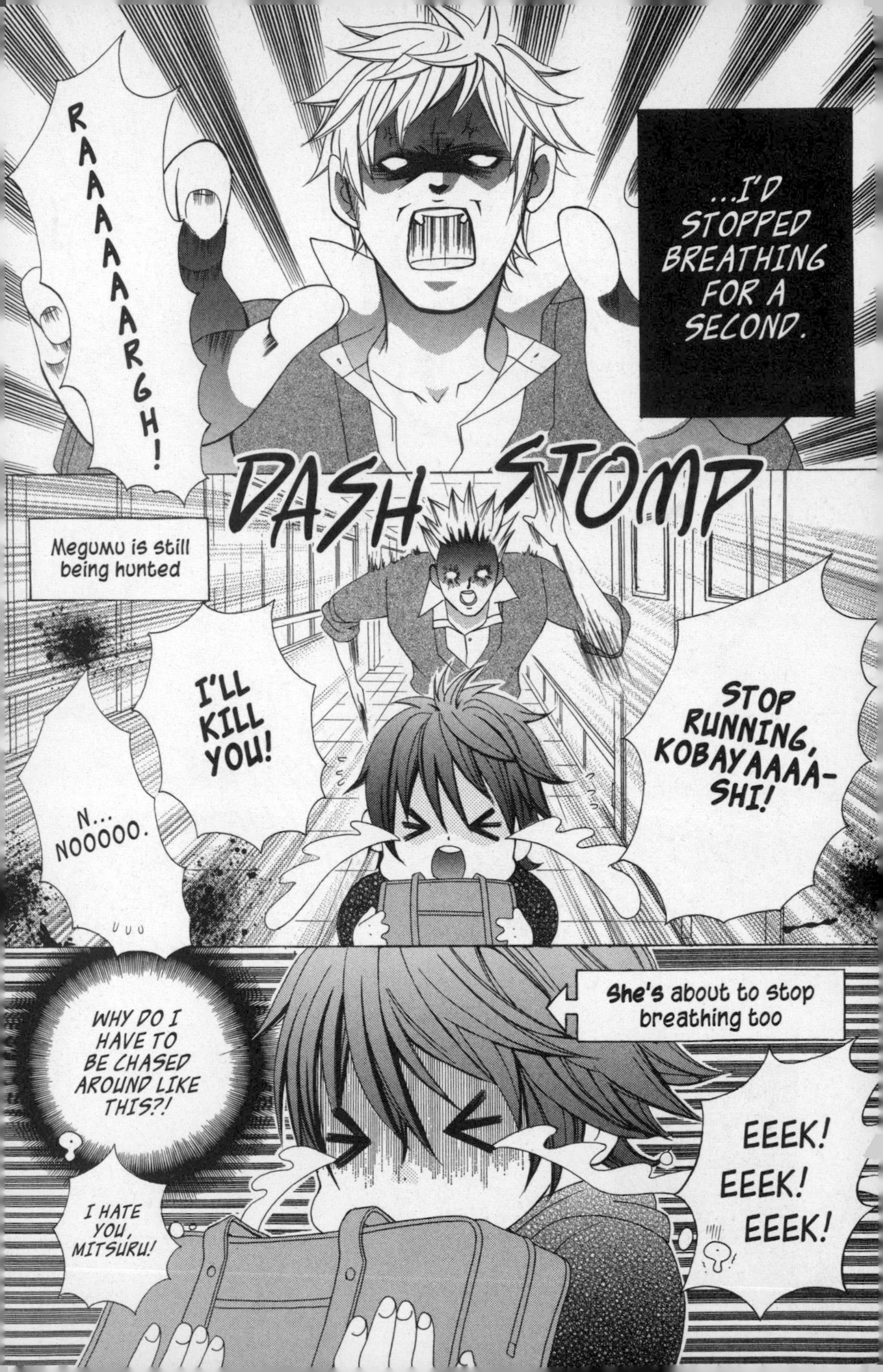
...I'D STOPPED BREATHING FOR A SECOND.
RAAAAAAARGH!
DASH STOMP
Megumu is still being hunted
STOP RUNNING, KOBAYAAAA-SHI!
I'LL KILL YOU!
N... NOOOOO.
She's about to stop breathing too
WHY DO I HAVE TO BE CHASED AROUND LIKE THIS?!
EEEK! EEEK! EEEK!
I HATE YOU, MITSURU!

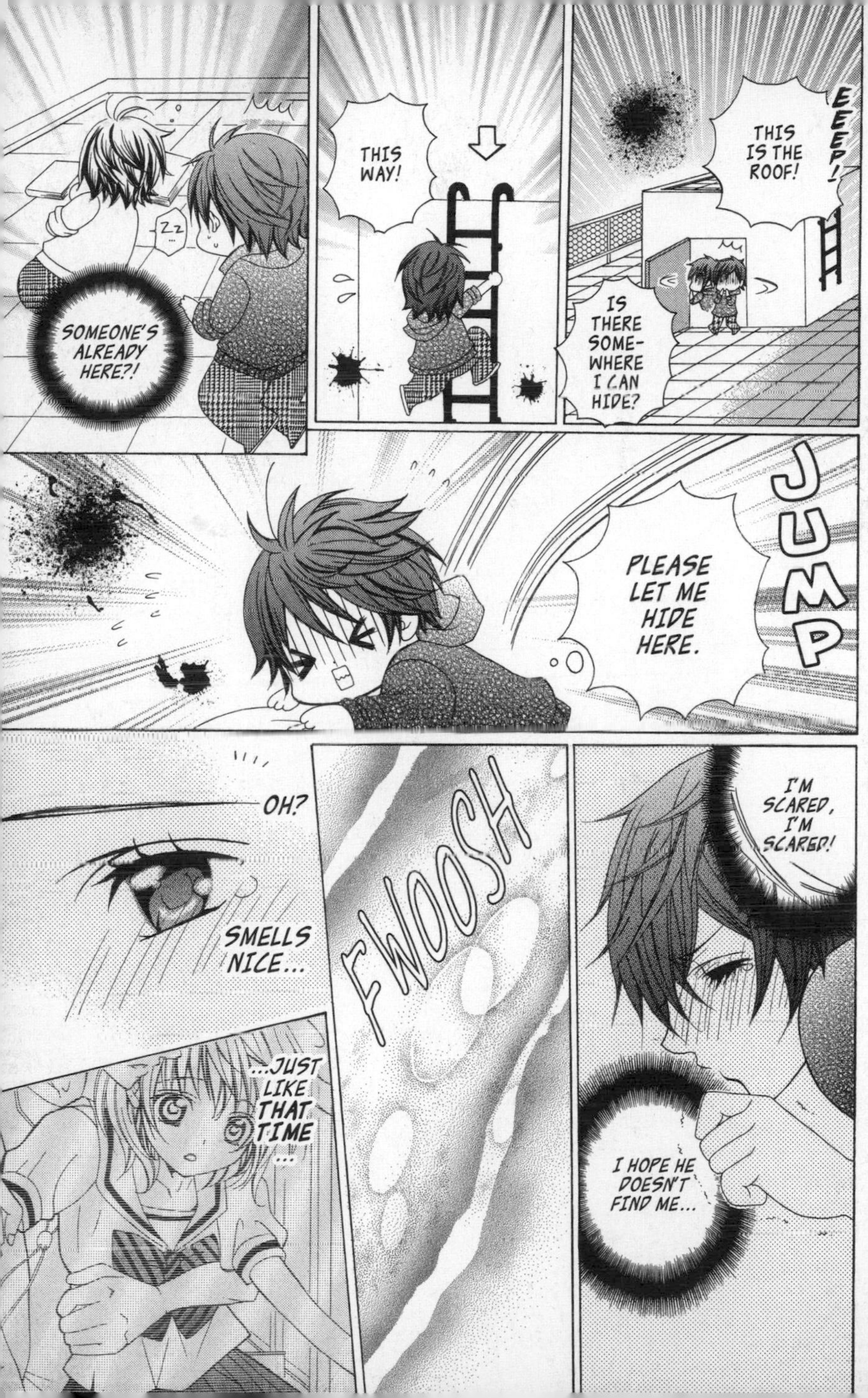
EEEP!
THIS IS THE ROOF!
IS THERE SOMEWHERE I CAN HIDE?
THIS WAY!
SOMEONE'S ALREADY HERE?!
Zz
JUMP
PLEASE LET ME HIDE HERE.
I'M SCARED, I'M SCARED!
I HOPE HE DOESN'T FIND ME...
FWOOSH
OH?
SMELLS NICE...
...JUST LIKE THAT TIME...

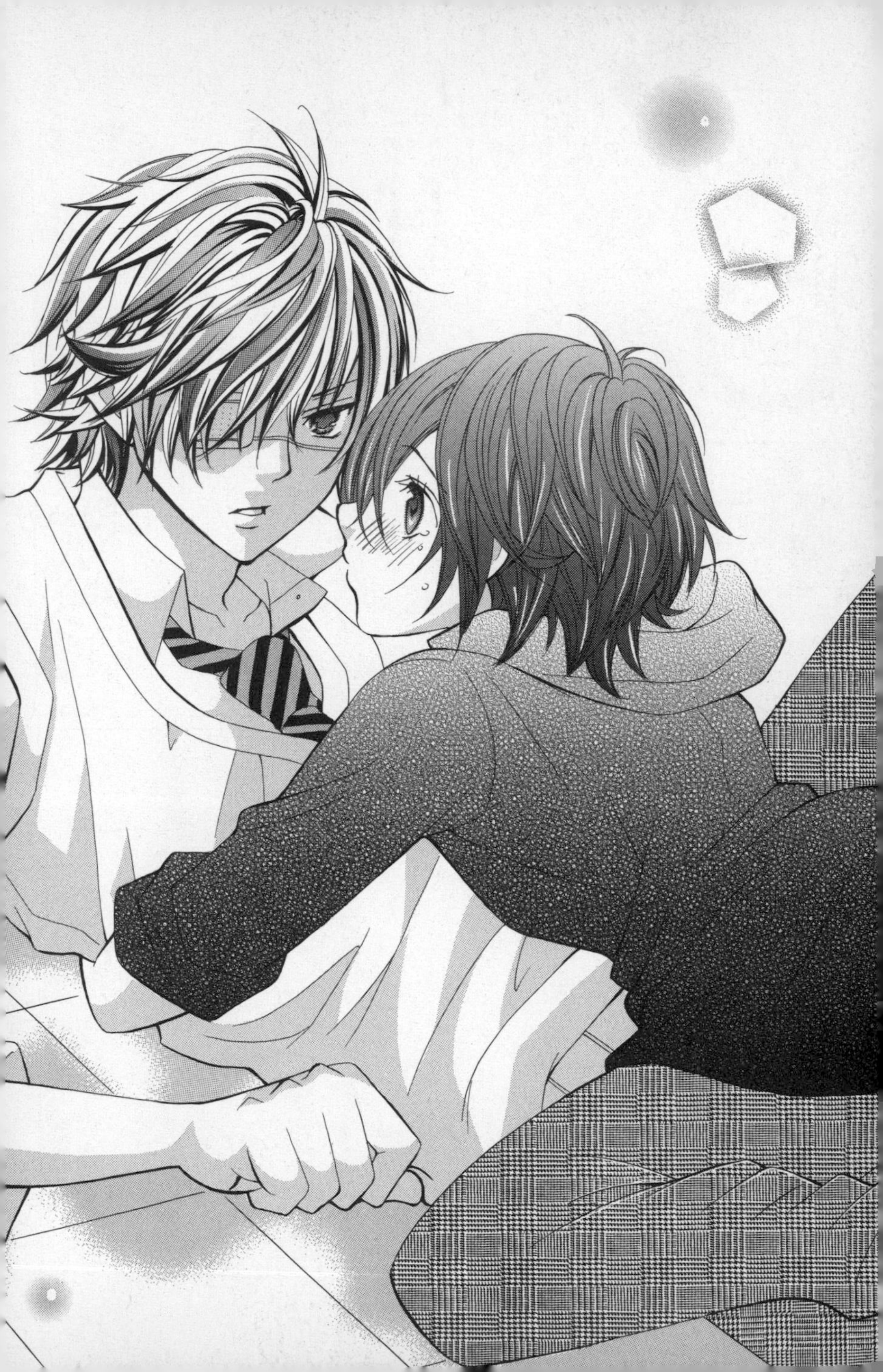

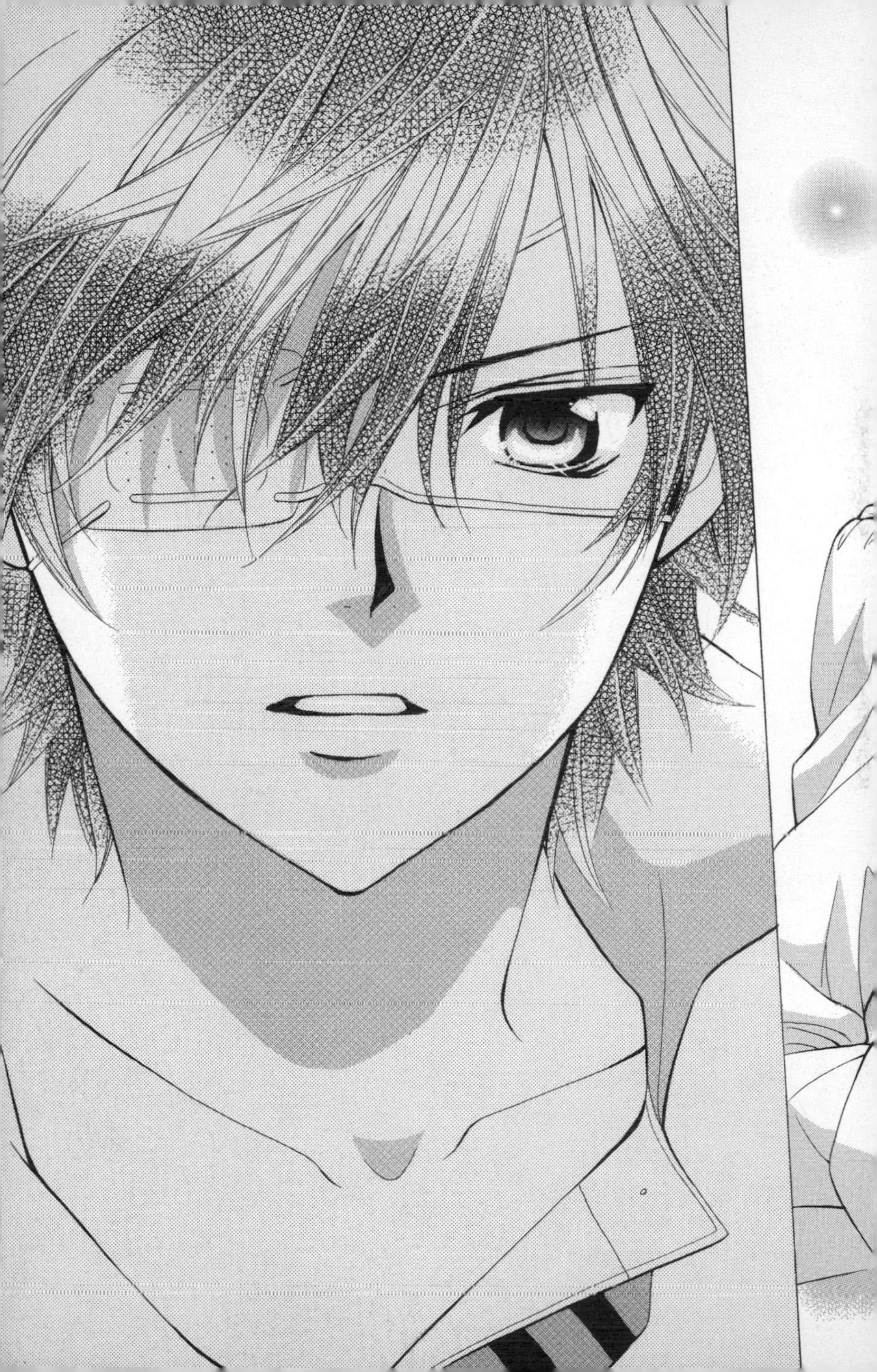

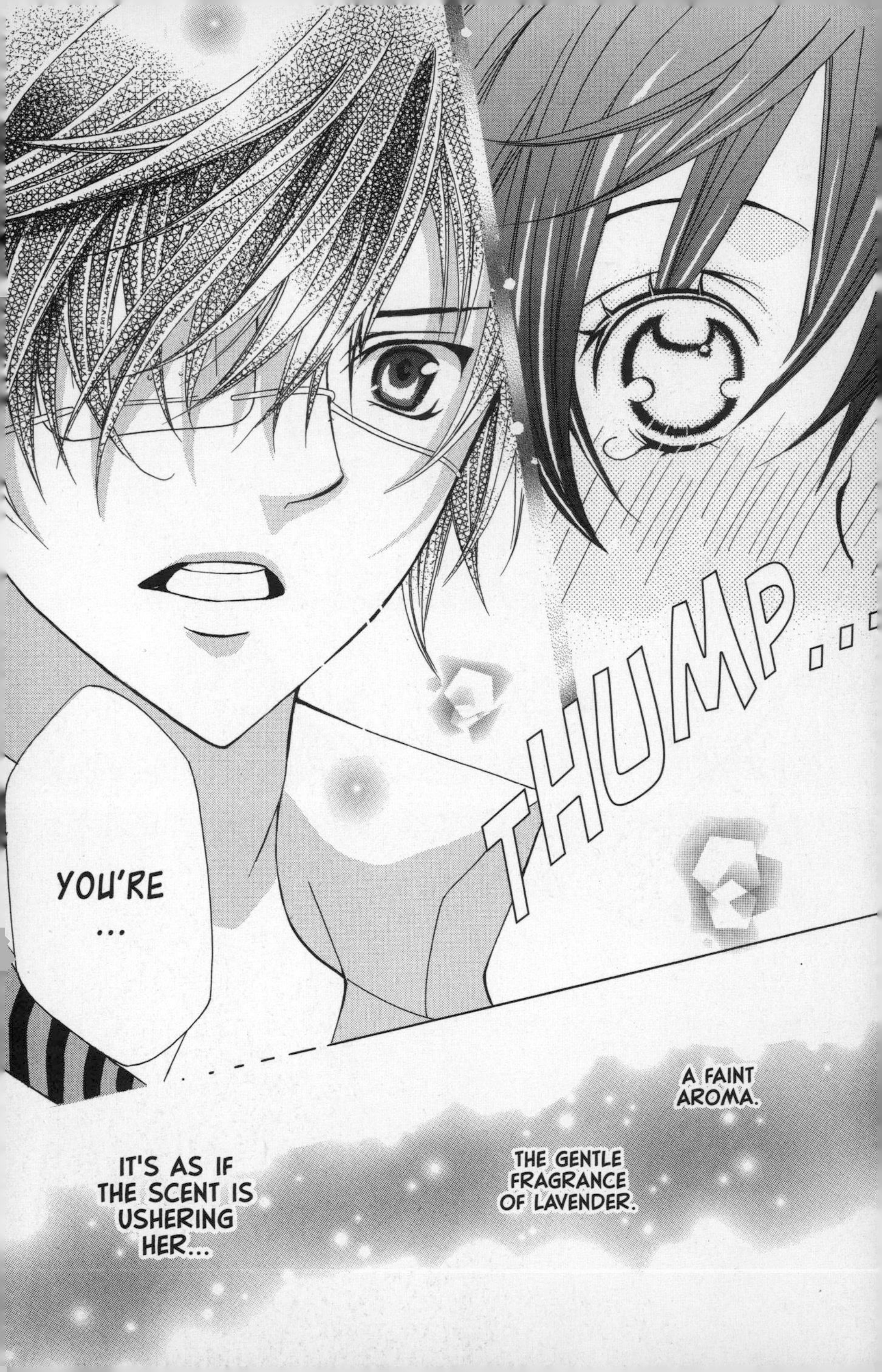
THUMP...
YOU'RE ...
A FAINT AROMA.
THE GENTLE FRAGRANCE OF LAVENDER.
IT'S AS IF THE SCENT IS USHERING HER...

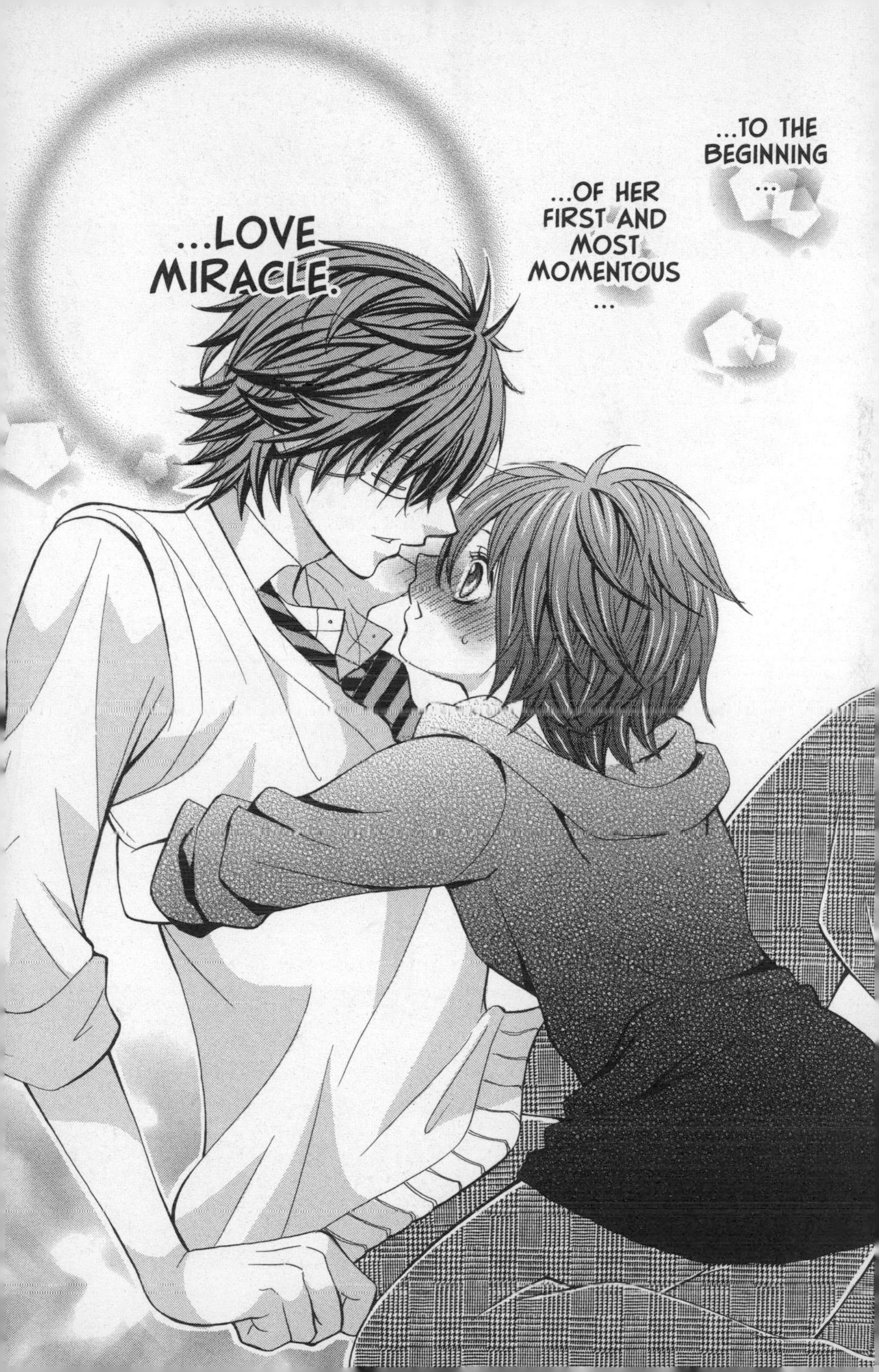
...TO THE BEGINNING ...
...OF HER FIRST AND MOST MOMENTOUS ...
...LOVE MIRACLE.

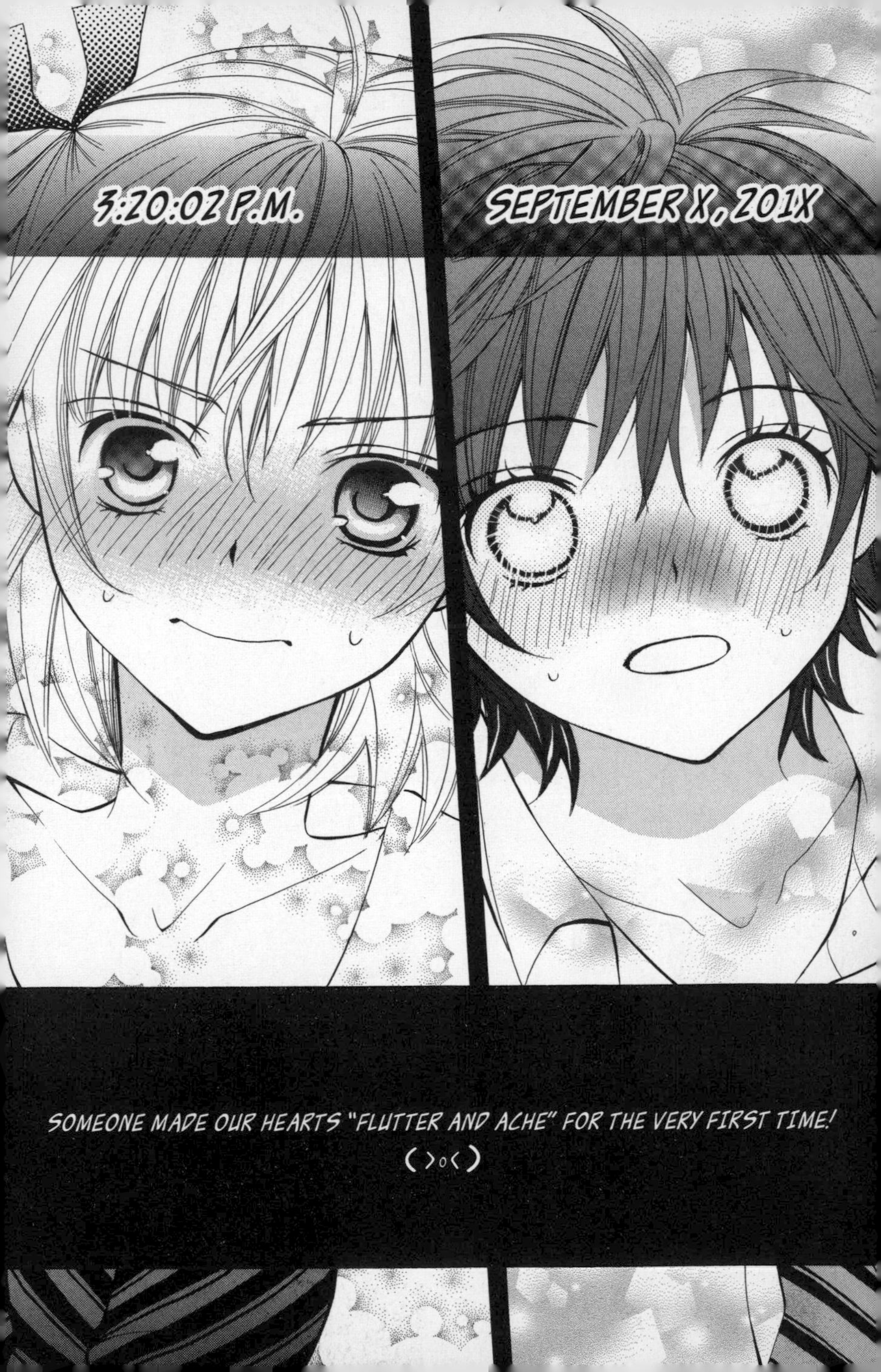
SEPTEMBER X, 201X
3:20:02 P.M.
SOMEONE MADE OUR HEARTS "FLUTTER AND ACHE" FOR THE VERY FIRST TIME!
(>o<)

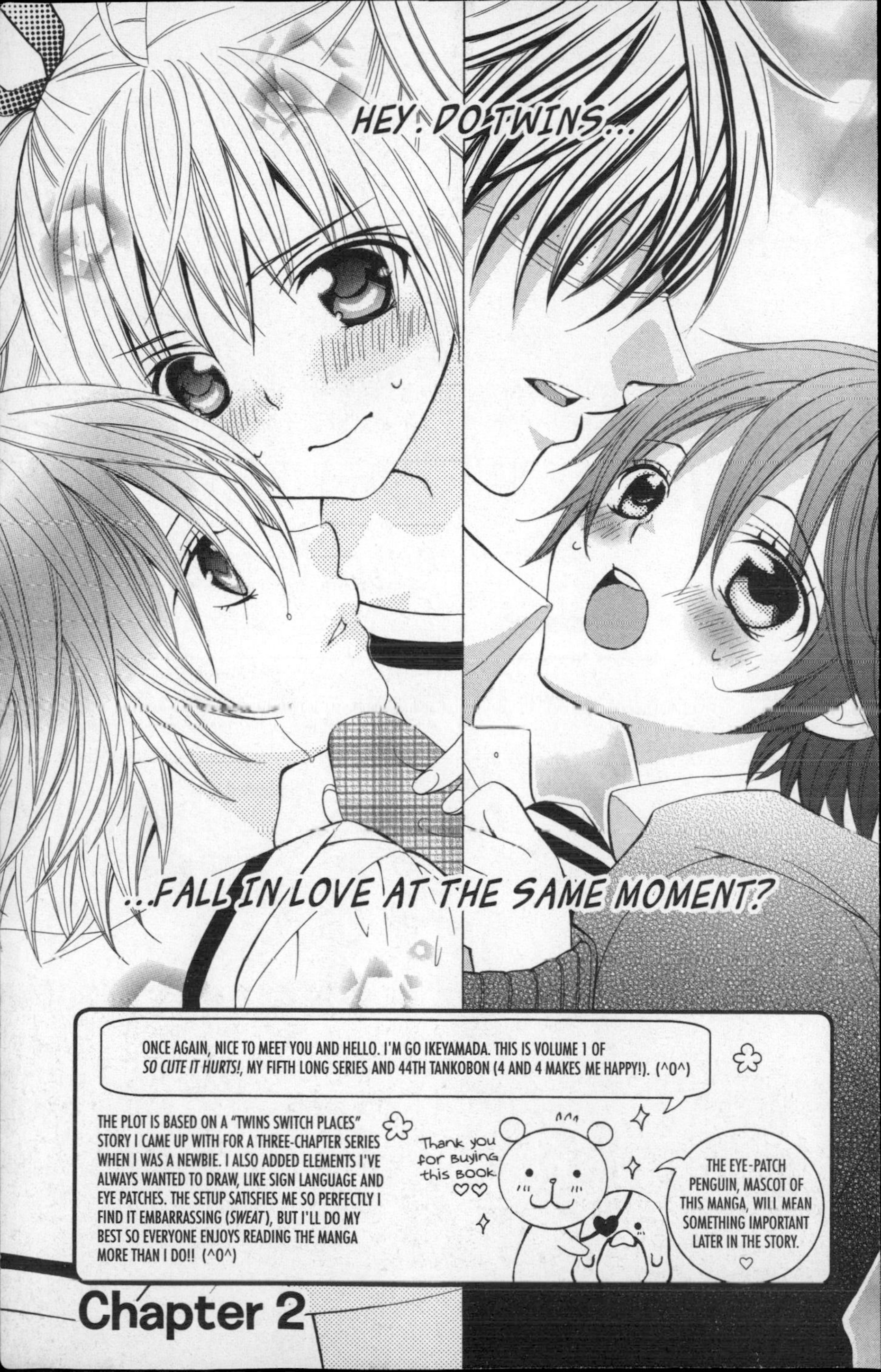
HEY. DO TWINS...
...FALL IN LOVE AT THE SAME MOMENT?
ONCE AGAIN, NICE TO MEET YOU AND HELLO. I'M GO IKEYAMADA. THIS IS VOLUME 1 OF *SO CUTE IT HURTS!*, MY FIFTH LONG SERIES AND 44TH TANKOBON (4 AND 4 MAKES ME HAPPY!). (^0^)
THE PLOT IS BASED ON A "TWINS SWITCH PLACES" STORY I CAME UP WITH FOR A THREE-CHAPTER SERIES WHEN I WAS A NEWBIE. I ALSO ADDED ELEMENTS I'VE ALWAYS WANTED TO DRAW, LIKE SIGN LANGUAGE AND EYE PATCHES. THE SETUP SATISFIES ME SO PERFECTLY I FIND IT EMBARRASSING (*SWEAT*), BUT I'LL DO MY BEST SO EVERYONE ENJOYS READING THE MANGA MORE THAN I DO!! (^0^)
Thank you for buying this book ♡♡
THE EYE-PATCH PENGUIN, MASCOT OF THIS MANGA, WILL MEAN SOMETHING IMPORTANT LATER IN THE STORY. ♡
Chapter 2

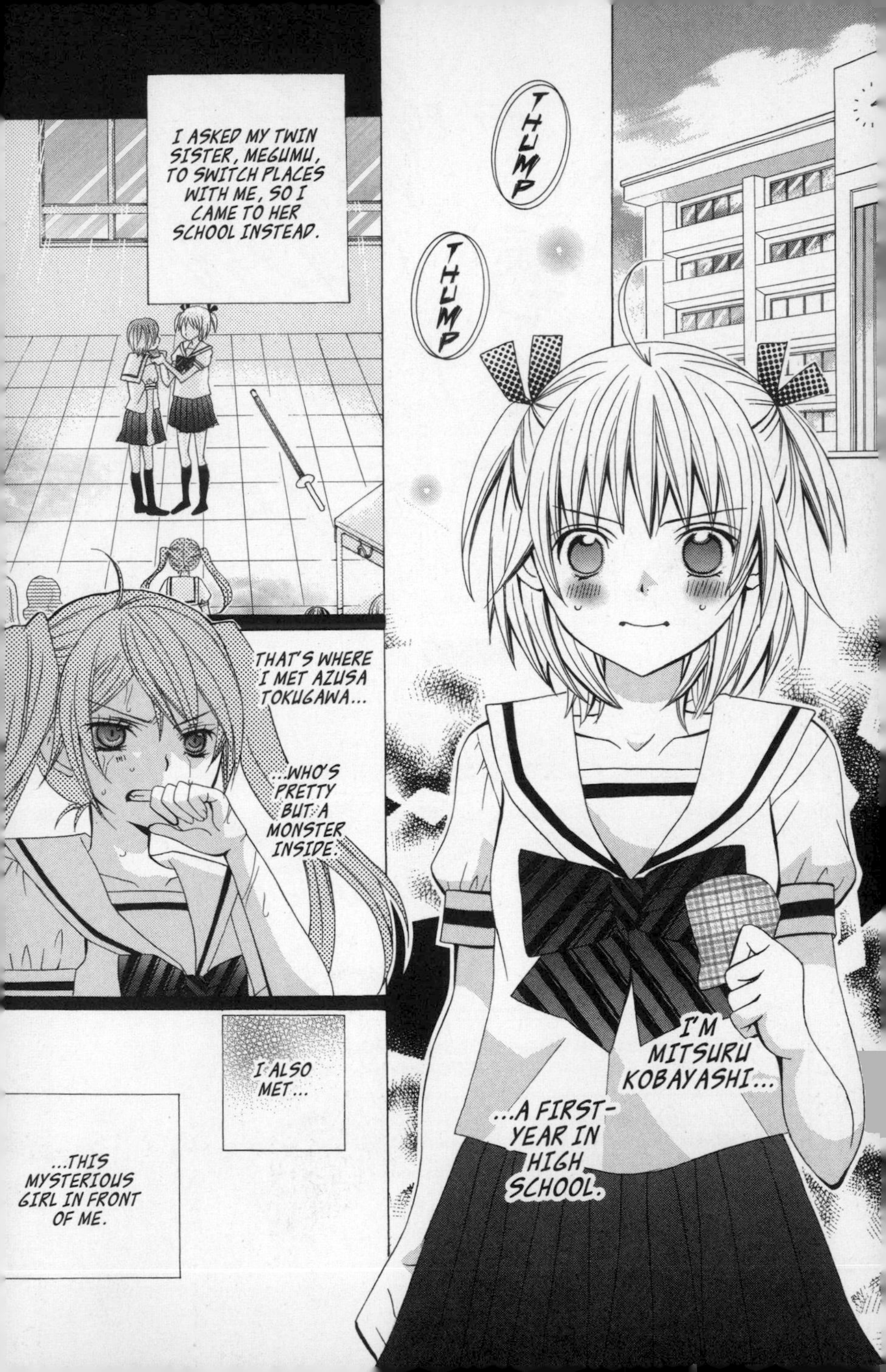
THUMP
THUMP
I'M MITSURU KOBAYASHI...
...A FIRST-YEAR IN HIGH SCHOOL.
I ASKED MY TWIN SISTER, MEGUMU, TO SWITCH PLACES WITH ME, SO I CAME TO HER SCHOOL INSTEAD.
THAT'S WHERE I MET AZUSA TOKUGAWA...
...WHO'S PRETTY BUT A MONSTER INSIDE.
I ALSO MET...
...THIS MYSTERIOUS GIRL IN FRONT OF ME.

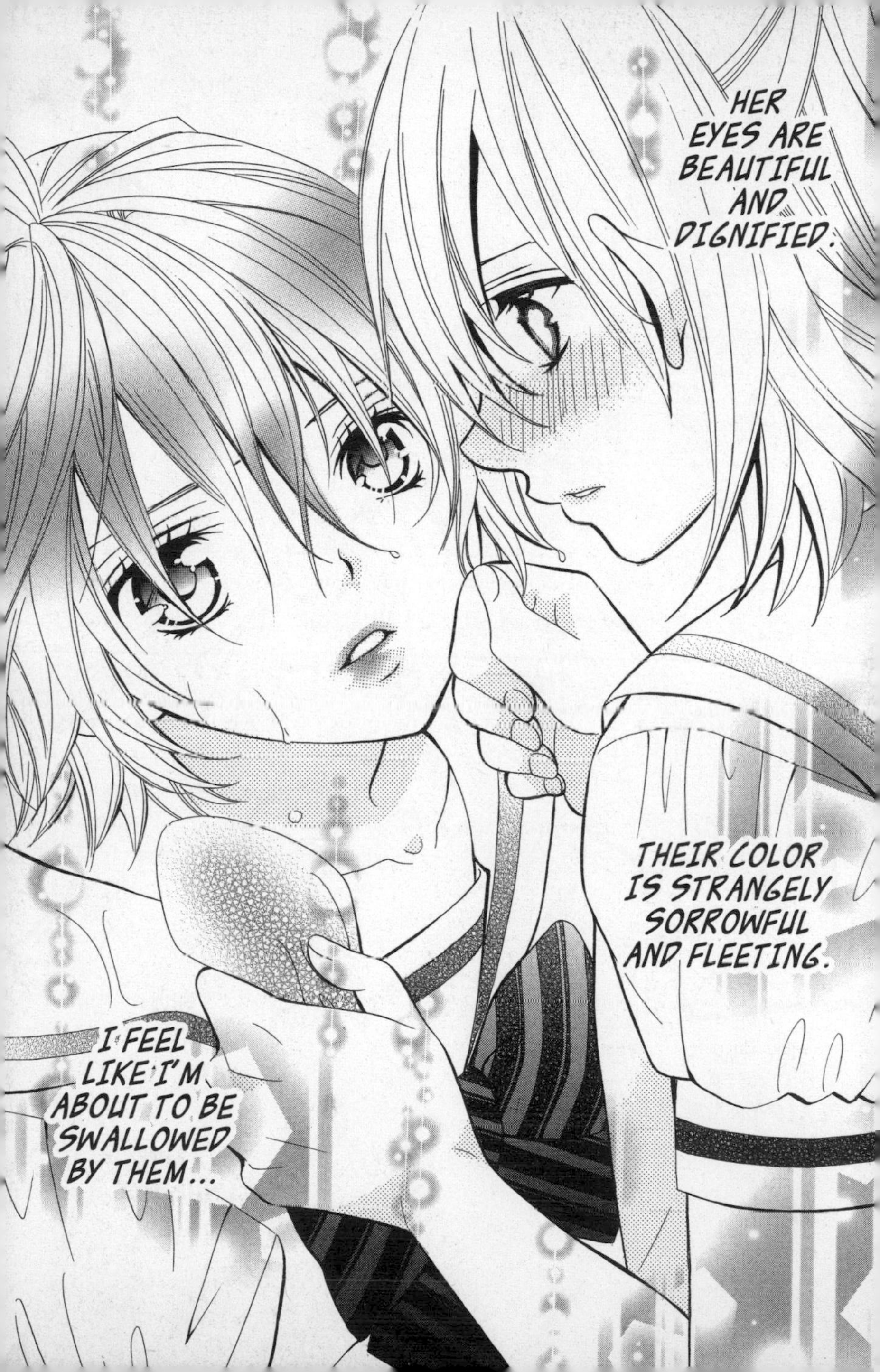
HER EYES ARE BEAUTIFUL AND DIGNIFIED.
THEIR COLOR IS STRANGELY SORROWFUL AND FLEETING.
I FEEL LIKE I'M ABOUT TO BE SWALLOWED BY THEM...

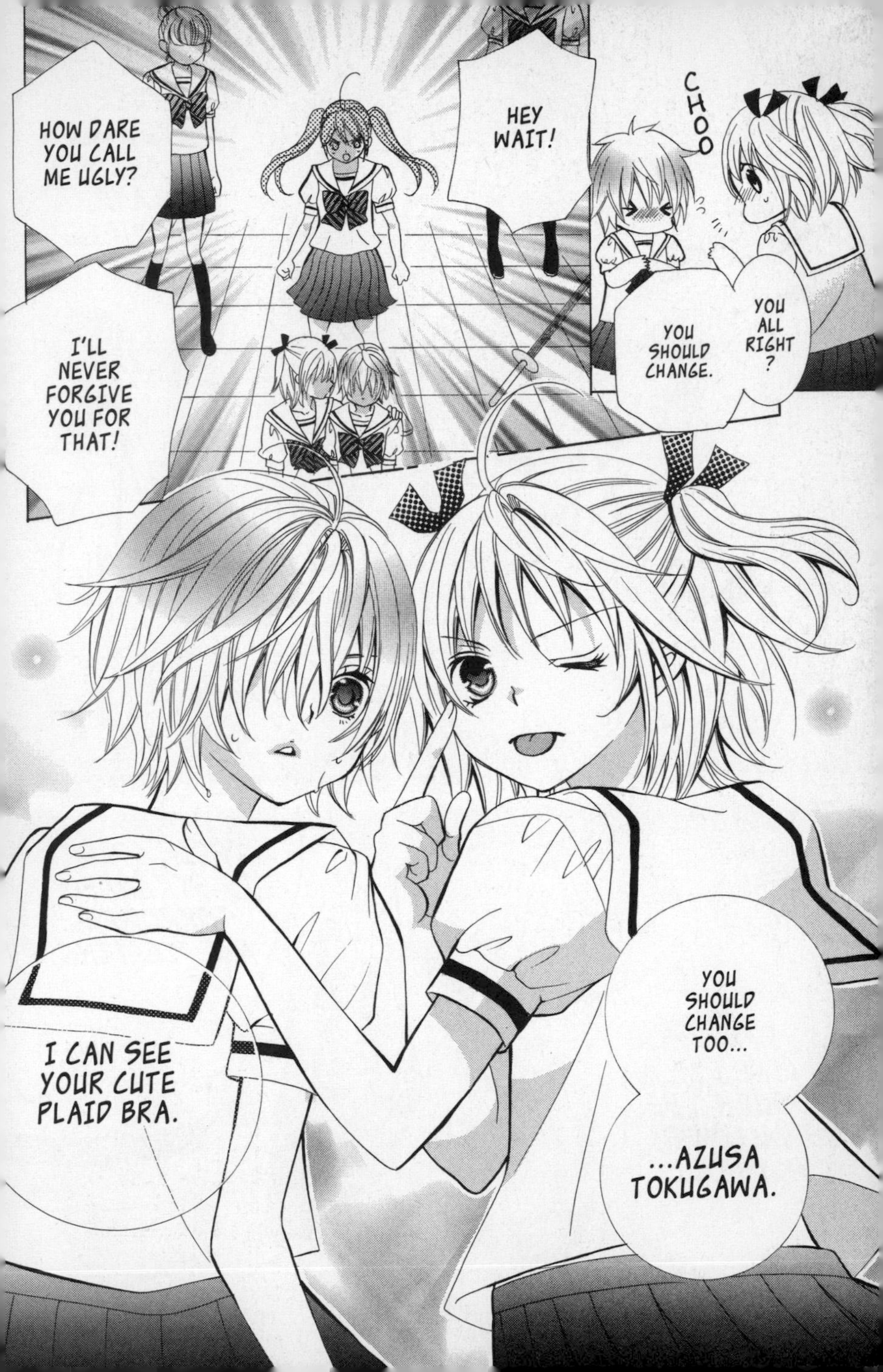
CHOO
YOU ALL RIGHT?
YOU SHOULD CHANGE.
HEY WAIT!
HOW DARE YOU CALL ME UGLY?
I'LL NEVER FORGIVE YOU FOR THAT!
YOU SHOULD CHANGE TOO...
...AZUSA TOKUGAWA.
I CAN SEE YOUR CUTE PLAID BRA.

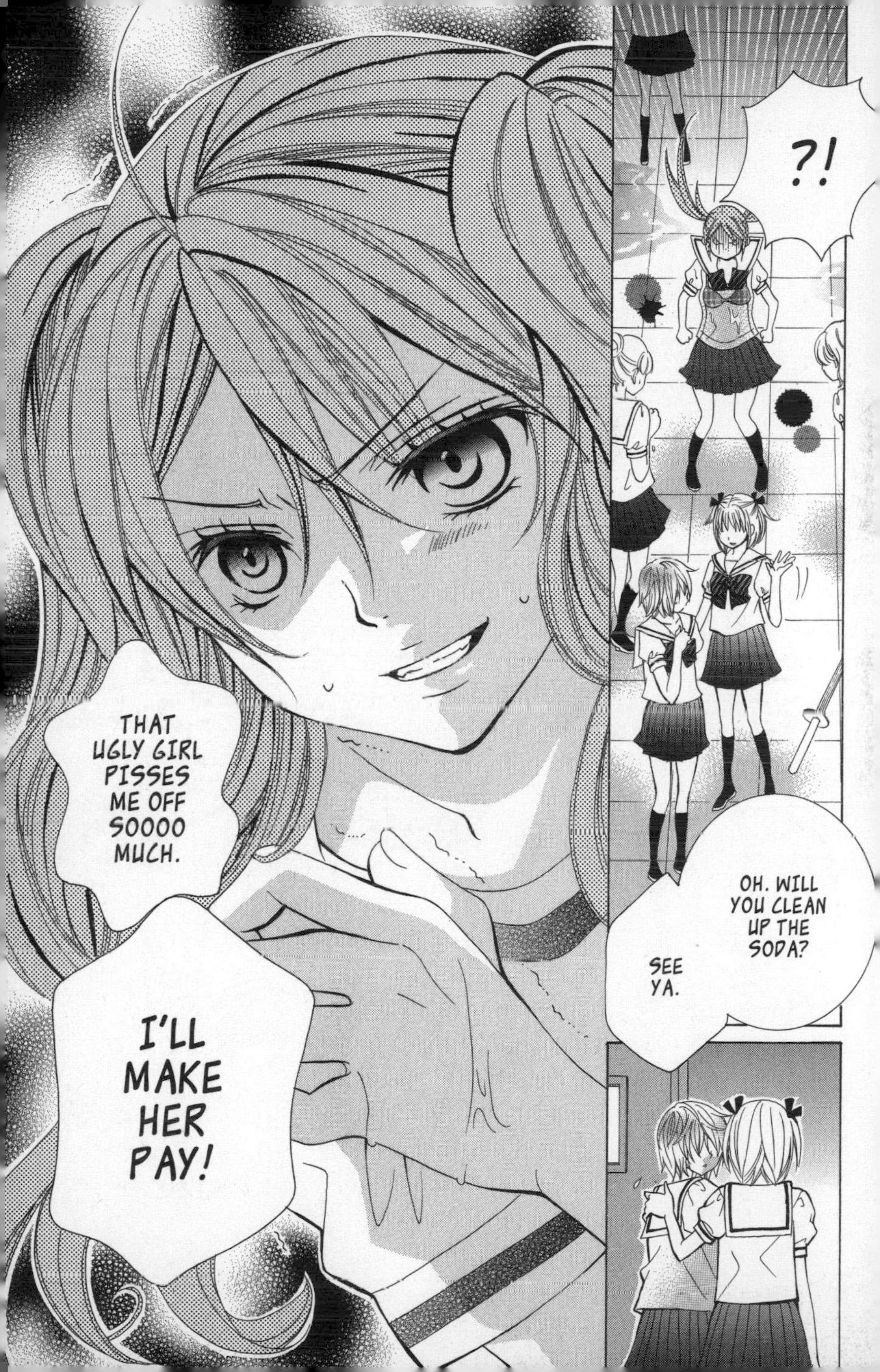
?!
OH. WILL YOU CLEAN UP THE SODA?
SEE YA.
THAT UGLY GIRL PISSES ME OFF SOOOO MUCH.
I'LL MAKE HER PAY!

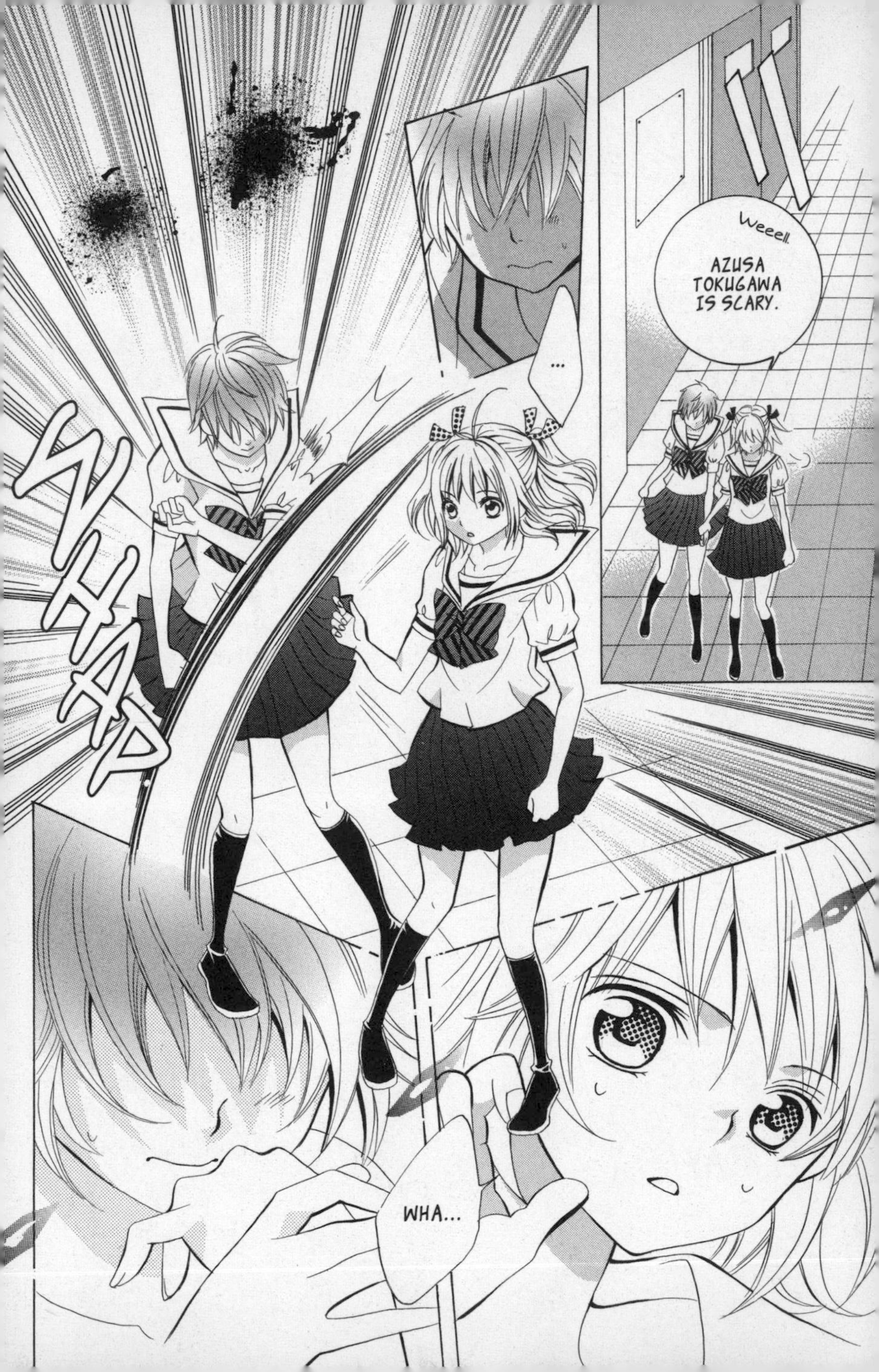
Weeell.
AZUSA TOKUGAWA IS SCARY.
...
WHAP
WHA...

A Slightly Serious Chat...

MY PREVIOUS SERIES *SUKI DESU SUZUKI-KUN* RAN FOR FOUR YEARS. AFTER THE SERIES WAS COMPLETE, I THOUGHT ABOUT TAKING TIME OFF OR REQUESTING A TRANSFER TO A MONTHLY MAGAZINE WITH FEWER DEADLINES.

(I LOVE *SHO-COMI*, BUT IT'S A SHOJO MANGA MAGAZINE WITH THE MOST DEADLINES IN JAPAN. IT'S BEEN TEN YEARS SINCE I BECAME A PROFESSIONAL MANGAKA, AND I'D LOST CONFIDENCE IN MY PHYSICAL STRENGTH...)

HOWEVER, MY YOUNG EDITOR EARNESTLY SAID, "I'VE BEEN SO LOOKING FORWARD TO WORKING ON A NEW SERIES WITH YOU!" AND WON ME OVER. I FELT HIS YOUTH AND PASSION WOULD COMPENSATE FOR WHAT I LACK.

MOREOVER, I DECIDED I'D DO MY BEST TO THE UTMOST LIMIT AS LONG AS THE MAGAZINE AND THE READERS WHO'VE NURTURED ME FROM MY DEBUT (PEOPLE I OWE SO MUCH TO STILL) NEED ME! AND SO I DECIDED TO START A NEW SERIES.

I'M APPREHENSIVE ABOUT A LOT OF THINGS LIKE MY PHYSICAL STRENGTH, BUT I'D LIKE TO DO MY BEST AND ENJOY DRAWING MY MANGA WITH THE HELP OF MY ASSISTANTS, MY EDITOR AND ALL OF YOU READERS!! (^o^)

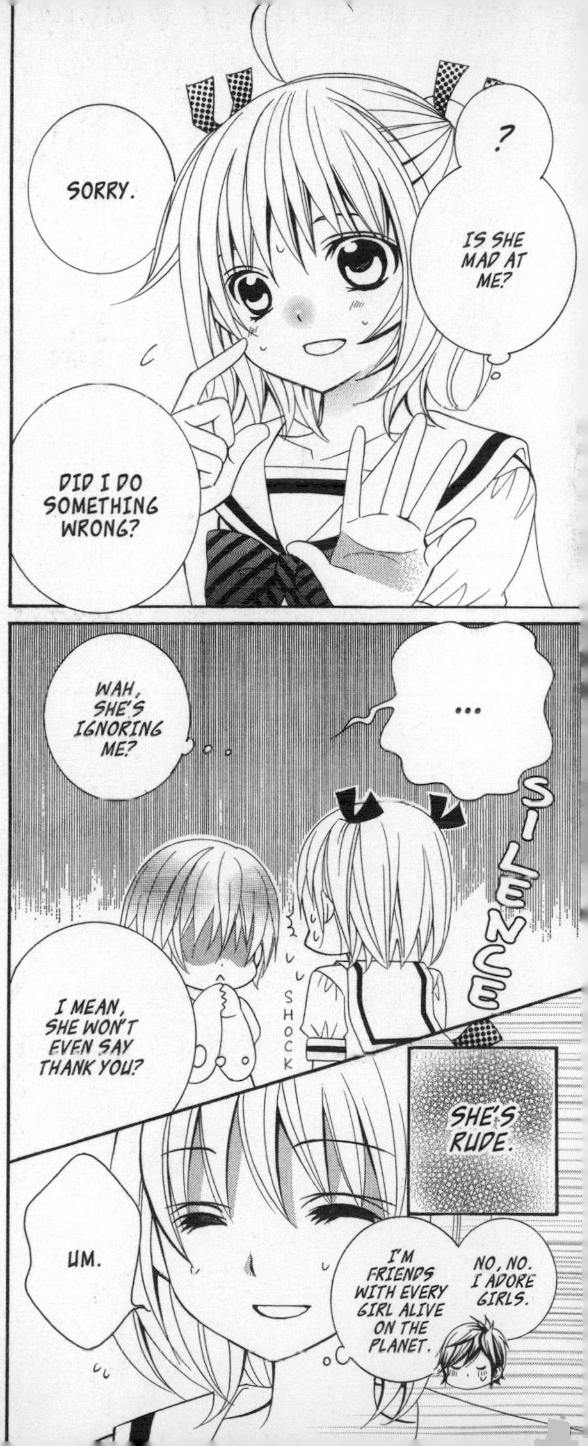
?
IS SHE MAD AT ME?
SORRY.
DID I DO SOMETHING WRONG?
...
SILENCE
WAH, SHE'S IGNORING ME?
SHOCK
I MEAN, SHE WON'T EVEN SAY THANK YOU?
SHE'S RUDE.
NO, NO. I ADORE GIRLS.
I'M FRIENDS WITH EVERY GIRL ALIVE ON THE PLANET.
UM.

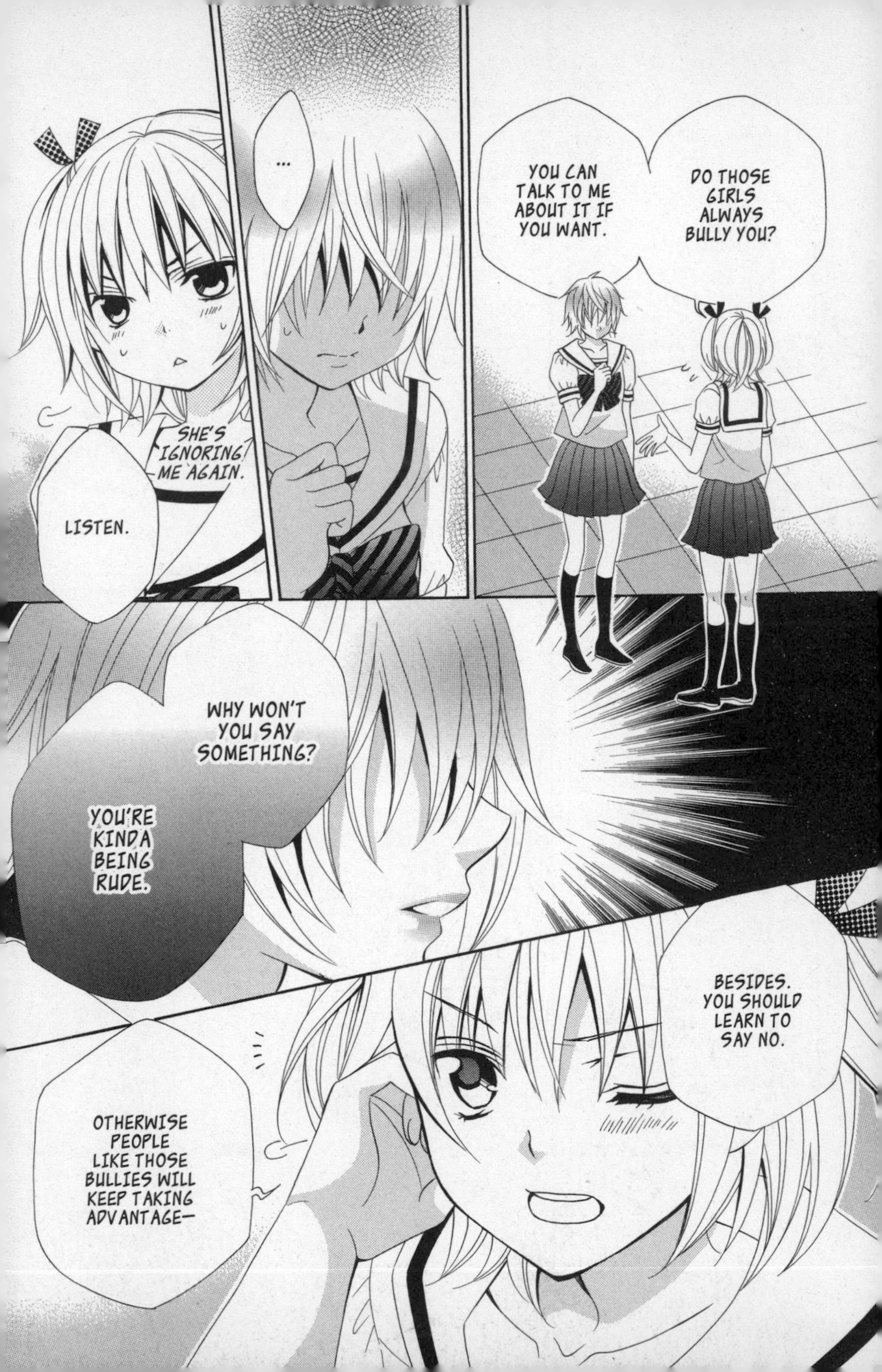
DO THOSE GIRLS ALWAYS BULLY YOU?
YOU CAN TALK TO ME ABOUT IT IF YOU WANT.
...
SHE'S IGNORING ME AGAIN.
LISTEN.
WHY WON'T YOU SAY SOMETHING?
YOU'RE KINDA BEING RUDE.
BESIDES. YOU SHOULD LEARN TO SAY NO.
OTHERWISE PEOPLE LIKE THOSE BULLIES WILL KEEP TAKING ADVANTAGE—

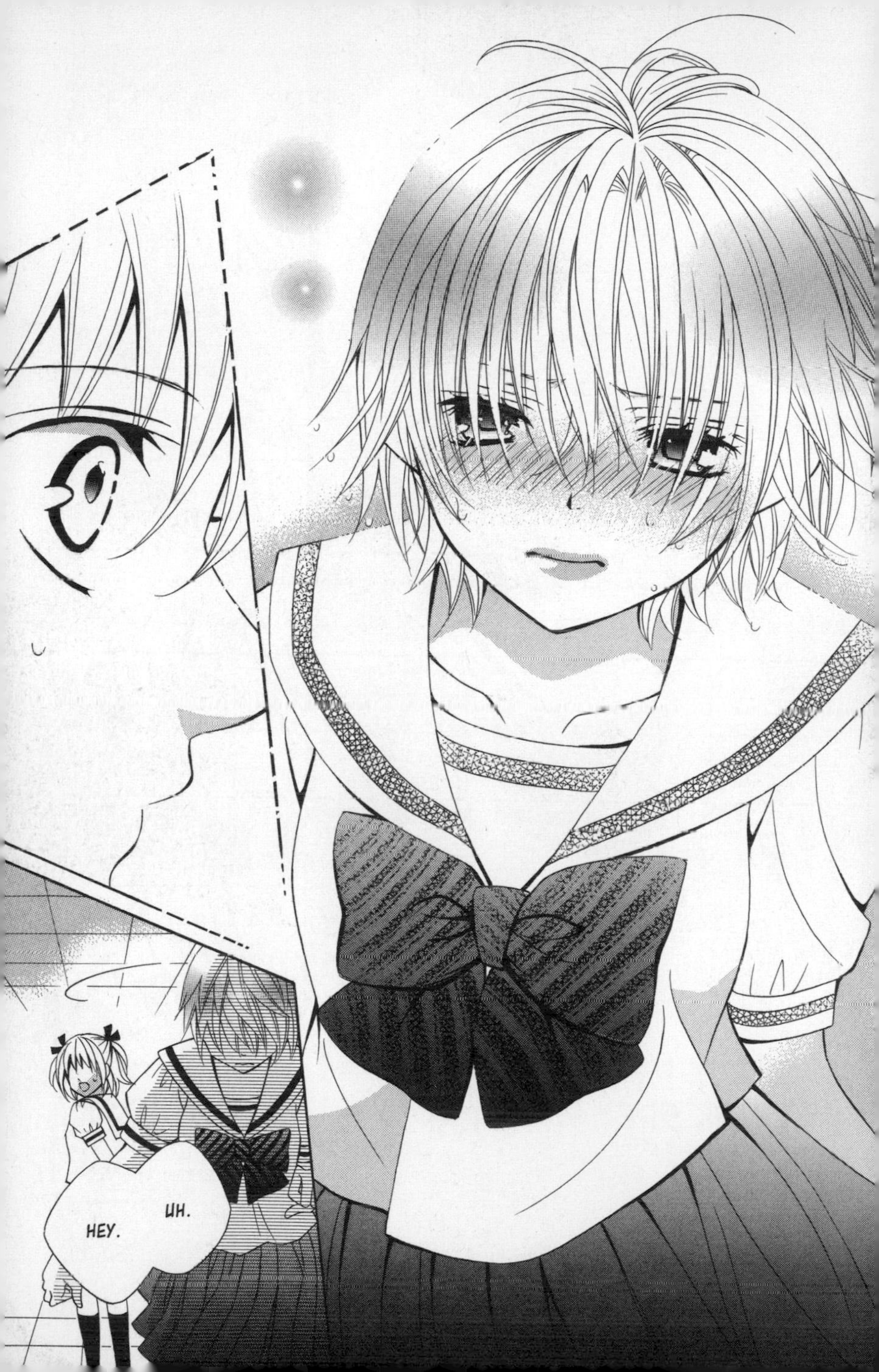
UH.
HEY.

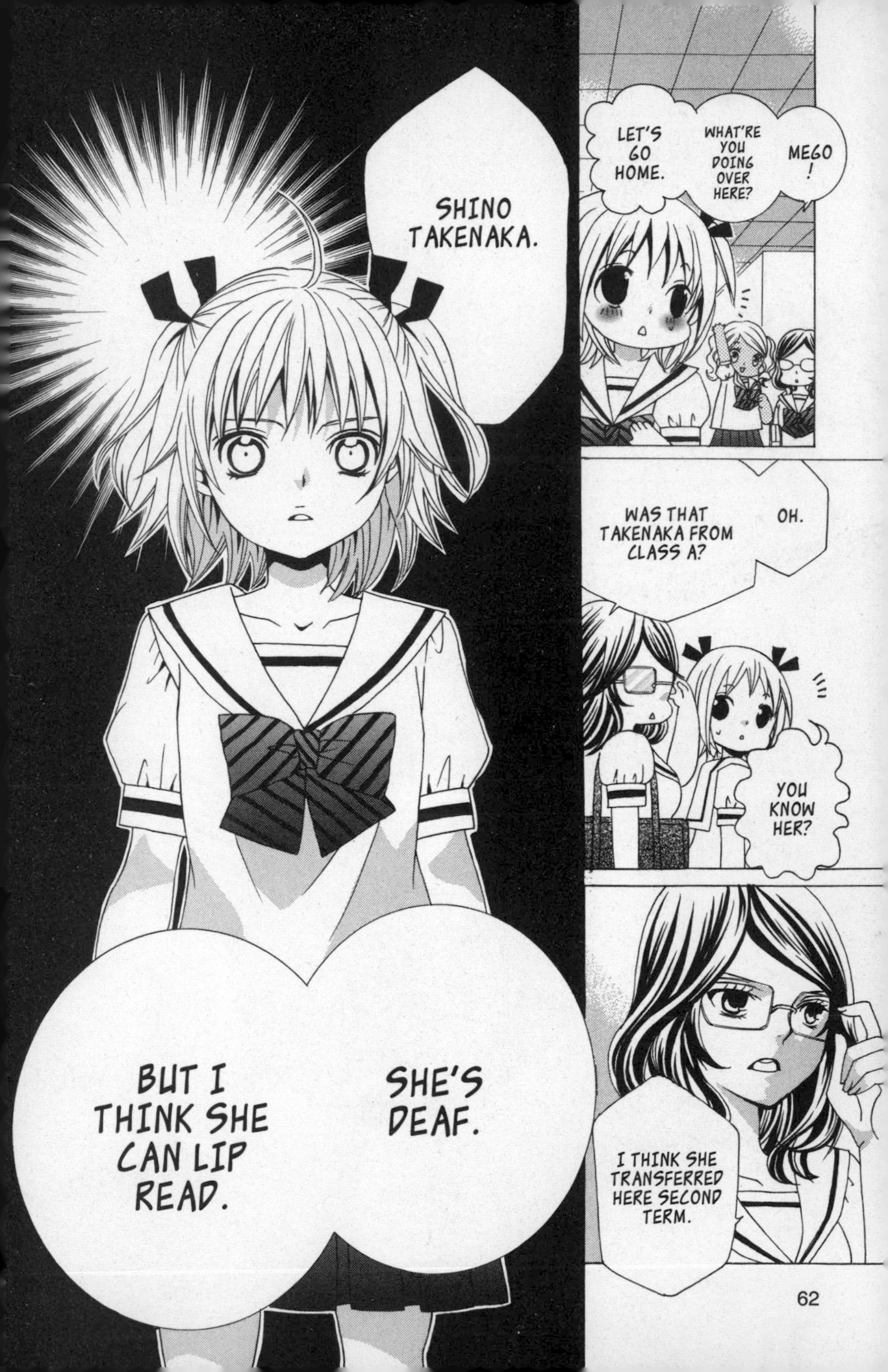
MEGO!
WHAT'RE YOU DOING OVER HERE?
LET'S GO HOME.
OH.
WAS THAT TAKENAKA FROM CLASS A?
YOU KNOW HER?
I THINK SHE TRANSFERRED HERE SECOND TERM.
SHINO TAKENAKA.
SHE'S DEAF.
BUT I THINK SHE CAN LIP READ.

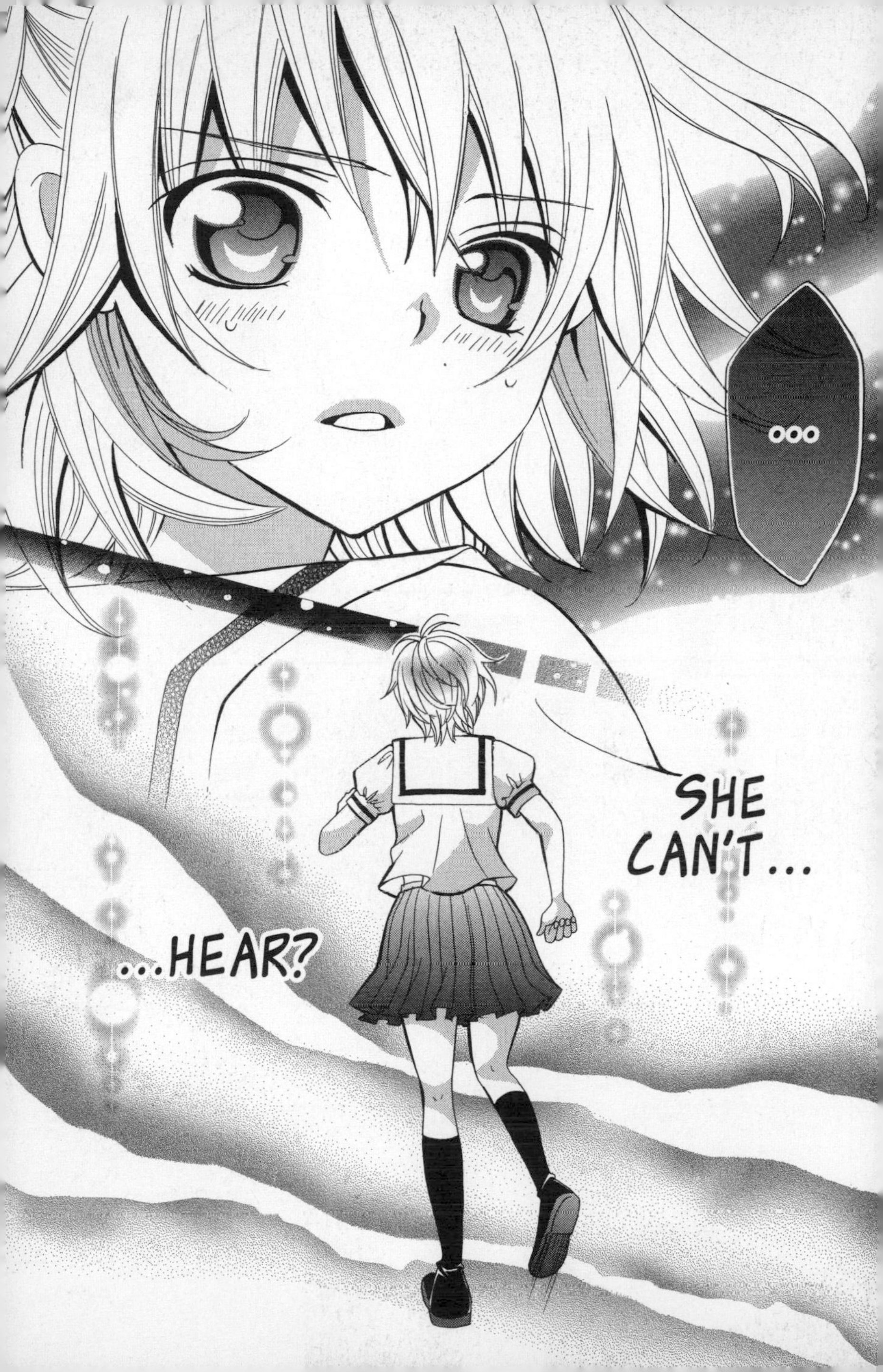
...
SHE CAN'T...
...HEAR?

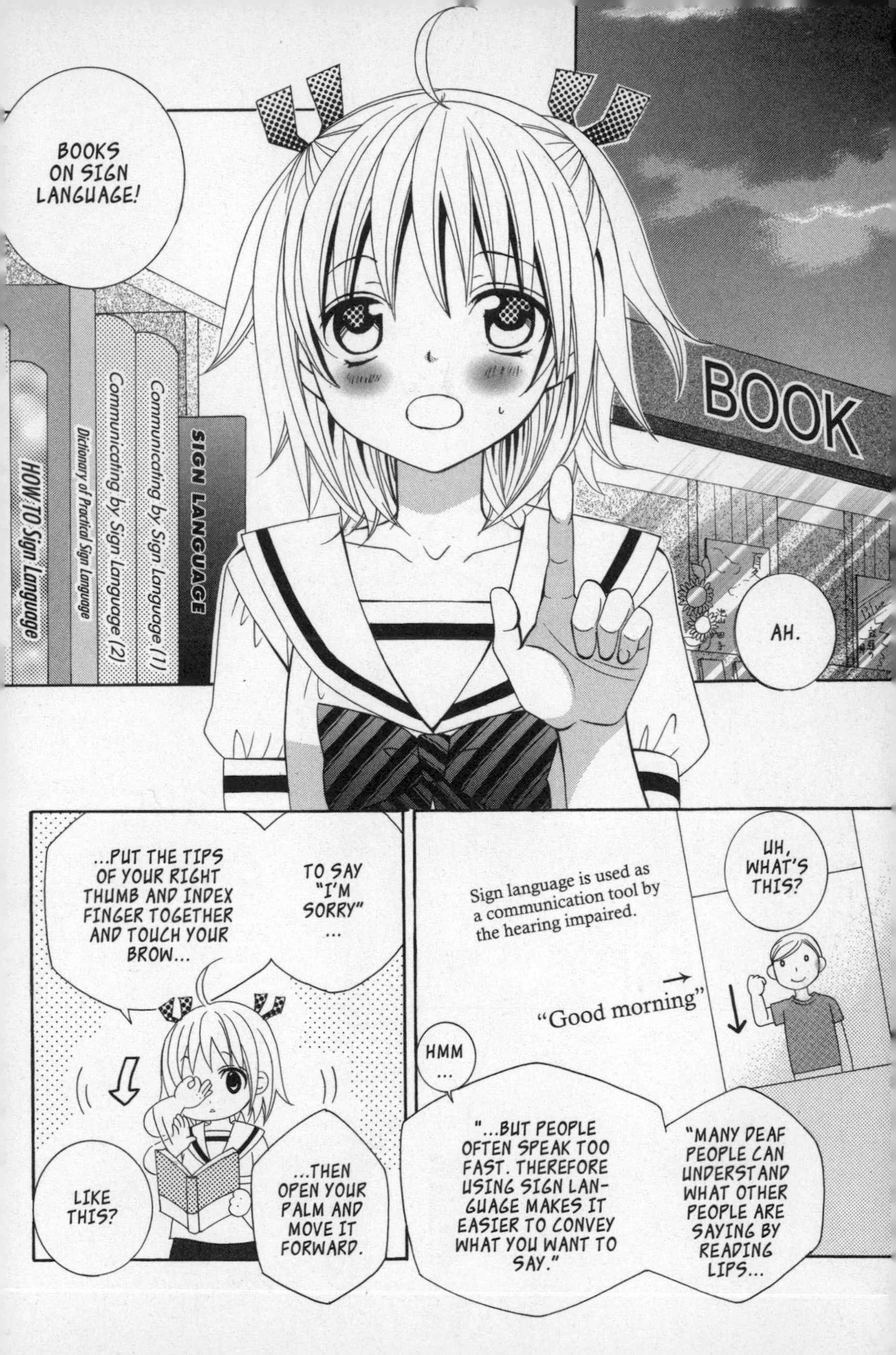
AH.
BOOKS ON SIGN LANGUAGE!
BOOK
SIGN LANGUAGE
Communicating by Sign Language (1)
Communicating by Sign Language (2)
Dictionary of Practical Sign Language
HOW TO Sign Language
UH, WHAT'S THIS?
Sign language is used as a communication tool by the hearing impaired.
"Good morning"
HMM...
"MANY DEAF PEOPLE CAN UNDERSTAND WHAT OTHER PEOPLE ARE SAYING BY READING LIPS...
"...BUT PEOPLE OFTEN SPEAK TOO FAST. THEREFORE USING SIGN LANGUAGE MAKES IT EASIER TO CONVEY WHAT YOU WANT TO SAY."
TO SAY "I'M SORRY"...
...PUT THE TIPS OF YOUR RIGHT THUMB AND INDEX FINGER TOGETHER AND TOUCH YOUR BROW...
...THEN OPEN YOUR PALM AND MOVE IT FORWARD.
LIKE THIS?

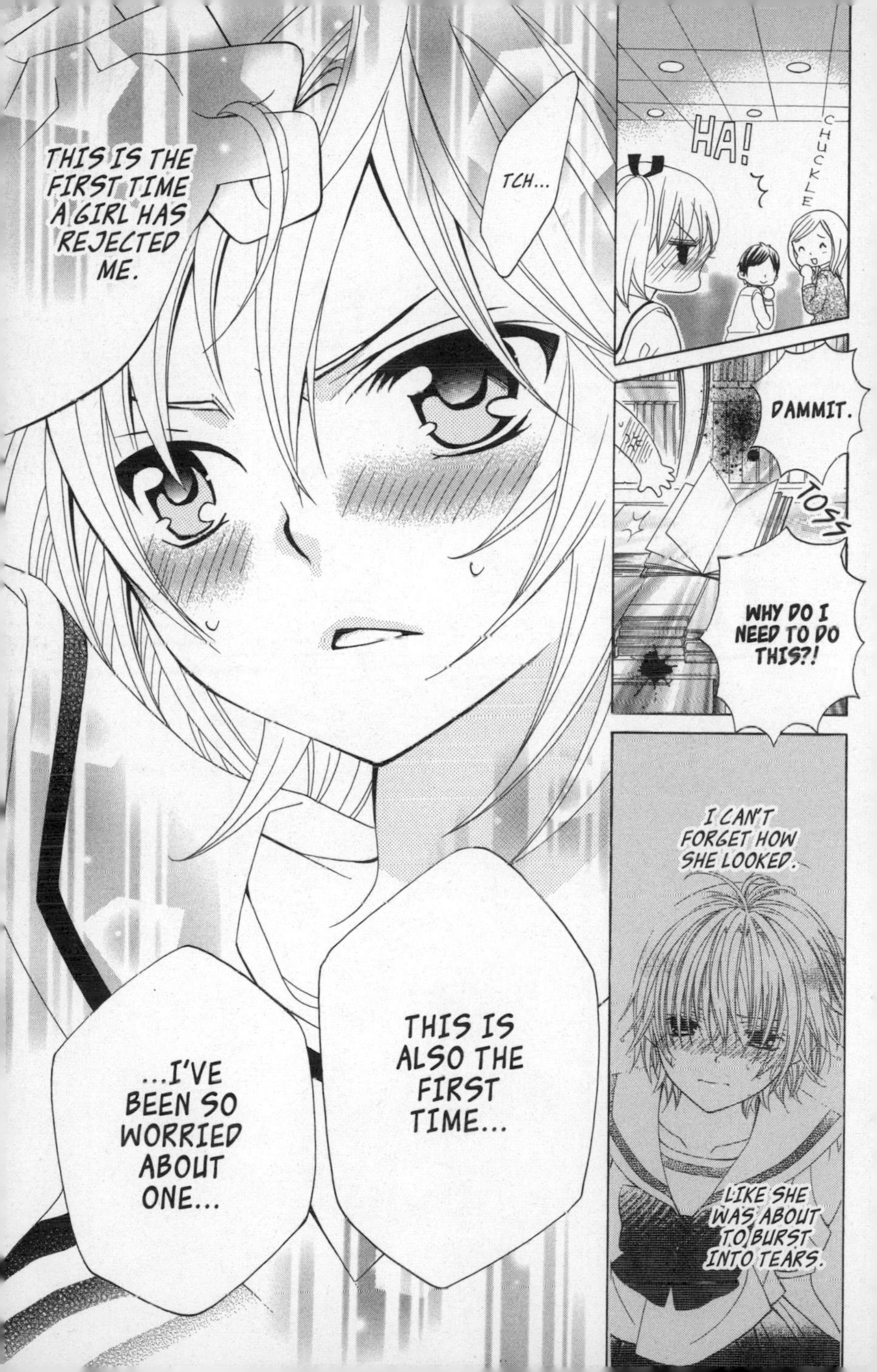
HA!
CHUCKLE
DAMMIT.
TOSS
WHY DO I NEED TO DO THIS?!
I CAN'T FORGET HOW SHE LOOKED.
LIKE SHE WAS ABOUT TO BURST INTO TEARS.
TCH...
THIS IS THE FIRST TIME A GIRL HAS REJECTED ME.
THIS IS ALSO THE FIRST TIME...
...I'VE BEEN SO WORRIED ABOUT ONE...

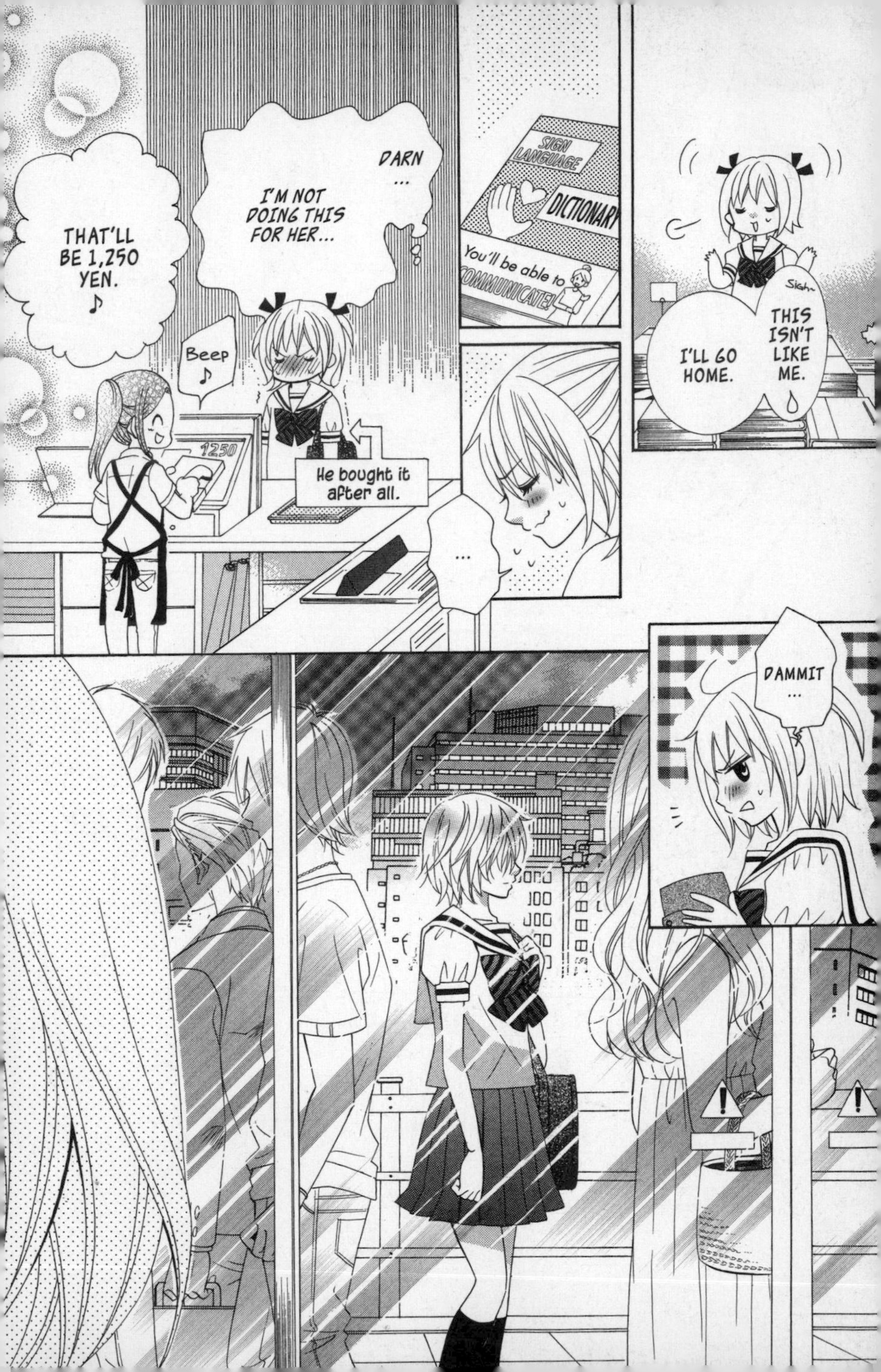
Sigh~
THIS ISN'T LIKE ME.
I'LL GO HOME.
SIGN LANGUAGE DICTIONARY
You'll be able to COMMUNICATE!
...
DARN ...
I'M NOT DOING THIS FOR HER...
Beep ♪
He bought it after all.
1250
THAT'LL BE 1,250 YEN. ♪
DAMMIT ...

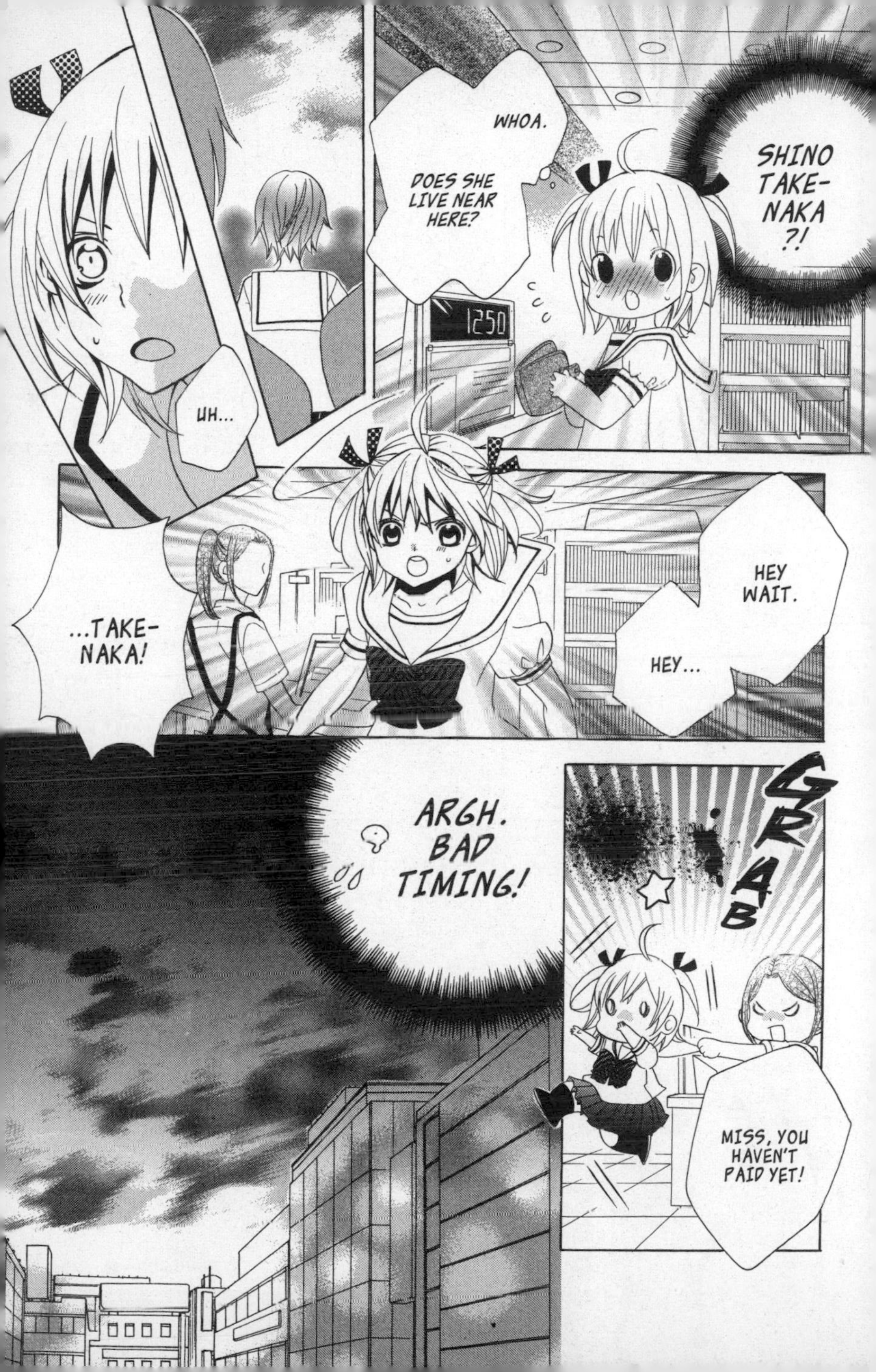
SHINO TAKE-NAKA?!
WHOA.
DOES SHE LIVE NEAR HERE?
1250
UH...
HEY WAIT.
HEY...
...TAKE-NAKA!
GRAB
MISS, YOU HAVEN'T PAID YET!
ARGH. BAD TIMING!

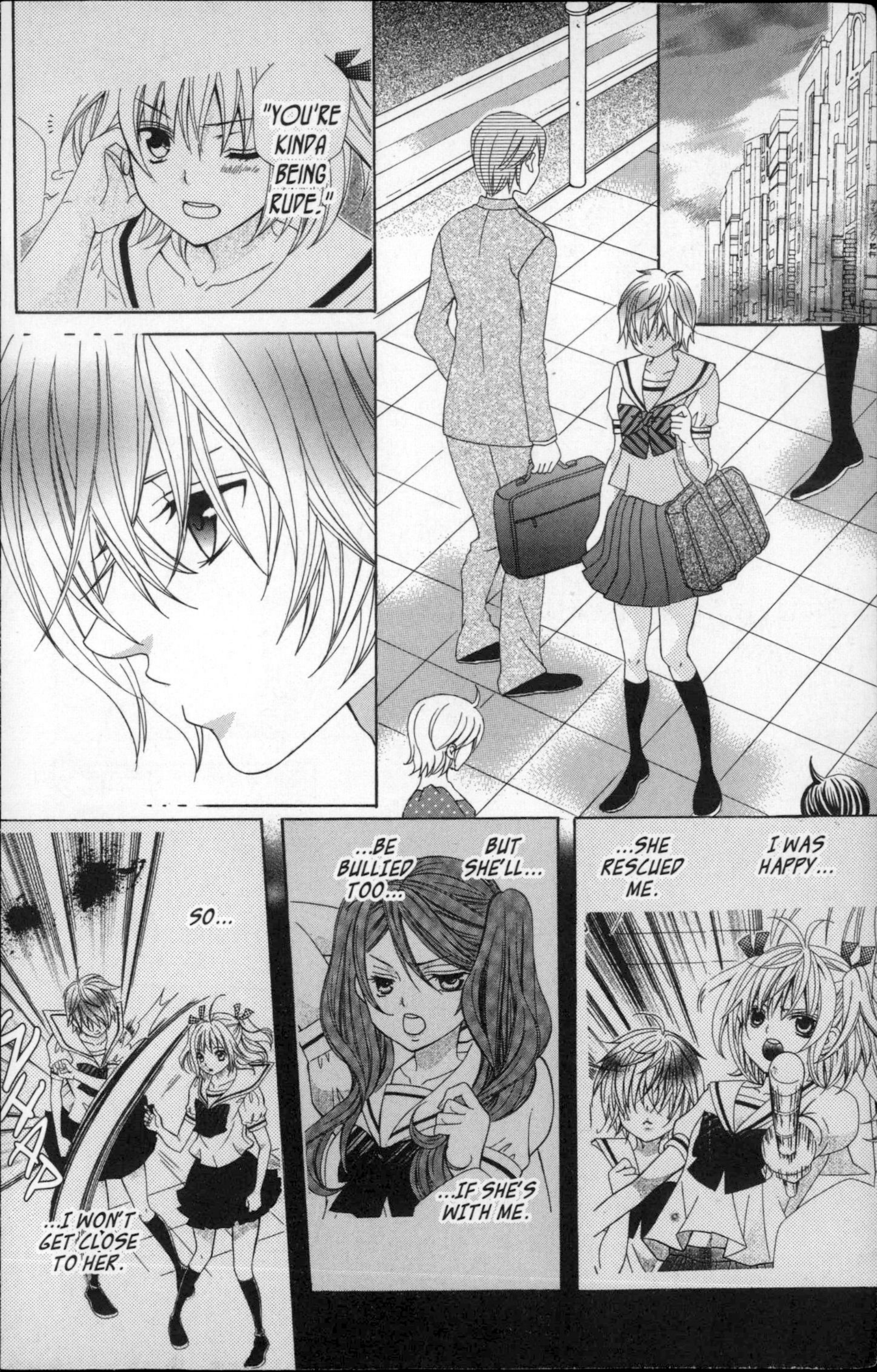
"YOU'RE KINDA BEING RUDE."
I WAS HAPPY...
...SHE RESCUED ME.
BUT SHE'LL...
...BE BULLIED TOO...
...IF SHE'S WITH ME.
SO...
...I WON'T GET CLOSE TO HER.

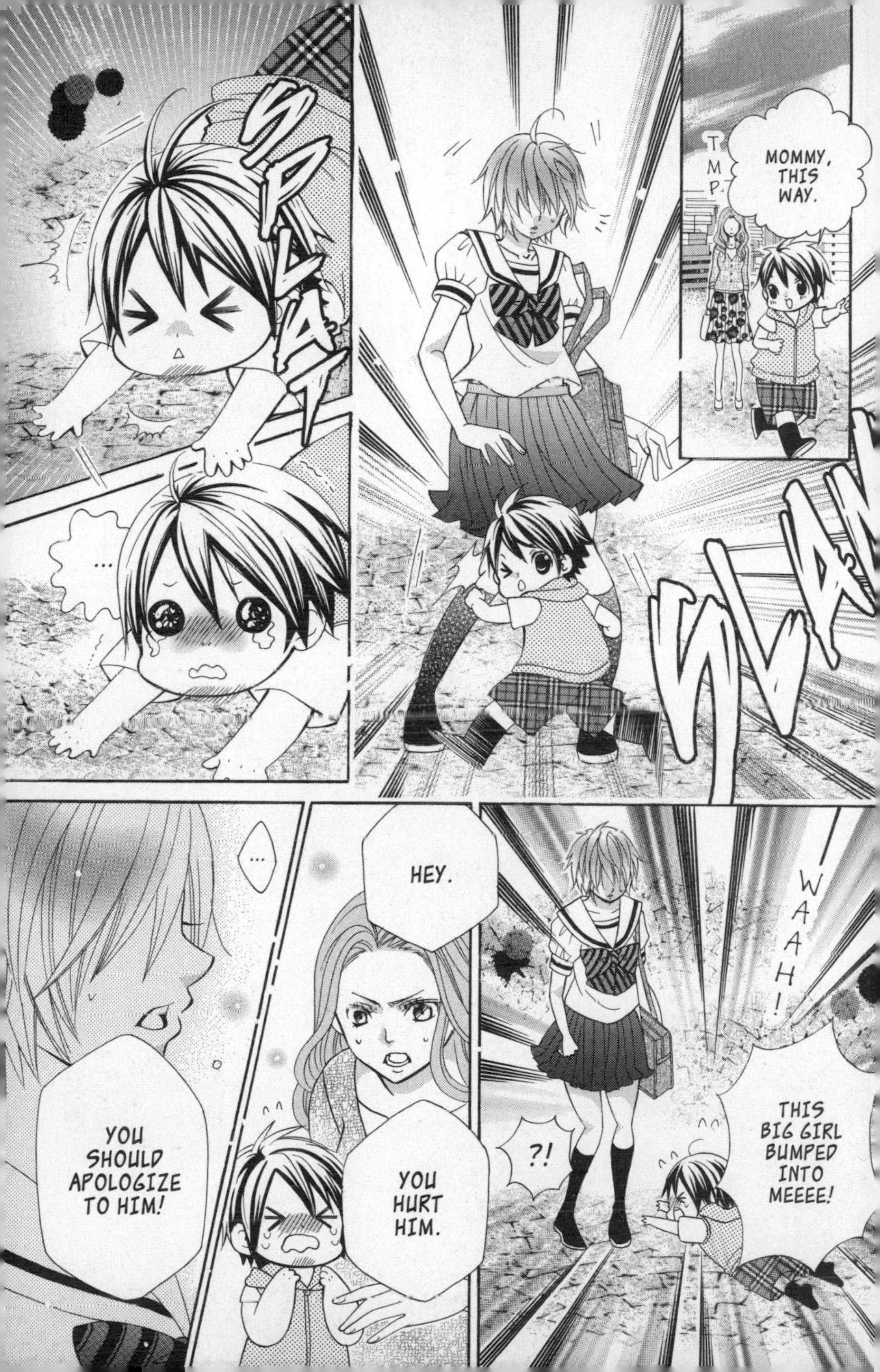
TMP
MOMMY, THIS WAY.
SPLAT
...
WAAH!
THIS BIG GIRL BUMPED INTO MEEEE!
?!
HEY.
YOU HURT HIM.
...
YOU SHOULD APOLOGIZE TO HIM!

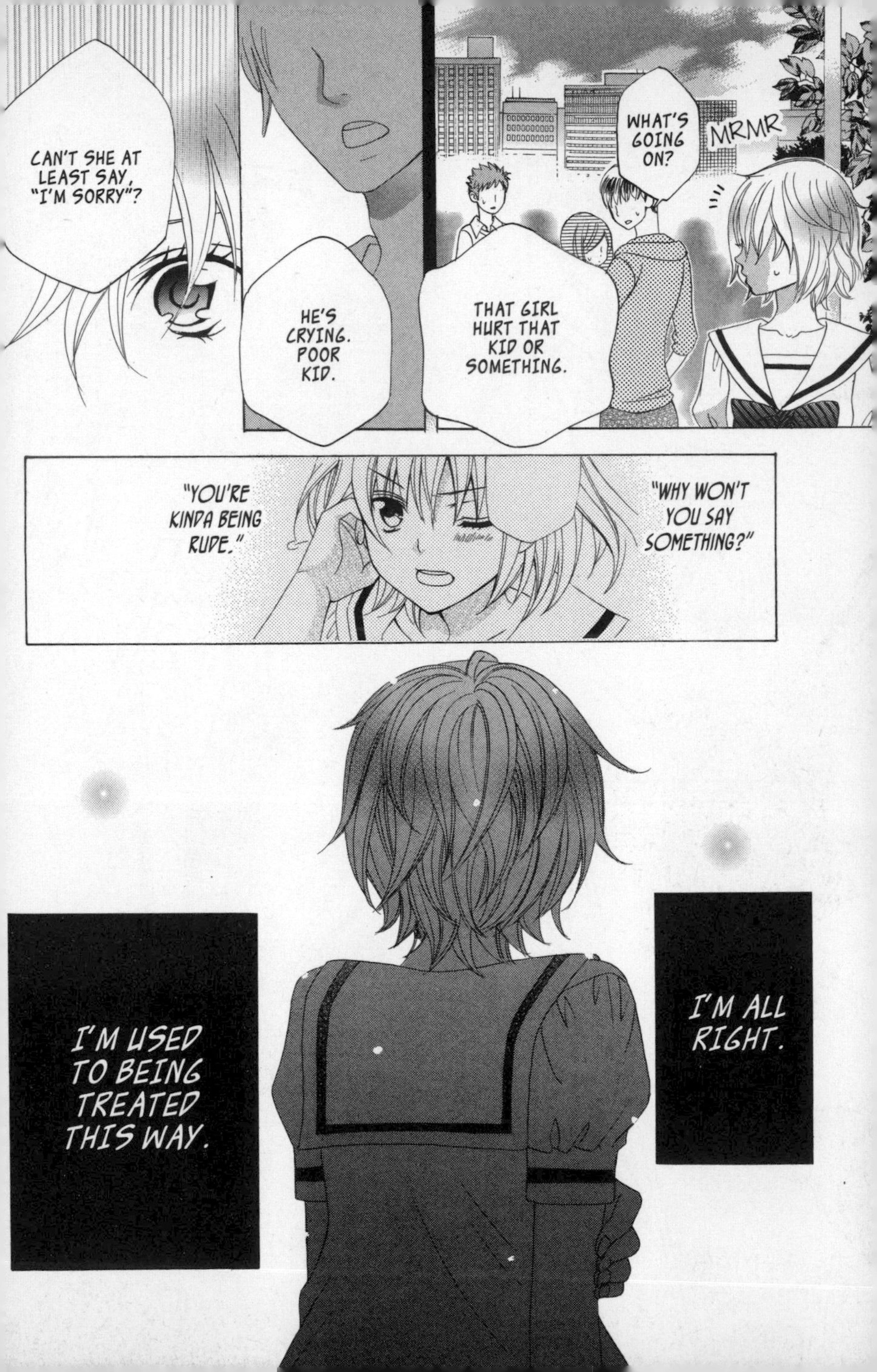
MRMR
WHAT'S GOING ON?
THAT GIRL HURT THAT KID OR SOMETHING.
HE'S CRYING. POOR KID.
CAN'T SHE AT LEAST SAY, "I'M SORRY"?
"WHY WON'T YOU SAY SOMETHING?"
"YOU'RE KINDA BEING RUDE."
I'M ALL RIGHT.
I'M USED TO BEING TREATED THIS WAY.

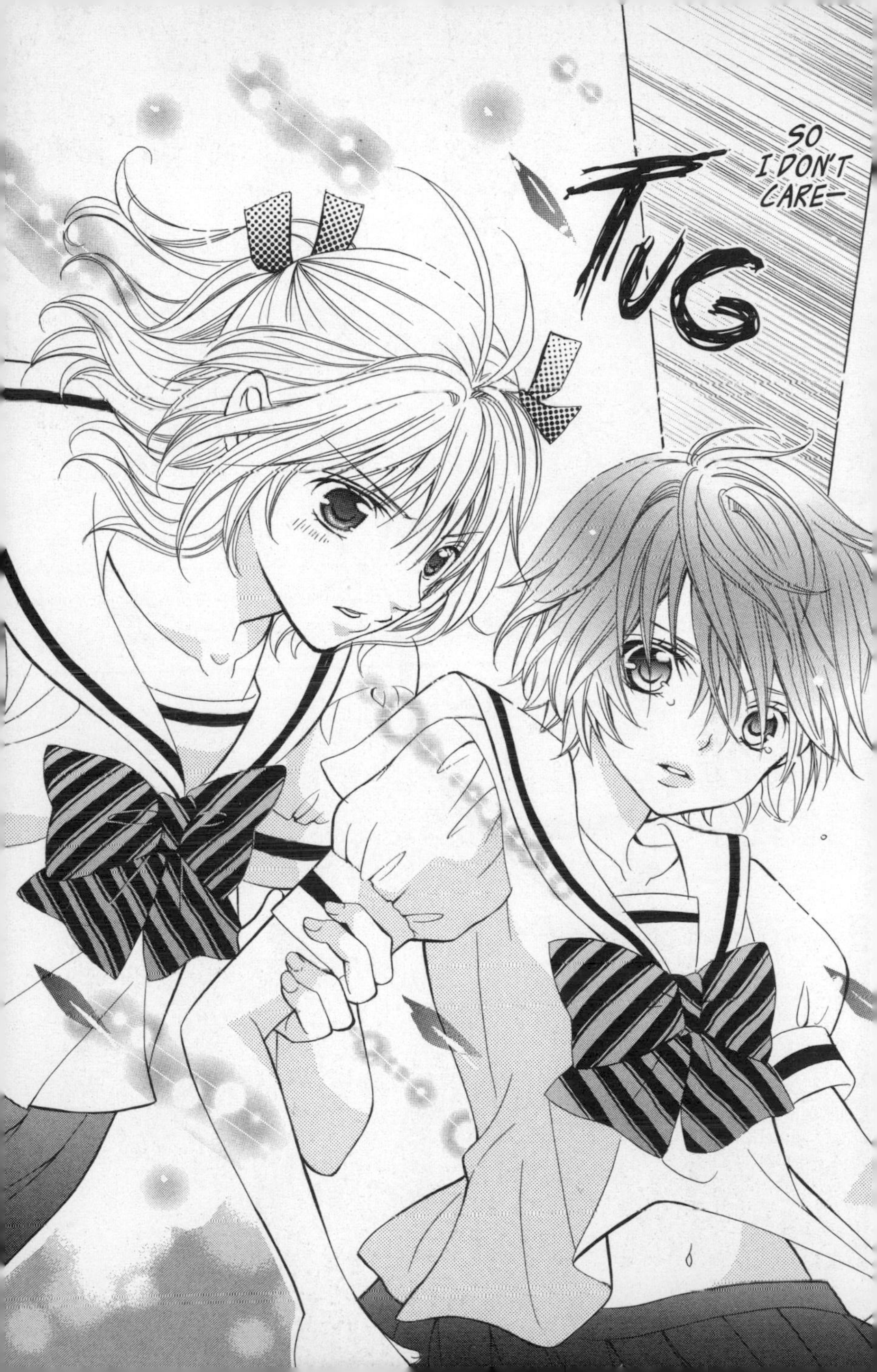
SO I DON'T CARE—
TUG

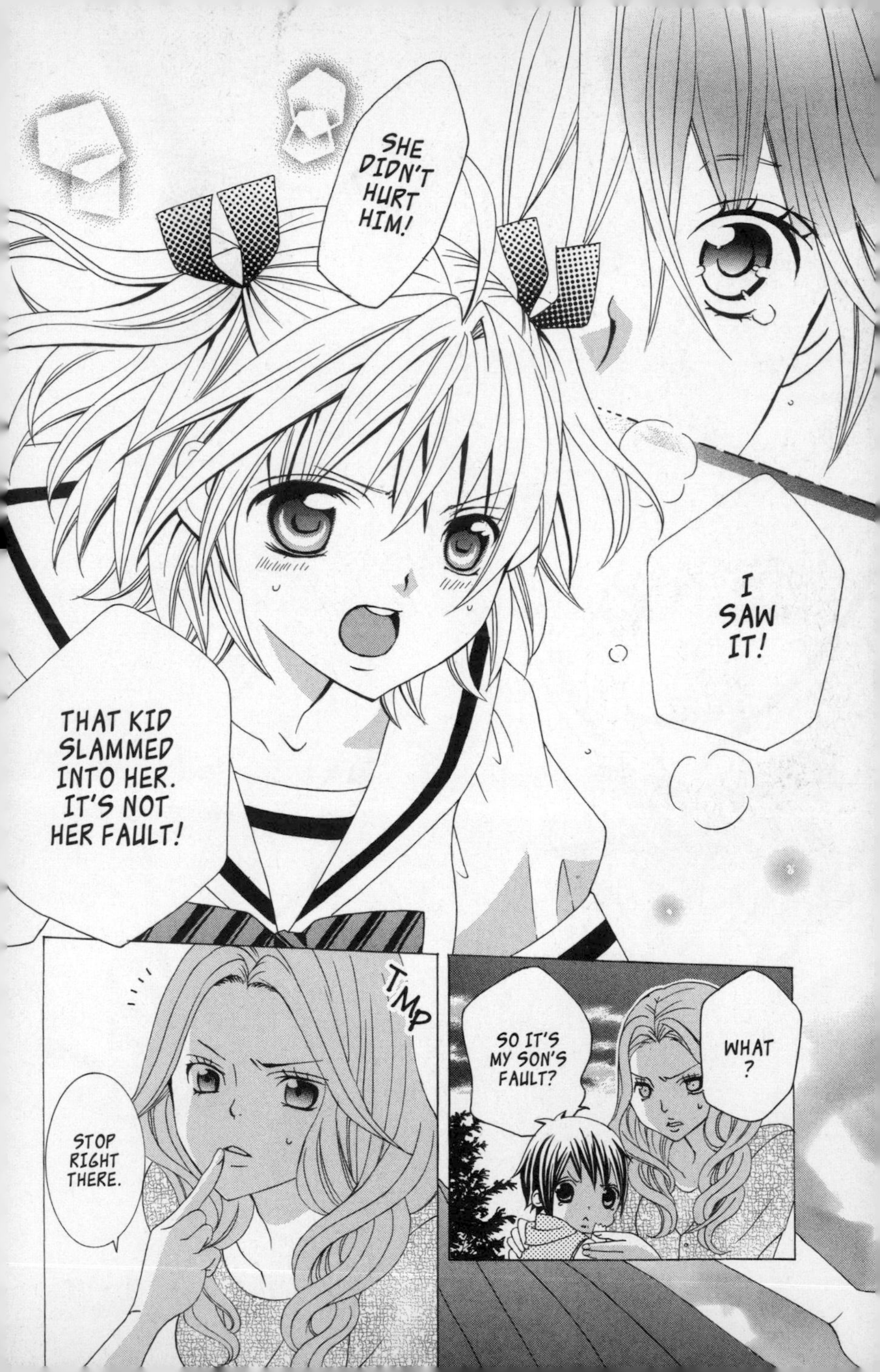
SHE DIDN'T HURT HIM!
I SAW IT!
THAT KID SLAMMED INTO HER. IT'S NOT HER FAULT!
WHAT?
SO IT'S MY SON'S FAULT?
TMP
STOP RIGHT THERE.

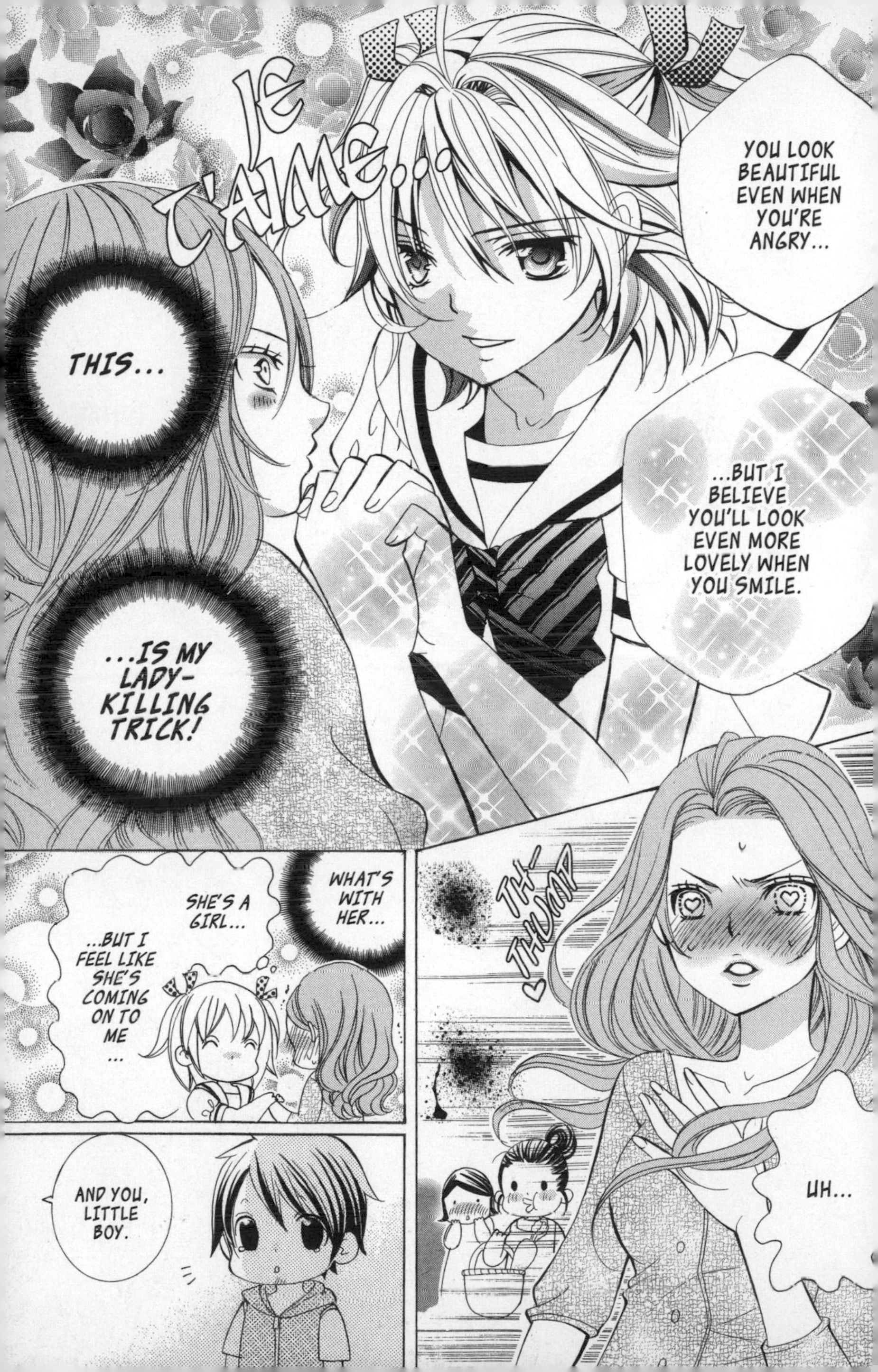
YOU LOOK BEAUTIFUL EVEN WHEN YOU'RE ANGRY...
JE T'AIME...
...BUT I BELIEVE YOU'LL LOOK EVEN MORE LOVELY WHEN YOU SMILE.
THIS...
...IS MY LADY-KILLING TRICK!
TH-THUMP
UH...
WHAT'S WITH HER...
SHE'S A GIRL...
...BUT I FEEL LIKE SHE'S COMING ON TO ME ...
AND YOU, LITTLE BOY.

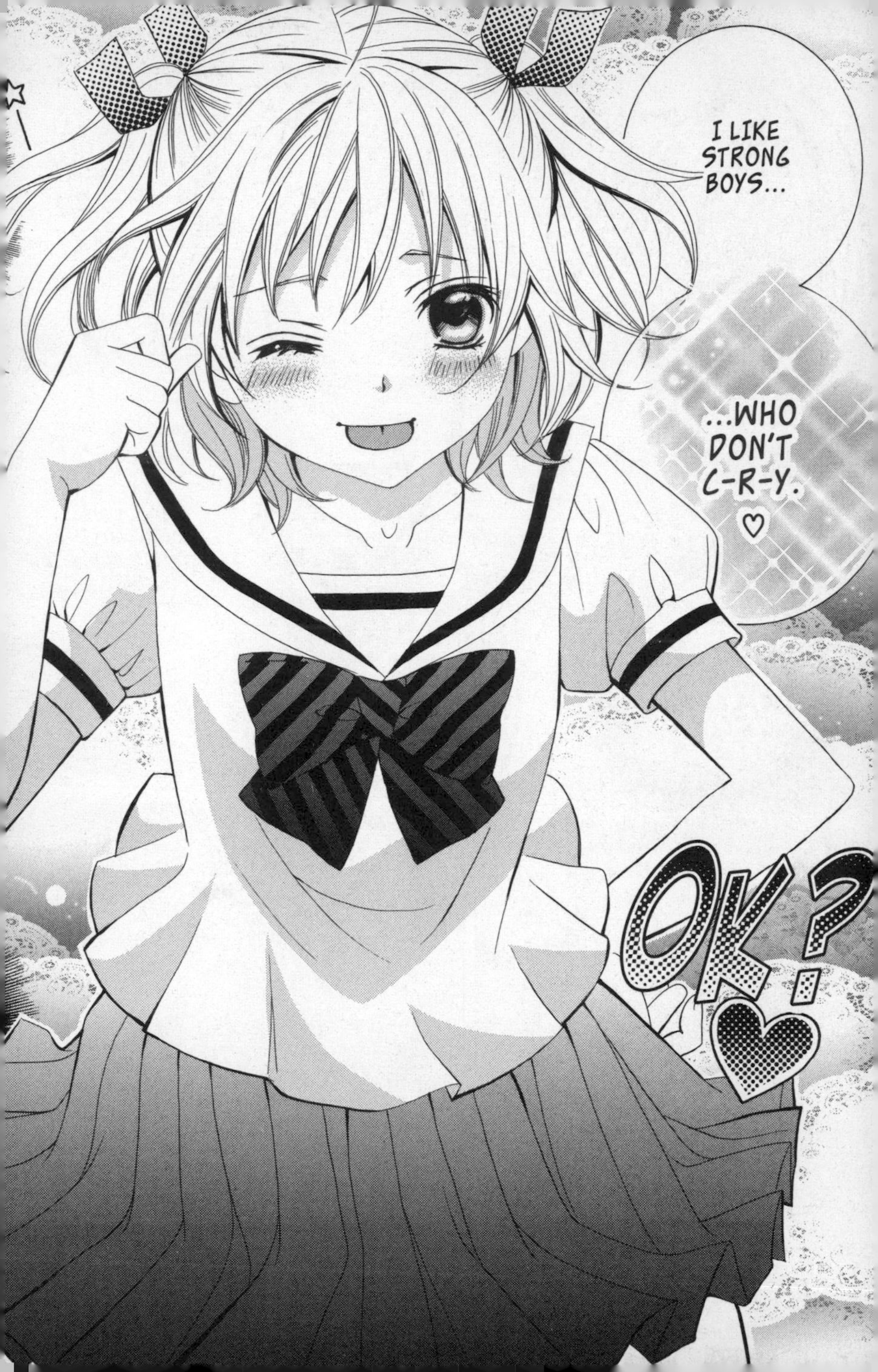
I LIKE STRONG BOYS...
...WHO DON'T C-R-Y. ♡
OK?♥

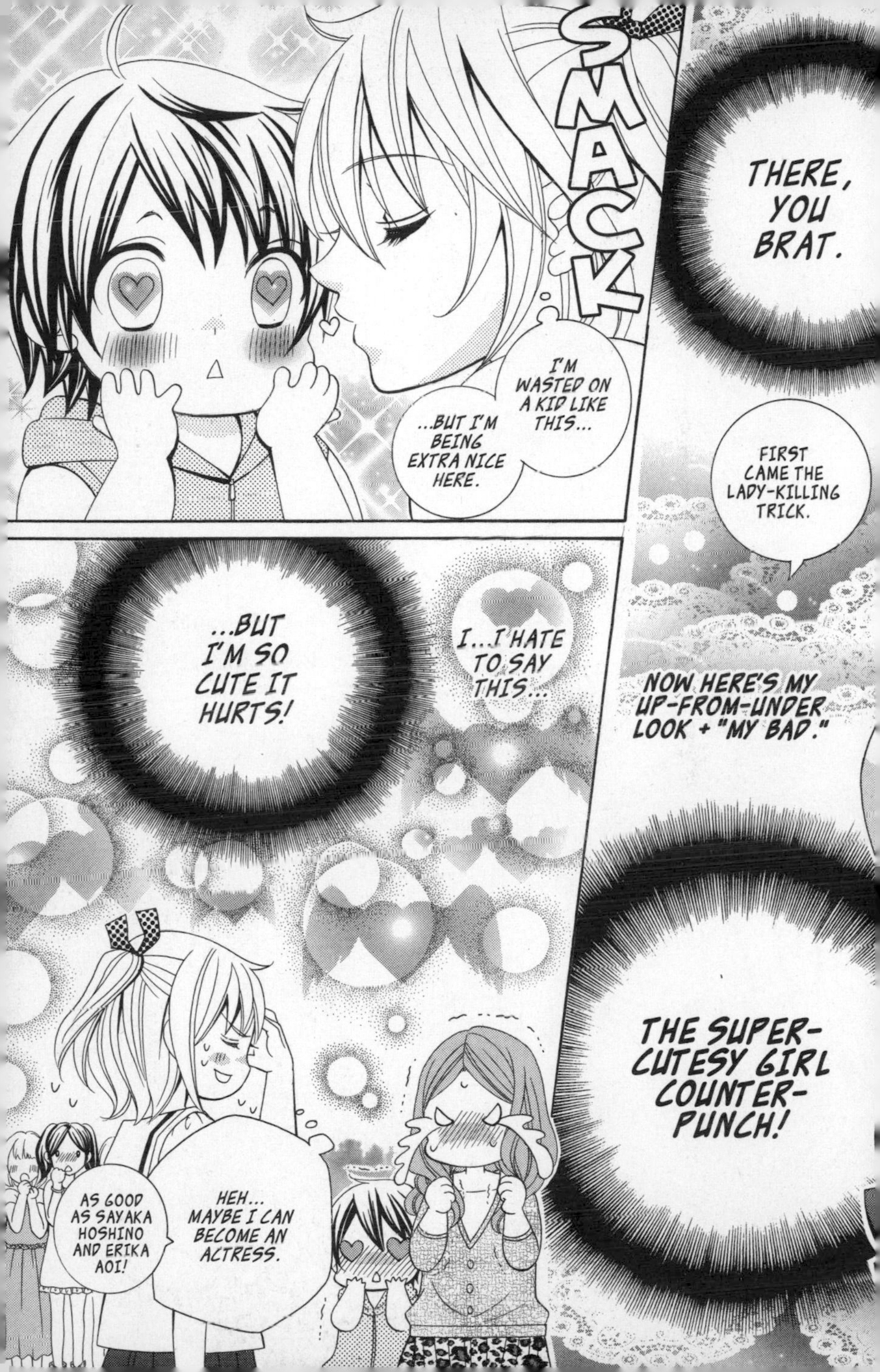
THERE, YOU BRAT.
FIRST CAME THE LADY-KILLING TRICK.
NOW HERE'S MY UP-FROM-UNDER LOOK + "MY BAD."
THE SUPER-CUTESY GIRL COUNTER-PUNCH!
SMACK
I'M WASTED ON A KID LIKE THIS...
...BUT I'M BEING EXTRA NICE HERE.
I...I HATE TO SAY THIS...
...BUT I'M SO CUTE IT HURTS!
HEH... MAYBE I CAN BECOME AN ACTRESS.
AS GOOD AS SAYAKA HOSHINO AND ERIKA AOI!

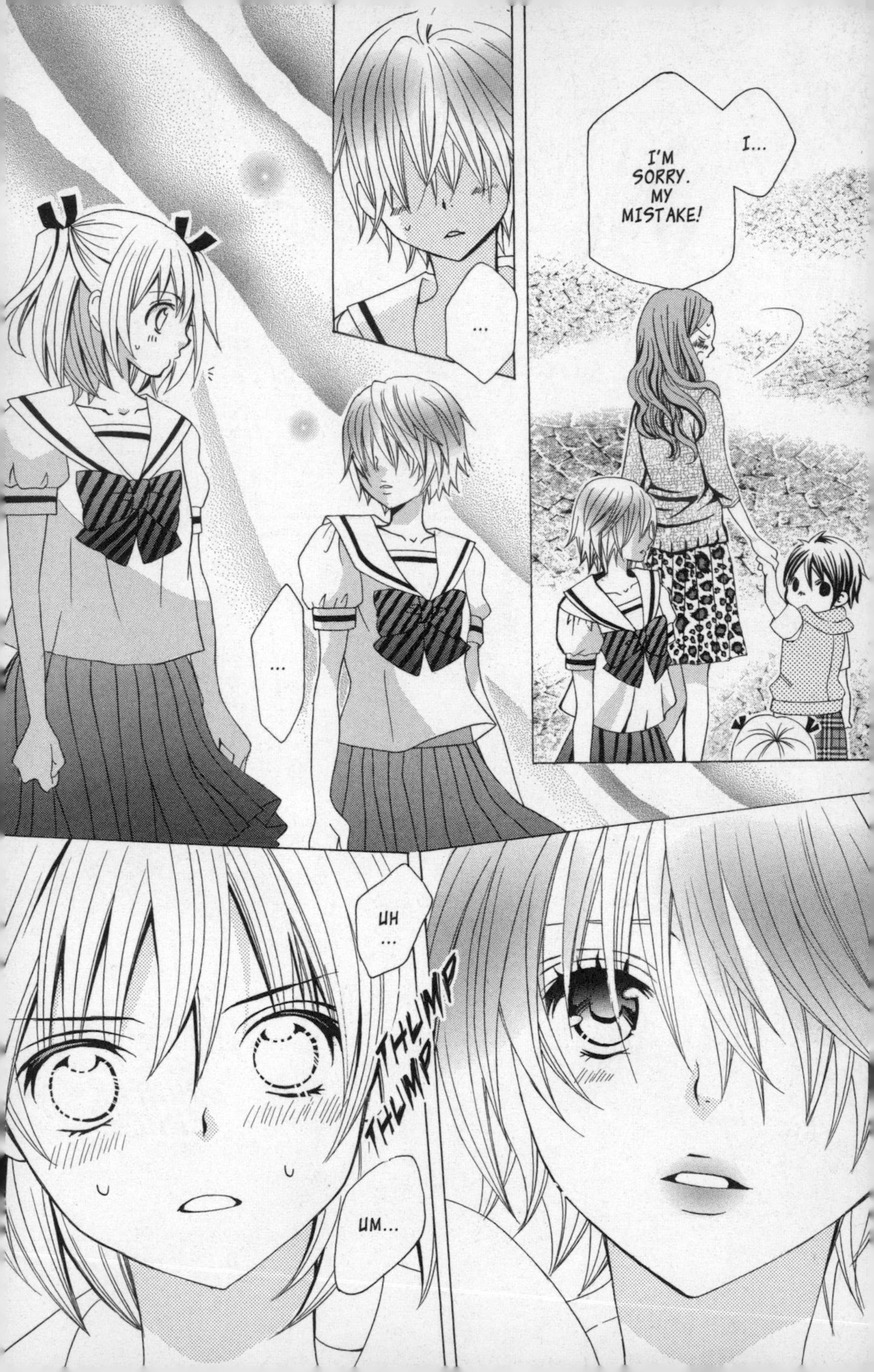
I...
I'M SORRY. MY MISTAKE!
...
...
UH ...
THUMP THUMP
UM...

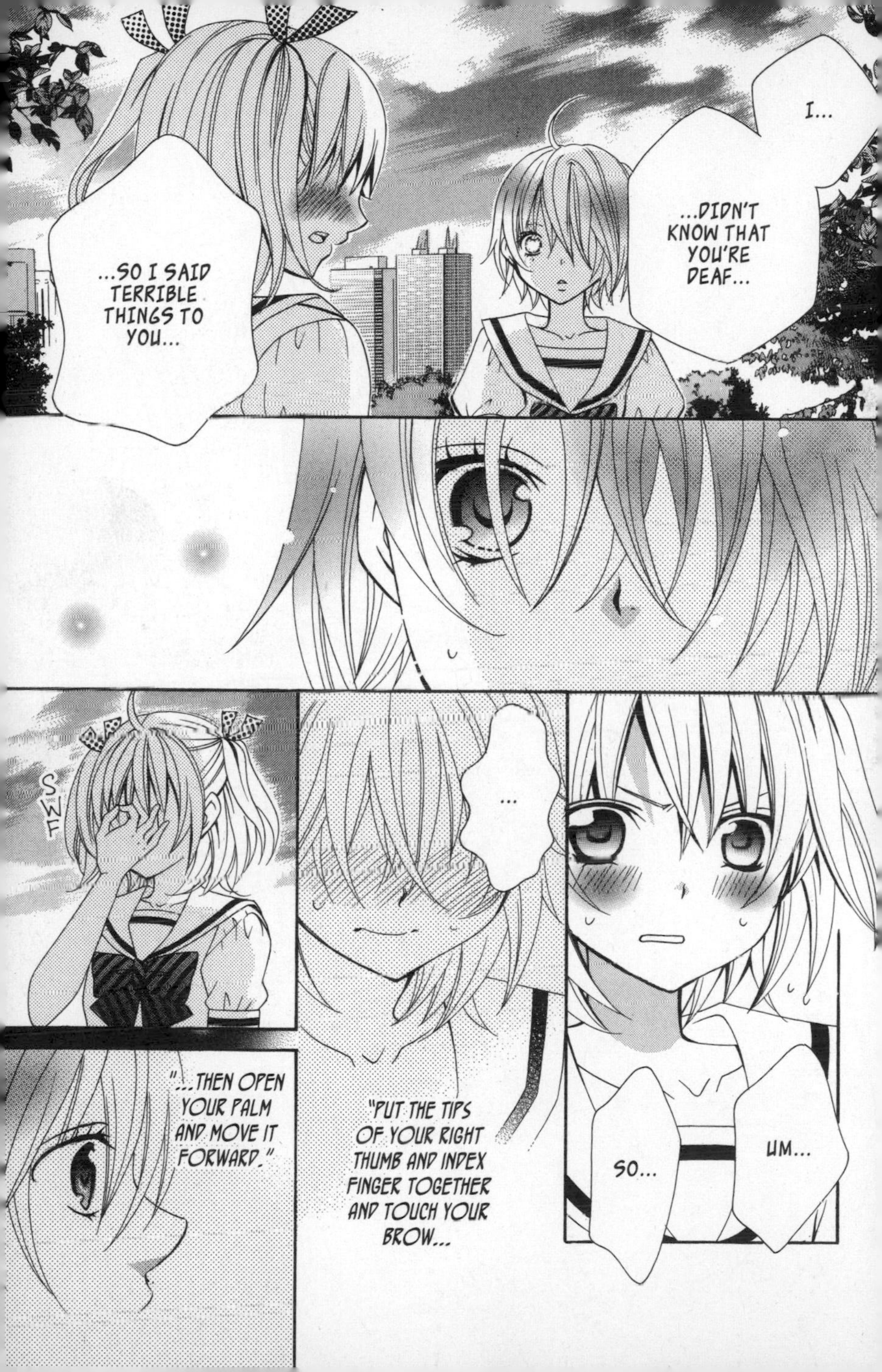
I...
...DIDN'T KNOW THAT YOU'RE DEAF...
...SO I SAID TERRIBLE THINGS TO YOU...
UM...
SO...
...
"PUT THE TIPS OF YOUR RIGHT THUMB AND INDEX FINGER TOGETHER AND TOUCH YOUR BROW...
SWF
"...THEN OPEN YOUR PALM AND MOVE IT FORWARD."

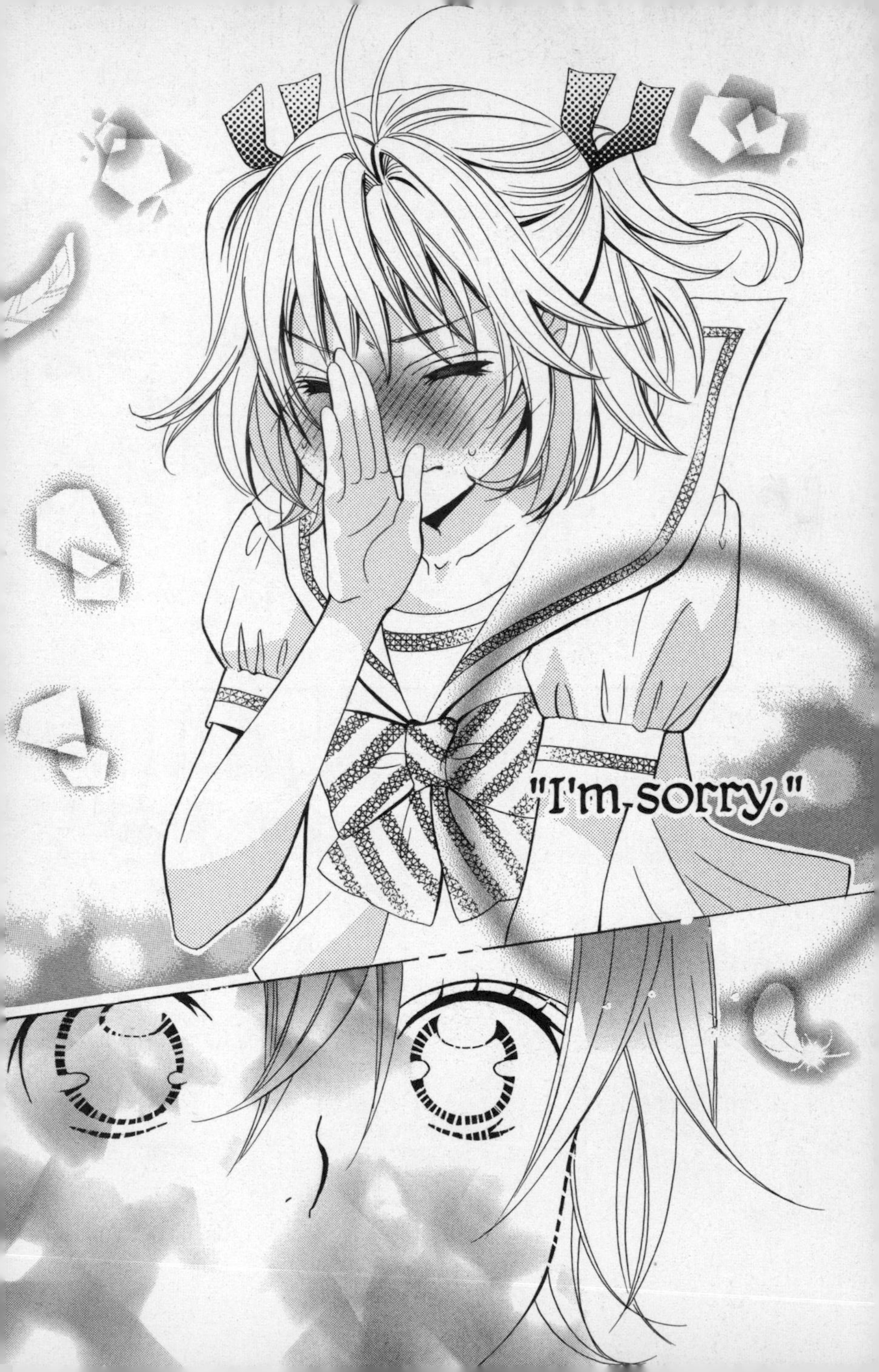
"I'm sorry."

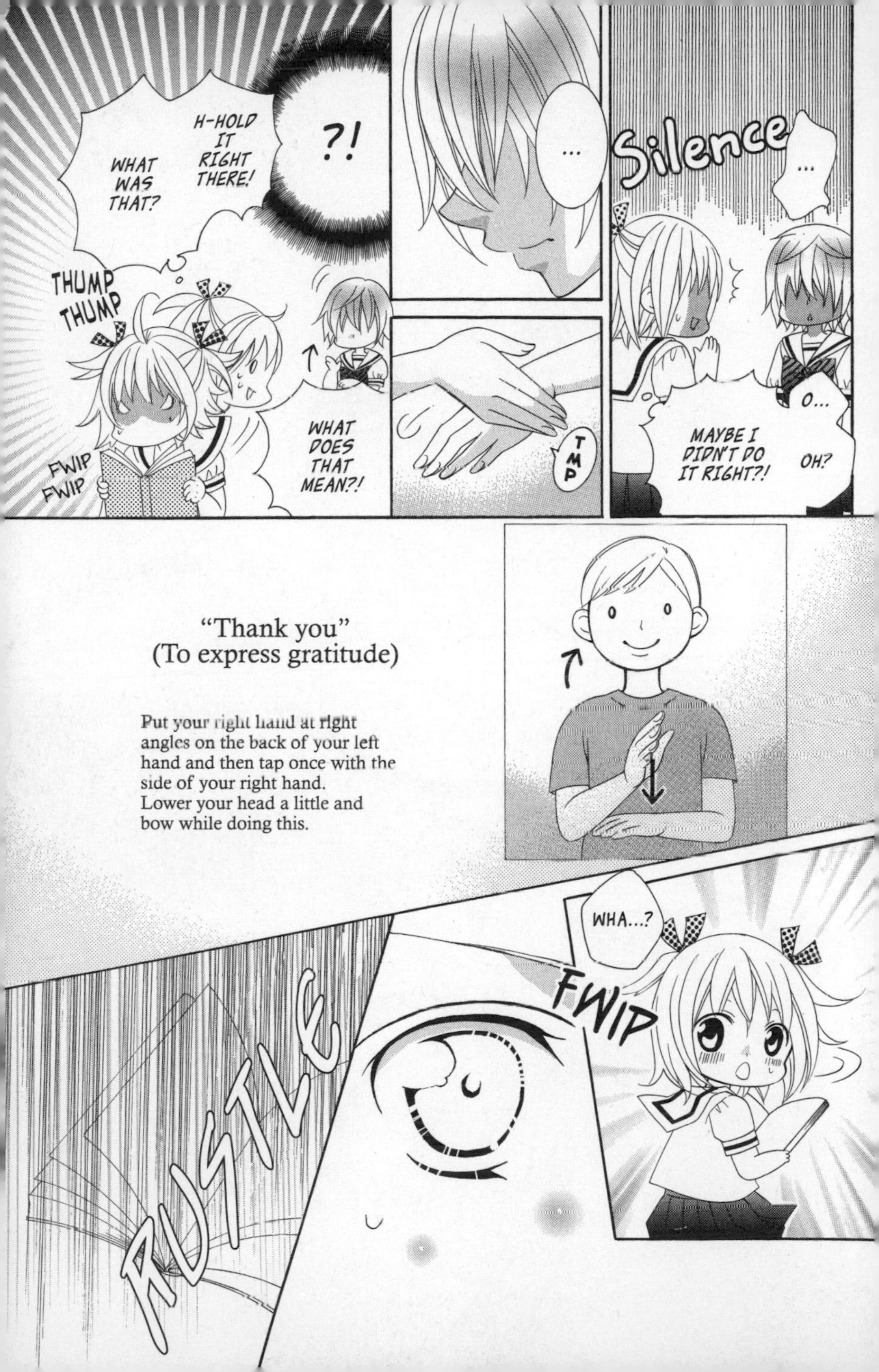
...
Silence
O... OH?
MAYBE I DIDN'T DO IT RIGHT?!
...
TMP
?!
H-HOLD IT RIGHT THERE!
WHAT WAS THAT?
THUMP THUMP
WHAT DOES THAT MEAN?!
FWIP FWIP
"Thank you"
(To express gratitude)
Put your right hand at right angles on the back of your left hand and then tap once with the side of your right hand. Lower your head a little and bow while doing this.
WHA...?
FWIP
RUSTLE

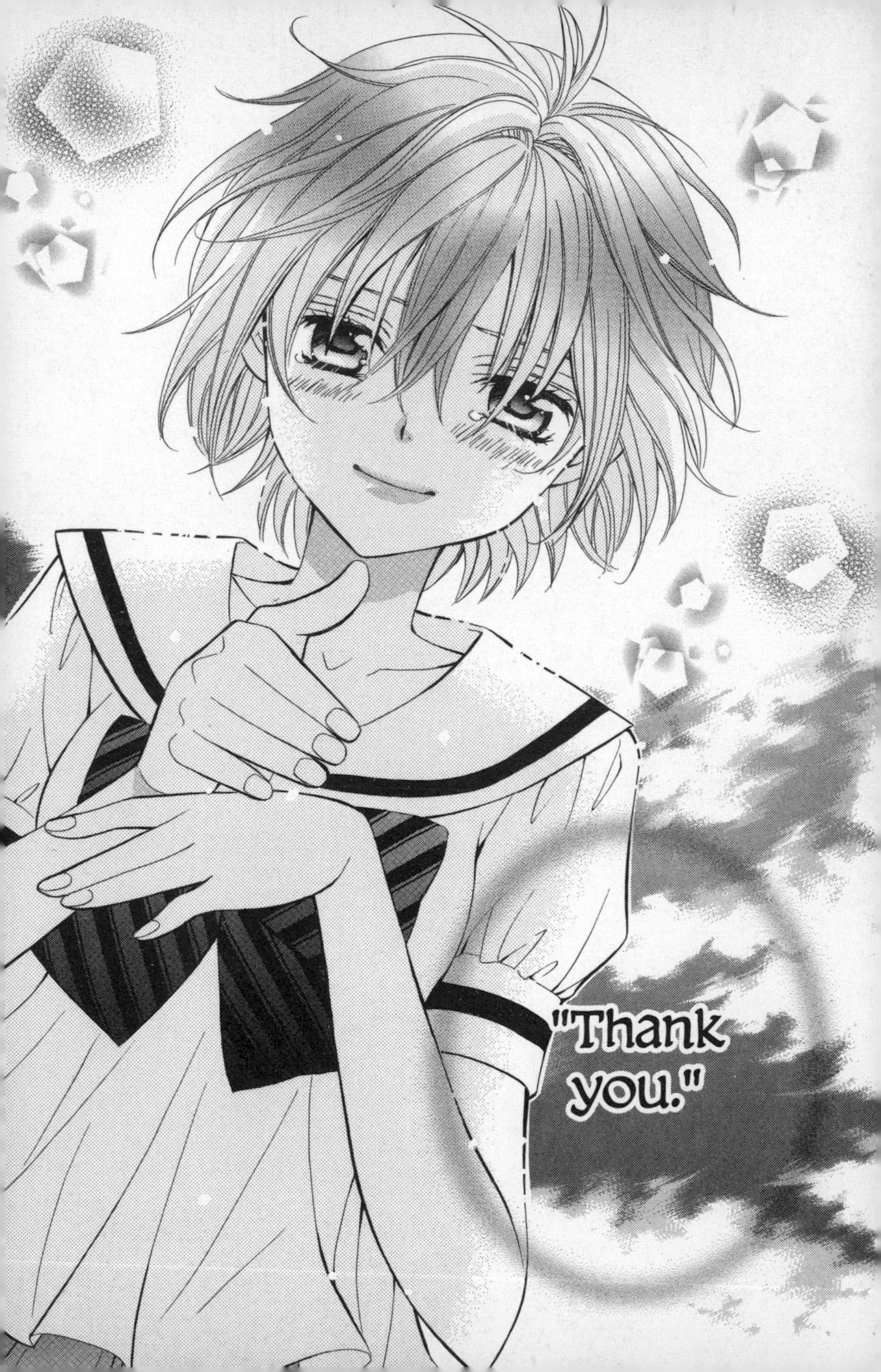
"Thank you."

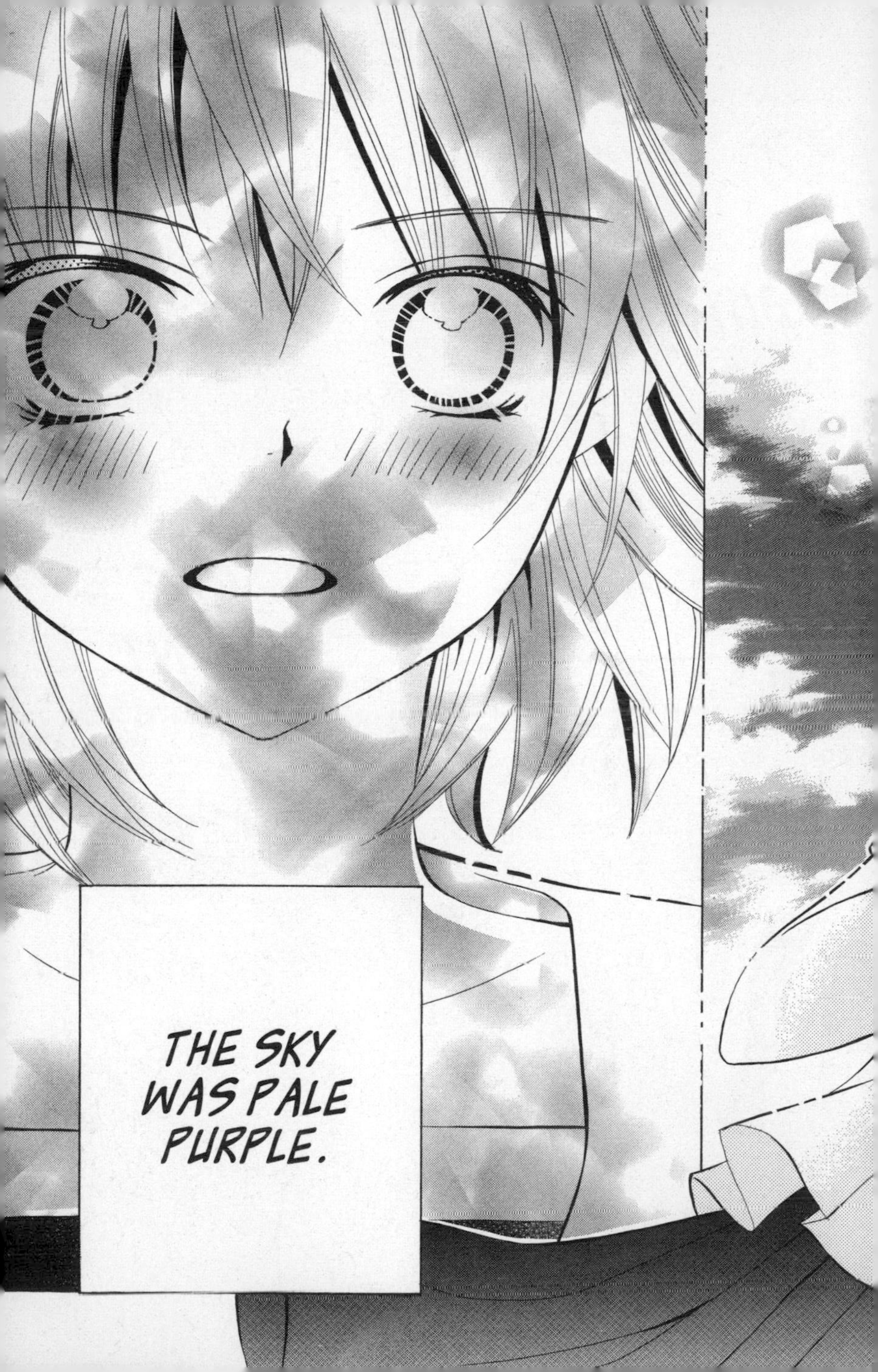
THE SKY WAS PALE PURPLE.

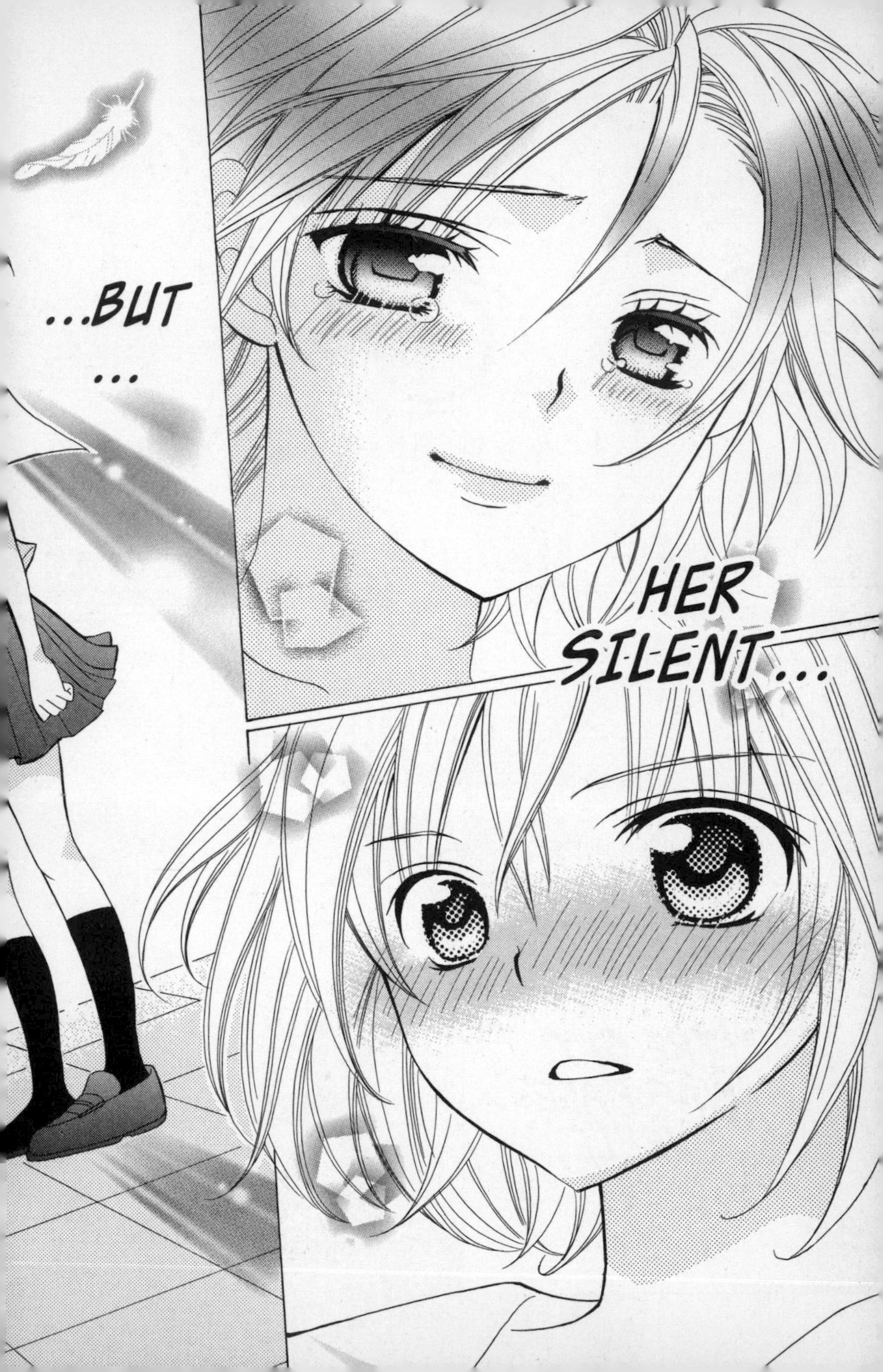
HER SILENT...
...BUT
...

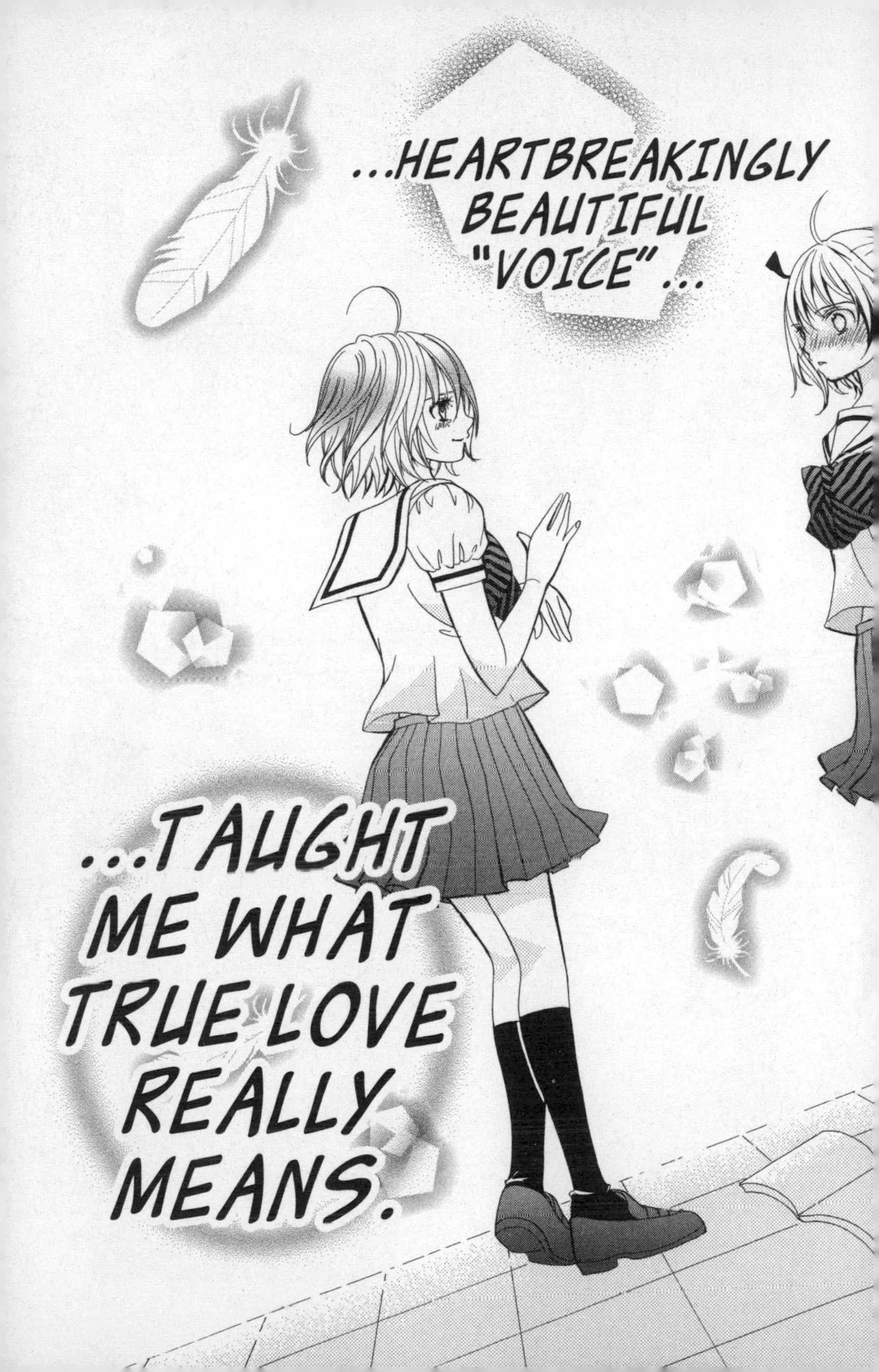
...HEARTBREAKINGLY BEAUTIFUL "VOICE"...
...TAUGHT ME WHAT TRUE LOVE REALLY MEANS.

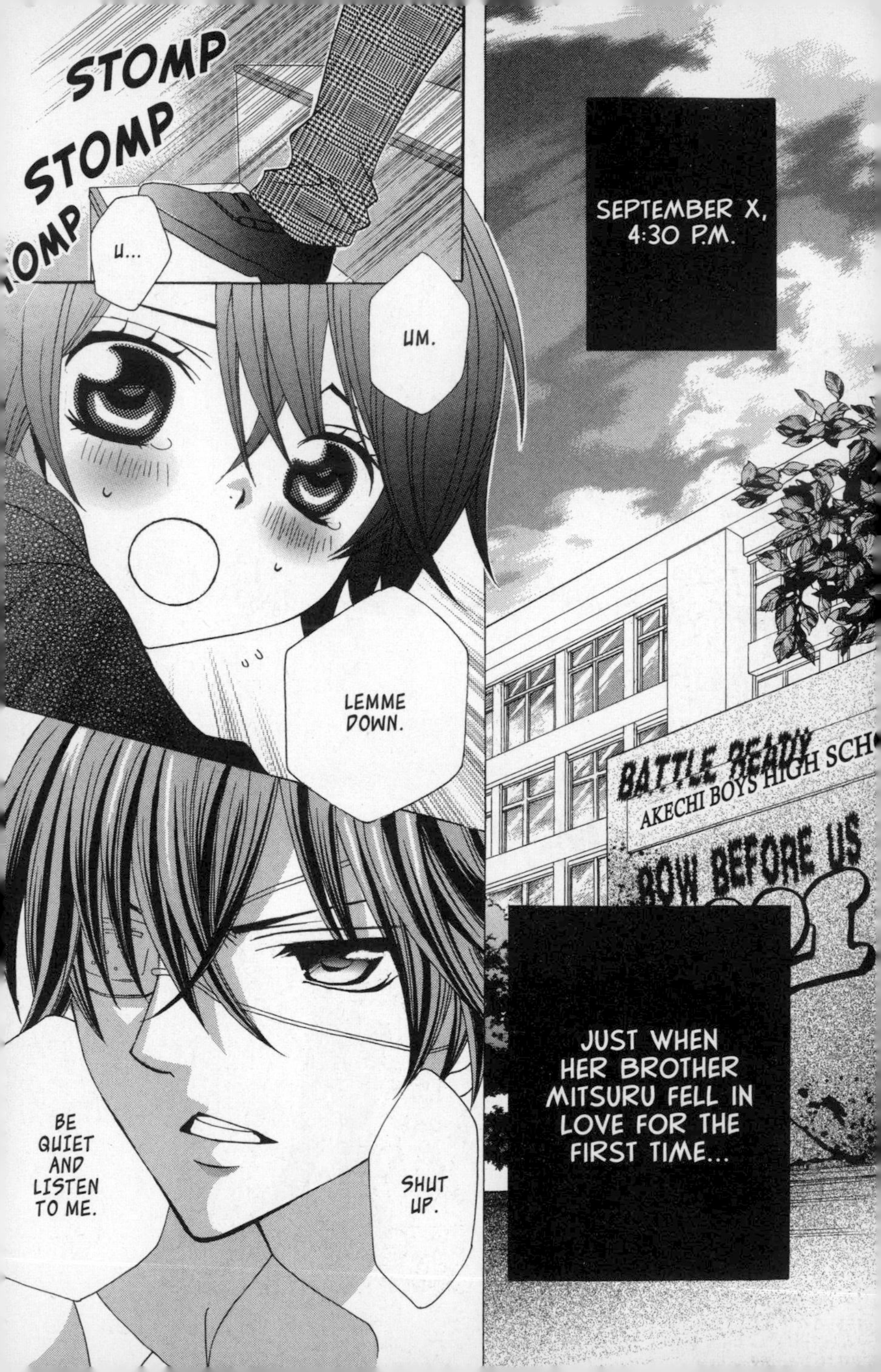
SEPTEMBER X, 4:30 P.M.
BATTLE READY
AKECHI BOYS HIGH SCH
BOW BEFORE US
JUST WHEN HER BROTHER MITSURU FELL IN LOVE FOR THE FIRST TIME...
STOMP
STOMP
OMP
U...
UM.
LEMME DOWN.
SHUT UP.
BE QUIET AND LISTEN TO ME.

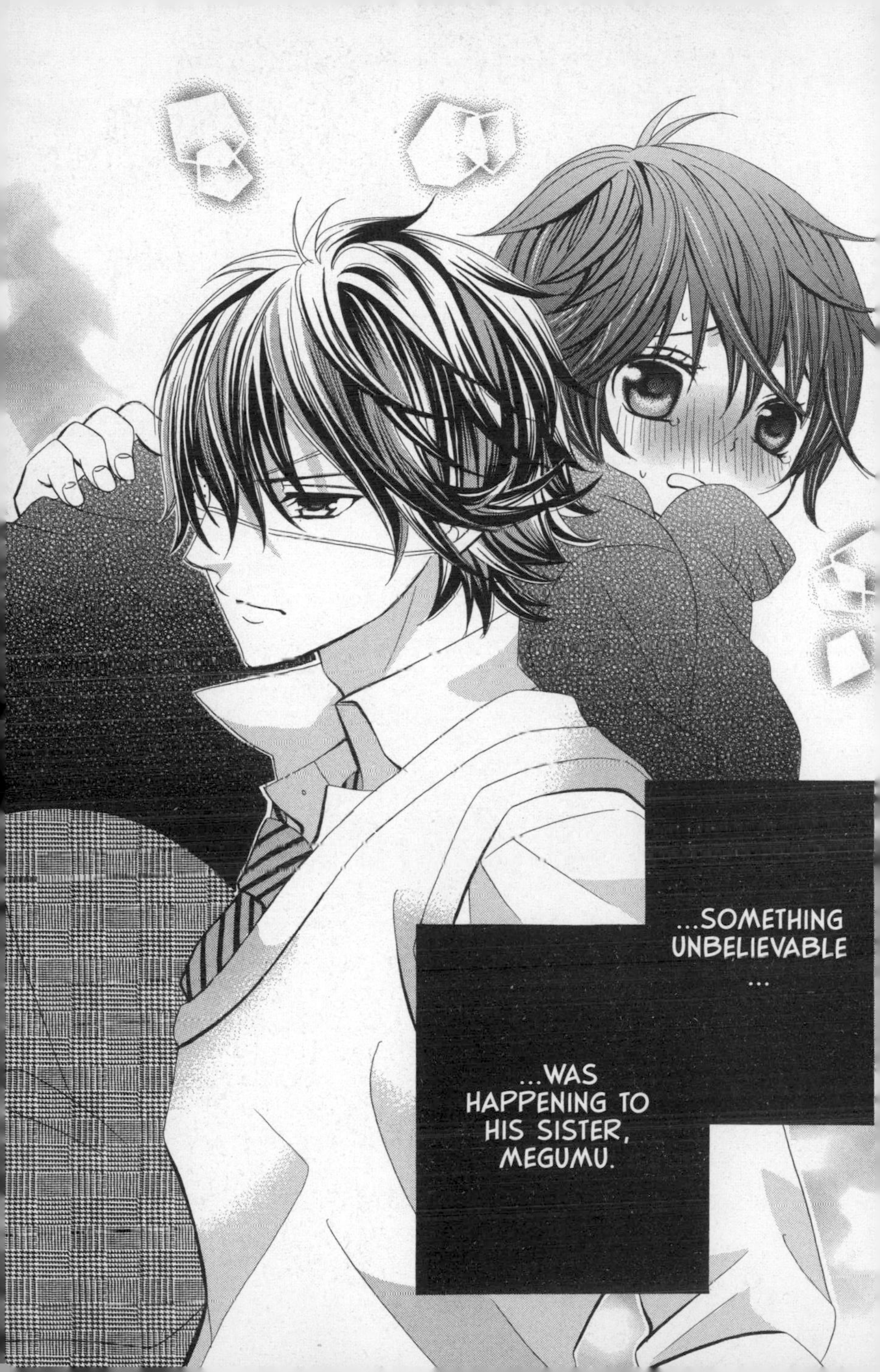
...SOMETHING UNBELIEVABLE ...
...WAS HAPPENING TO HIS SISTER, MEGUMU.

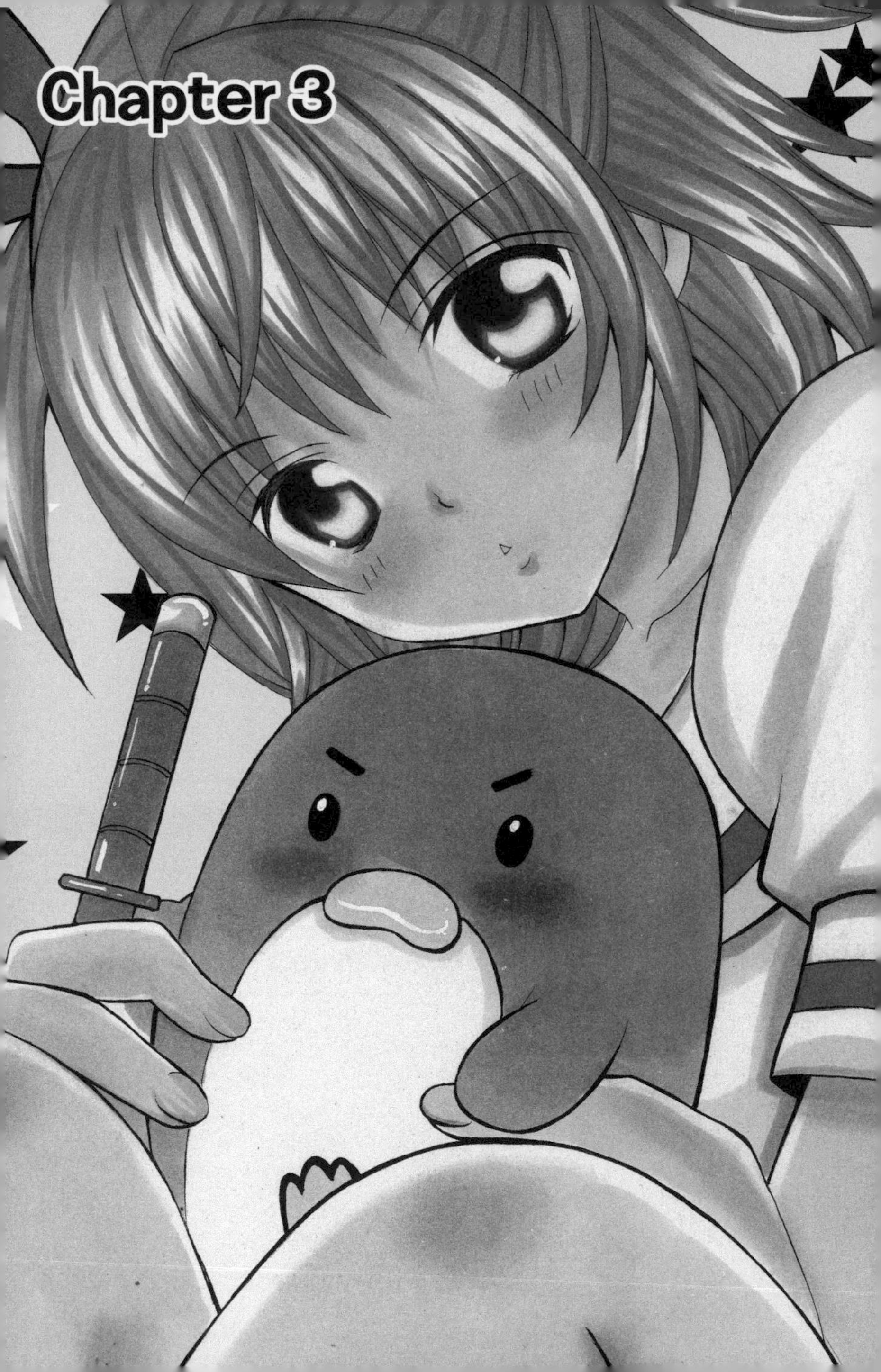
Chapter 3

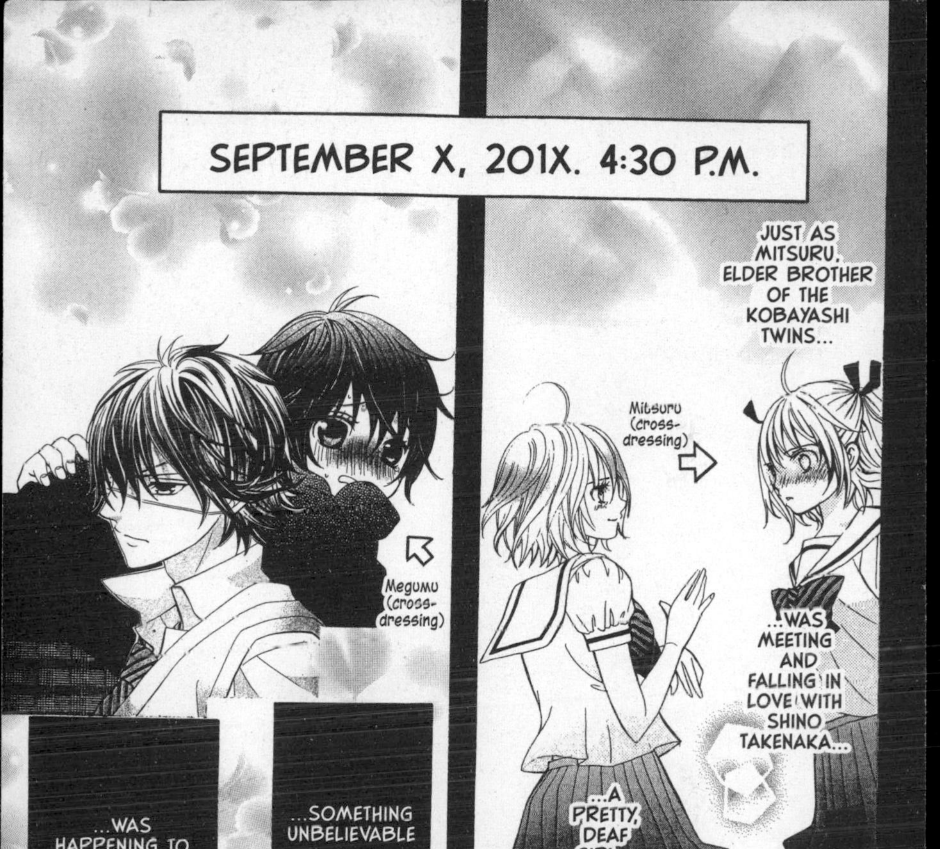
SEPTEMBER X, 201X. 4:30 P.M.
JUST AS MITSURU, ELDER BROTHER OF THE KOBAYASHI TWINS...
Mitsuru (cross-dressing)
...WAS MEETING AND FALLING IN LOVE WITH SHINO TAKENAKA...
...A PRETTY, DEAF GIRL...
Megumu (cross-dressing)
...SOMETHING UNBELIEVABLE ...
...WAS HAPPENING TO HIS SISTER, MEGUMU.

I HAVE ALWAYS LOVED EYE PATCH CHARACTERS. (LIKE KEN WATANABE'S *DOKUGANRYU MASAMUNE* TV DRAMA, XIAHOU DUN OF *RECORDS OF THE THREE KINGDOMS*, MASAMUNE-SAMA OF *SENGOKU BASARA*...)

I'VE ALWAYS WANTED TO DRAW AN EYE PATCH CHARACTER, AND I FELT NOW WAS THE PERFECT TIMING TO DRAW ONE. (>_<)

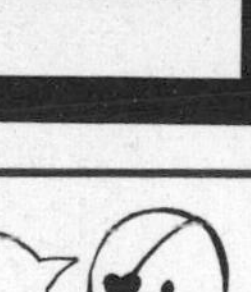

WHEN I ASKED MY FRIENDS AND MY EDITOR WHAT THEY THOUGHT, THEY WERE ALL APPALLED AS THEY APPARENTLY IMAGINED SOMETHING LIKE A PIRATE'S EYE PATCH.

WHEN I SUBMITTED A DRAWING OF SANADA WEARING AN ORDINARY MEDICAL EYE PATCH (I CHOSE THE BEST ONE FROM THE SEVERAL I'D DRAWN), EVERYONE SUDDENLY CHANGED THEIR MIND AND SAID, "THAT'S SEXY AND COOL!" AND I WAS GIVEN THE GO-AHEAD. (*SMILE*)

I WAS MOST WORRIED ABOUT MY READERS' REACTIONS, BUT THEY SEEM TO LIKE IT MORE THAN I EXPECTED, SO I'M VERY RELIEVED. (^o^) I'M SECRETLY HOPING THE EYE PATCH WILL BE MADE INTO A *SHO-COMI* FUROKU GIFT SOMEDAY. LOL.

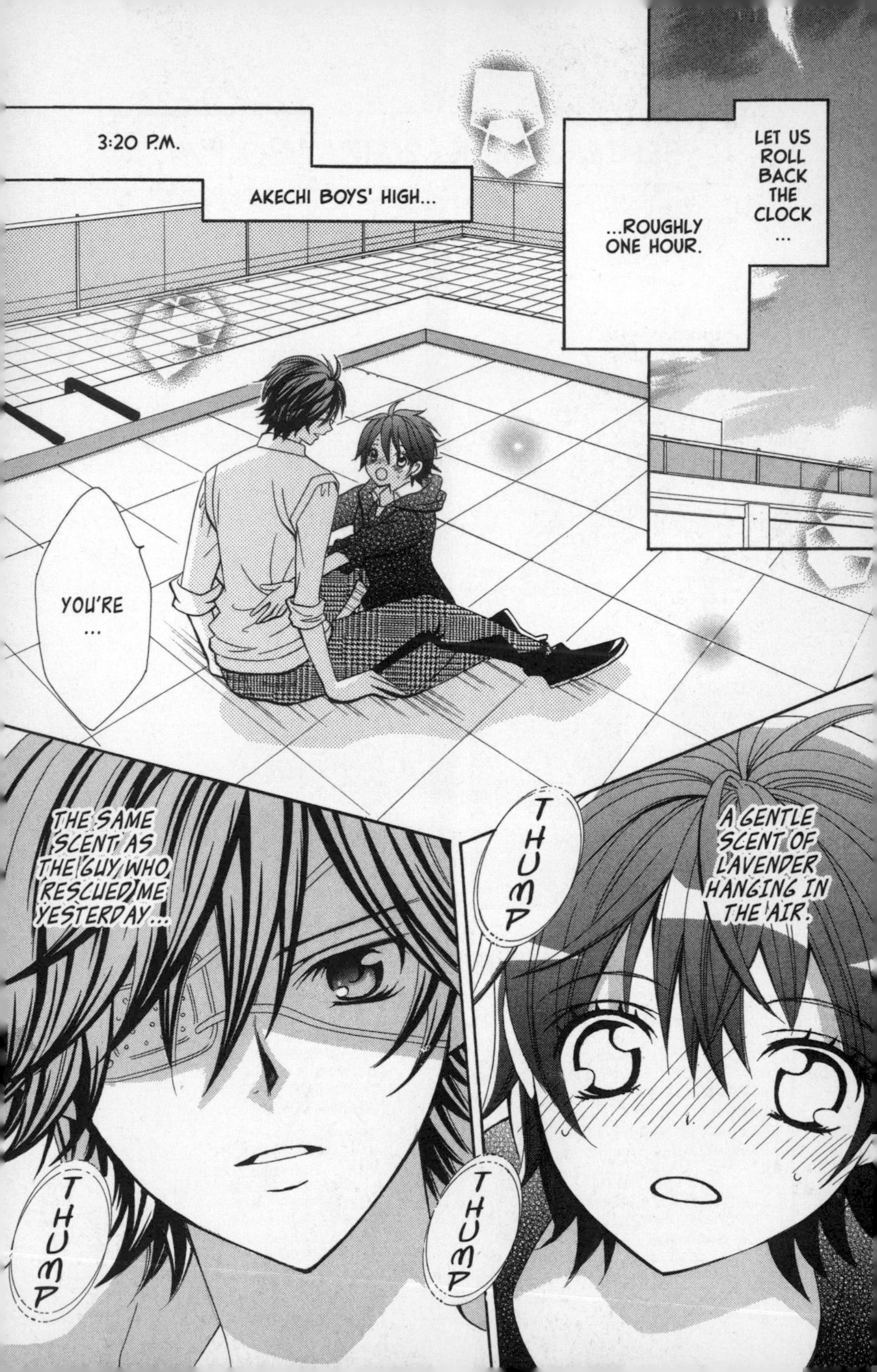
LET US ROLL BACK THE CLOCK ...
...ROUGHLY ONE HOUR.
3:20 P.M.
AKECHI BOYS' HIGH...
YOU'RE ...
A GENTLE SCENT OF LAVENDER HANGING IN THE AIR.
THUMP
THE SAME SCENT AS THE GUY WHO RESCUED ME YESTERDAY...
THUMP
THUMP

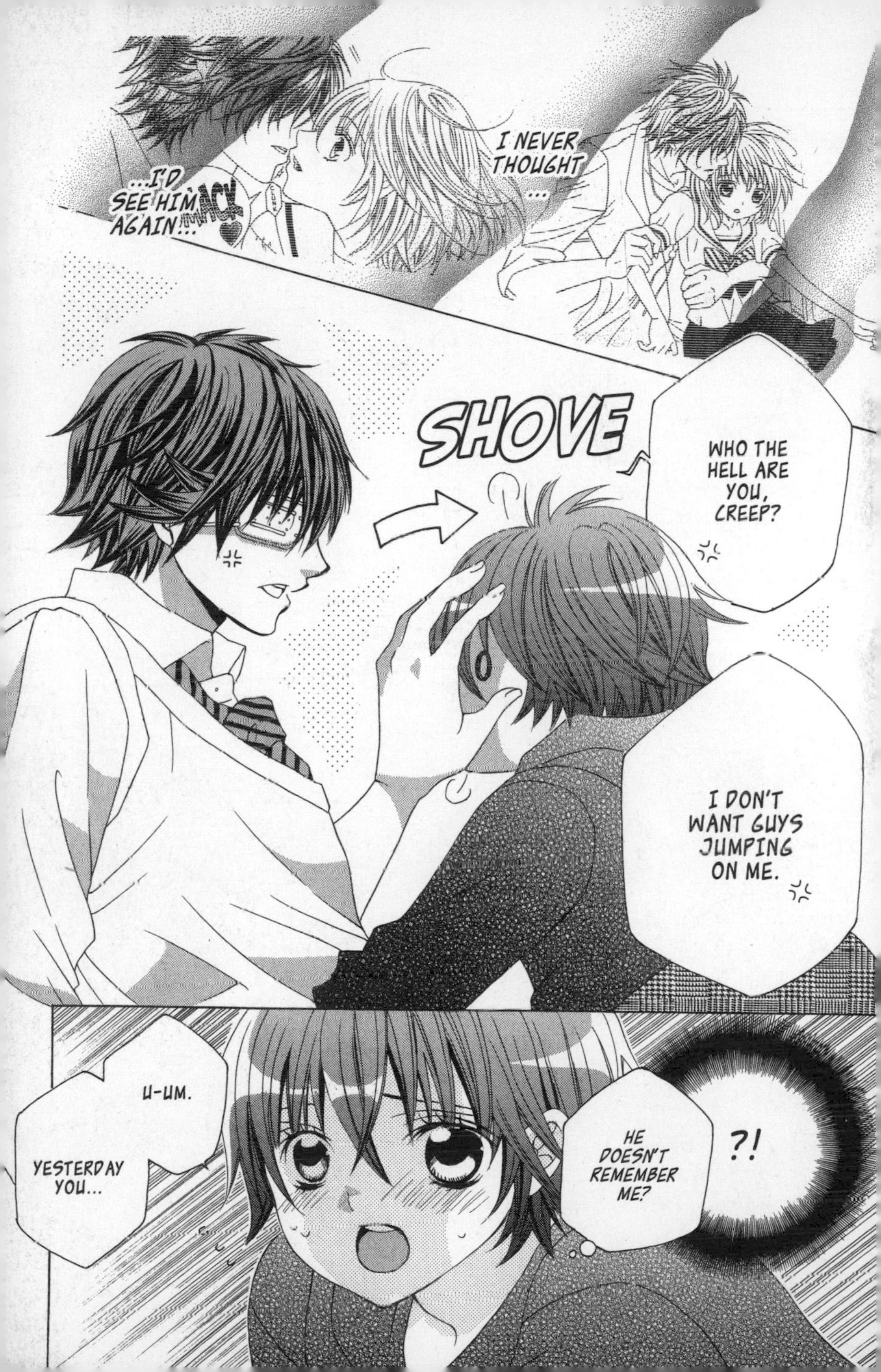
I NEVER THOUGHT ...
...I'D SEE HIM AGAIN...
MACK
WHO THE HELL ARE YOU, CREEP?
SHOVE
I DON'T WANT GUYS JUMPING ON ME.
?!
HE DOESN'T REMEMBER ME?
U-UM.
YESTERDAY YOU...

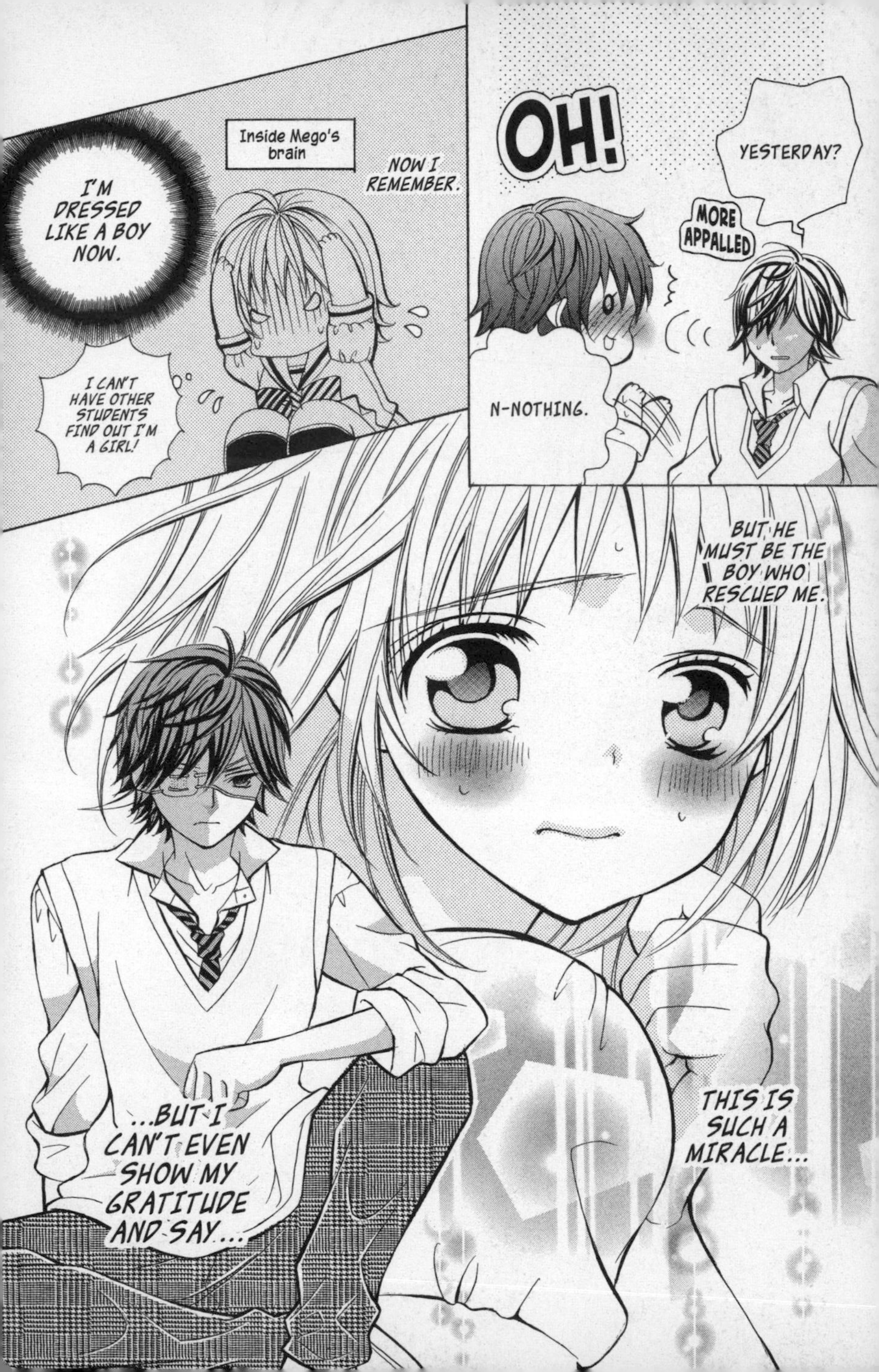
YESTERDAY?
OH!
MORE APPALLED
N-NOTHING.
NOW I REMEMBER.
Inside Mego's brain
I'M DRESSED LIKE A BOY NOW.
I CAN'T HAVE OTHER STUDENTS FIND OUT I'M A GIRL!
BUT HE MUST BE THE BOY WHO RESCUED ME.
THIS IS SUCH A MIRACLE...
...BUT I CAN'T EVEN SHOW MY GRATITUDE AND SAY...

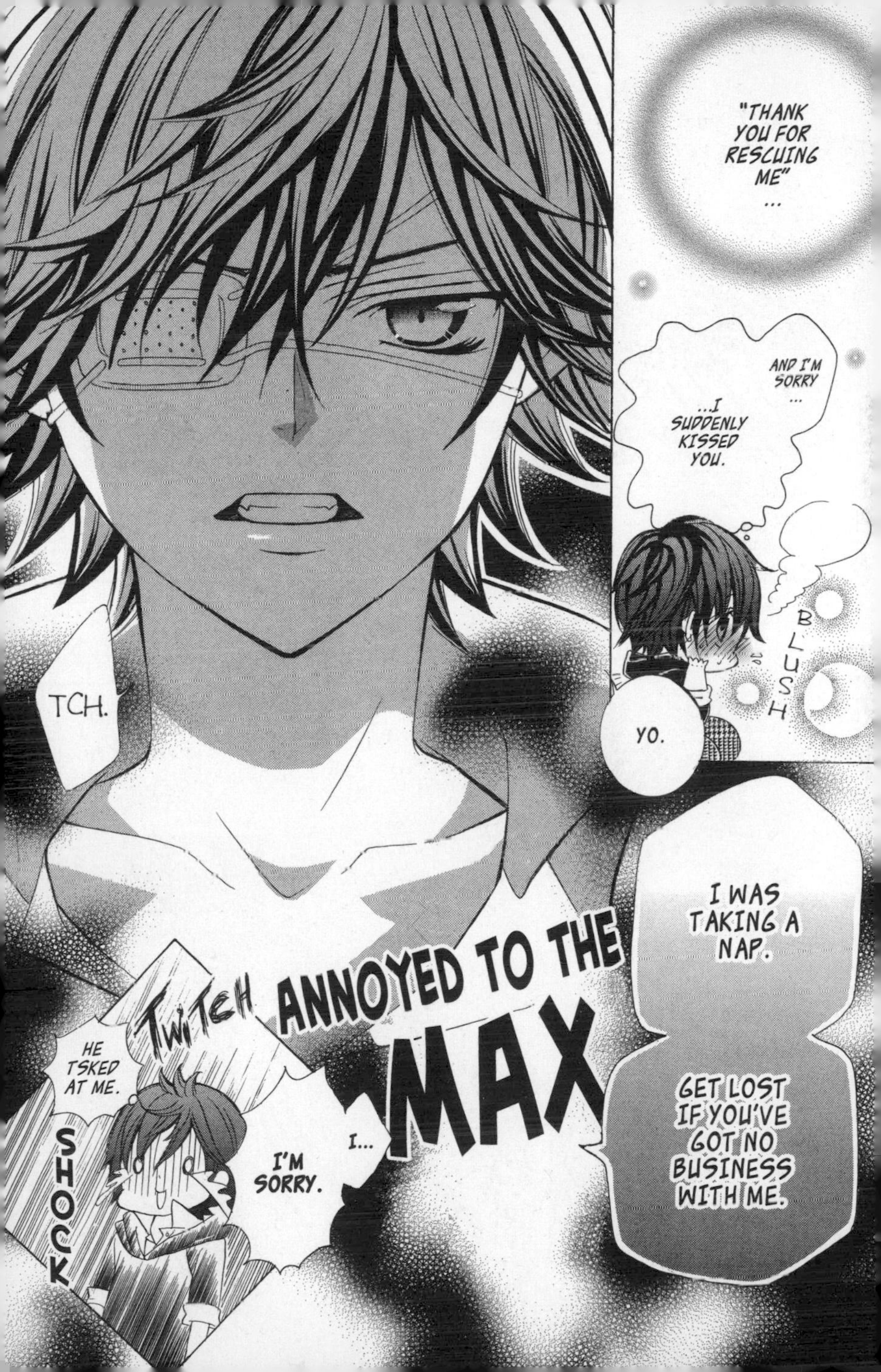
"THANK YOU FOR RESCUING ME" ...
AND I'M SORRY ...
...I SUDDENLY KISSED YOU.
BLUSH
YO.
TCH.
I WAS TAKING A NAP.
GET LOST IF YOU'VE GOT NO BUSINESS WITH ME.
ANNOYED TO THE MAX
TWITCH
I...
I'M SORRY.
HE TSKED AT ME.
SHOCK

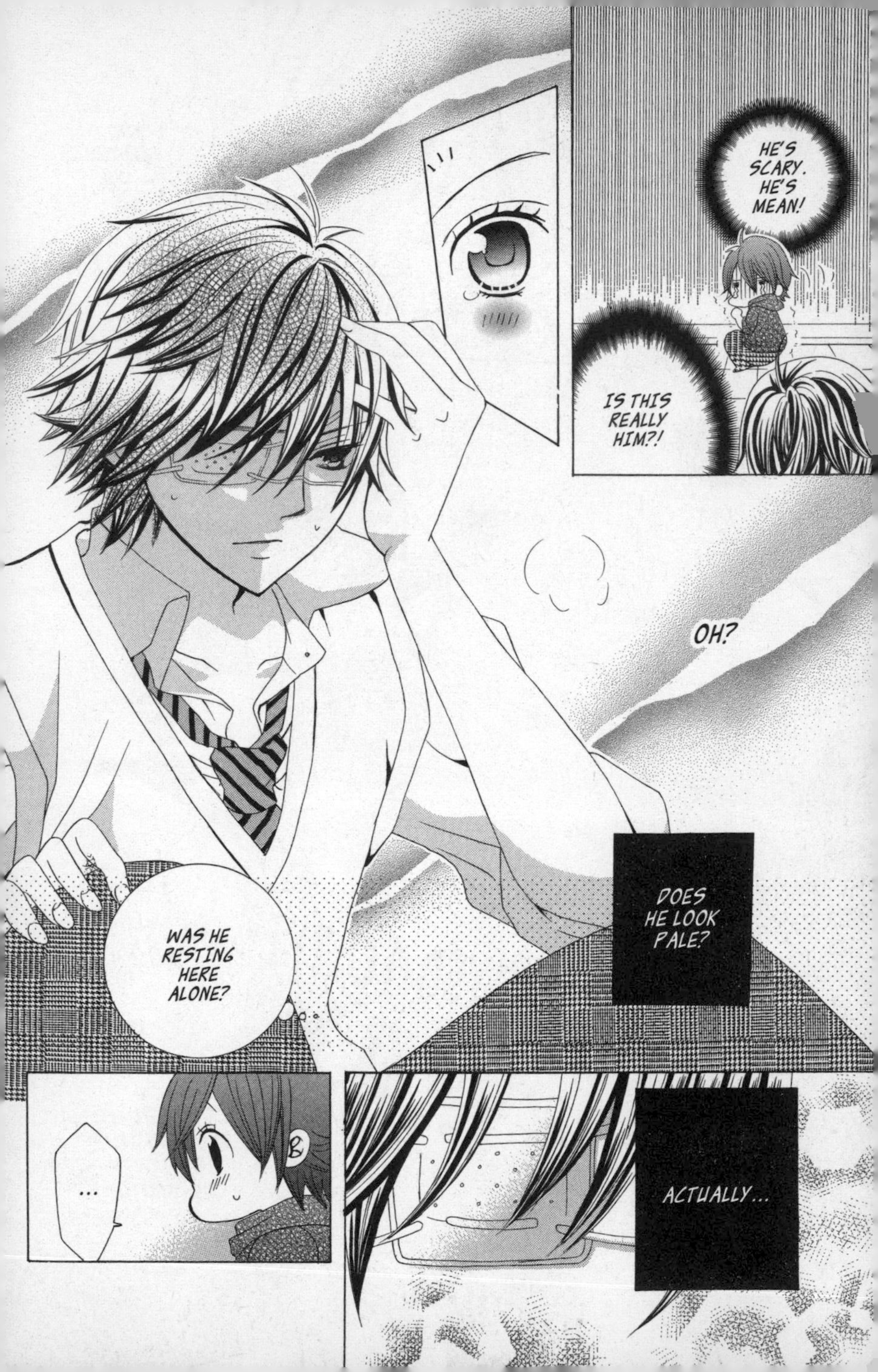
HE'S SCARY. HE'S MEAN!
IS THIS REALLY HIM?!
OH?
DOES HE LOOK PALE?
WAS HE RESTING HERE ALONE?
ACTUALLY...
...

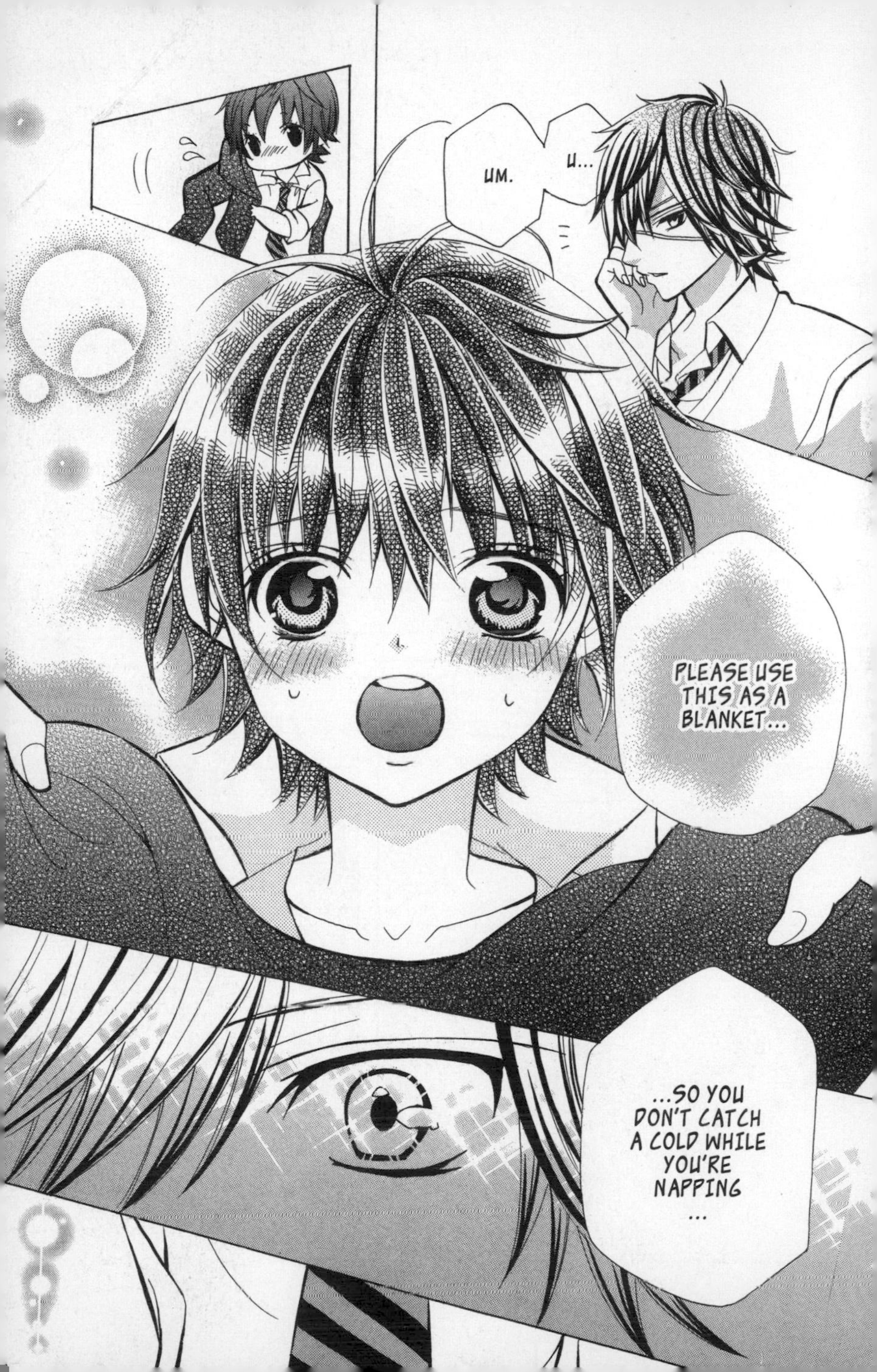
U...
UM.
PLEASE USE THIS AS A BLANKET...
...SO YOU DON'T CATCH A COLD WHILE YOU'RE NAPPING ...

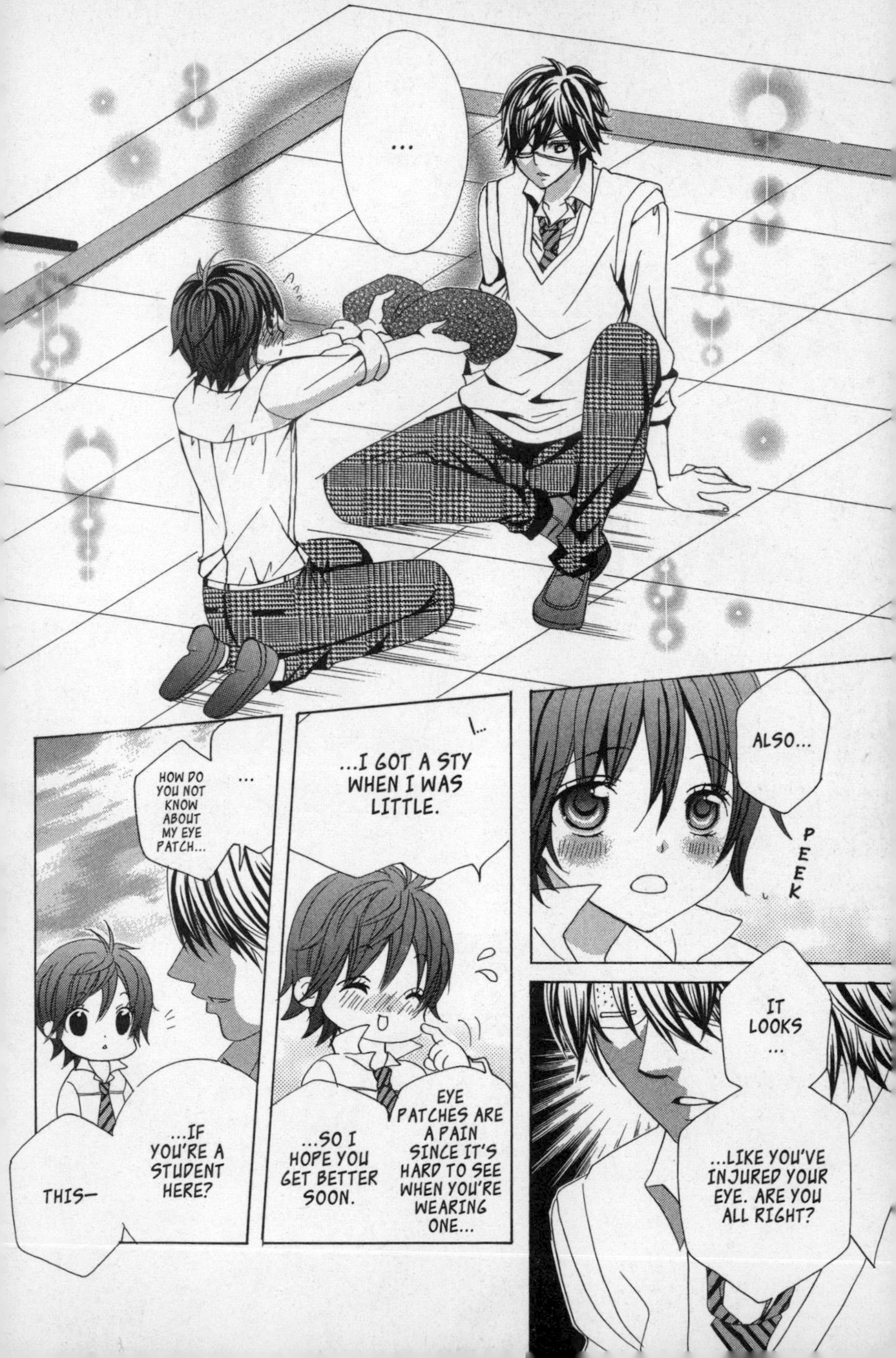
...
ALSO...
PEEK
IT LOOKS...
...LIKE YOU'VE INJURED YOUR EYE. ARE YOU ALL RIGHT?
I...
...I GOT A STY WHEN I WAS LITTLE.
EYE PATCHES ARE A PAIN SINCE IT'S HARD TO SEE WHEN YOU'RE WEARING ONE...
...SO I HOPE YOU GET BETTER SOON.
...
HOW DO YOU NOT KNOW ABOUT MY EYE PATCH...
...IF YOU'RE A STUDENT HERE?
THIS—

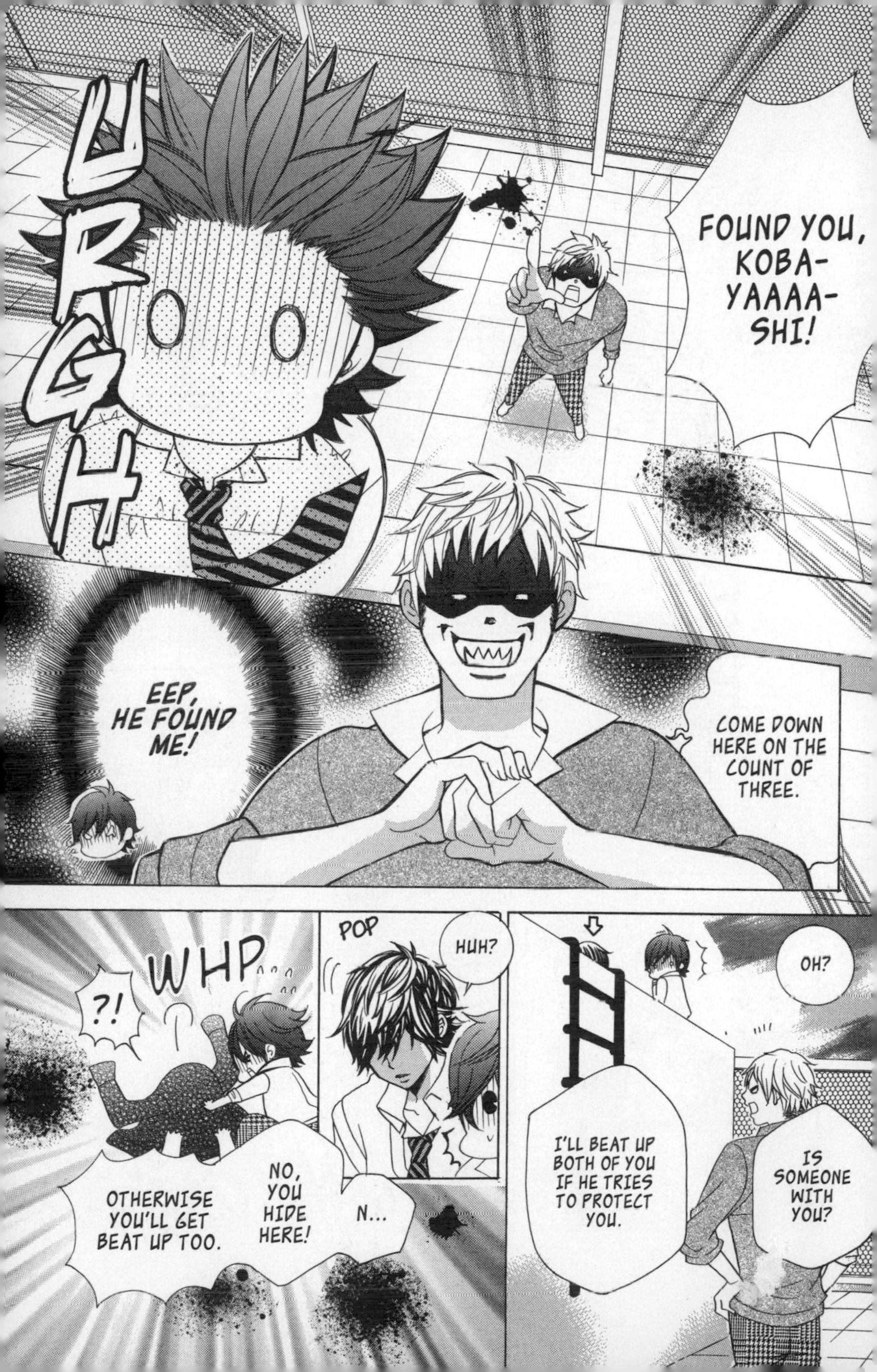
FOUND YOU, KOBA-YAAAA-SHI!
URGH
COME DOWN HERE ON THE COUNT OF THREE.
EEP, HE FOUND ME!
OH?
IS SOMEONE WITH YOU?
I'LL BEAT UP BOTH OF YOU IF HE TRIES TO PROTECT YOU.
POP
HUH?
N...
WHP
?!
NO, YOU HIDE HERE!
OTHERWISE YOU'LL GET BEAT UP TOO.

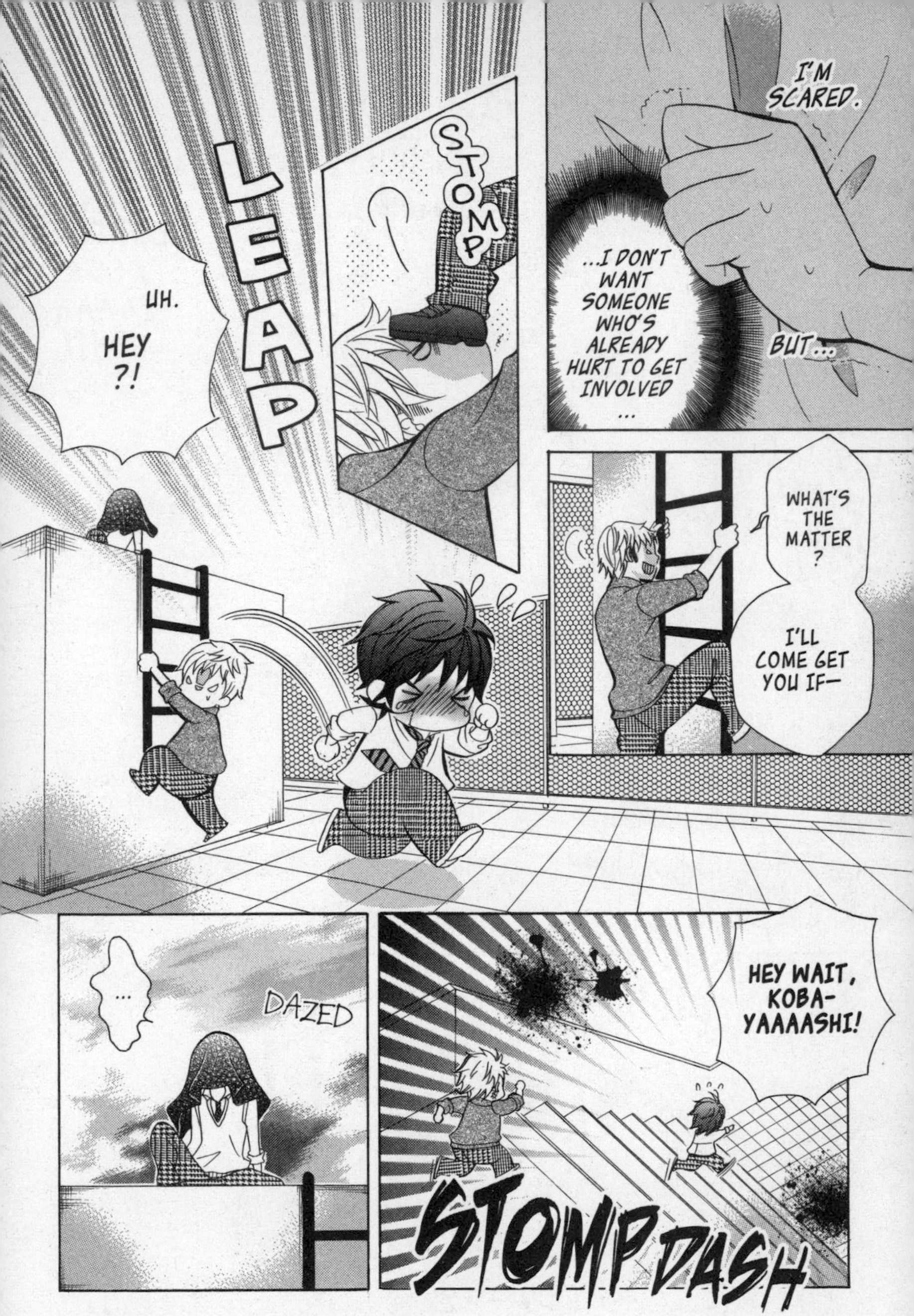

I'M SCARED.
BUT...
...I DON'T WANT SOMEONE WHO'S ALREADY HURT TO GET INVOLVED...
WHAT'S THE MATTER?
I'LL COME GET YOU IF—
STOMP
LEAP
UH.
HEY?!
HEY WAIT, KOBA-YAAAASHI!
STOMP
DASH
...
DAZED

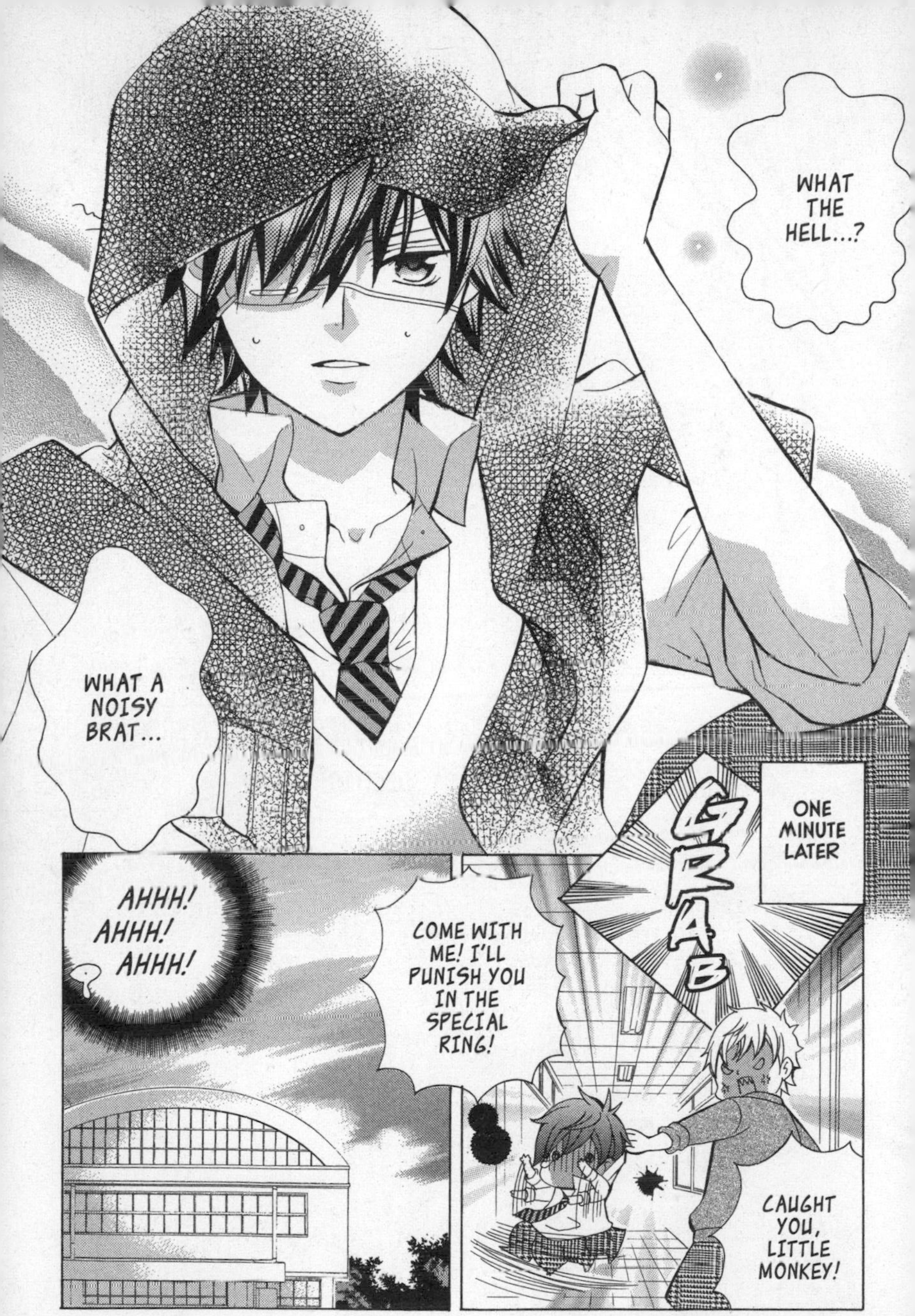
WHAT THE HELL...?
WHAT A NOISY BRAT...
ONE MINUTE LATER
GRAB
CAUGHT YOU, LITTLE MONKEY!
COME WITH ME! I'LL PUNISH YOU IN THE SPECIAL RING!
AHHH! AHHH! AHHH!

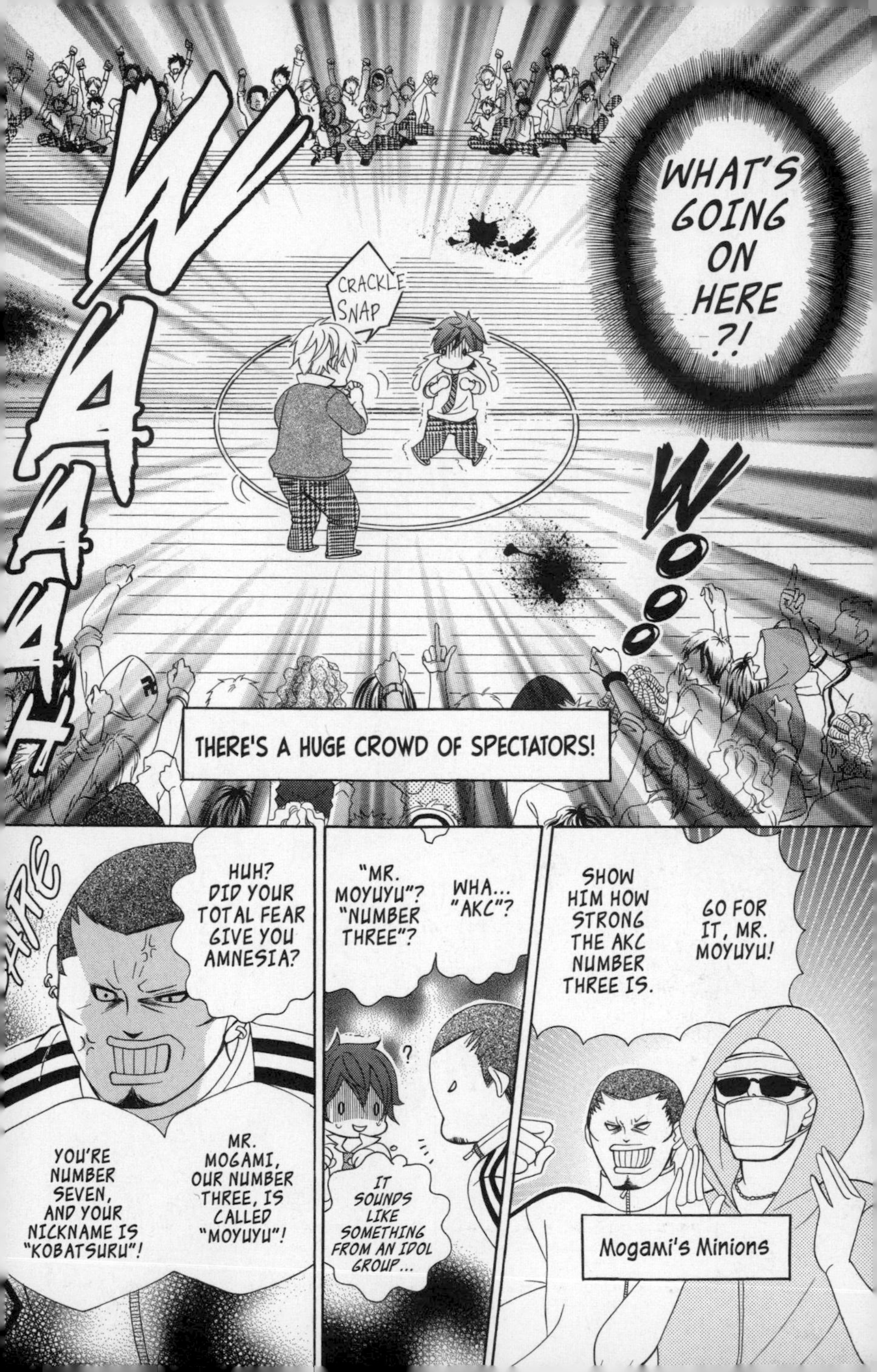
WHAT'S GOING ON HERE?!
CRACKLE SNAP
WOOOOO
WAAAA
THERE'S A HUGE CROWD OF SPECTATORS!
GO FOR IT, MR. MOYUYU!
SHOW HIM HOW STRONG THE AKC NUMBER THREE IS.
Mogami's Minions
WHA... "AKC"?
"MR. MOYUYU"? "NUMBER THREE"?
IT SOUNDS LIKE SOMETHING FROM AN IDOL GROUP...
HUH? DID YOUR TOTAL FEAR GIVE YOU AMNESIA?
MR. MOGAMI, OUR NUMBER THREE, IS CALLED "MOYUYU"!
YOU'RE NUMBER SEVEN, AND YOUR NICKNAME IS "KOBATSURU"!

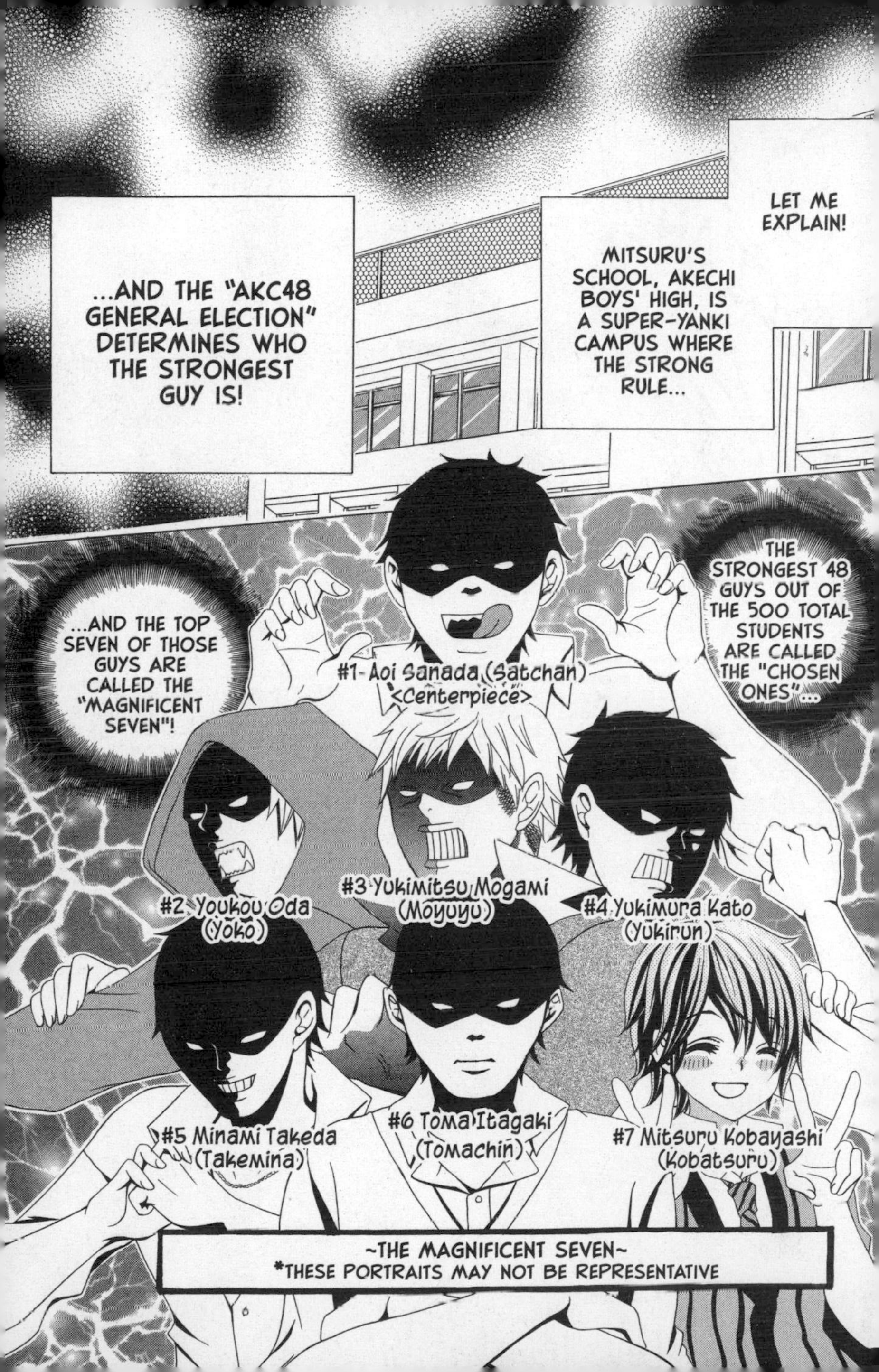
LET ME EXPLAIN!
MITSURU'S SCHOOL, AKECHI BOYS' HIGH, IS A SUPER-YANKI CAMPUS WHERE THE STRONG RULE...
...AND THE "AKC48 GENERAL ELECTION" DETERMINES WHO THE STRONGEST GUY IS!
THE STRONGEST 48 GUYS OUT OF THE 500 TOTAL STUDENTS ARE CALLED THE "CHOSEN ONES"...
...AND THE TOP SEVEN OF THOSE GUYS ARE CALLED THE "MAGNIFICENT SEVEN"!
#1- Aoi Sanada (Satchan) <Centerpiece>
#4 Yukimura Kato (Yukirun)
#3 Yukimitsu Mogami (Moyuyu)
#2 Youkou Oda (Yoko)
#7 Mitsuru Kobayashi (Kobatsuru)
#6 Toma Itagaki (Tomachin)
#5 Minami Takeda (Takemina)
~THE MAGNIFICENT SEVEN~
*THESE PORTRAITS MAY NOT BE REPRESENTATIVE

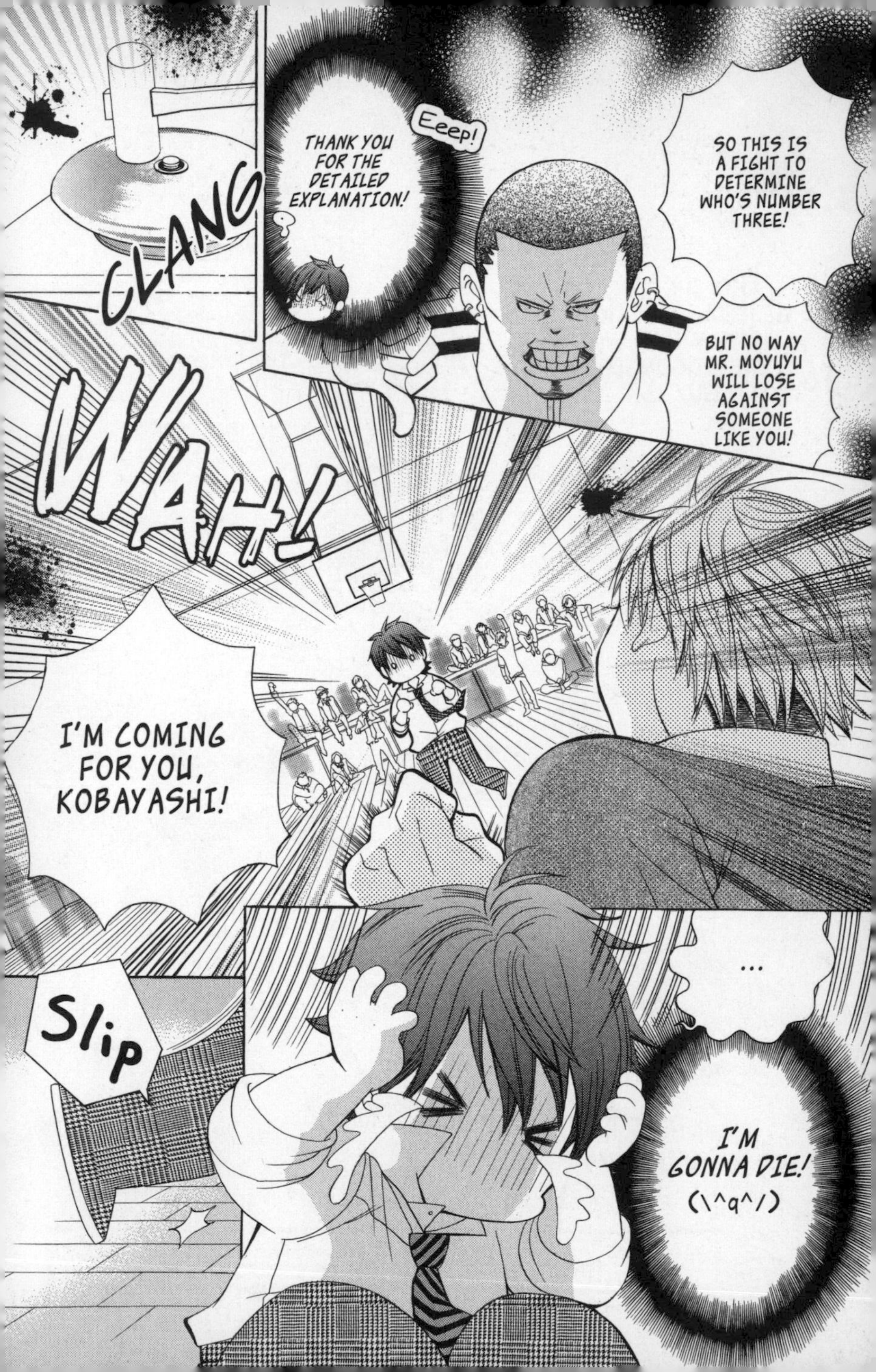
SO THIS IS A FIGHT TO DETERMINE WHO'S NUMBER THREE!
BUT NO WAY MR. MOYUYU WILL LOSE AGAINST SOMEONE LIKE YOU!
Eeep!
THANK YOU FOR THE DETAILED EXPLANATION!
CLANG
WAH!
I'M COMING FOR YOU, KOBAYASHI!
...
I'M GONNA DIE! (\^q^/)
Slip

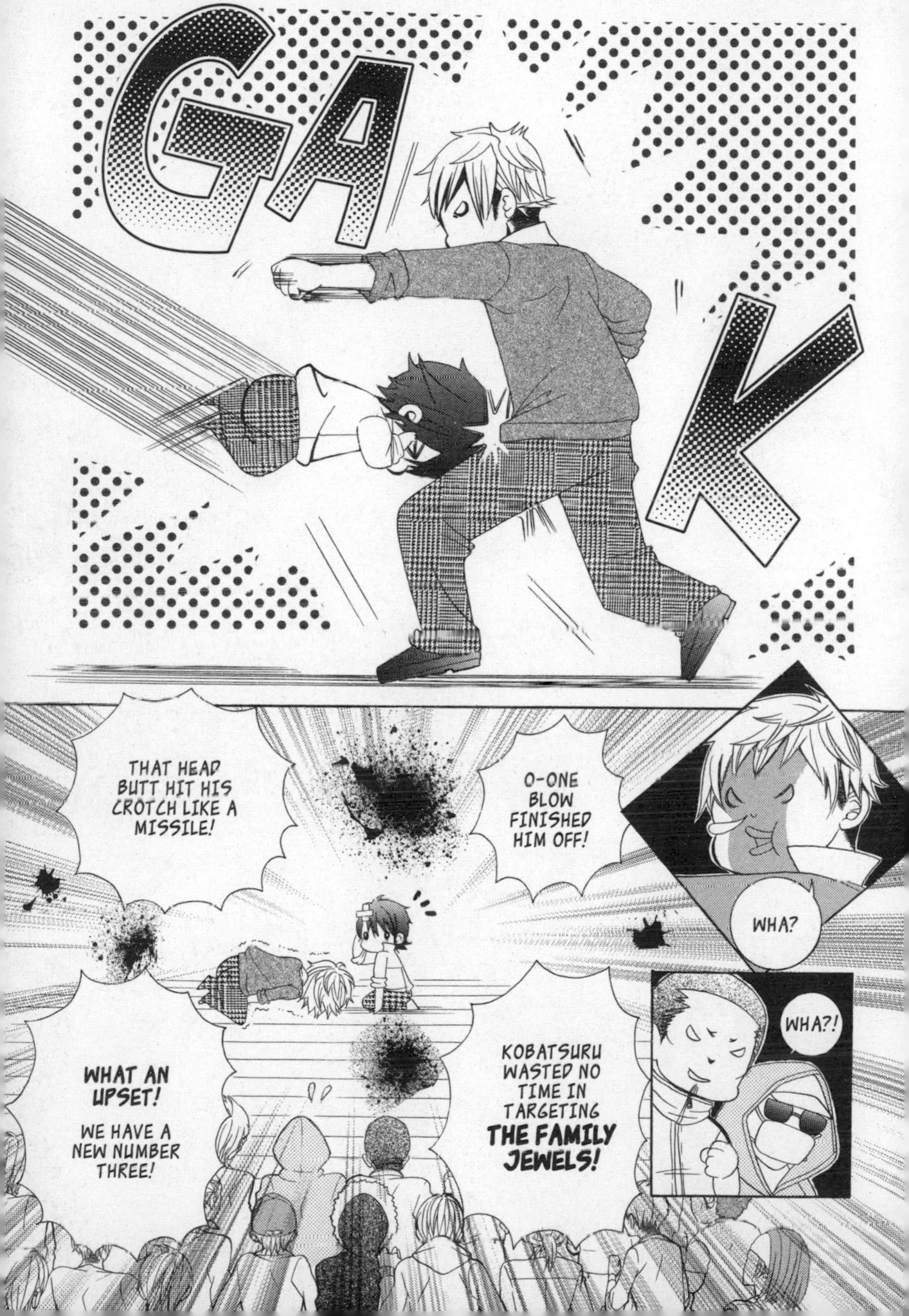
GAK
WHA?
WHA?!
O-ONE BLOW FINISHED HIM OFF!
THAT HEAD BUTT HIT HIS CROTCH LIKE A MISSILE!
KOBATSURU WASTED NO TIME IN TARGETING **THE FAMILY JEWELS!**
WHAT AN UPSET!
WE HAVE A NEW NUMBER THREE!

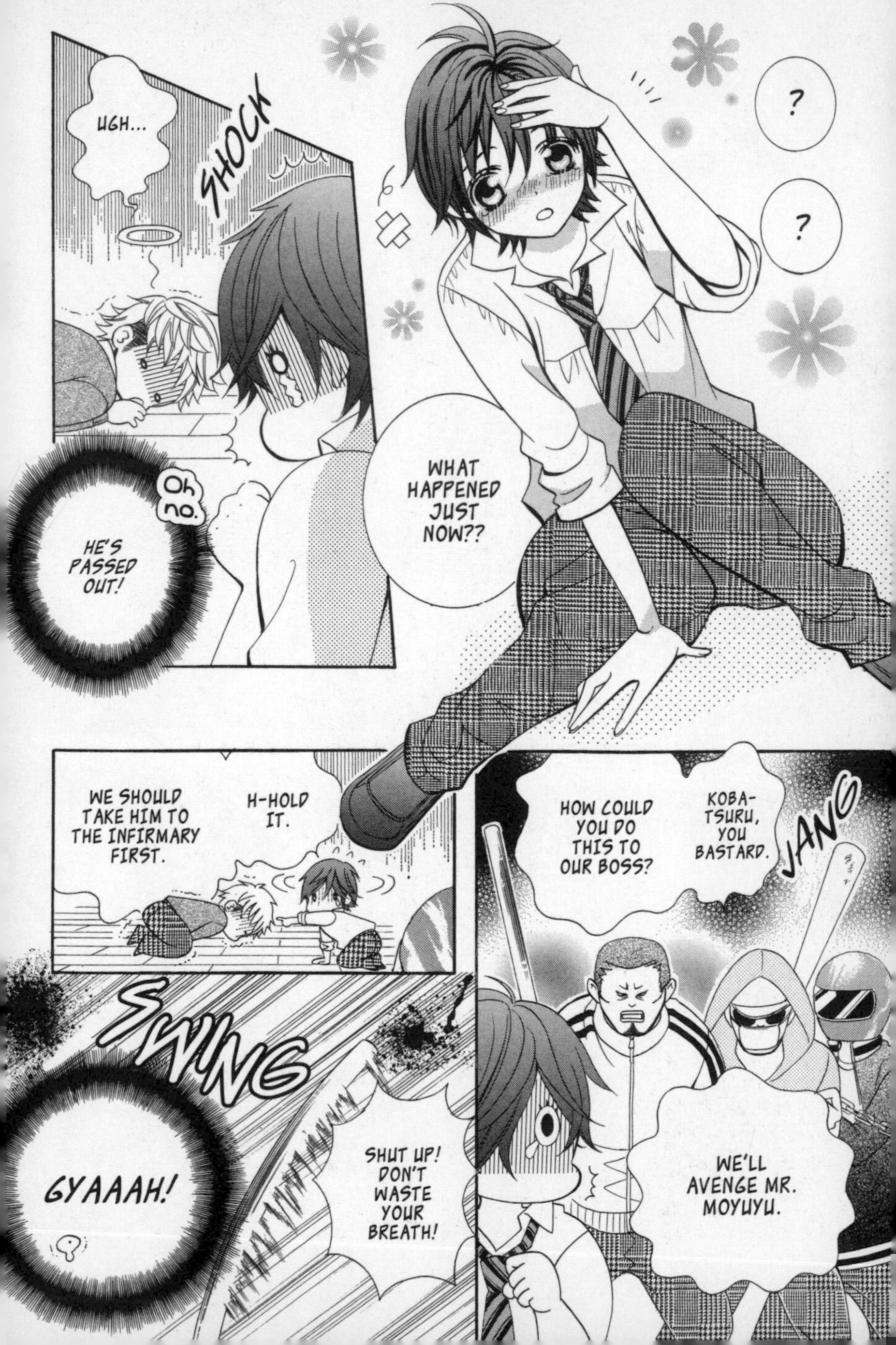
?
?
WHAT HAPPENED JUST NOW??
UGH...
SHOCK
Oh no.
HE'S PASSED OUT!
KOBA-TSURU, YOU BASTARD.
JANG
HOW COULD YOU DO THIS TO OUR BOSS?
WE'LL AVENGE MR. MOYUYU.
H-HOLD IT.
WE SHOULD TAKE HIM TO THE INFIRMARY FIRST.
SHUT UP! DON'T WASTE YOUR BREATH!
SWING
GYAAAH!

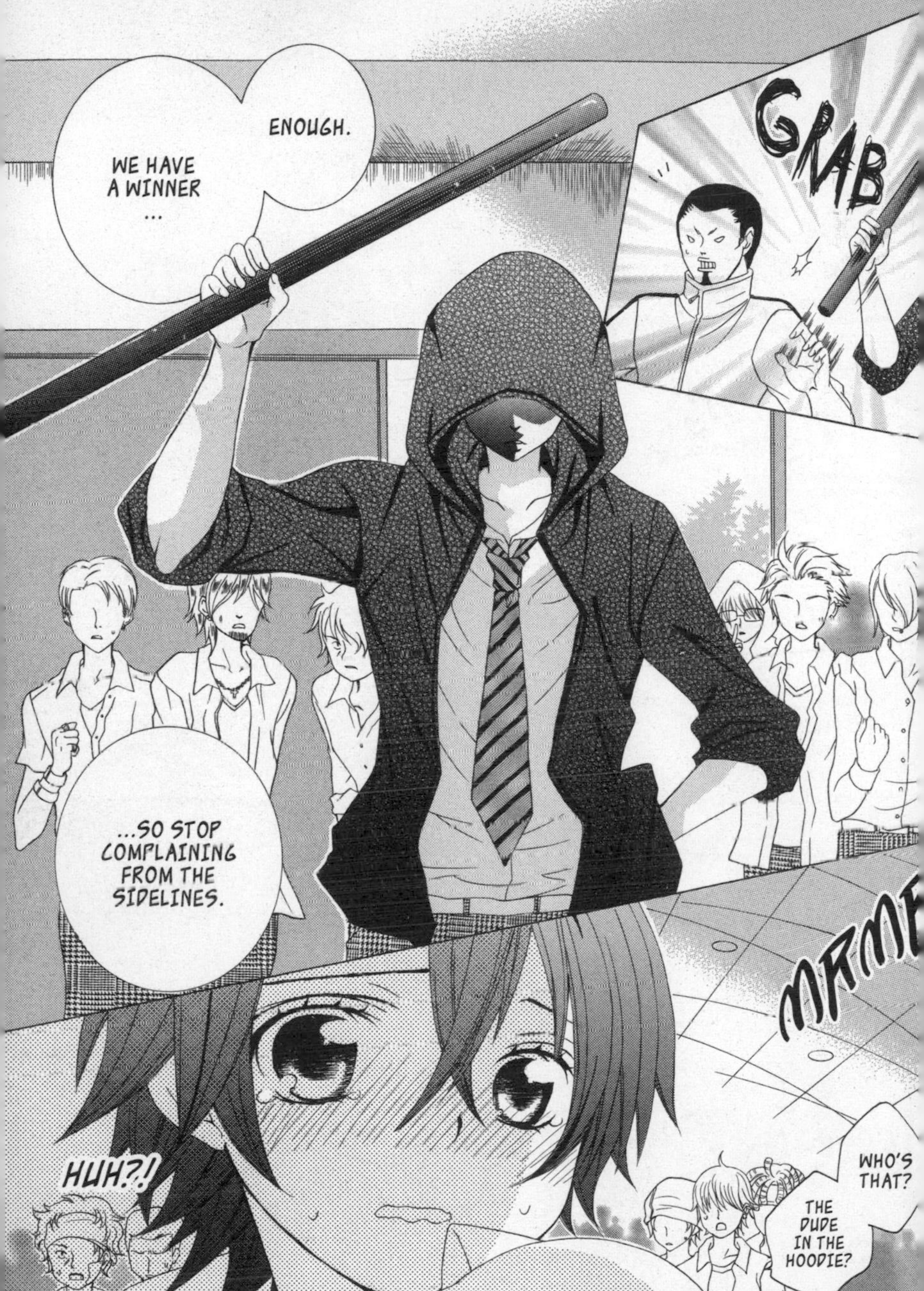
GRAB
ENOUGH.
WE HAVE A WINNER ...
...SO STOP COMPLAINING FROM THE SIDELINES.
WHO'S THAT?
THE DUDE IN THE HOODIE?
HUH?!

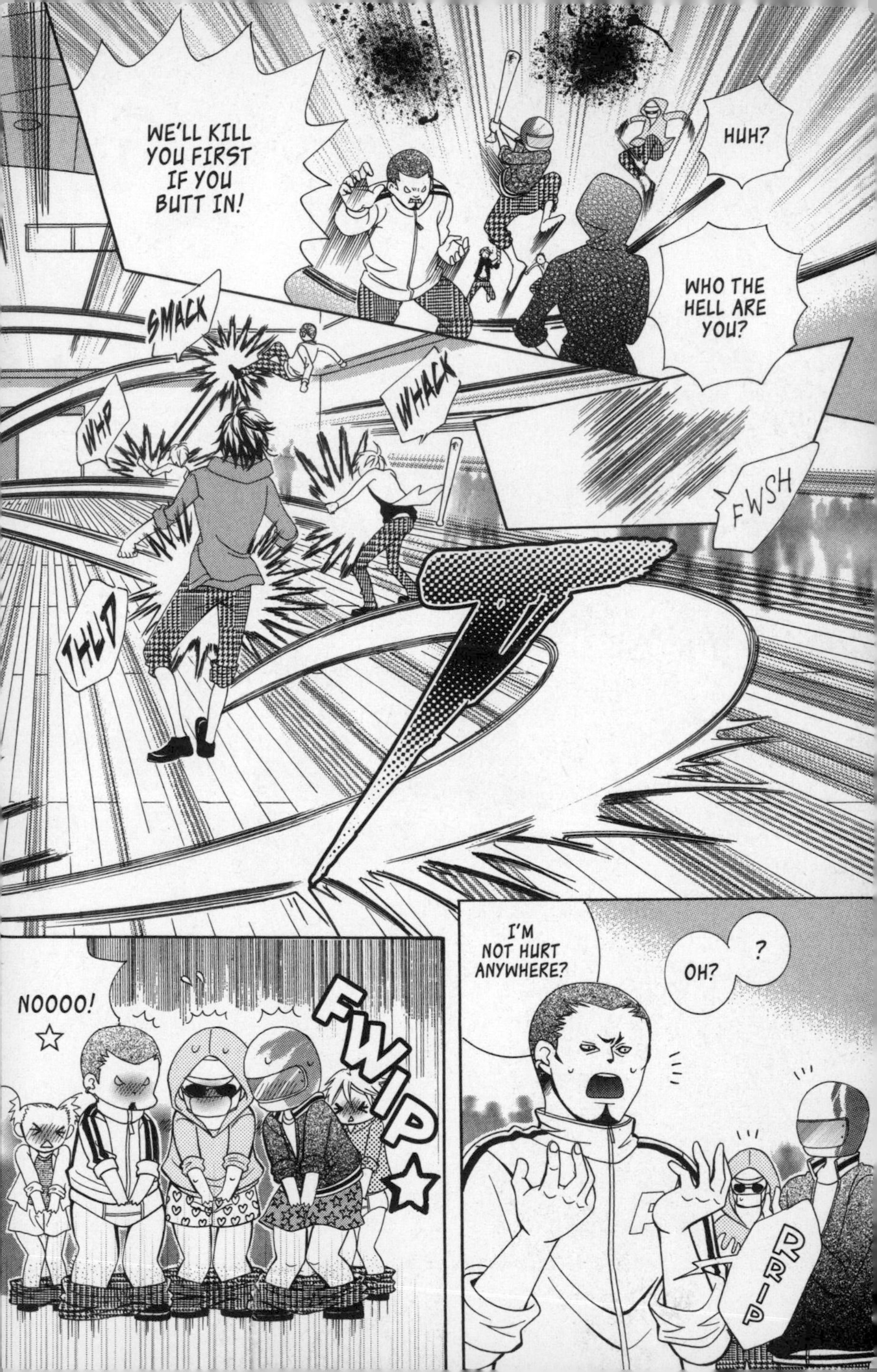
HUH?
WHO THE HELL ARE YOU?
WE'LL KILL YOU FIRST IF YOU BUTT IN!
FWSH
WHACK
SMACK
WHP
THUD
?
OH?
I'M NOT HURT ANYWHERE?
RRIP
FWIP☆
NOOOO! ☆

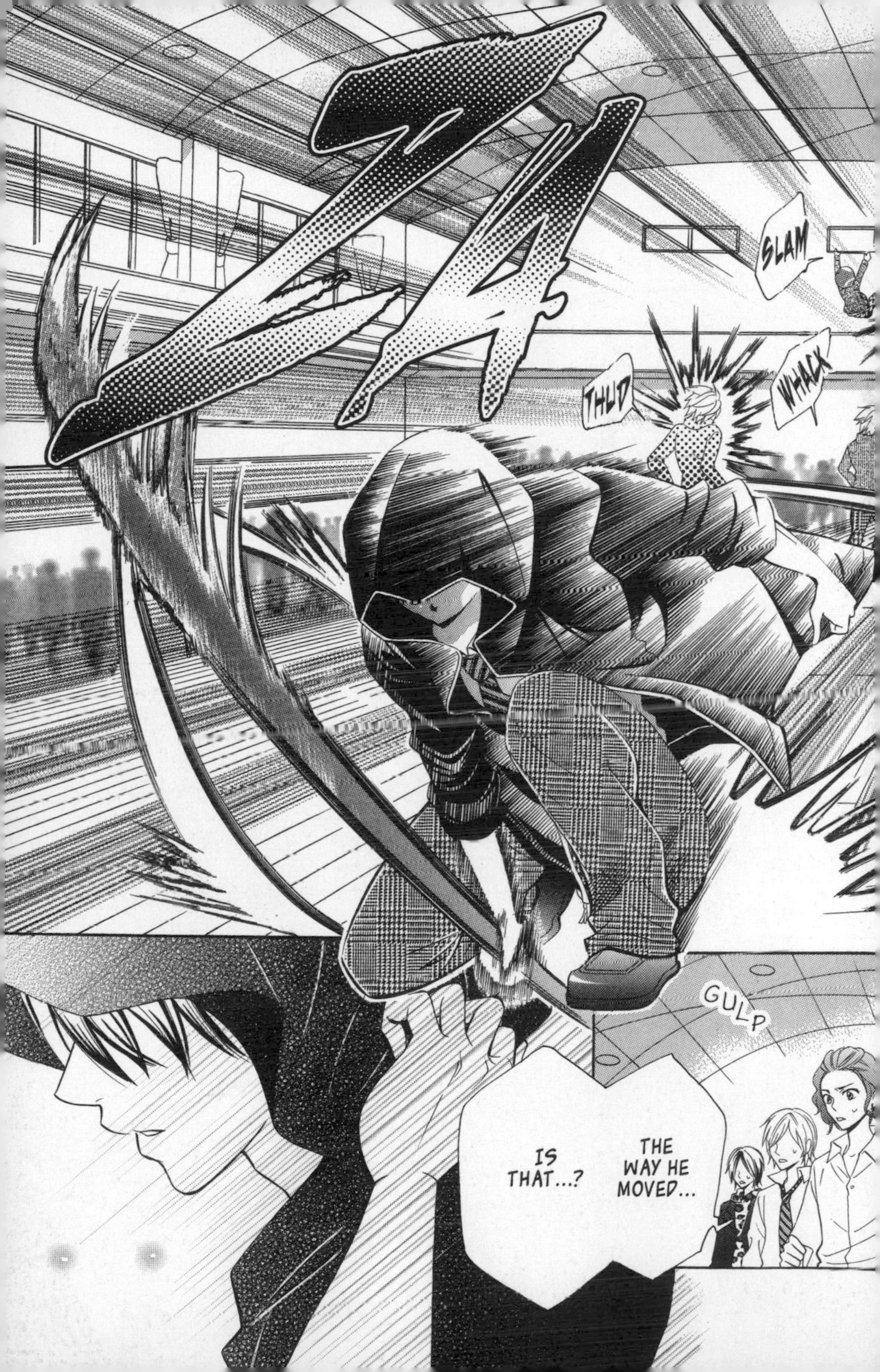
SLAM
WHACK
THUD
GULP
THE WAY HE MOVED...
IS THAT...?

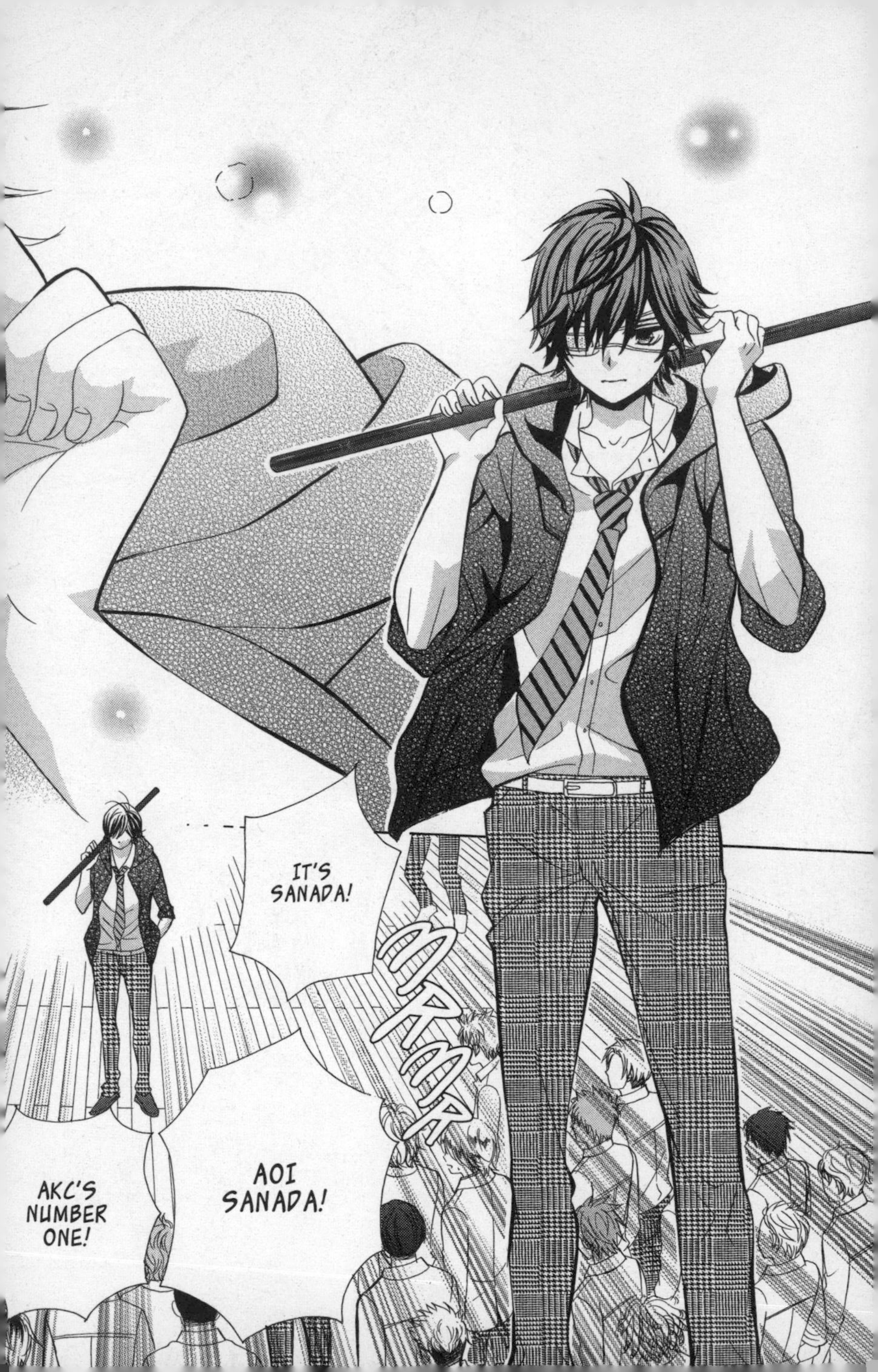
IT'S SANADA!
MRMR
AOI SANADA!
AKC'S NUMBER ONE!

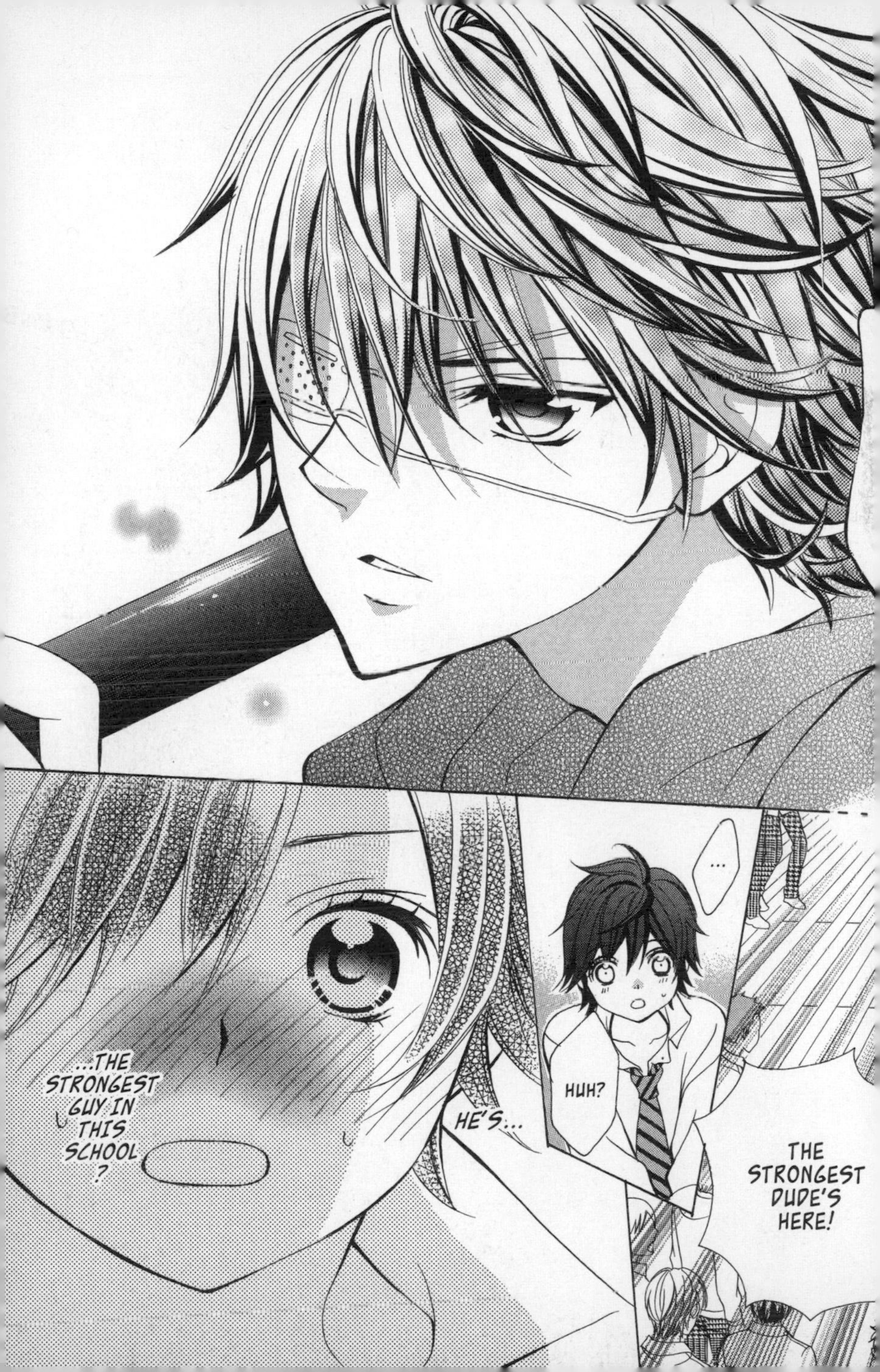
THE STRONGEST DUDE'S HERE!
...
HUH?
HE'S...
...THE STRONGEST GUY IN THIS SCHOOL?

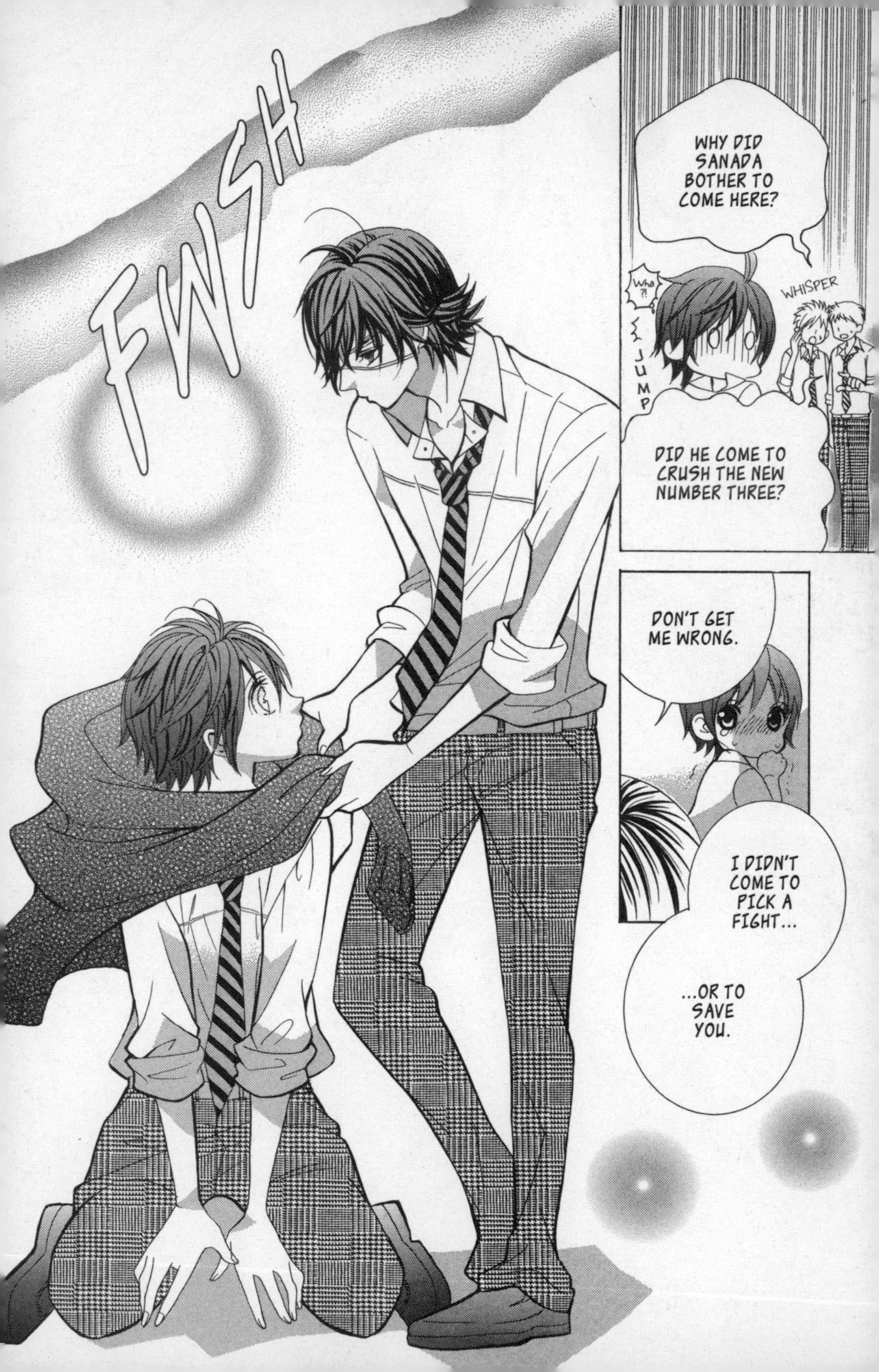
WHY DID SANADA BOTHER TO COME HERE?
WHISPER
Wha?!
JUMP
DID HE COME TO CRUSH THE NEW NUMBER THREE?
DON'T GET ME WRONG.
I DIDN'T COME TO PICK A FIGHT...
...OR TO SAVE YOU.
FWSH

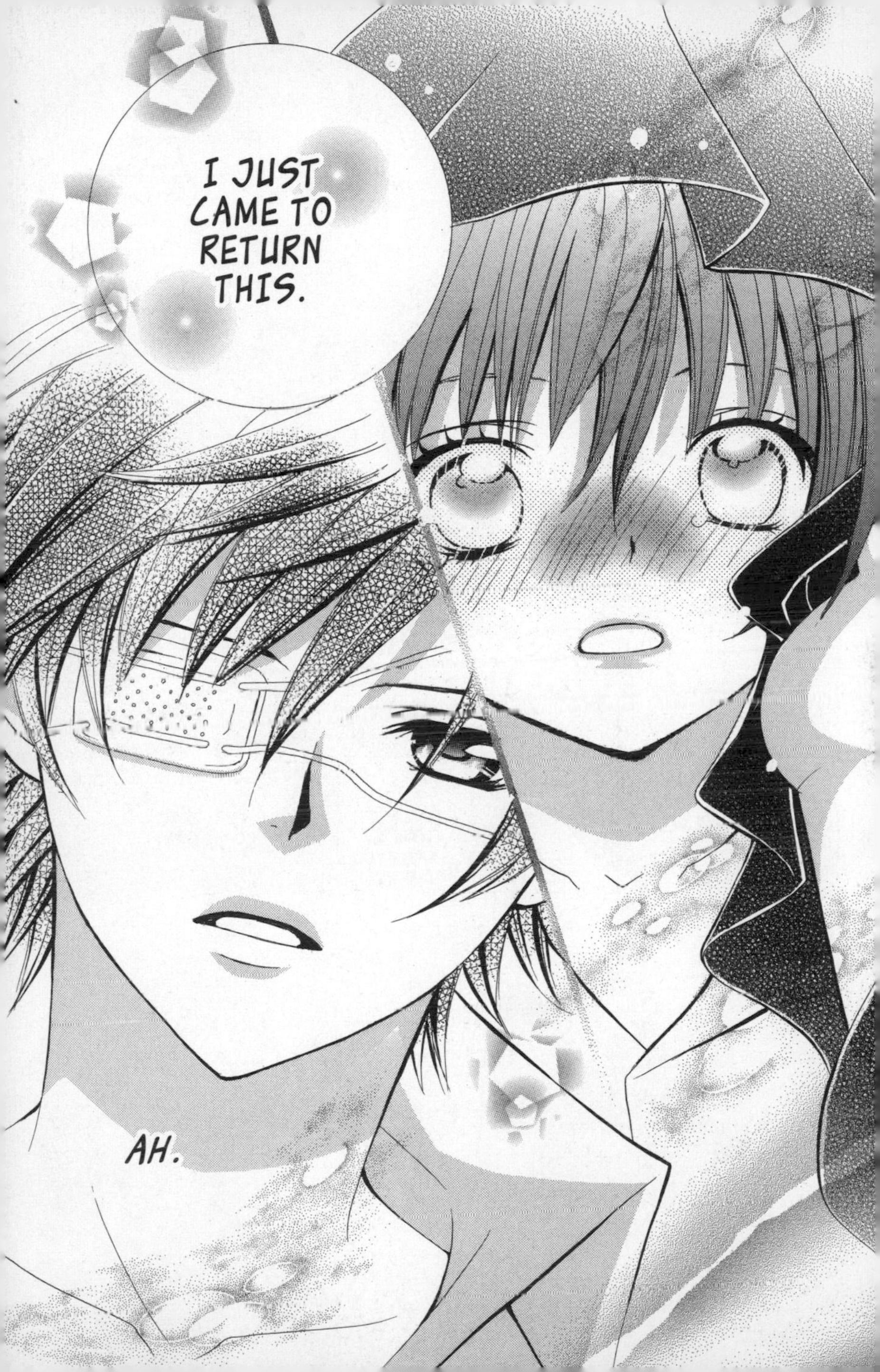
I JUST CAME TO RETURN THIS.
AH.

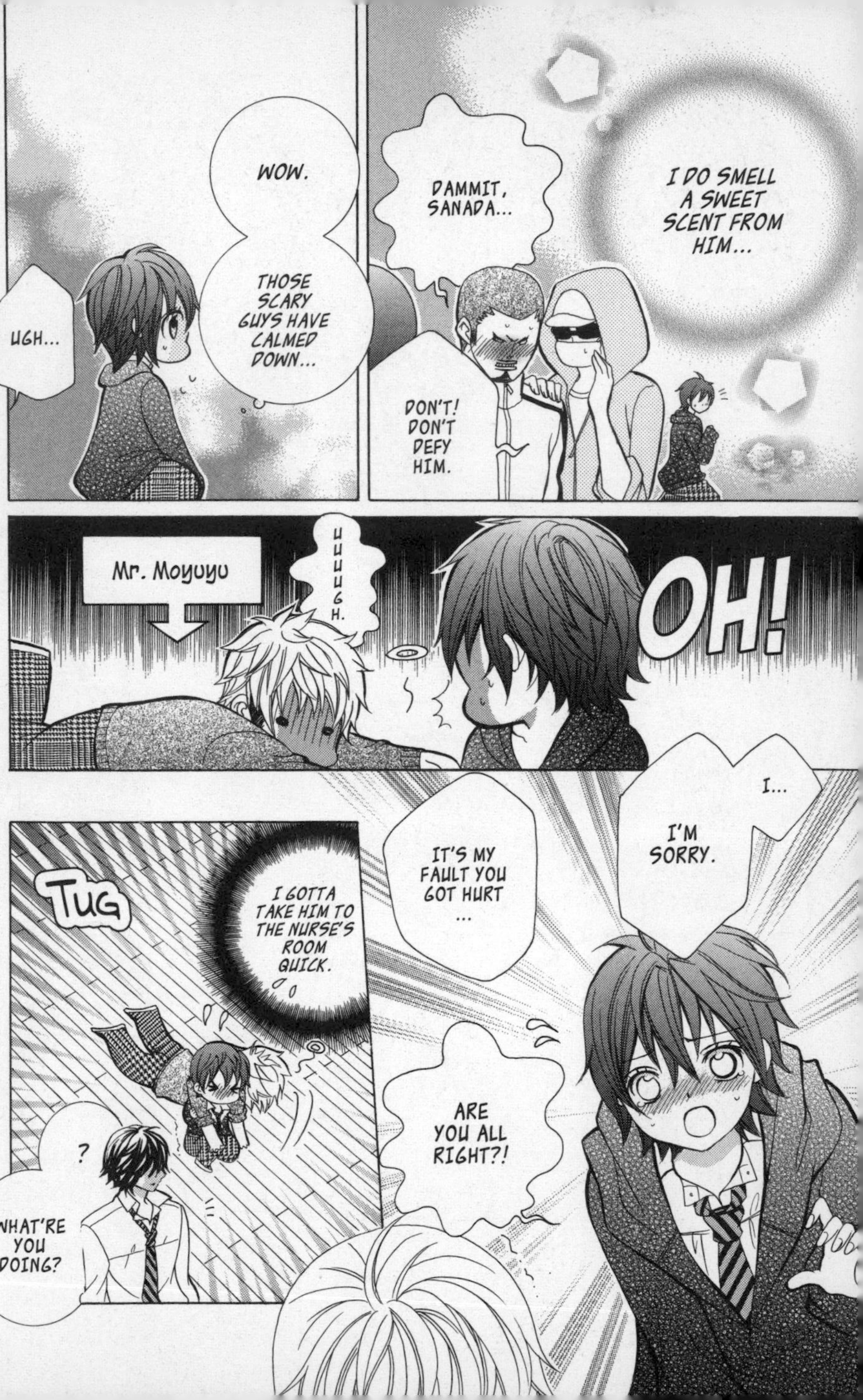
I DO SMELL A SWEET SCENT FROM HIM...
DAMMIT, SANADA...
DON'T! DON'T DEFY HIM.
WOW.
THOSE SCARY GUYS HAVE CALMED DOWN...
UGH...
OH!
UUUUUGH.
Mr. Moyuyu
I...
I'M SORRY.
IT'S MY FAULT YOU GOT HURT...
ARE YOU ALL RIGHT?!
TUG
I GOTTA TAKE HIM TO THE NURSE'S ROOM QUICK.
?
WHAT'RE YOU DOING?

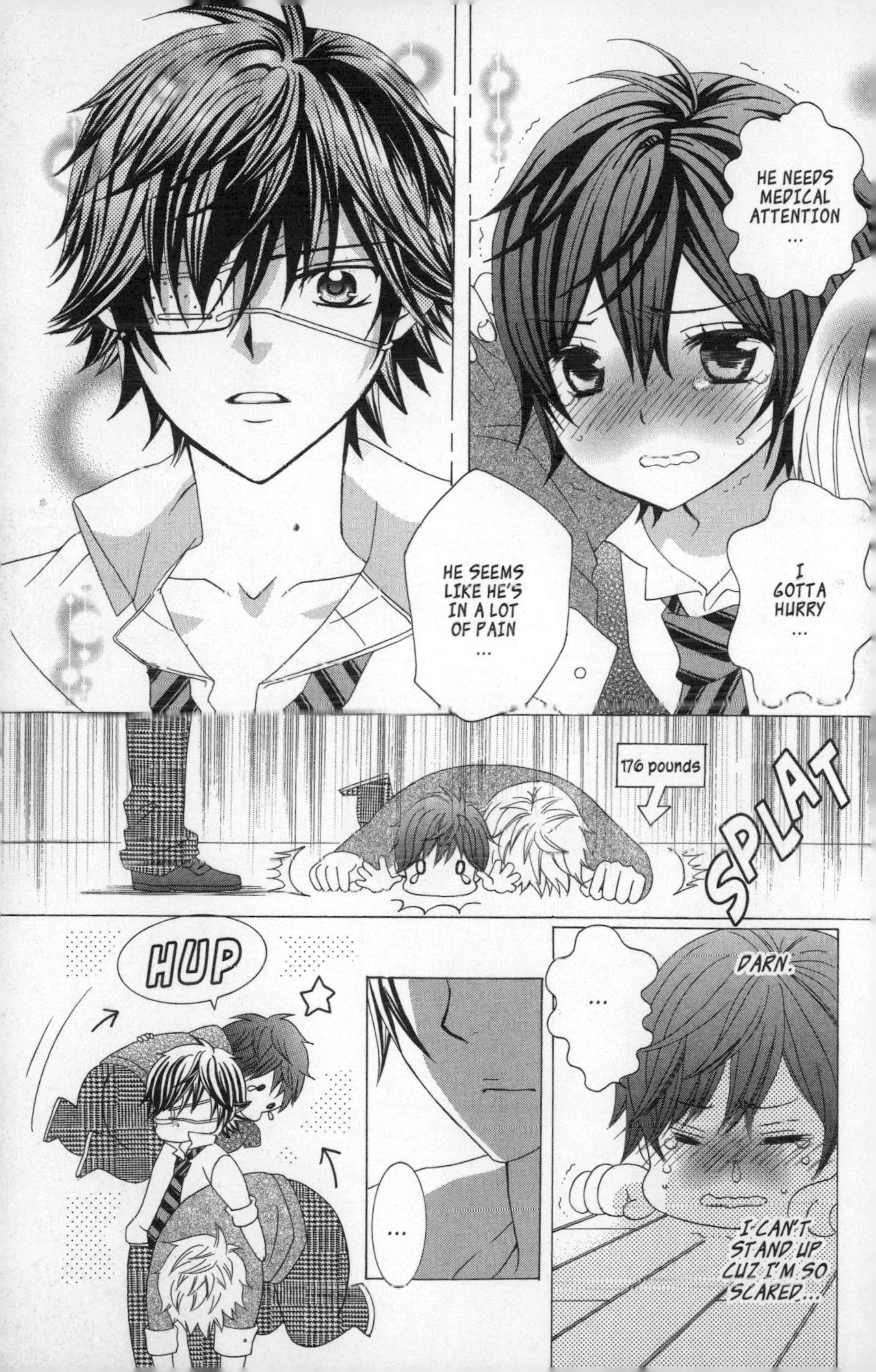
HE NEEDS MEDICAL ATTENTION ...
I GOTTA HURRY ...
HE SEEMS LIKE HE'S IN A LOT OF PAIN ...
176 pounds
SPLAT
...
DARN.
I CAN'T STAND UP CUZ I'M SO SCARED...
...
HUP

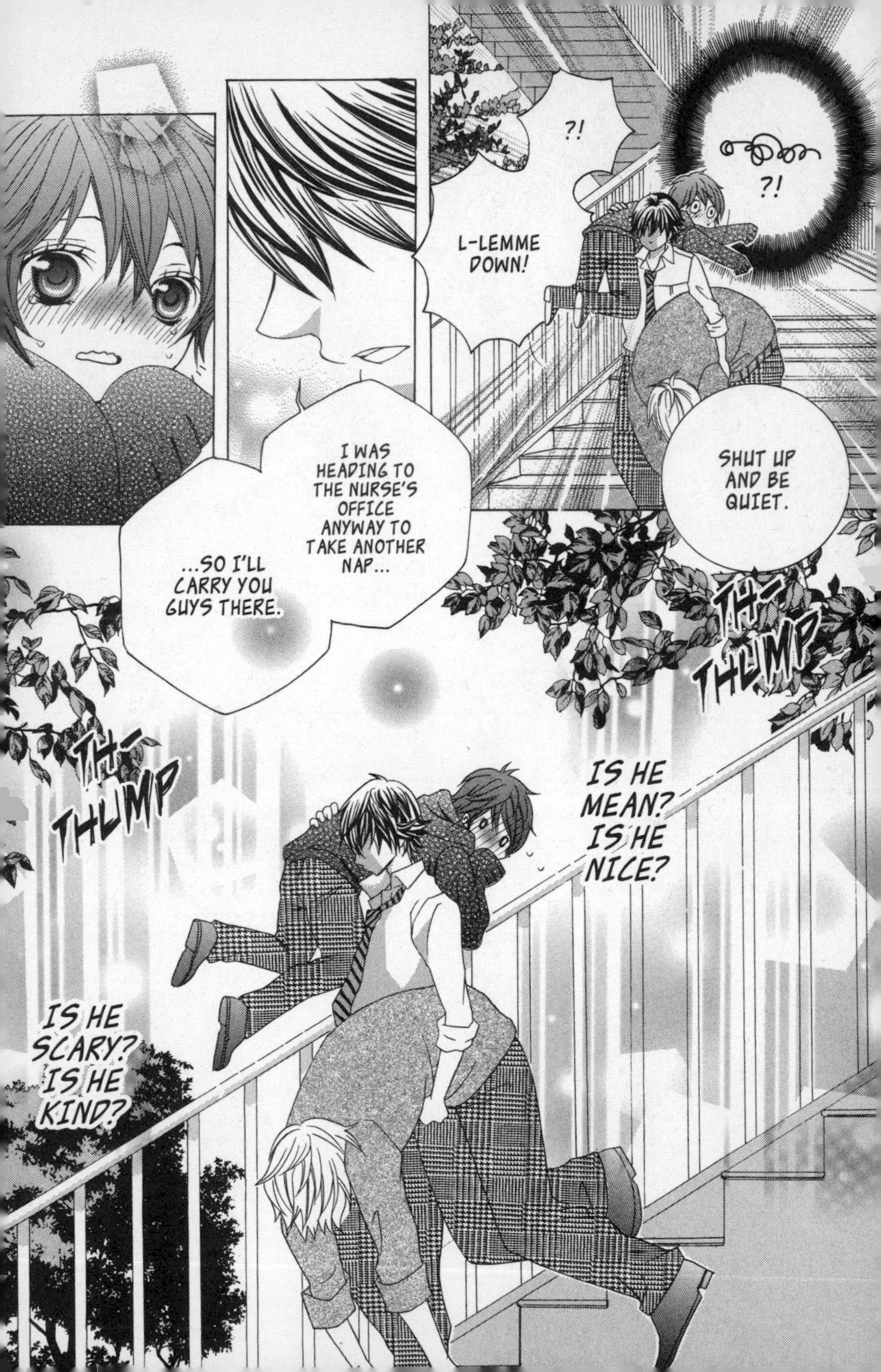
?!
?!
L-LEMME DOWN!
SHUT UP AND BE QUIET.
I WAS HEADING TO THE NURSE'S OFFICE ANYWAY TO TAKE ANOTHER NAP...
...SO I'LL CARRY YOU GUYS THERE.
TH-THUMP
IS HE MEAN? IS HE NICE?
TH-THUMP
IS HE SCARY? IS HE KIND?

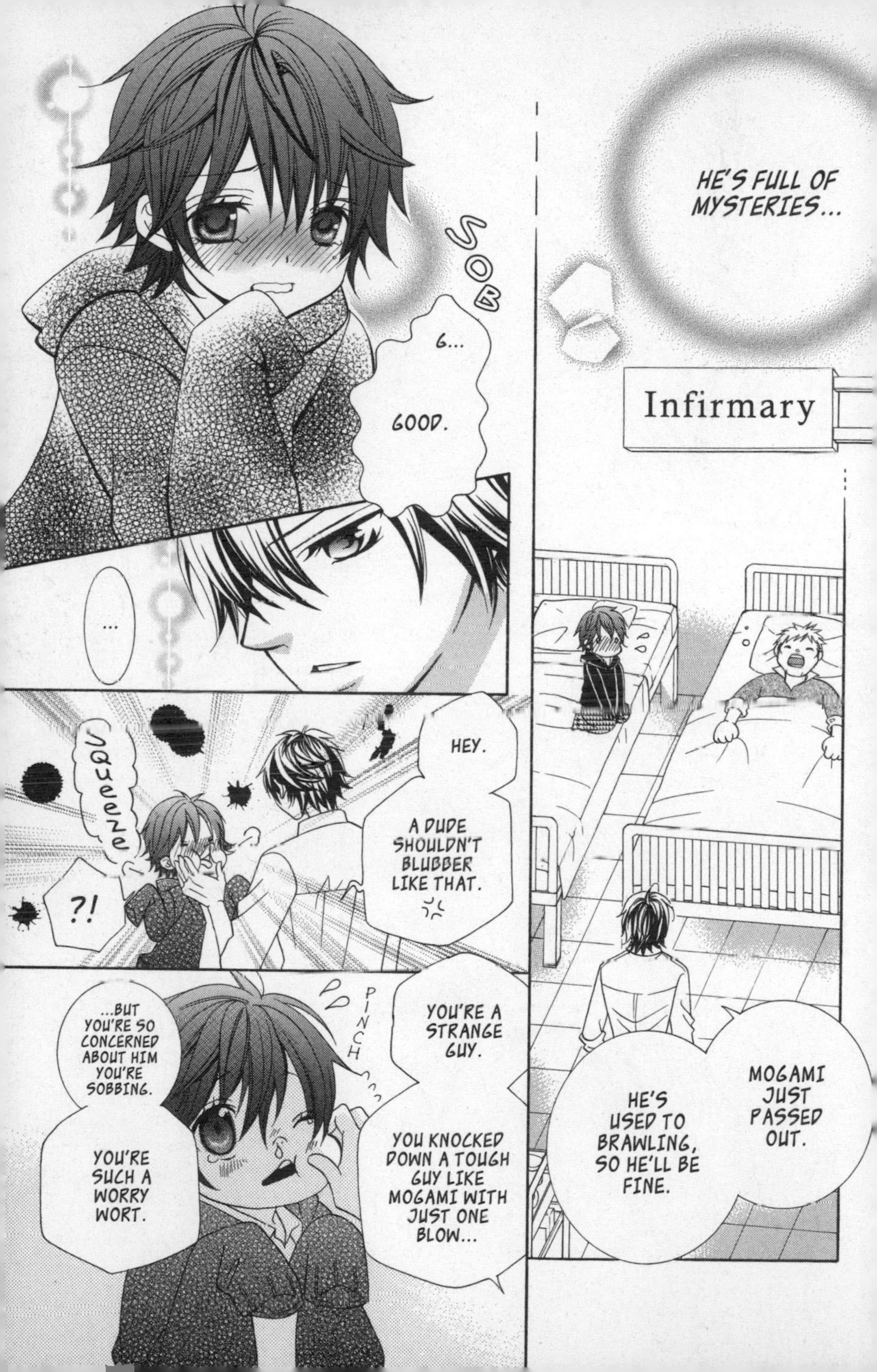
HE'S FULL OF MYSTERIES...
Infirmary
MOGAMI JUST PASSED OUT.
HE'S USED TO BRAWLING, SO HE'LL BE FINE.
SOB
G...
GOOD.
...
HEY.
A DUDE SHOULDN'T BLUBBER LIKE THAT.
Squeeze
?!
YOU'RE A STRANGE GUY.
PINCH
YOU KNOCKED DOWN A TOUGH GUY LIKE MOGAMI WITH JUST ONE BLOW...
...BUT YOU'RE SO CONCERNED ABOUT HIM YOU'RE SOBBING.
YOU'RE SUCH A WORRY WORT.

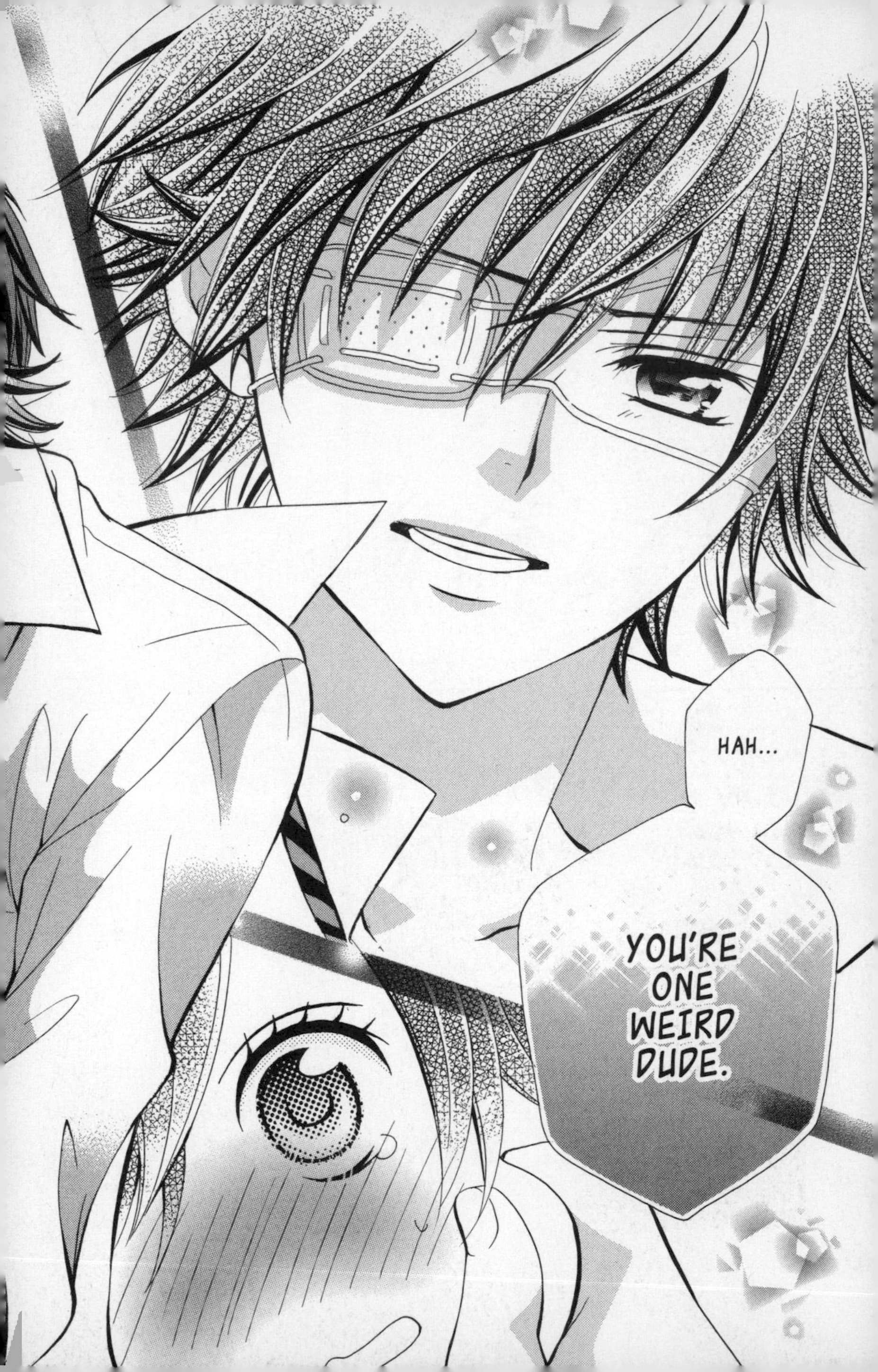
HAH...
YOU'RE ONE WEIRD DUDE.

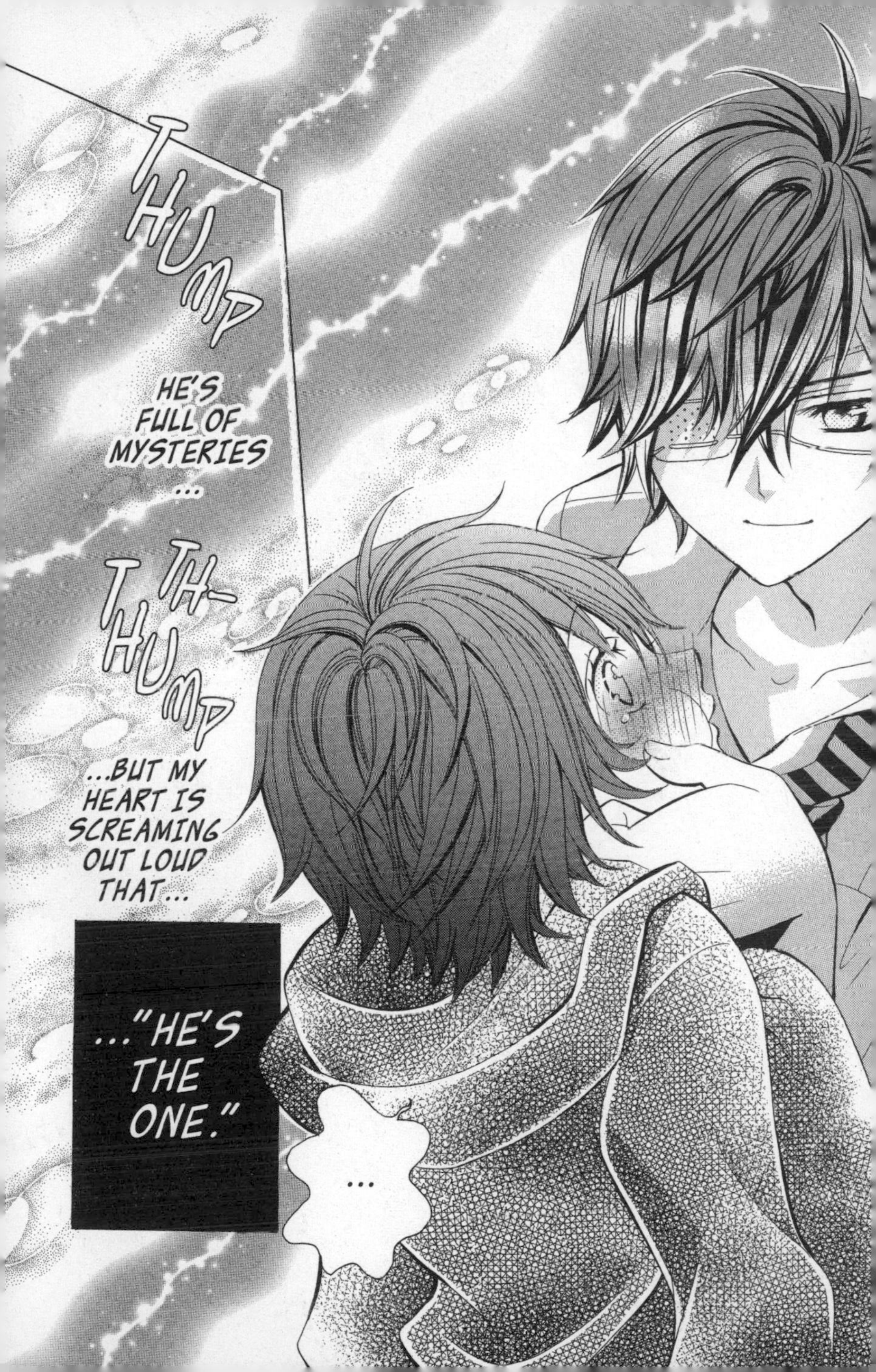
THUMP
HE'S FULL OF MYSTERIES...
TH-THUMP
...BUT MY HEART IS SCREAMING OUT LOUD THAT...
..."HE'S THE ONE."
...

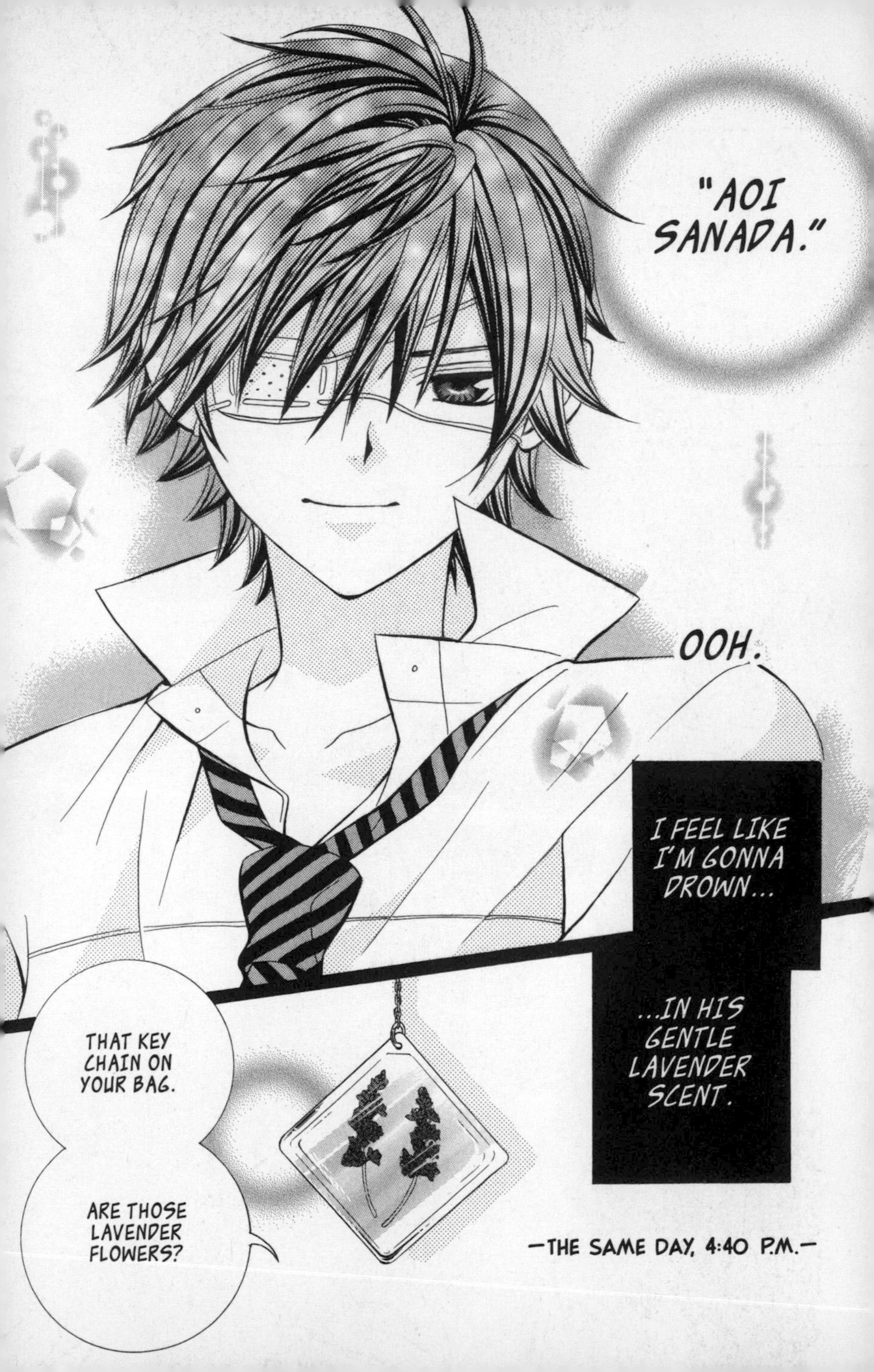
"AOI SANADA."
OOH.
I FEEL LIKE I'M GONNA DROWN...
...IN HIS GENTLE LAVENDER SCENT.
—THE SAME DAY, 4:40 P.M.—
THAT KEY CHAIN ON YOUR BAG.
ARE THOSE LAVENDER FLOWERS?

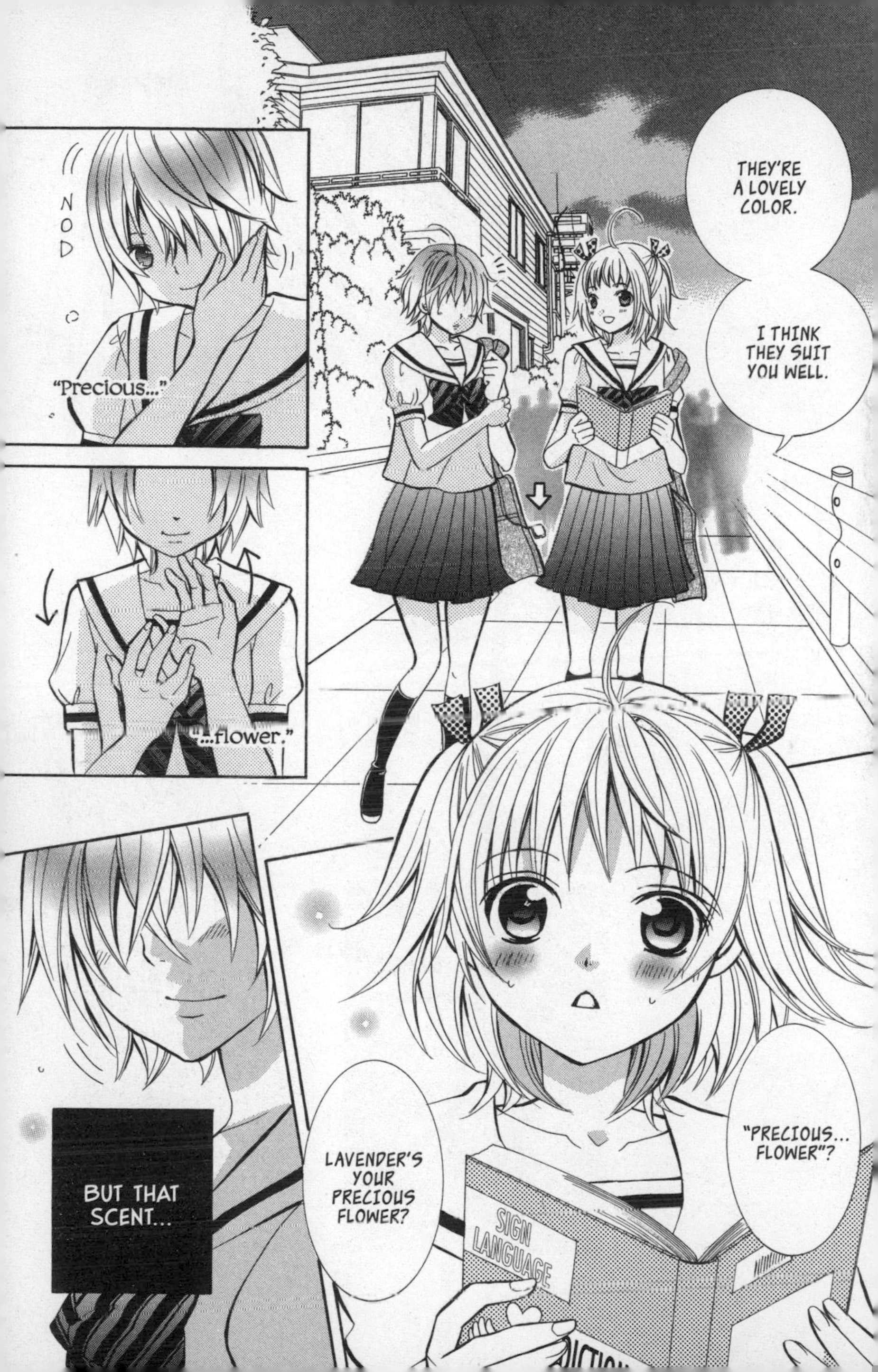
THEY'RE A LOVELY COLOR.
I THINK THEY SUIT YOU WELL.
NOD
"Precious..."
"...flower."
"PRECIOUS... FLOWER"?
LAVENDER'S YOUR PRECIOUS FLOWER?
SIGN LANGUAGE
BUT THAT SCENT...

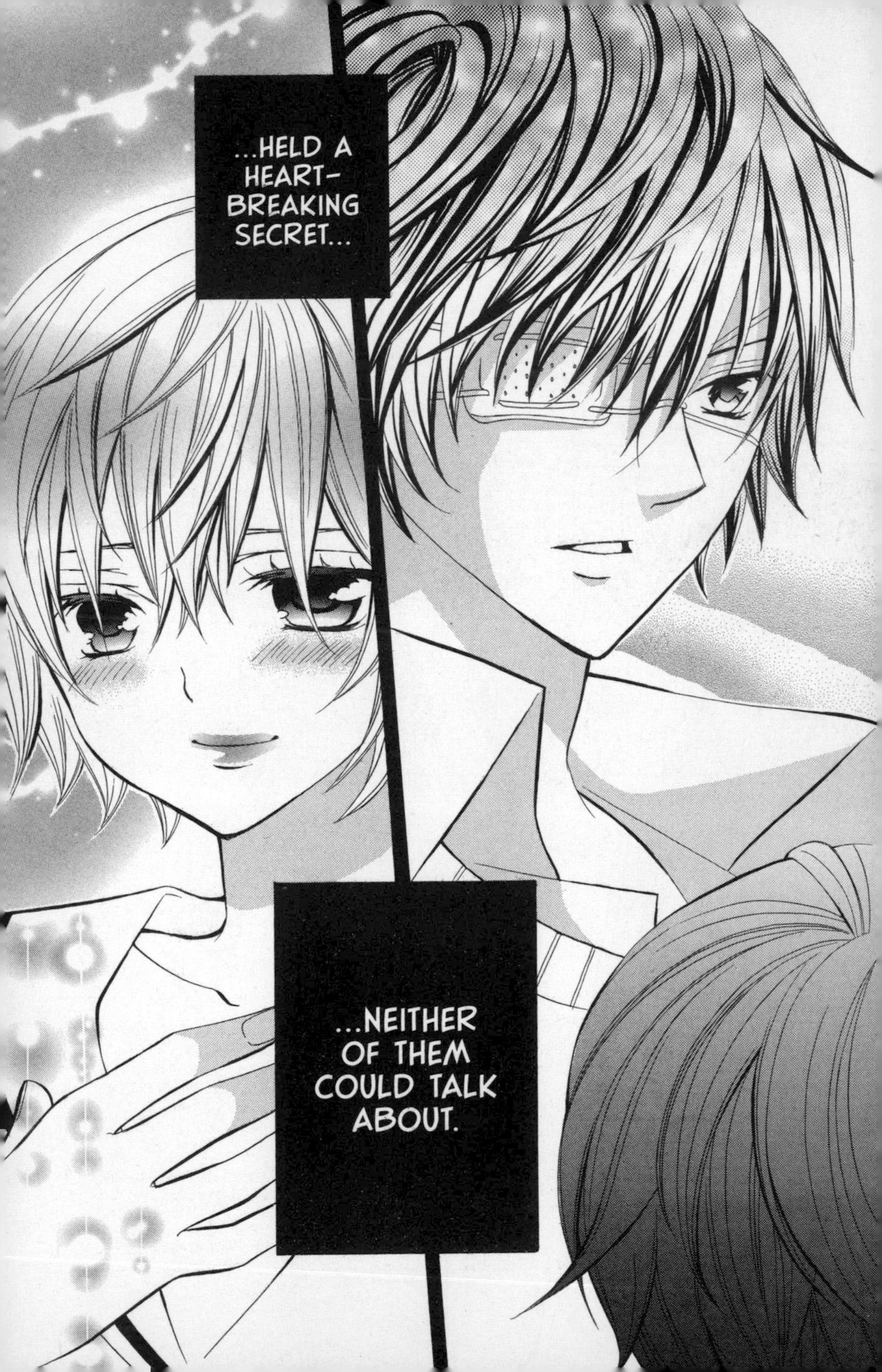
...HELD A HEART-BREAKING SECRET...
...NEITHER OF THEM COULD TALK ABOUT.

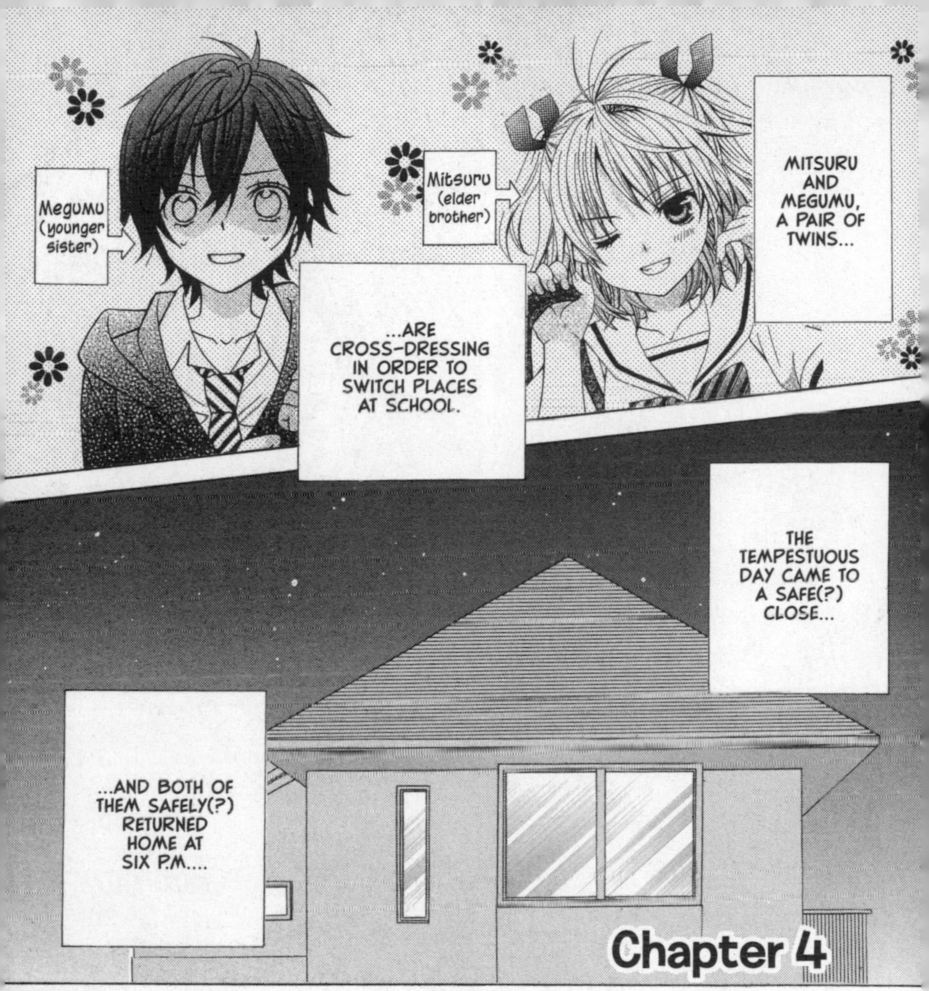
MITSURU AND MEGUMU, A PAIR OF TWINS...
Mitsuru (elder brother)
Megumu (younger sister)
...ARE CROSS-DRESSING IN ORDER TO SWITCH PLACES AT SCHOOL.
THE TEMPESTUOUS DAY CAME TO A SAFE(?) CLOSE...
...AND BOTH OF THEM SAFELY(?) RETURNED HOME AT SIX P.M....
Chapter 4

About sign language

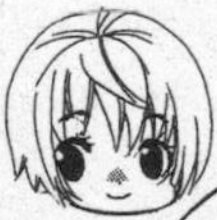

WHEN I WAS A STUDENT, THERE WERE MANY TV DRAMAS THAT FEATURED SIGN LANGUAGE. I WAS VERY MOVED AND PRACTICED SIGN LANGUAGE AT SCHOOL WITH MY FRIENDS.

AFTER I BECAME A MANGAKA, I WANTED TO DRAW A MANGA THAT FEATURED SIGN LANGUAGE, BUT I DIDN'T FEEL AN INEXPERIENCED MANGAKA LIKE ME WOULD BE ABLE TO FULLY PORTRAY THE SUBJECT MATTER.

NOW THAT I'VE BEEN A MANGAKA FOR TEN YEARS, I WANT TO CHALLENGE MYSELF TO DRAW WHAT I WANT SO I DON'T HAVE ANY REGRETS LATER ON. I'M HAPPY IF I CAN CONVEY MY FEELINGS THE BEST I CAN.

SIGN LANGUAGE DIFFERS FROM COUNTRY TO COUNTRY, AND SOMETIMES IT'S EVEN DIFFERENT WITHIN ONE COUNTRY. I WOULD LIKE TO PORTRAY SIGN LANGUAGE BY STUDYING TOGETHER WITH MITSURU AND MEGO.

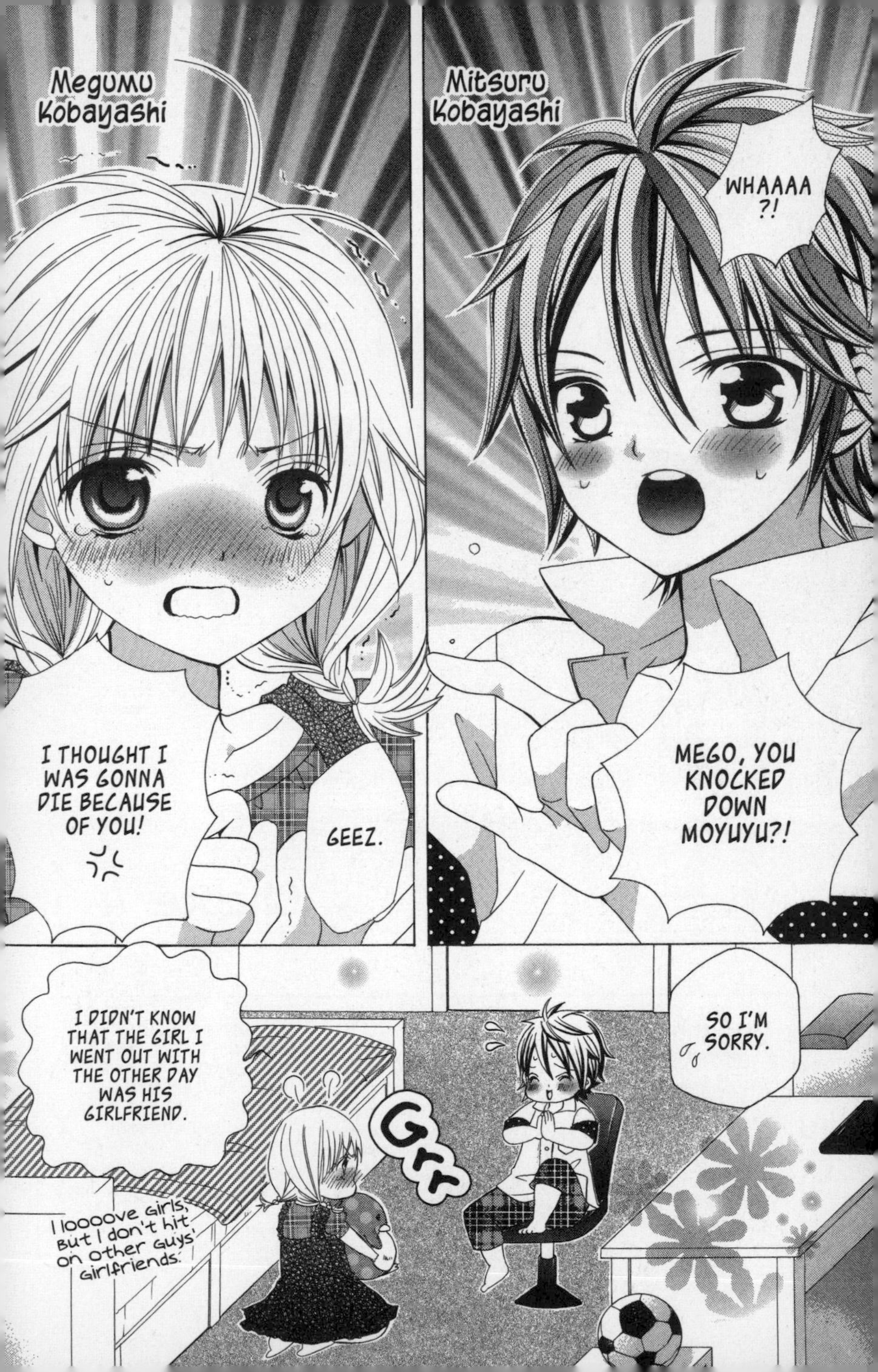
Mitsuru Kobayashi
WHAAAA?!
MEGO, YOU KNOCKED DOWN MOYUYU?!
Megumu Kobayashi
GEEZ.
I THOUGHT I WAS GONNA DIE BECAUSE OF YOU!
SO I'M SORRY.
I DIDN'T KNOW THAT THE GIRL I WENT OUT WITH THE OTHER DAY WAS HIS GIRLFRIEND.
Grr
I loooove girls, but I don't hit on other guys' girlfriends.

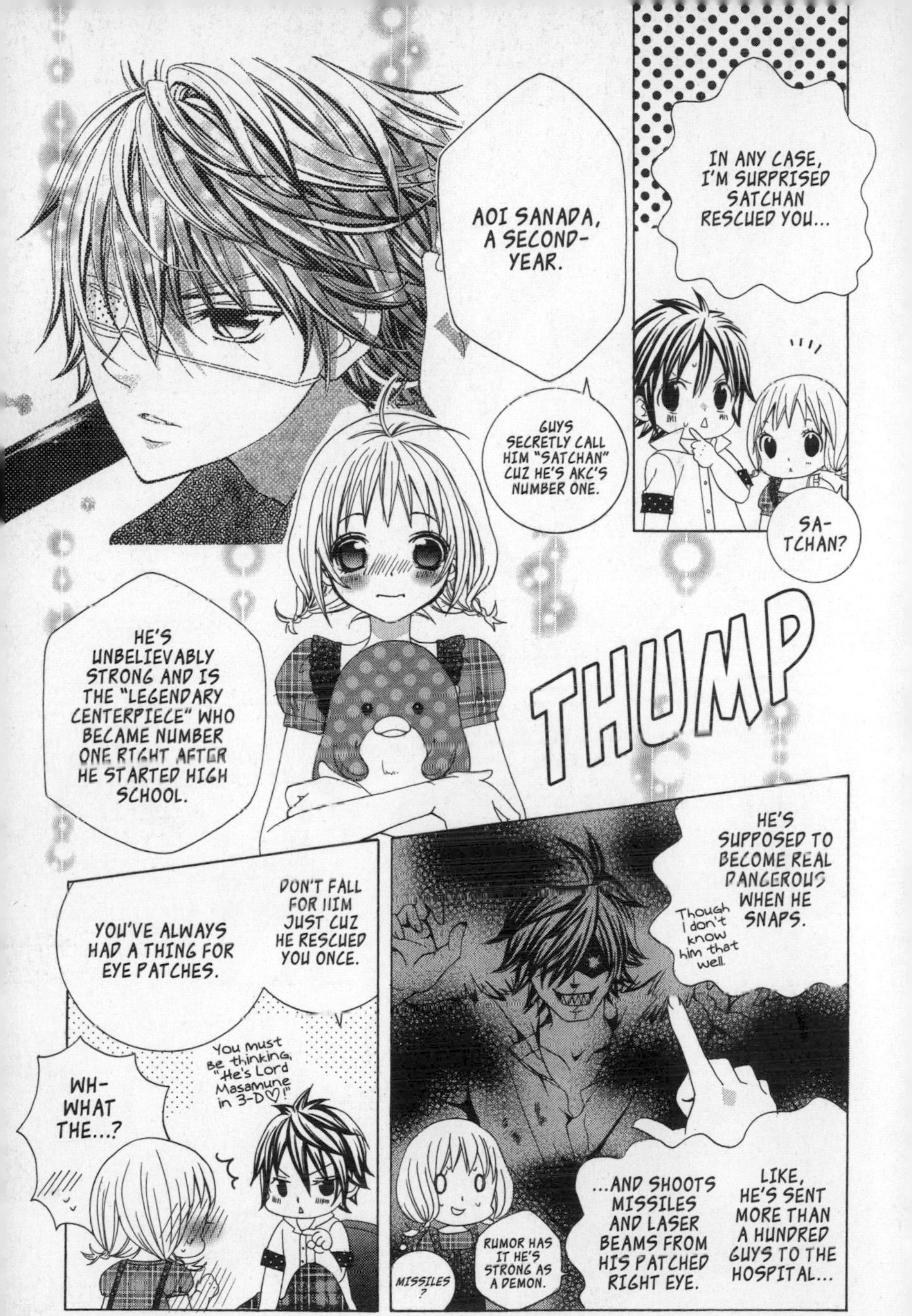

IN ANY CASE, I'M SURPRISED SATCHAN RESCUED YOU...
SA-TCHAN?
AOI SANADA, A SECOND-YEAR.
GUYS SECRETLY CALL HIM "SATCHAN" CUZ HE'S AKC'S NUMBER ONE.
HE'S UNBELIEVABLY STRONG AND IS THE "LEGENDARY CENTERPIECE" WHO BECAME NUMBER ONE RIGHT AFTER HE STARTED HIGH SCHOOL.
THUMP
HE'S SUPPOSED TO BECOME REAL DANGEROUS WHEN HE SNAPS.
Though I don't know him that well.
LIKE, HE'S SENT MORE THAN A HUNDRED GUYS TO THE HOSPITAL...
...AND SHOOTS MISSILES AND LASER BEAMS FROM HIS PATCHED RIGHT EYE.
RUMOR HAS IT HE'S STRONG AS A DEMON.
MISSILES?
DON'T FALL FOR HIM JUST CUZ HE RESCUED YOU ONCE.
YOU'VE ALWAYS HAD A THING FOR EYE PATCHES.
You must be thinking, "He's Lord Masamune in 3-D♡!"
WH-WHAT THE...?

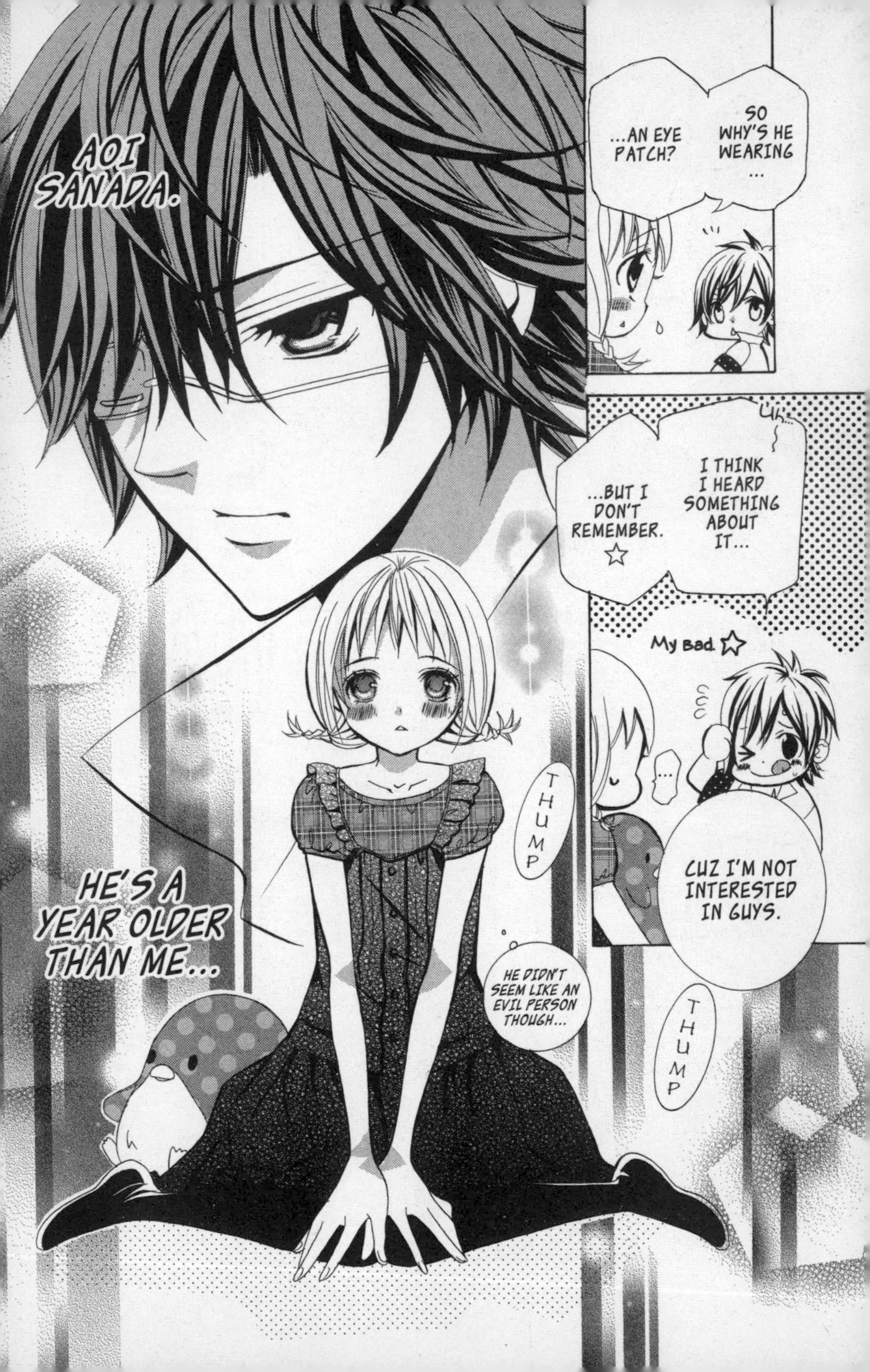
SO WHY'S HE WEARING ...
...AN EYE PATCH?
Uh...
I THINK I HEARD SOMETHING ABOUT IT...
...BUT I DON'T REMEMBER. ☆
My bad ☆
...
CUZ I'M NOT INTERESTED IN GUYS.
AOI SANADA.
HE'S A YEAR OLDER THAN ME...
THUMP
HE DIDN'T SEEM LIKE AN EVIL PERSON THOUGH...
THUMP

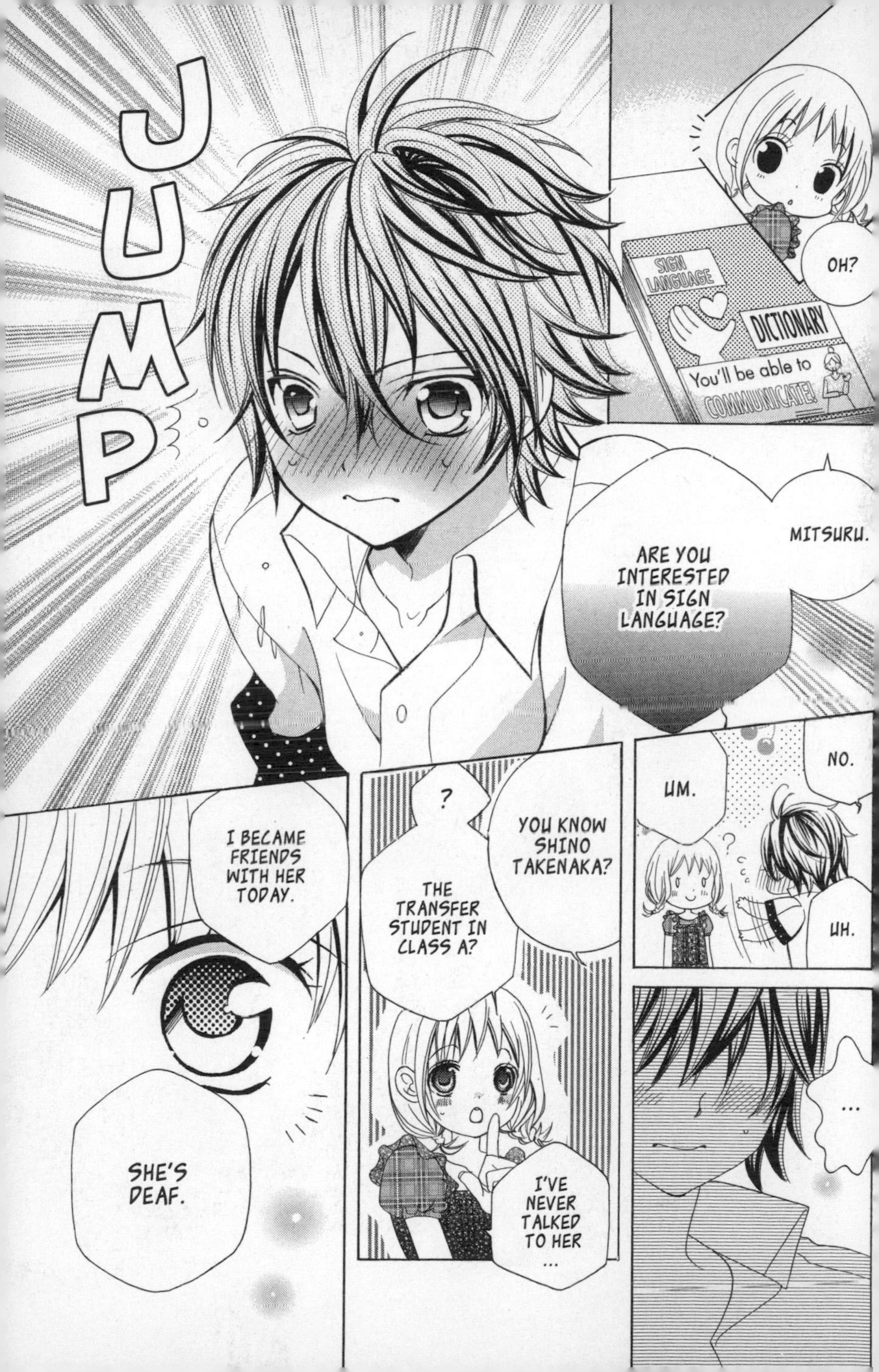
OH?
SIGN LANGUAGE
DICTIONARY
You'll be able to COMMUNICATE!
MITSURU.
ARE YOU INTERESTED IN SIGN LANGUAGE?
JUMP
NO.
UM.
UH.
...
YOU KNOW SHINO TAKENAKA?
?
THE TRANSFER STUDENT IN CLASS A?
I'VE NEVER TALKED TO HER ...
I BECAME FRIENDS WITH HER TODAY.
SHE'S DEAF.

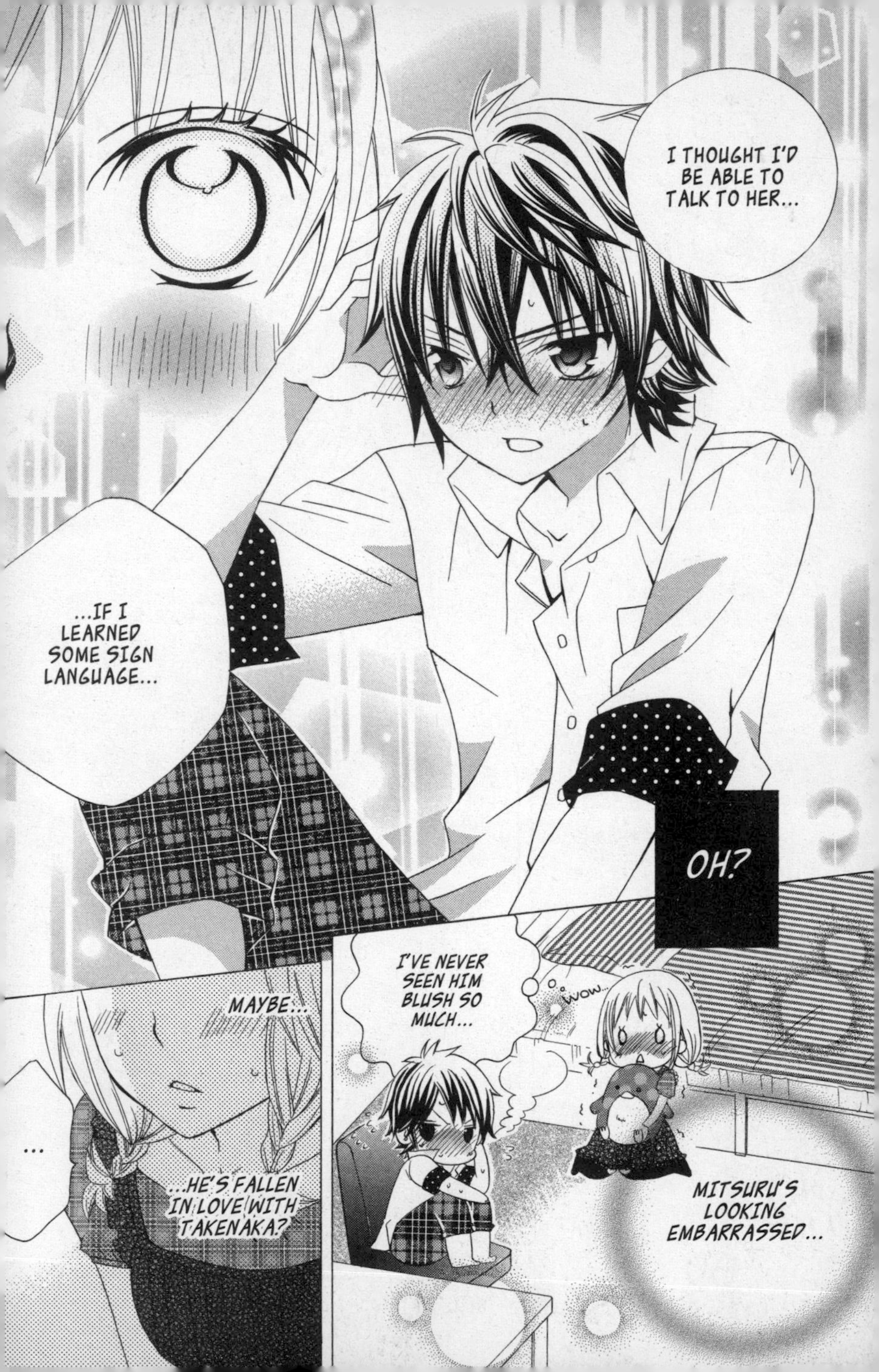
I THOUGHT I'D BE ABLE TO TALK TO HER...
...IF I LEARNED SOME SIGN LANGUAGE...
OH?
WOW...
I'VE NEVER SEEN HIM BLUSH SO MUCH...
MITSURU'S LOOKING EMBARRASSED...
MAYBE...
...
...HE'S FALLEN IN LOVE WITH TAKENAKA?

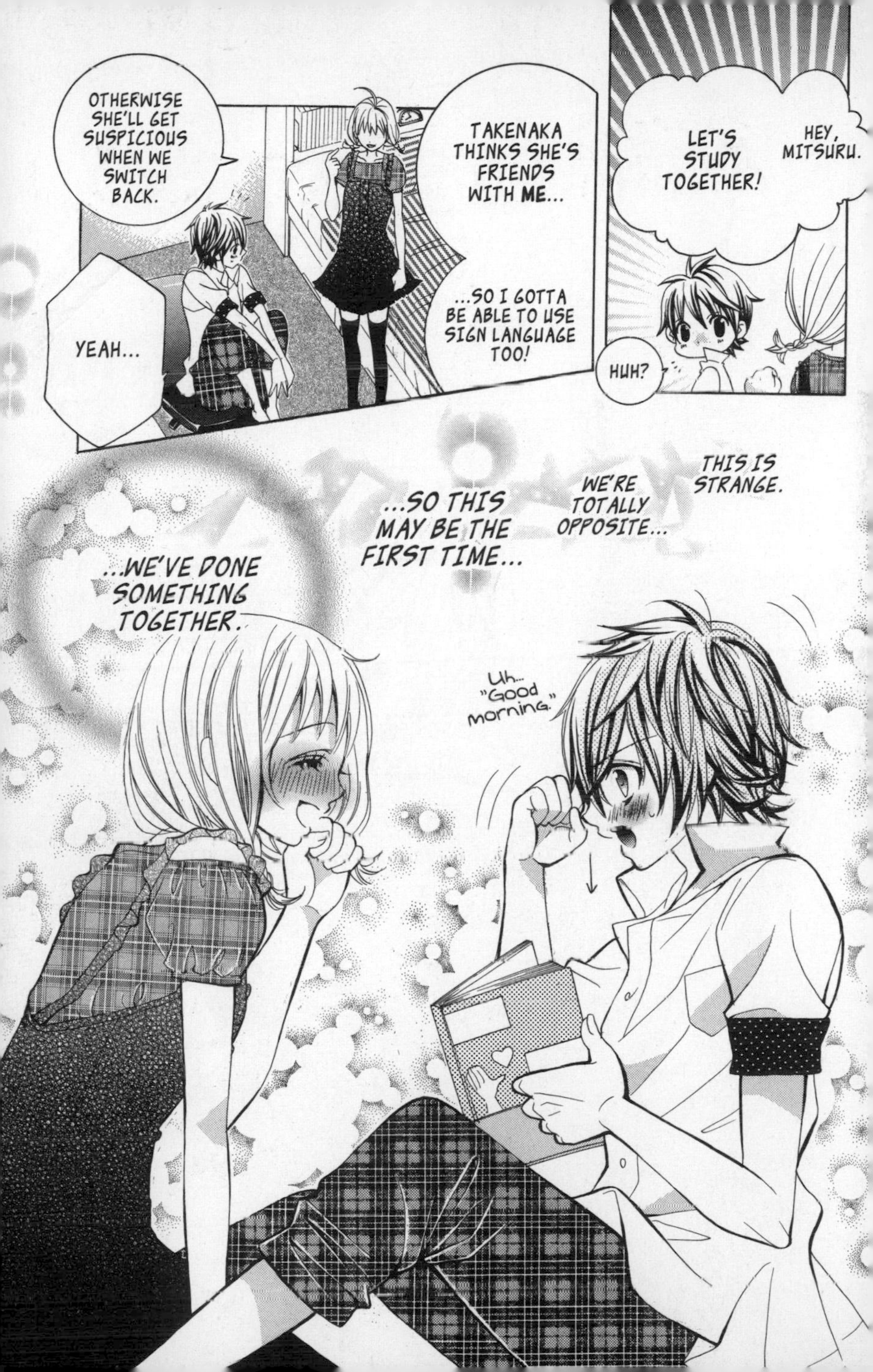
HEY, MITSURU.
LET'S STUDY TOGETHER!
HUH?
TAKENAKA THINKS SHE'S FRIENDS WITH ME...
...SO I GOTTA BE ABLE TO USE SIGN LANGUAGE TOO!
OTHERWISE SHE'LL GET SUSPICIOUS WHEN WE SWITCH BACK.
YEAH...
THIS IS STRANGE.
WE'RE TOTALLY OPPOSITE...
...SO THIS MAY BE THE FIRST TIME...
...WE'VE DONE SOMETHING TOGETHER.
Uh... "Good morning."

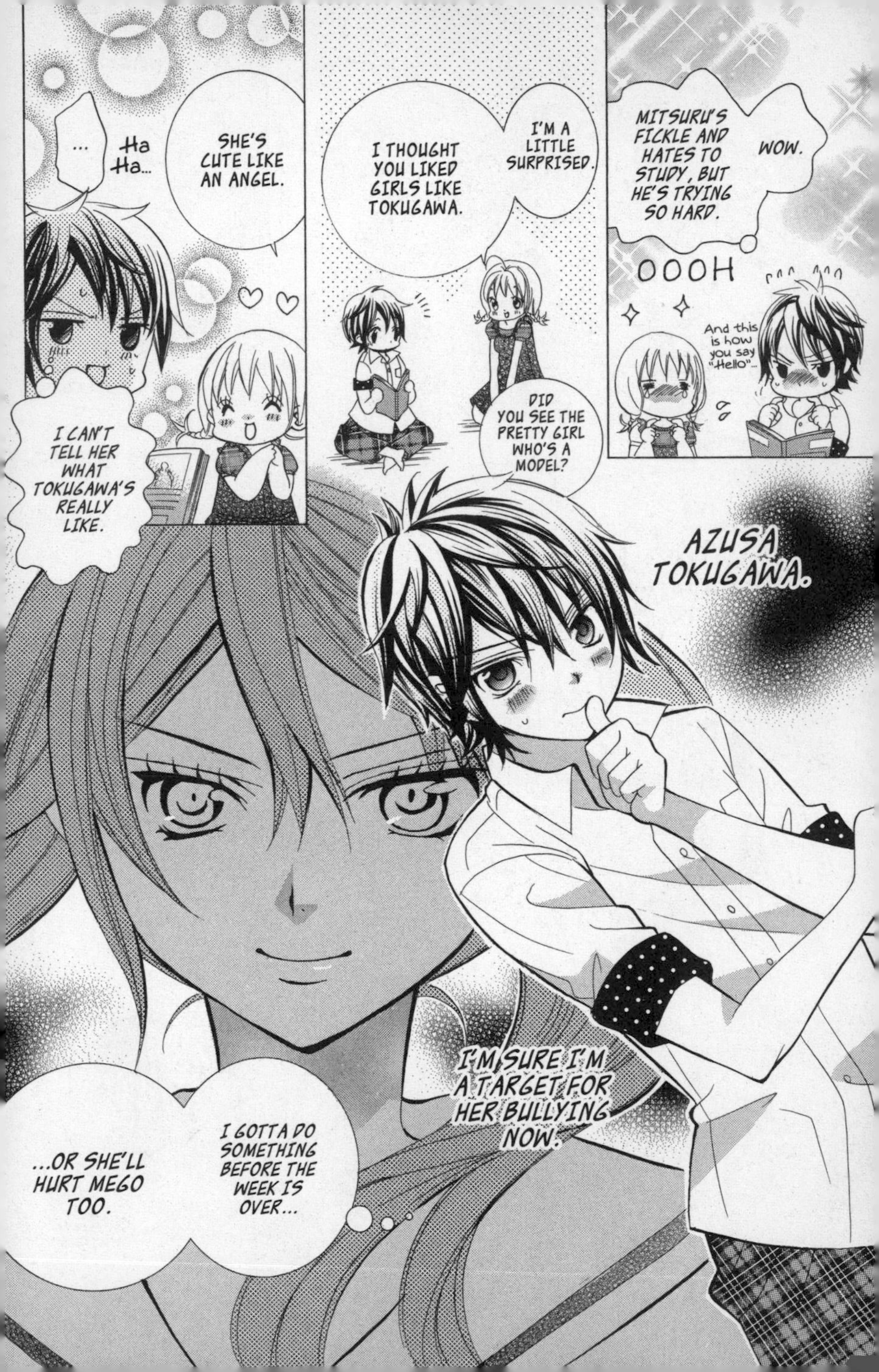
WOW.
MITSURU'S FICKLE AND HATES TO STUDY, BUT HE'S TRYING SO HARD.
OOOH
And this is how you say "Hello"...
I'M A LITTLE SURPRISED.
I THOUGHT YOU LIKED GIRLS LIKE TOKUGAWA.
DID YOU SEE THE PRETTY GIRL WHO'S A MODEL?
SHE'S CUTE LIKE AN ANGEL.
Ha Ha...
...
I CAN'T TELL HER WHAT TOKUGAWA'S REALLY LIKE.
AZUSA TOKUGAWA.
I'M SURE I'M A TARGET FOR HER BULLYING NOW.
I GOTTA DO SOMETHING BEFORE THE WEEK IS OVER...
...OR SHE'LL HURT MEGO TOO.

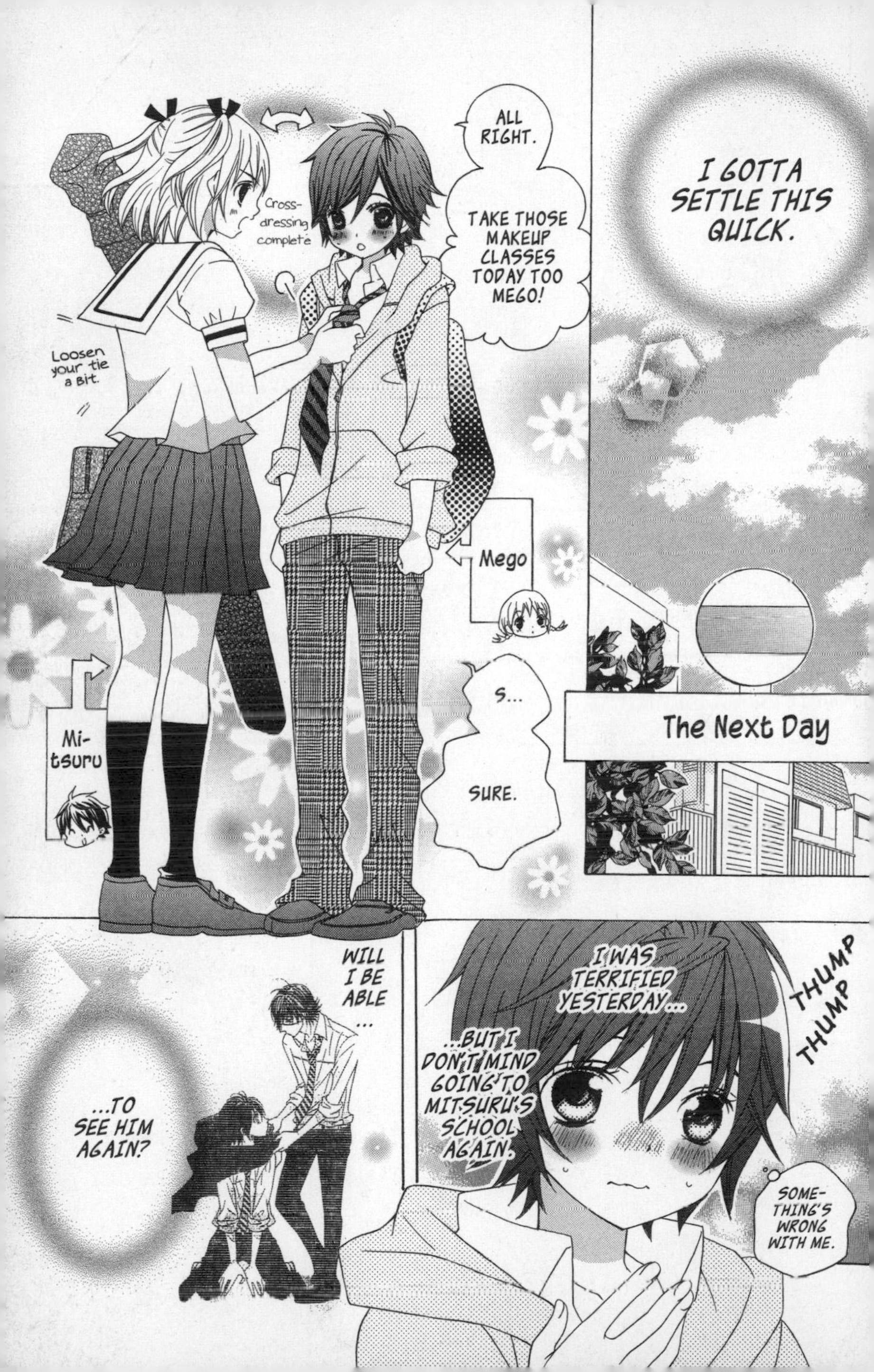
I GOTTA SETTLE THIS QUICK.
The Next Day
ALL RIGHT.
TAKE THOSE MAKEUP CLASSES TODAY TOO MEGO!
Cross-dressing complete
Mego
S...
SURE.
Loosen your tie a bit.
Mi-tsuru
I WAS TERRIFIED YESTERDAY...
THUMP THUMP
...BUT I DON'T MIND GOING TO MITSURU'S SCHOOL AGAIN.
SOME-THING'S WRONG WITH ME.
WILL I BE ABLE...
...TO SEE HIM AGAIN?

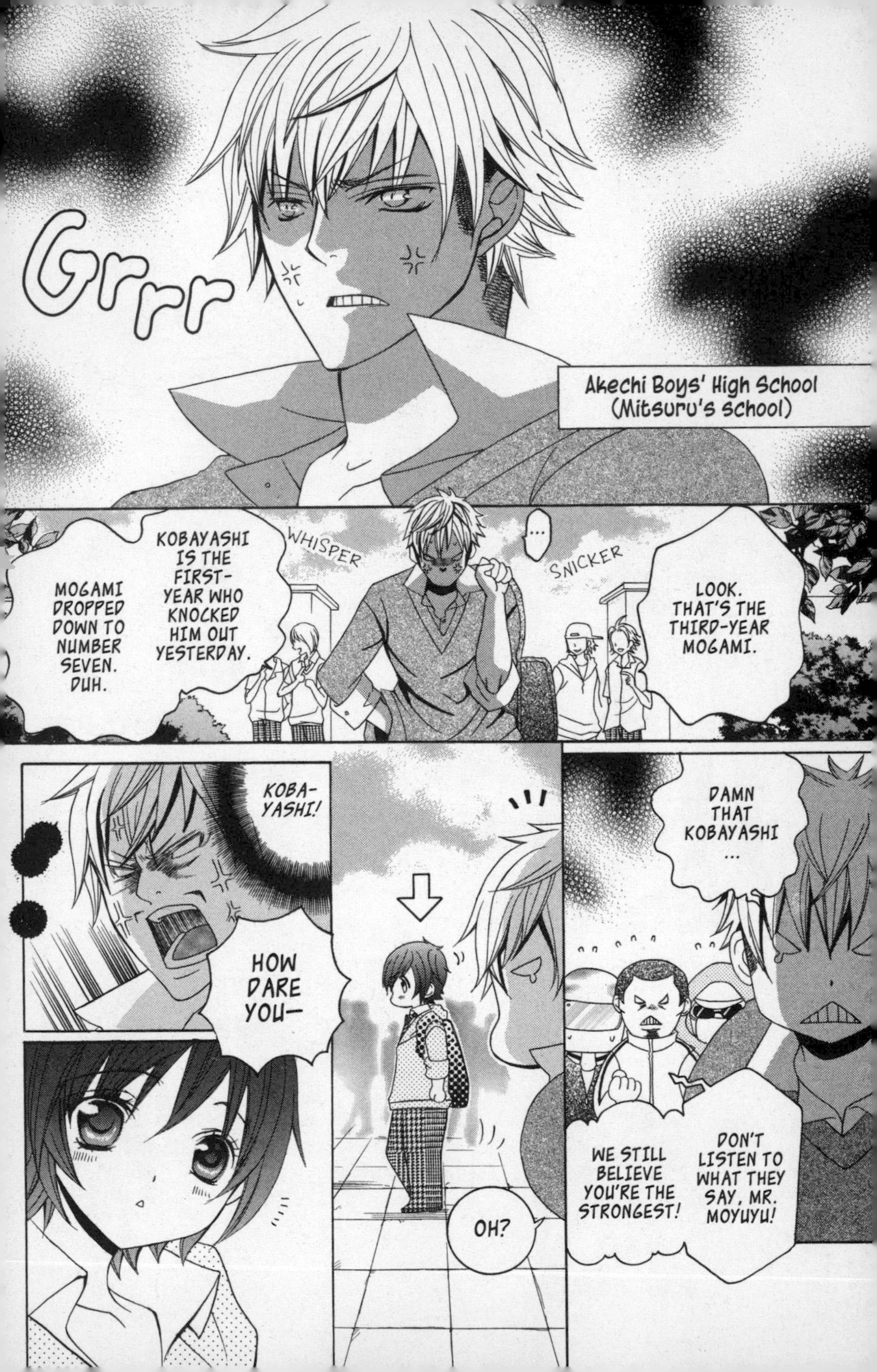
Akechi Boys' High School (Mitsuru's school)
Grrr
LOOK. THAT'S THE THIRD-YEAR MOGAMI.
SNICKER
...
WHISPER
KOBAYASHI IS THE FIRST-YEAR WHO KNOCKED HIM OUT YESTERDAY.
MOGAMI DROPPED DOWN TO NUMBER SEVEN. DUH.
DAMN THAT KOBAYASHI ...
DON'T LISTEN TO WHAT THEY SAY, MR. MOYUYU!
WE STILL BELIEVE YOU'RE THE STRONGEST!
OH?
KOBA-YASHI!
HOW DARE YOU—

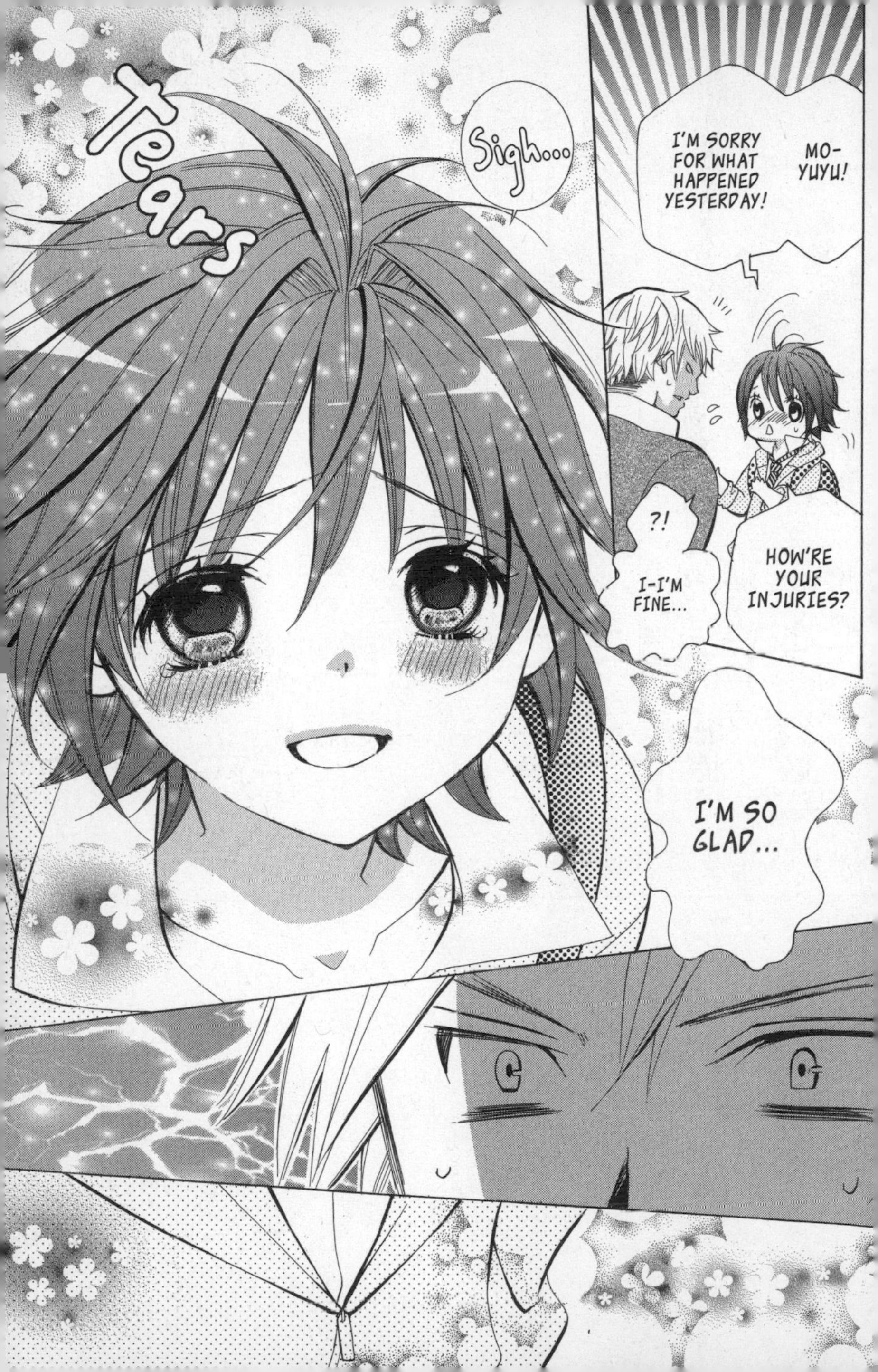
MO-YUYU!
I'M SORRY FOR WHAT HAPPENED YESTERDAY!
HOW'RE YOUR INJURIES?
?!
I-I'M FINE...
Sigh...
tears
I'M SO GLAD...

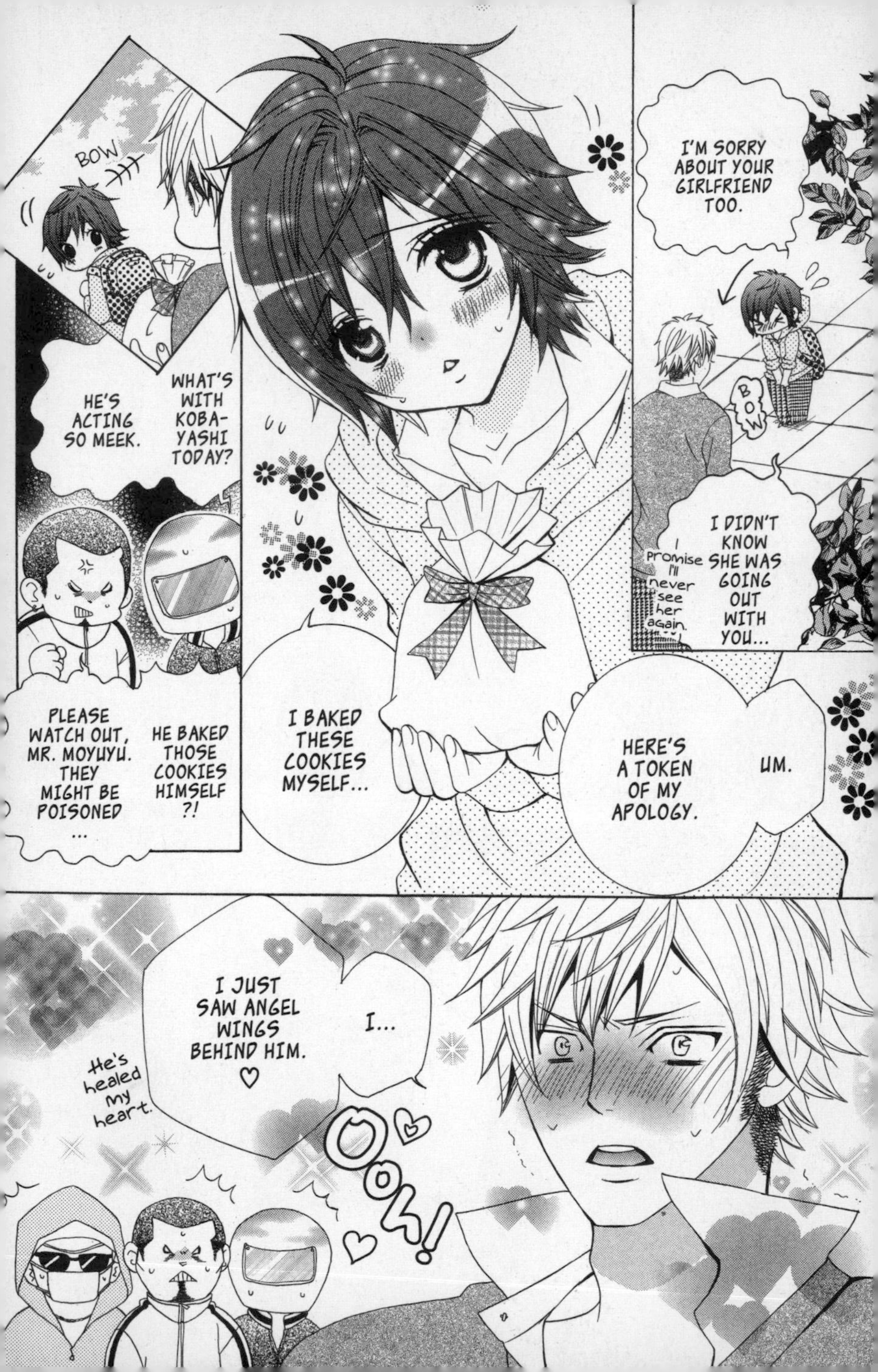
I'M SORRY ABOUT YOUR GIRLFRIEND TOO.
BOW
I DIDN'T KNOW SHE WAS GOING OUT WITH YOU...
I promise I'll never see her again.
UM.
HERE'S A TOKEN OF MY APOLOGY.
I BAKED THESE COOKIES MYSELF...
BOW
WHAT'S WITH KOBA-YASHI TODAY?
HE'S ACTING SO MEEK.
HE BAKED THOSE COOKIES HIMSELF?!
PLEASE WATCH OUT, MR. MOYUYU. THEY MIGHT BE POISONED...
I...
I JUST SAW ANGEL WINGS BEHIND HIM. ♡
OOH!
He's healed my heart.

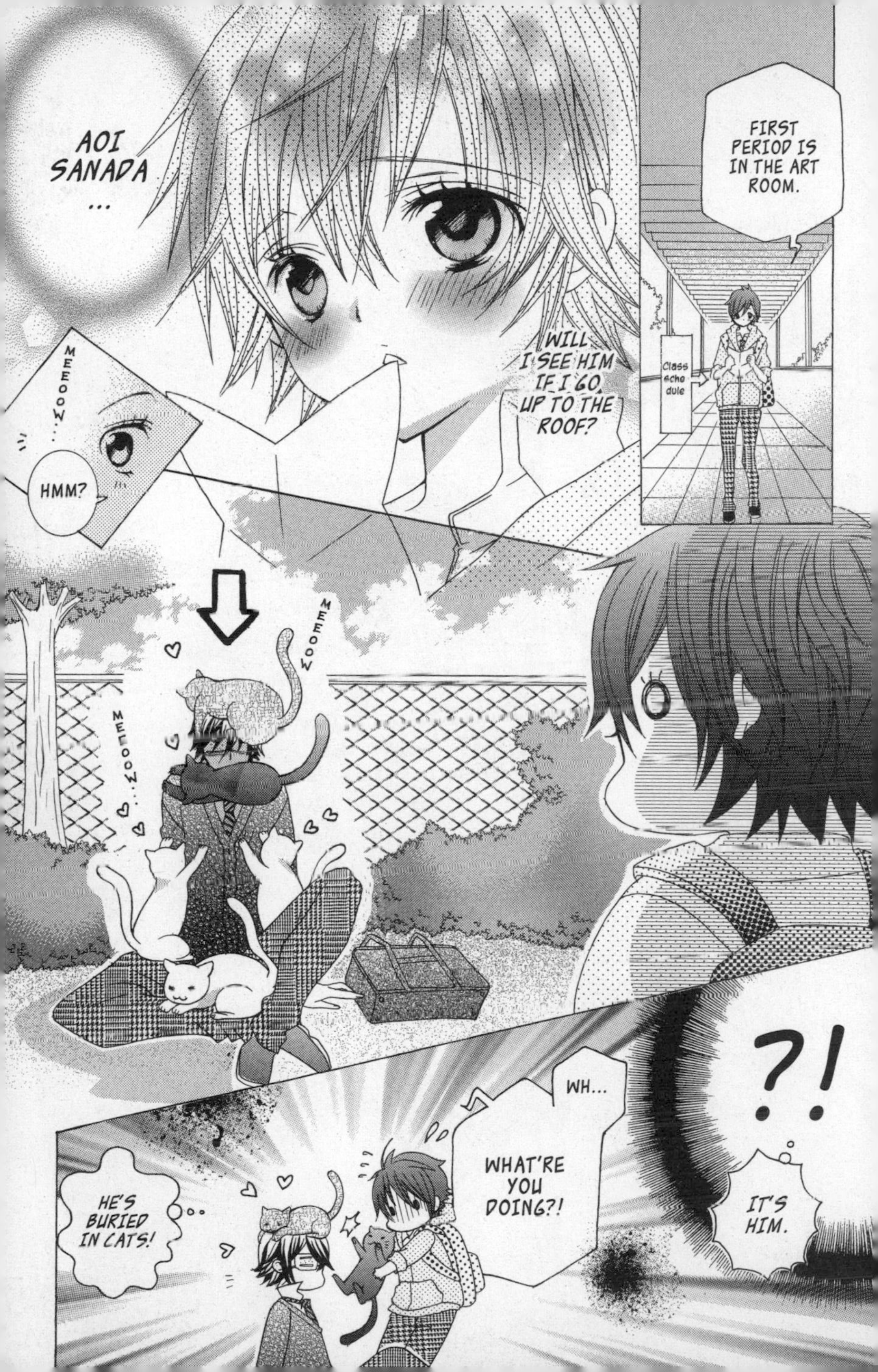

FIRST PERIOD IS IN THE ART ROOM.
Class schedule
WILL I SEE HIM IF I GO UP TO THE ROOF?
AOI SANADA ...
MEEOOW...
HMM?
MEEOOW
MEEOOW...
?!
IT'S HIM.
WH...
WHAT'RE YOU DOING?!
HE'S BURIED IN CATS!

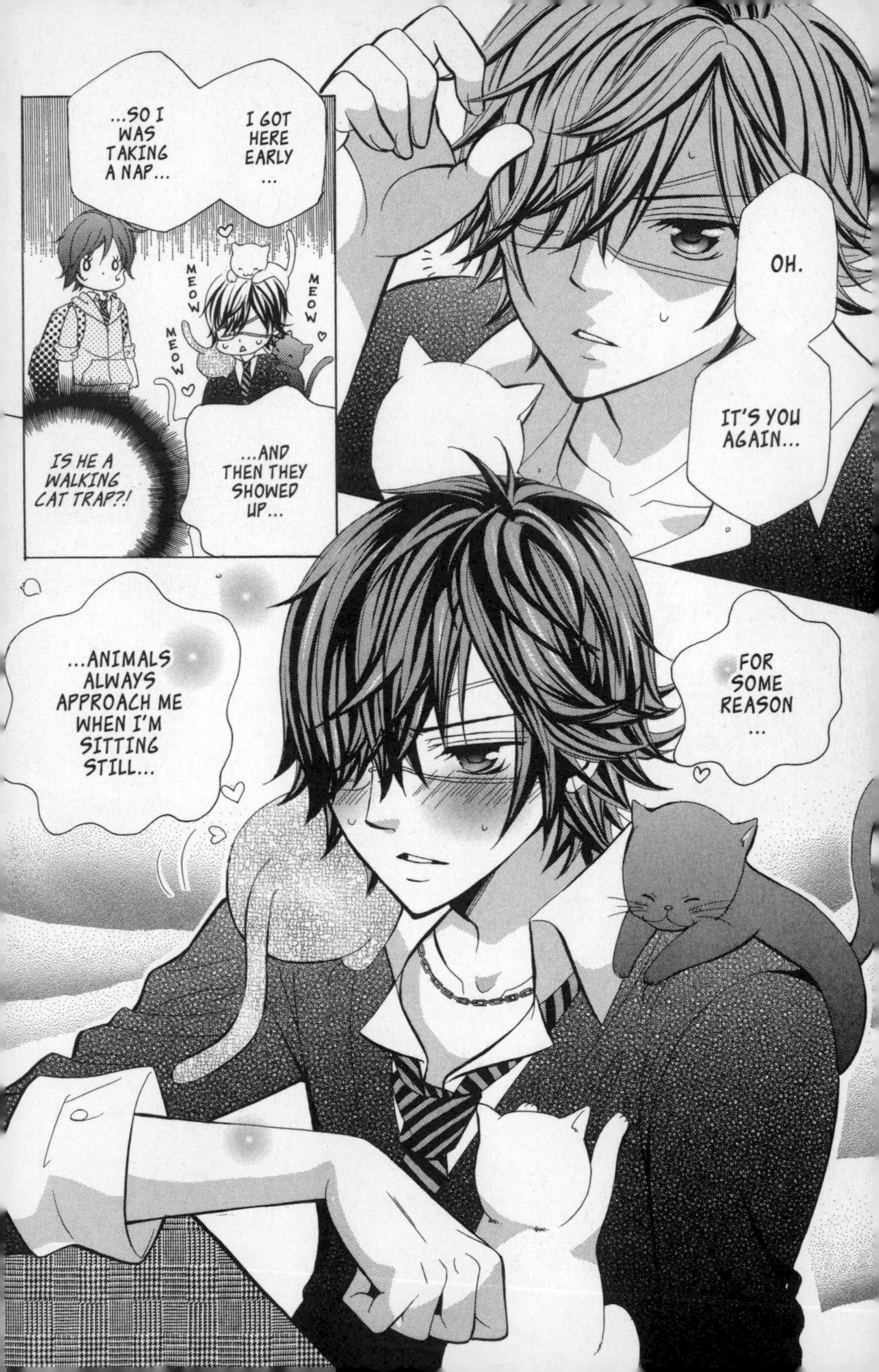
OH.
IT'S YOU AGAIN...
I GOT HERE EARLY ...
...SO I WAS TAKING A NAP...
MEOW
MEOW
MEOW
...AND THEN THEY SHOWED UP...
IS HE A WALKING CAT TRAP?!
FOR SOME REASON ...
...ANIMALS ALWAYS APPROACH ME WHEN I'M SITTING STILL...

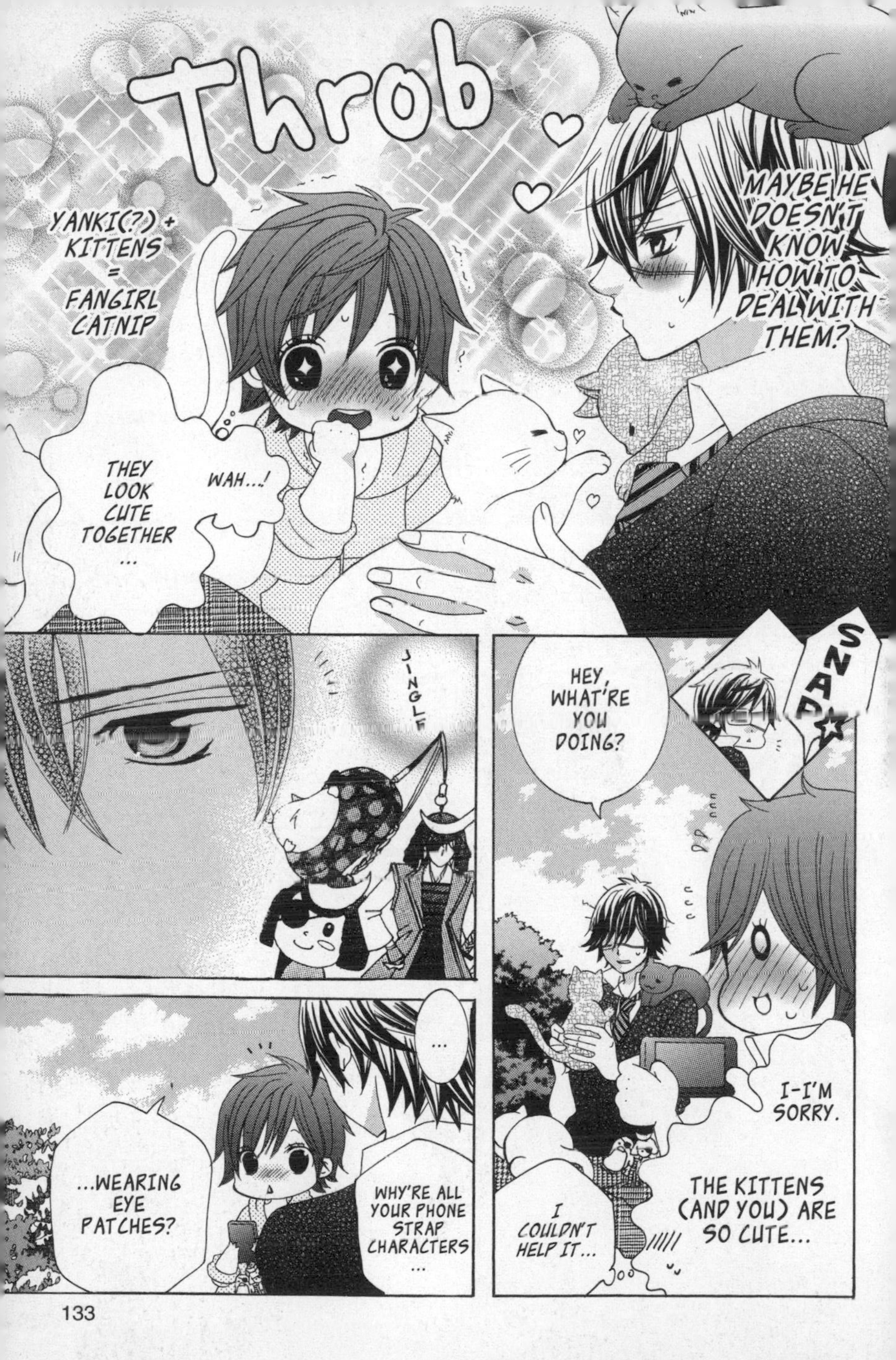
Throb
MAYBE HE DOESN'T KNOW HOW TO DEAL WITH THEM?
YANKI(?) + KITTENS = FANGIRL CATNIP
WAH...!
THEY LOOK CUTE TOGETHER ...
SNAP☆
HEY, WHAT'RE YOU DOING?
I-I'M SORRY.
THE KITTENS (AND YOU) ARE SO CUTE...
I COULDN'T HELP IT...
JINGLE
...
WHY'RE ALL YOUR PHONE STRAP CHARACTERS ...
...WEARING EYE PATCHES?

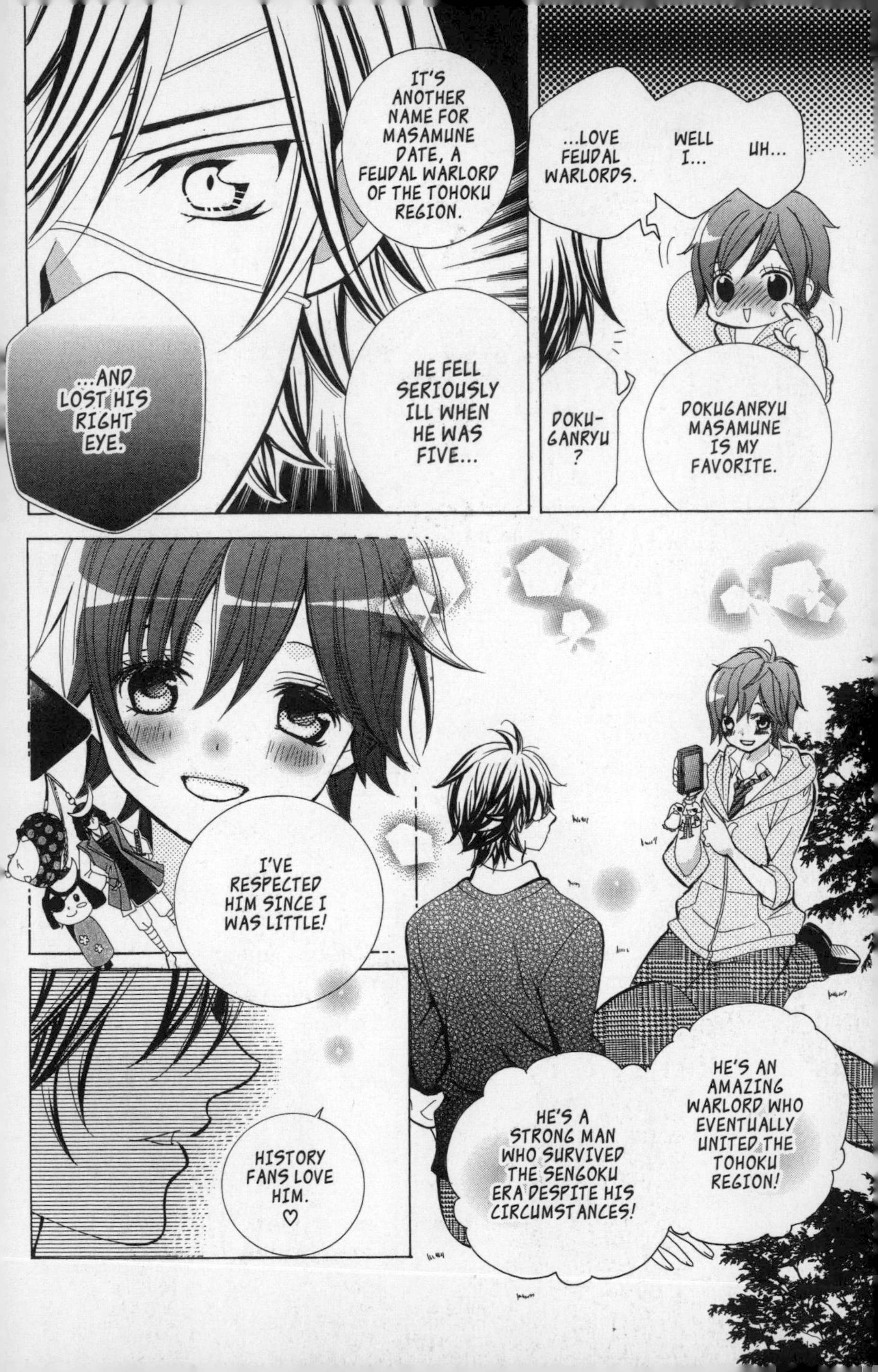
UH...
WELL I...
...LOVE FEUDAL WARLORDS.
DOKUGANRYU MASAMUNE IS MY FAVORITE.
DOKU-GANRYU?
IT'S ANOTHER NAME FOR MASAMUNE DATE, A FEUDAL WARLORD OF THE TOHOKU REGION.
HE FELL SERIOUSLY ILL WHEN HE WAS FIVE...
...AND LOST HIS RIGHT EYE.
HE'S AN AMAZING WARLORD WHO EVENTUALLY UNITED THE TOHOKU REGION!
HE'S A STRONG MAN WHO SURVIVED THE SENGOKU ERA DESPITE HIS CIRCUMSTANCES!
I'VE RESPECTED HIM SINCE I WAS LITTLE!
HISTORY FANS LOVE HIM. ♡

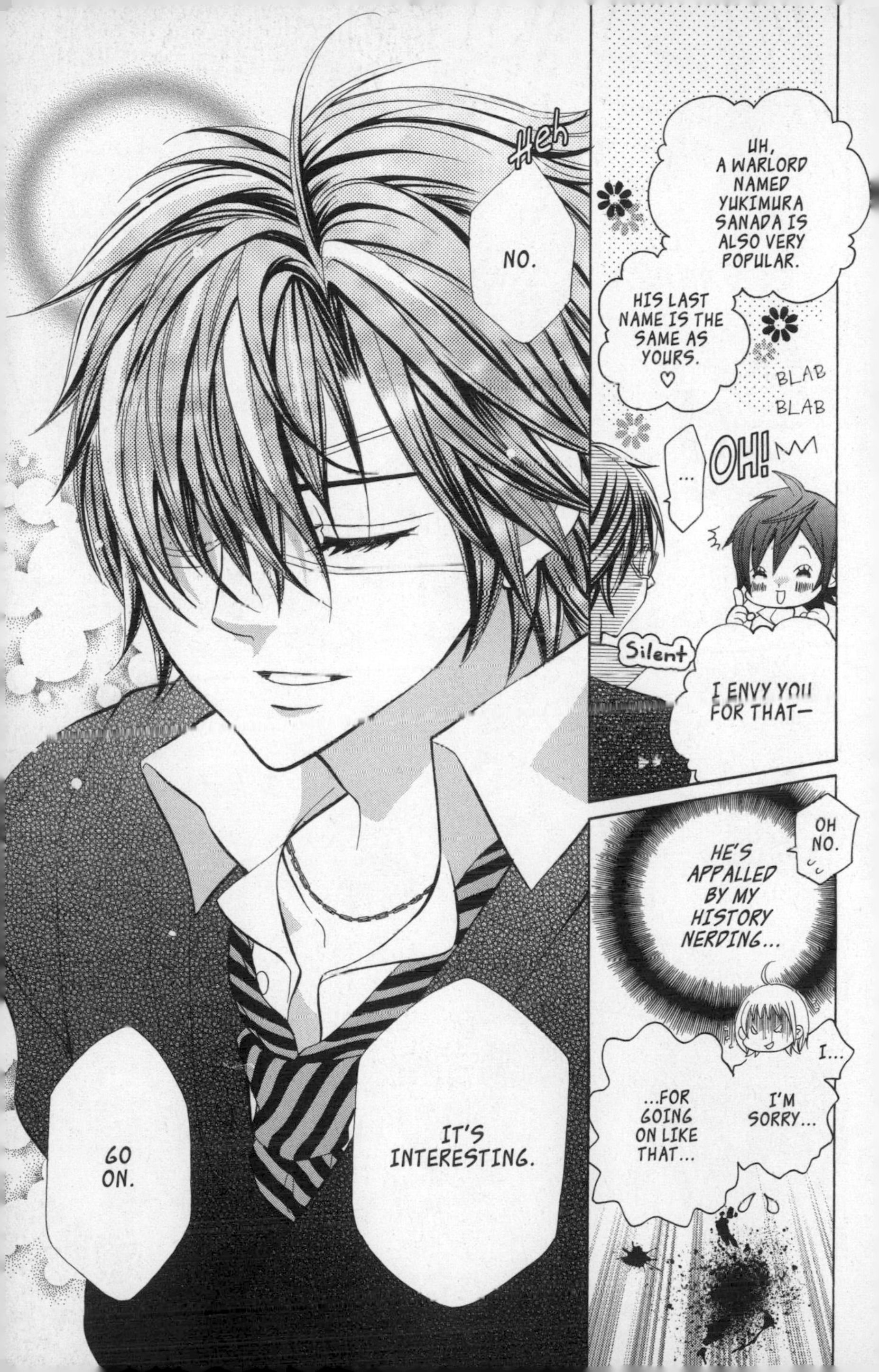

UH, A WARLORD NAMED YUKIMURA SANADA IS ALSO VERY POPULAR.
HIS LAST NAME IS THE SAME AS YOURS. ♡
BLAB BLAB
...
OH!
Silent
I ENVY YOU FOR THAT—
OH NO.
HE'S APPALLED BY MY HISTORY NERDING...
I...
I'M SORRY...
...FOR GOING ON LIKE THAT...
Heh
NO.
IT'S INTERESTING.
GO ON.

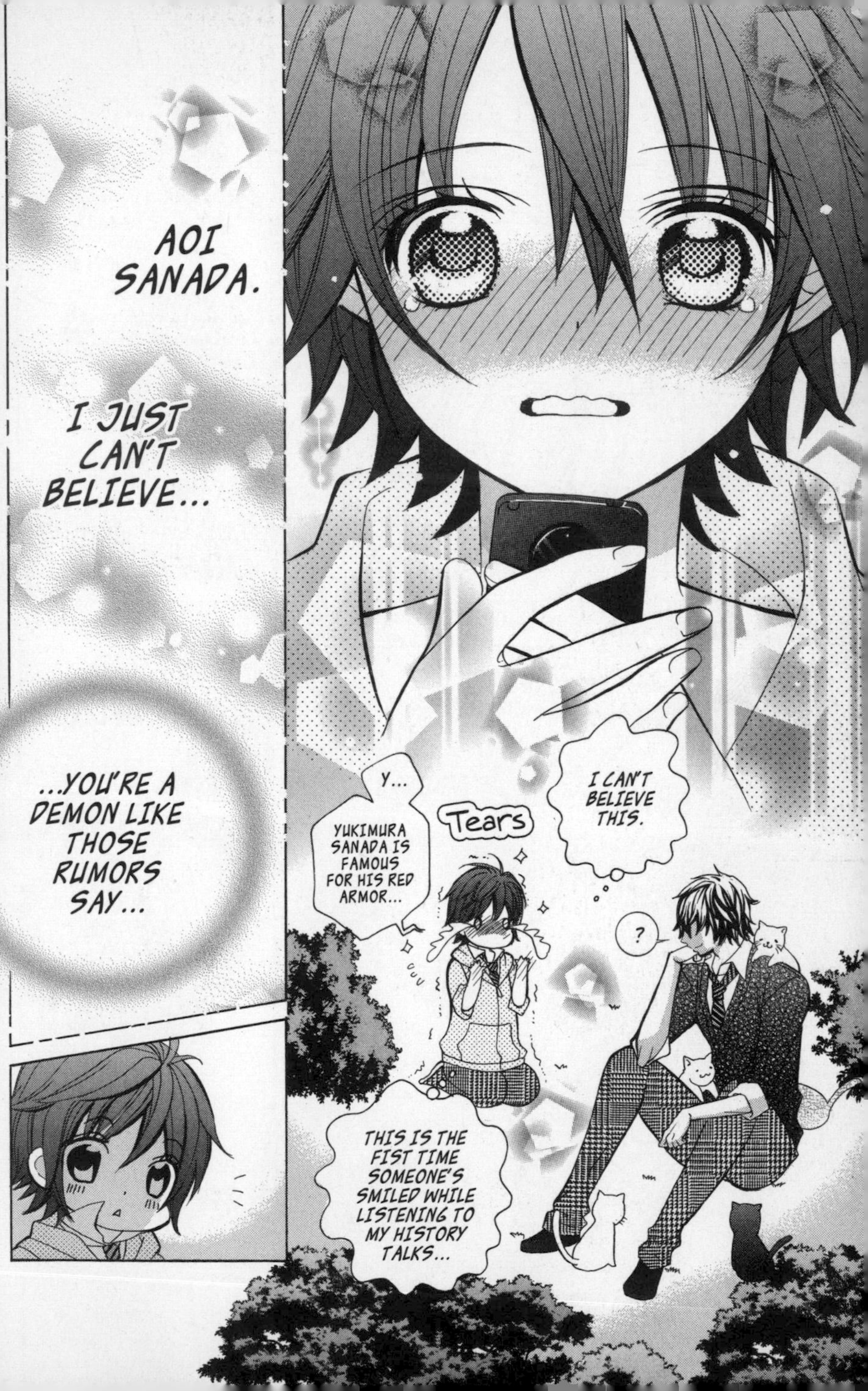
I CAN'T BELIEVE THIS.
Y...
Tears
YUKIMURA SANADA IS FAMOUS FOR HIS RED ARMOR...
?
THIS IS THE FIST TIME SOMEONE'S SMILED WHILE LISTENING TO MY HISTORY TALKS...
AOI SANADA.
I JUST CAN'T BELIEVE...
...YOU'RE A DEMON LIKE THOSE RUMORS SAY...

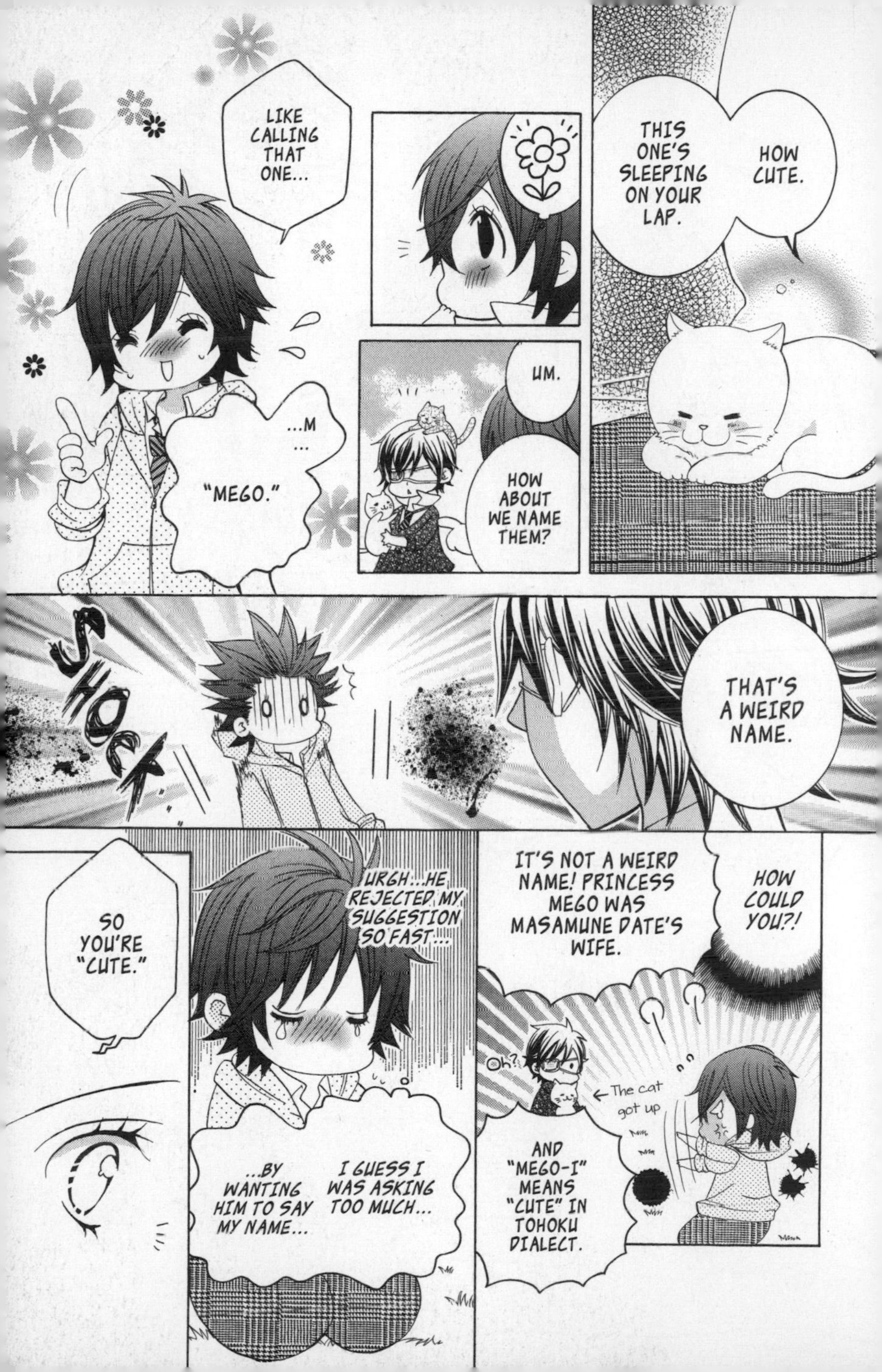
HOW CUTE.
THIS ONE'S SLEEPING ON YOUR LAP.
UM.
HOW ABOUT WE NAME THEM?
LIKE CALLING THAT ONE...
...M ...
"MEGO."
THAT'S A WEIRD NAME.
SHOCK
HOW COULD YOU?!
IT'S NOT A WEIRD NAME! PRINCESS MEGO WAS MASAMUNE DATE'S WIFE.
Oh?
← The cat got up
AND "MEGO-I" MEANS "CUTE" IN TOHOKU DIALECT.
URGH...HE REJECTED MY SUGGESTION SO FAST...
I GUESS I WAS ASKING TOO MUCH...
...BY WANTING HIM TO SAY MY NAME...
SO YOU'RE "CUTE."

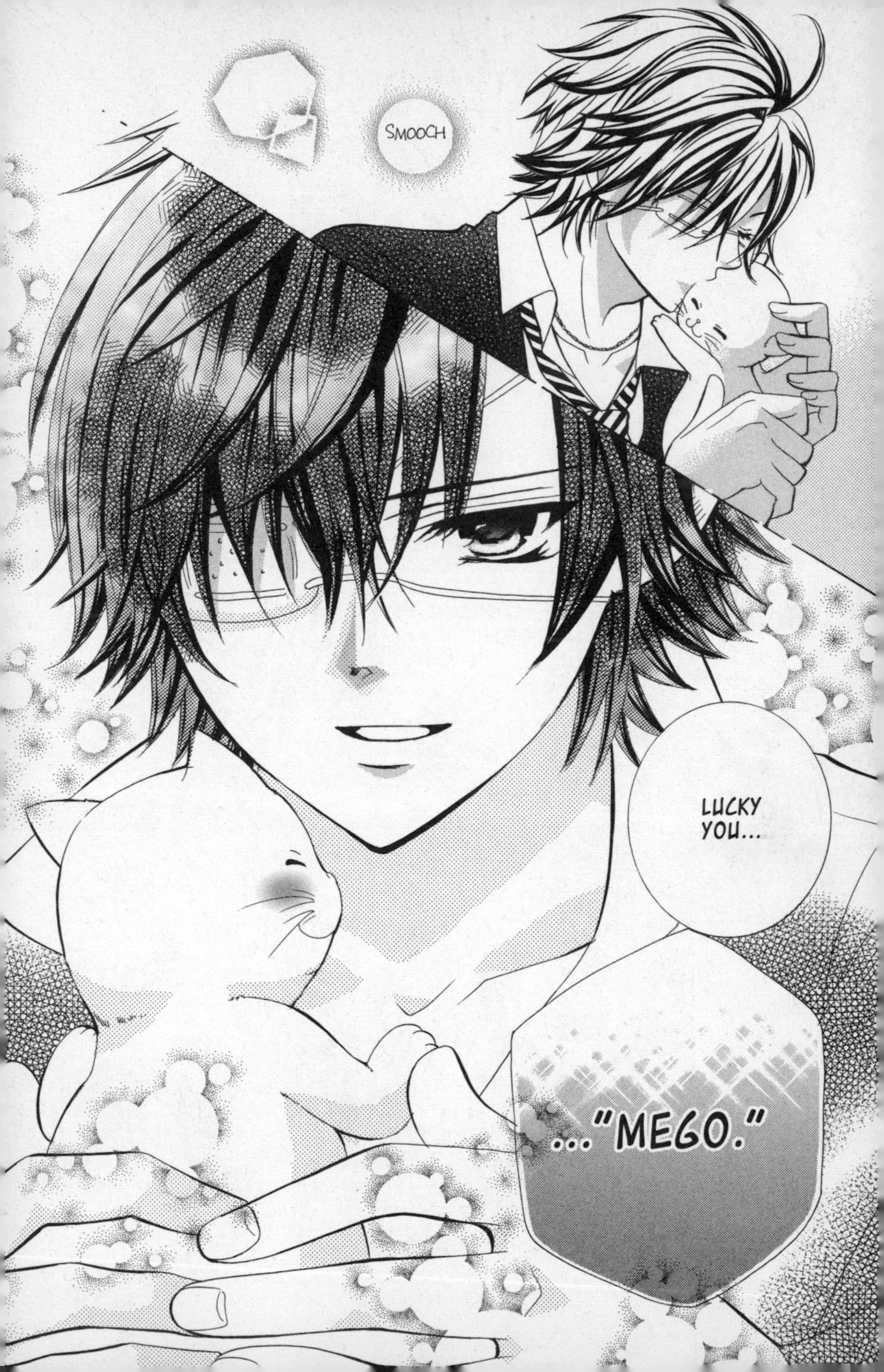
SMOOCH
LUCKY YOU...
..."MEGO."

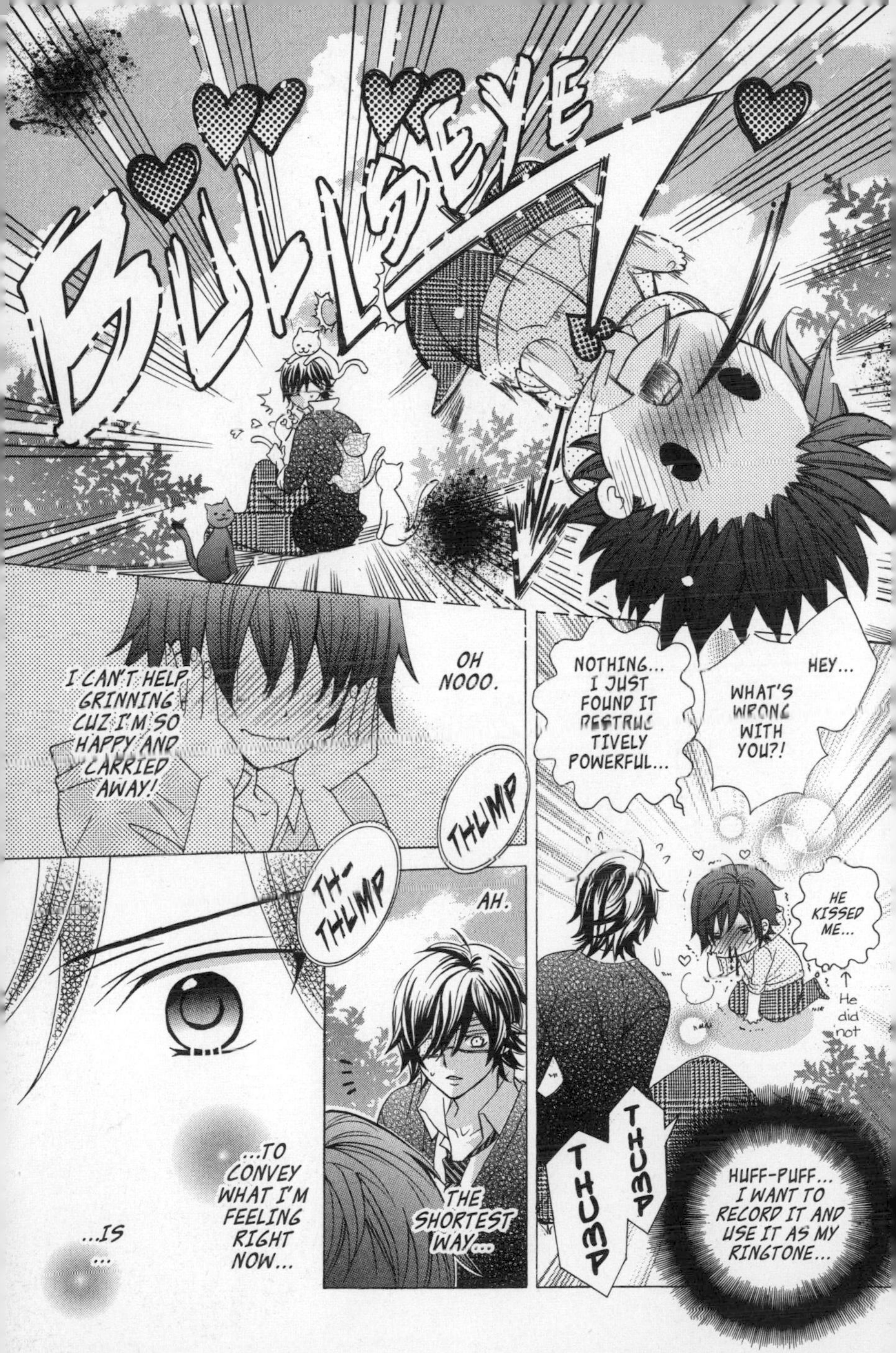
BULLSEYE
HEY...
WHAT'S WRONG WITH YOU?!
NOTHING... I JUST FOUND IT DESTRUCTIVELY POWERFUL...
HE KISSED ME...
↑ He did not
THUMP THUMP THUMP
HUFF-PUFF... I WANT TO RECORD IT AND USE IT AS MY RINGTONE...
OH NOOO.
I CAN'T HELP GRINNING CUZ I'M SO HAPPY AND CARRIED AWAY!
THUMP
TH-THUMP
AH.
THE SHORTEST WAY...
...TO CONVEY WHAT I'M FEELING RIGHT NOW...
...IS ...

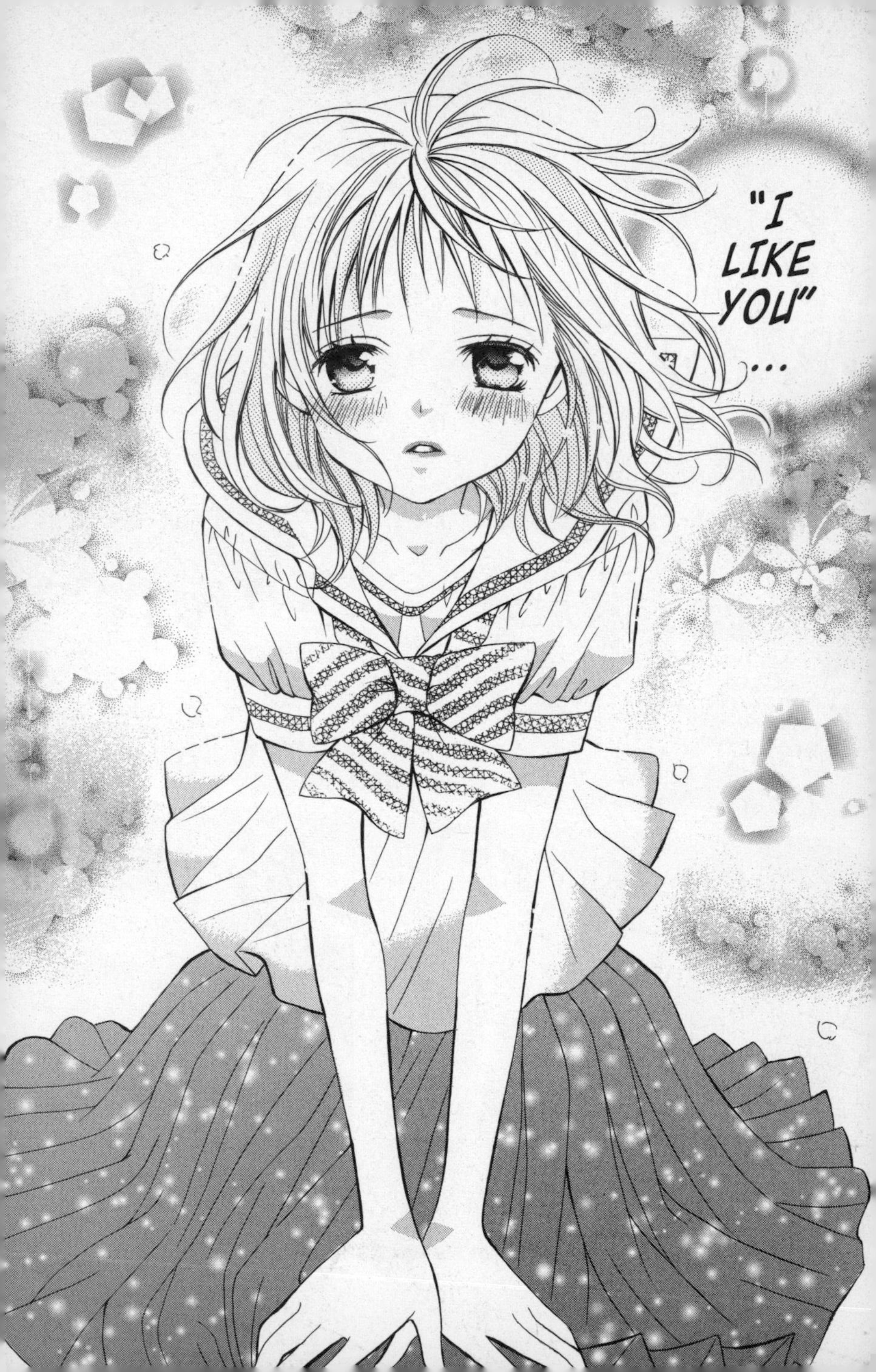
"I LIKE YOU"...

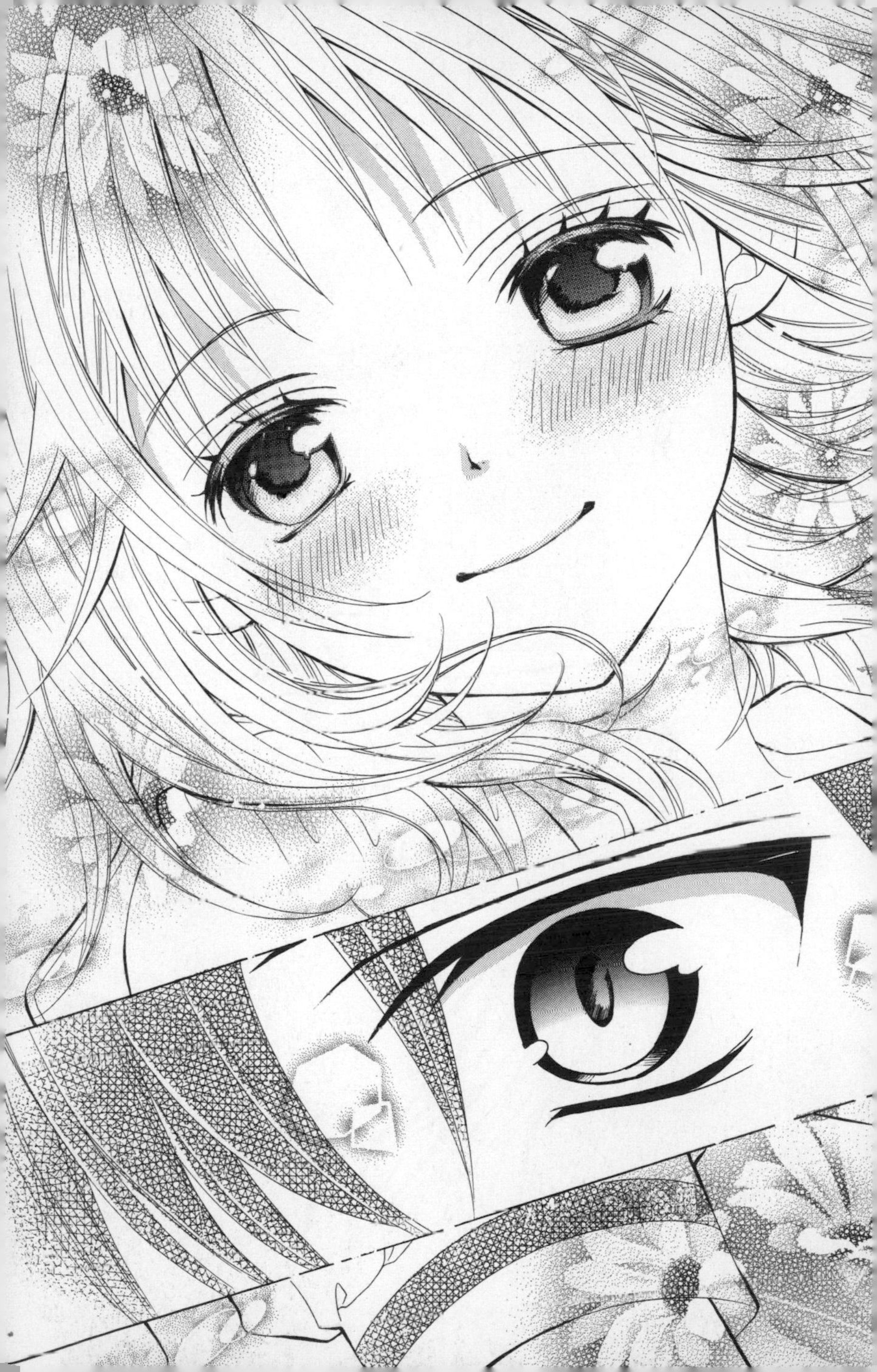

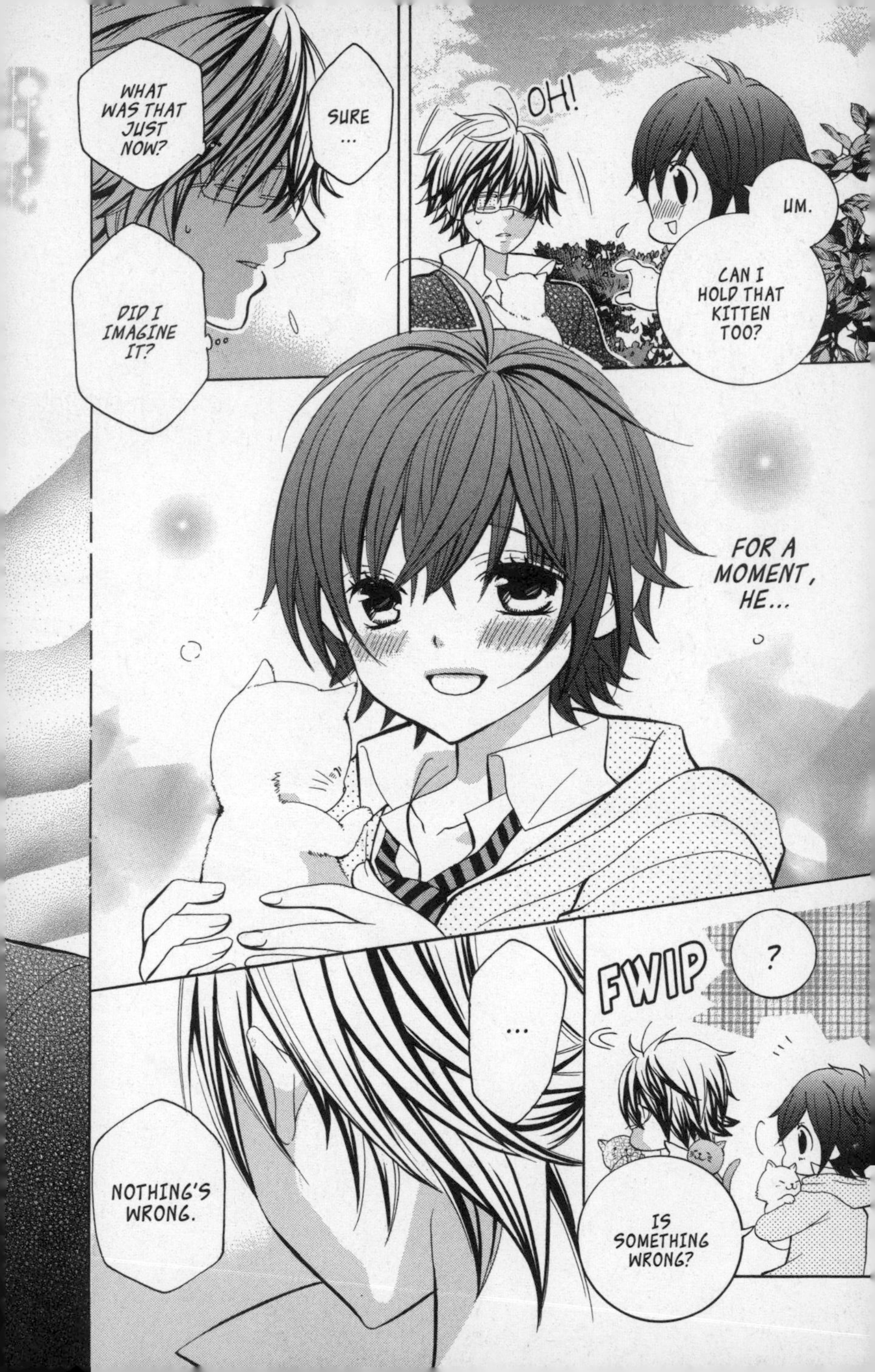
OH!
UM.
CAN I HOLD THAT KITTEN TOO?
SURE...
WHAT WAS THAT JUST NOW?
DID I IMAGINE IT?
FOR A MOMENT, HE...
FWIP
?
IS SOMETHING WRONG?
...
NOTHING'S WRONG.

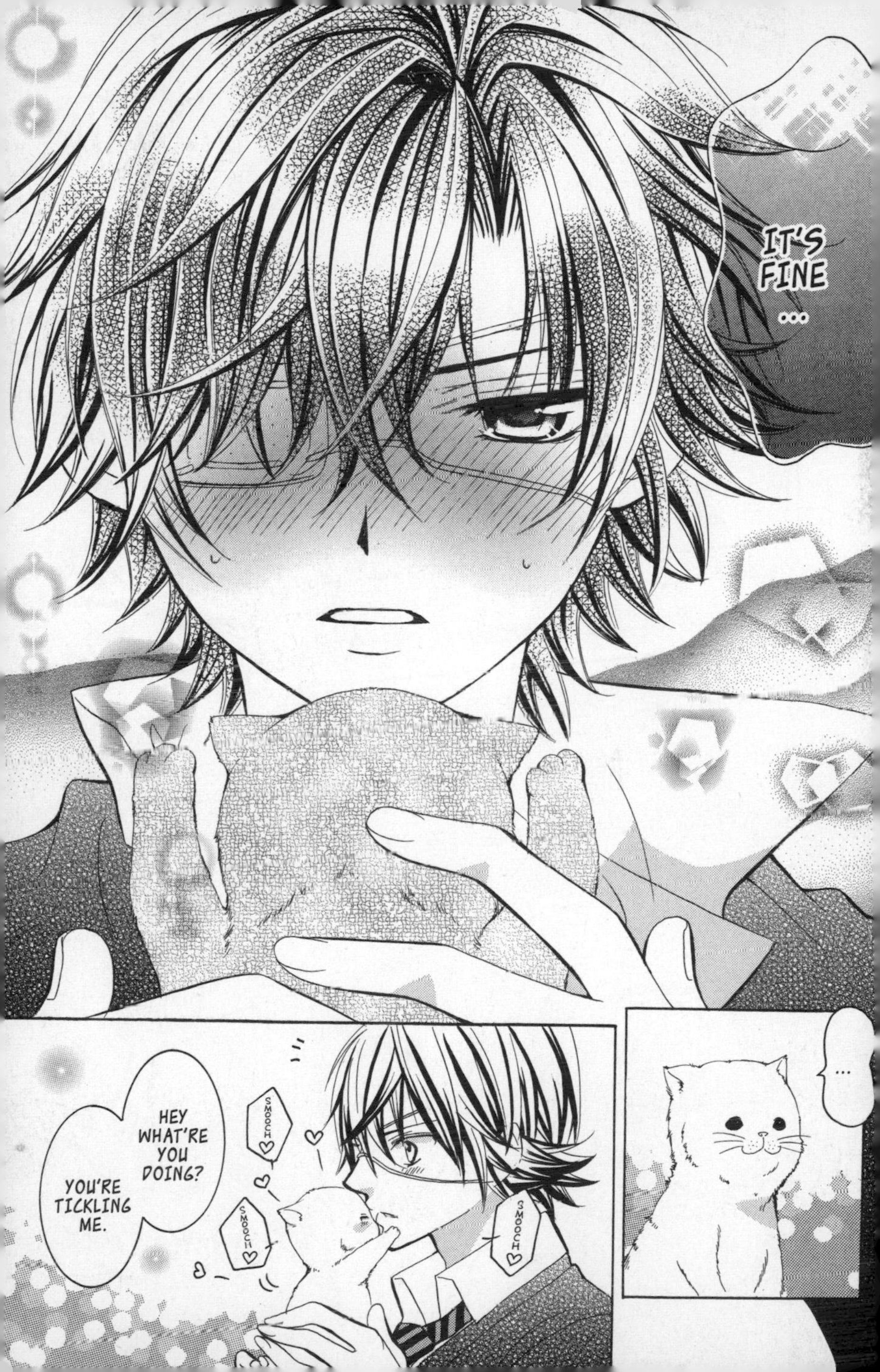
IT'S FINE ...
...
SMOOCH ♡
SMOOCH ♡
SMOOCH ♡
HEY WHAT'RE YOU DOING?
YOU'RE TICKLING ME.

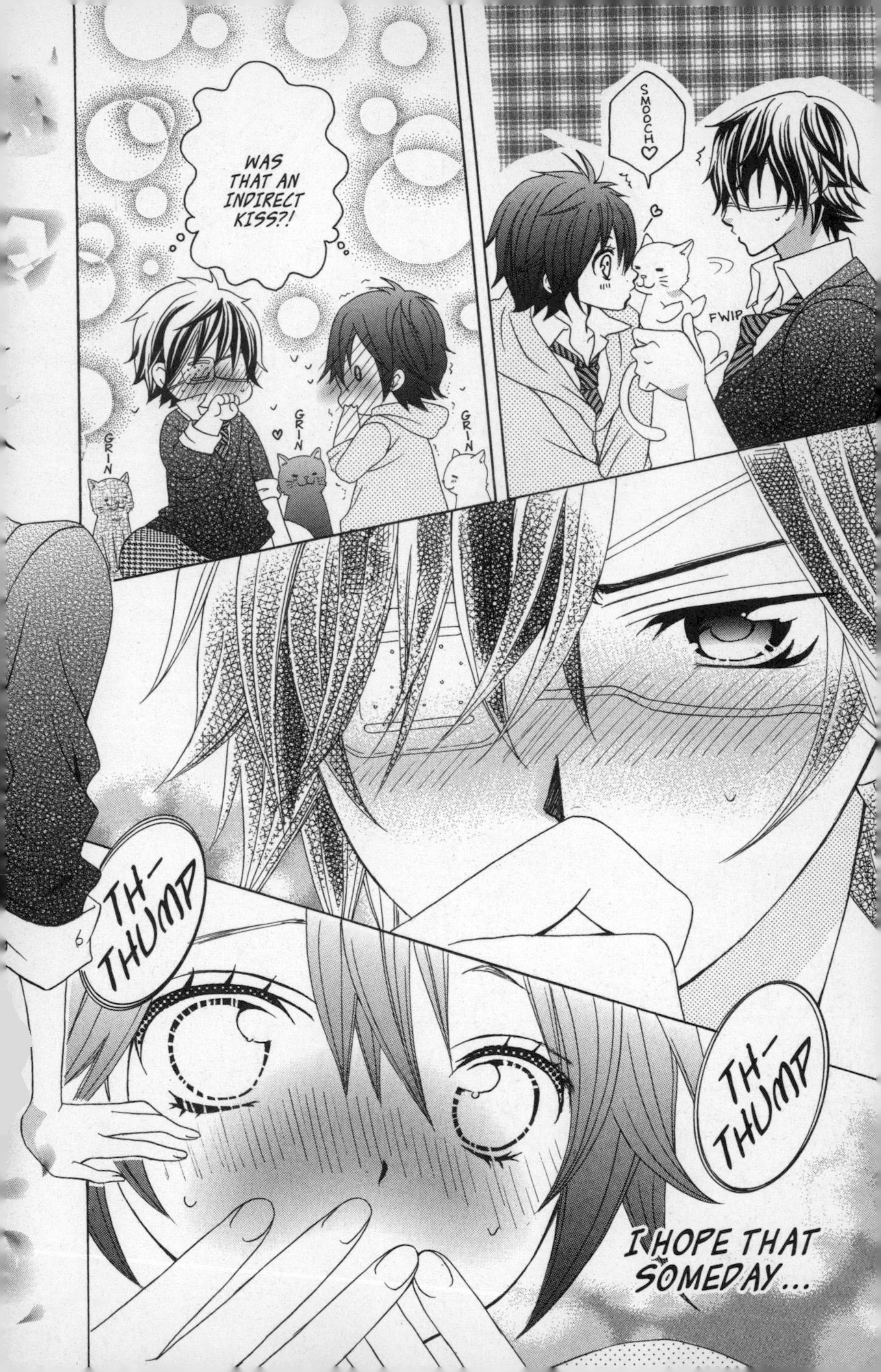
SMOOCH♡
FWIP
WAS THAT AN INDIRECT KISS?!
GRIN
GRIN
GRIN
TH-THUMP
TH-THUMP
I HOPE THAT SOMEDAY...

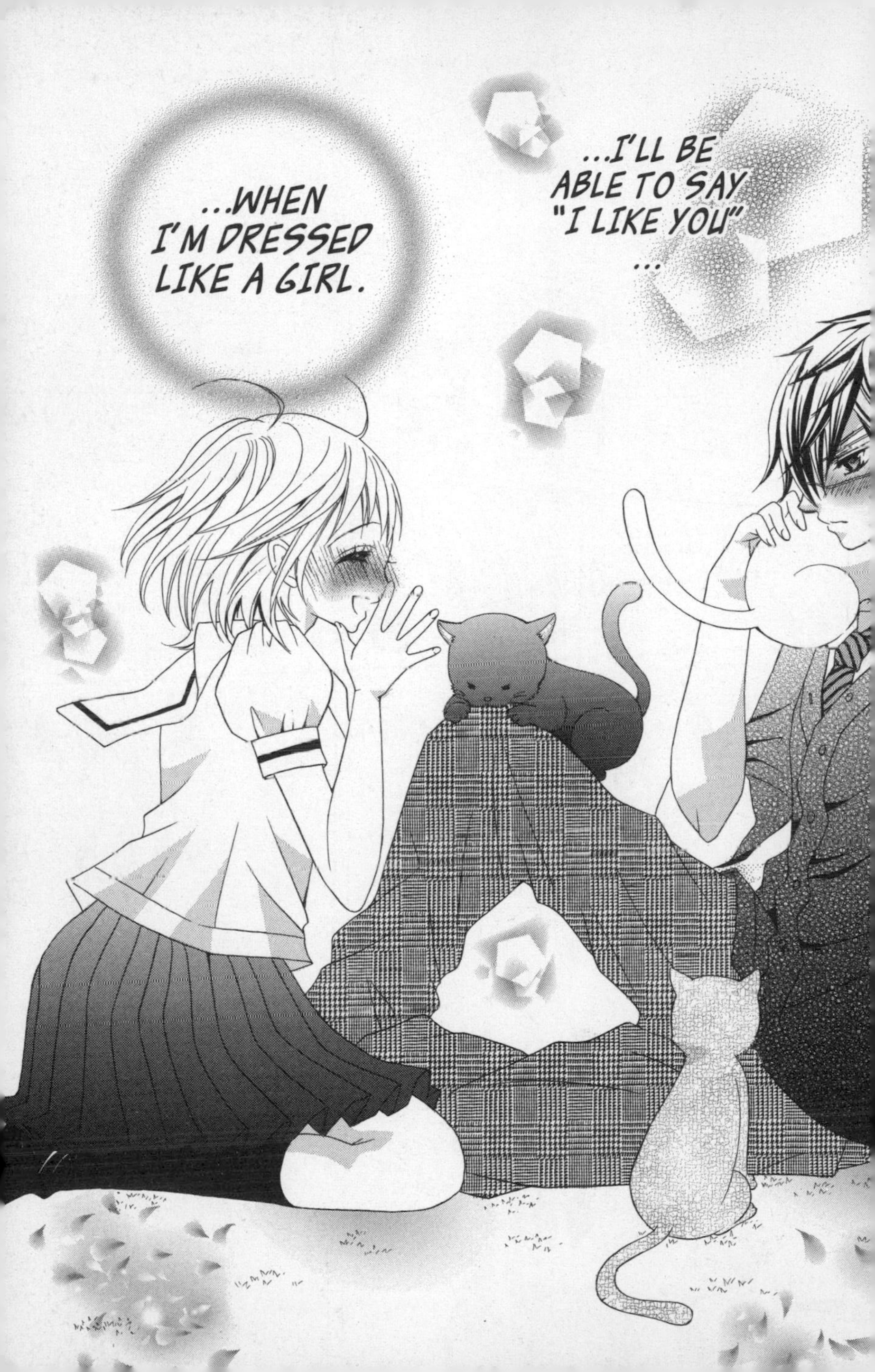
...I'LL BE ABLE TO SAY "I LIKE YOU"...
...WHEN I'M DRESSED LIKE A GIRL.

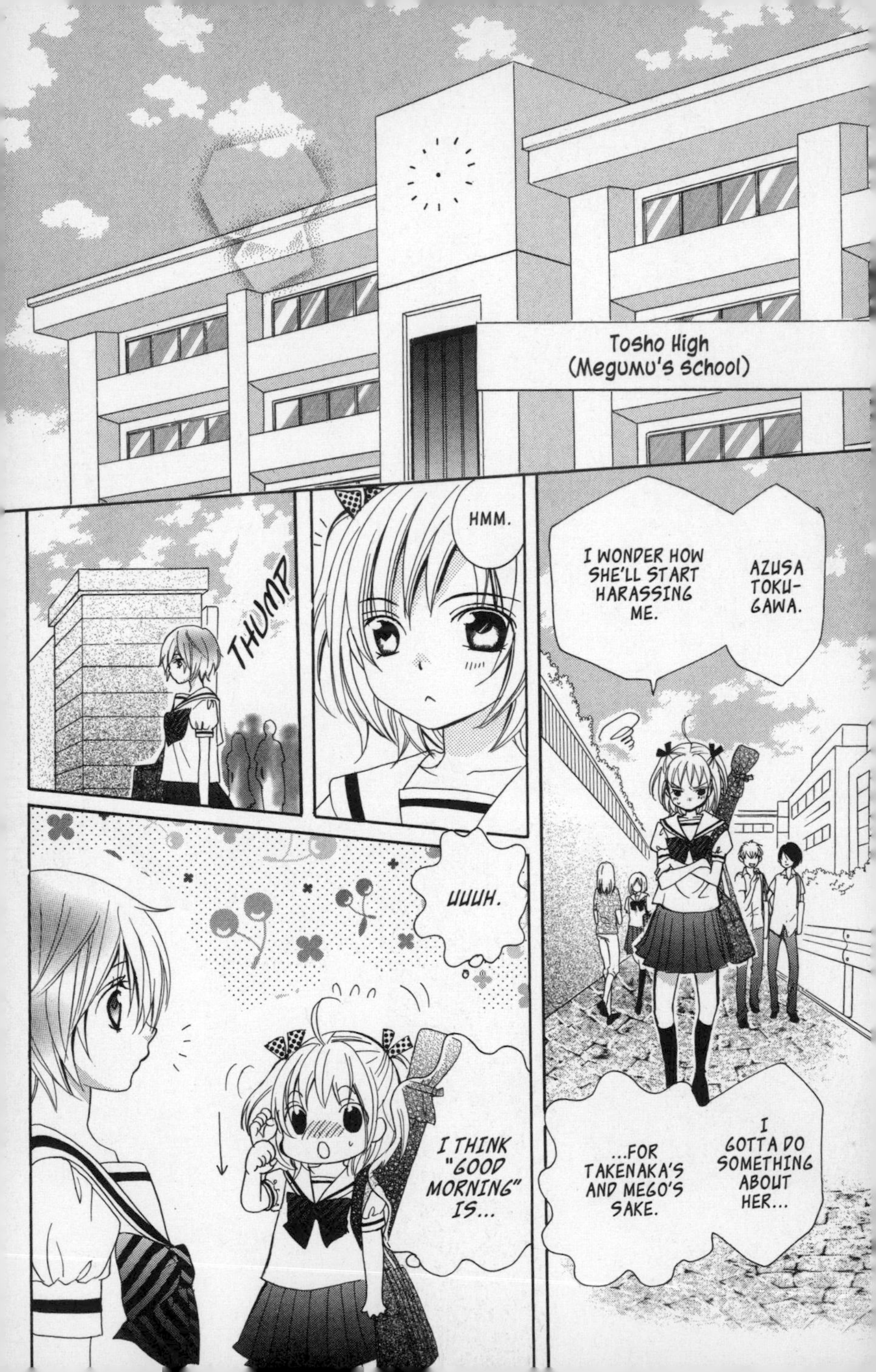
Tosho High
(Megumu's school)
AZUSA TOKU-GAWA.
I WONDER HOW SHE'LL START HARASSING ME.
I GOTTA DO SOMETHING ABOUT HER...
...FOR TAKENAKA'S AND MEGO'S SAKE.
HMM.
THUMP
UUUH.
I THINK "GOOD MORNING" IS...

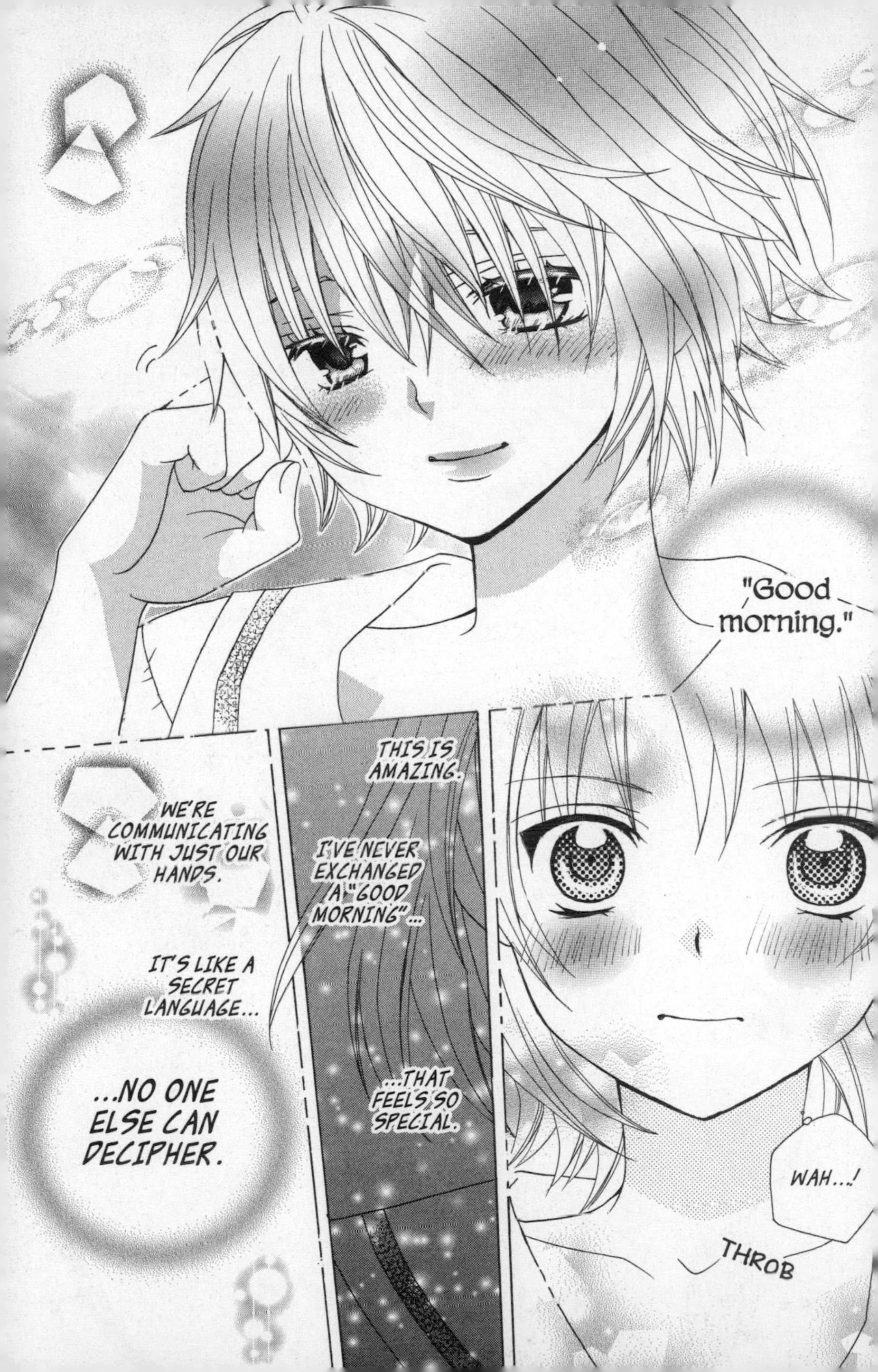
"Good morning."
WAH...!
THROB
THIS IS AMAZING.
I'VE NEVER EXCHANGED A "GOOD MORNING"...
...THAT FEELS SO SPECIAL.
WE'RE COMMUNICATING WITH JUST OUR HANDS.
IT'S LIKE A SECRET LANGUAGE...
...NO ONE ELSE CAN DECIPHER.

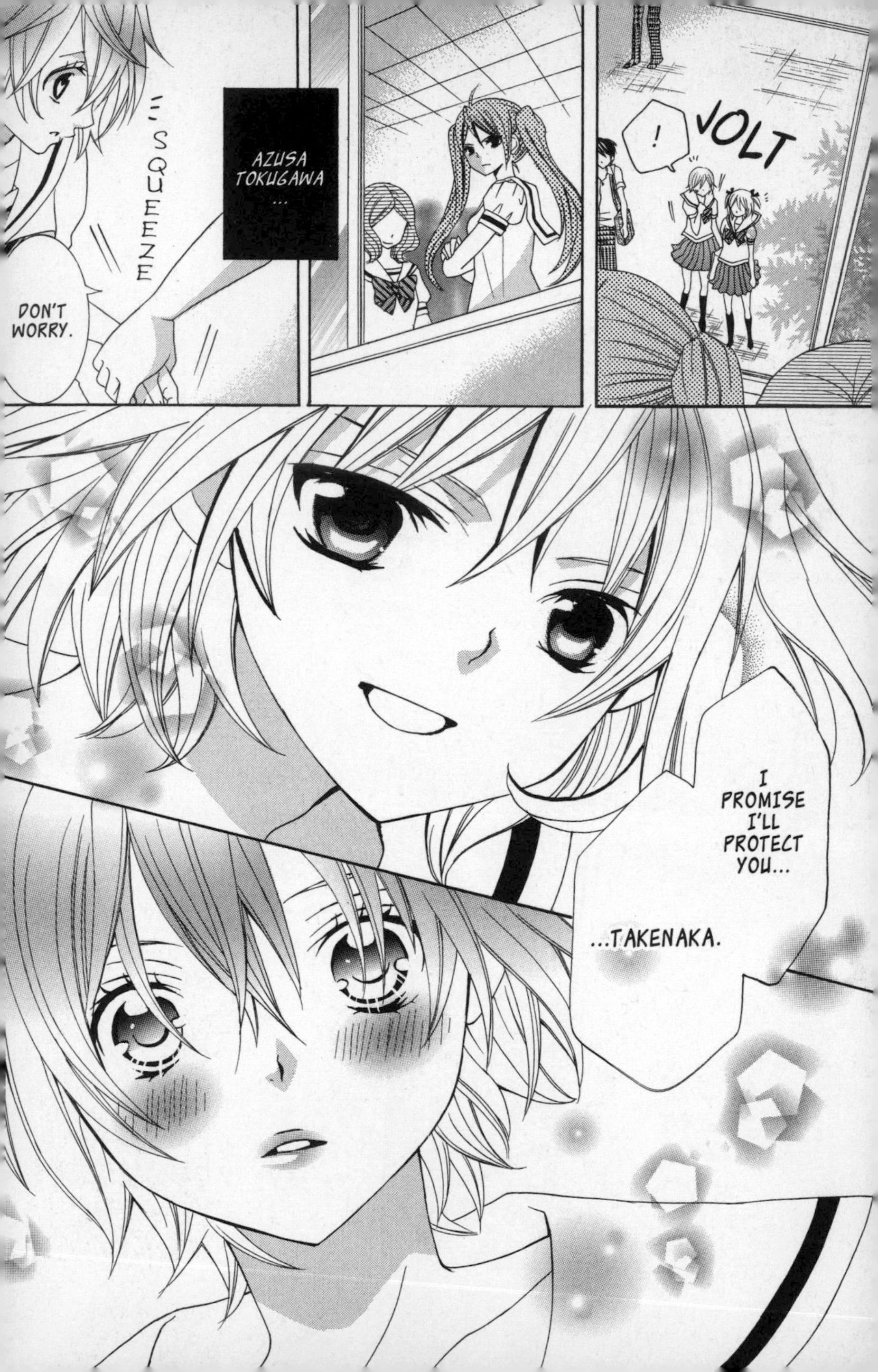
VOLT
!
AZUSA TOKUGAWA ...
SQUEEZE
DON'T WORRY.
I PROMISE I'LL PROTECT YOU...
...TAKENAKA.

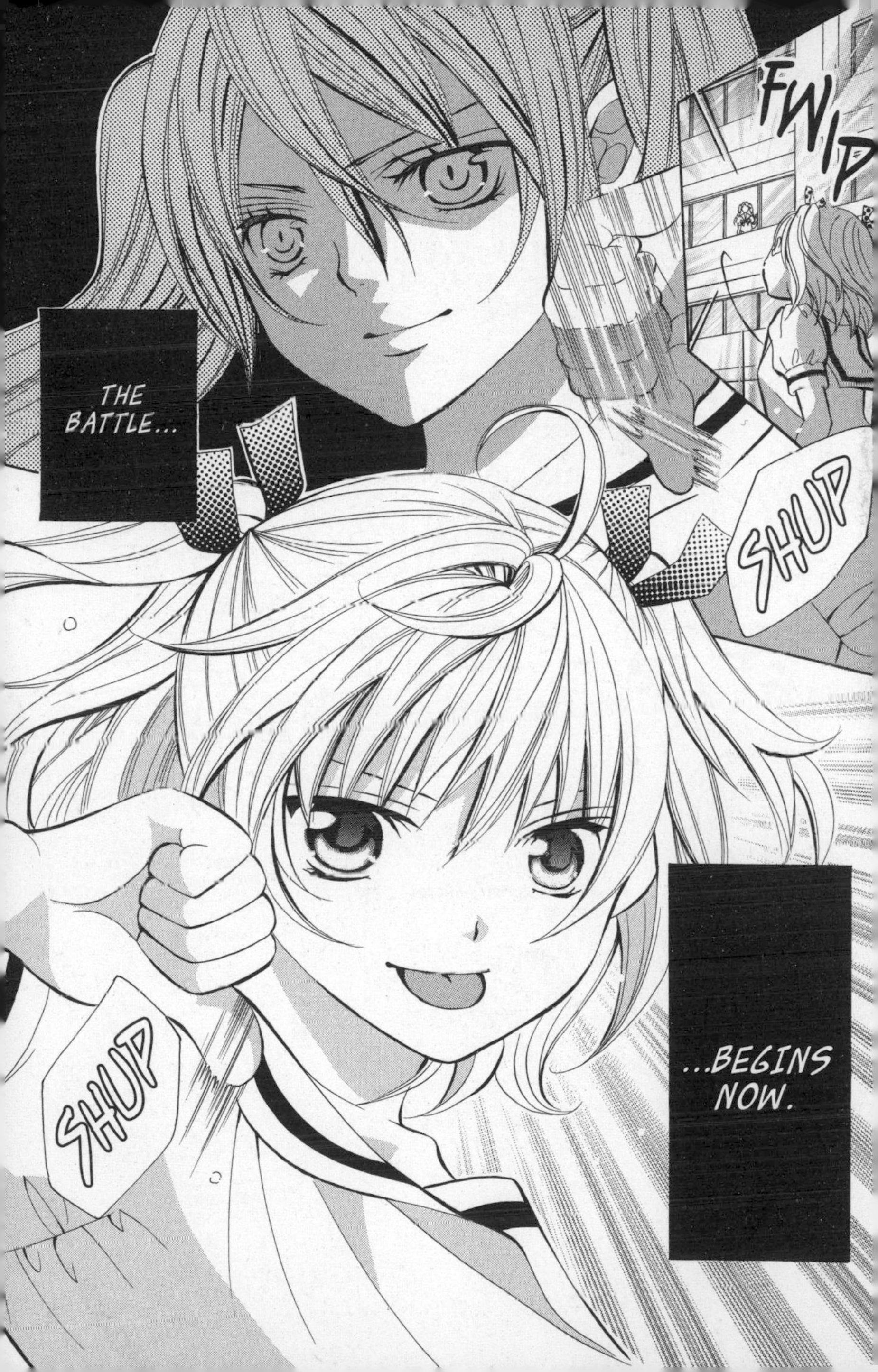
FWIP
SHUP
THE BATTLE...
...BEGINS NOW.
SHUP

So Cute! Fan Art Feature

EVERYONE'S DRAWINGS ARE SO CUTE, THEY HURT!!

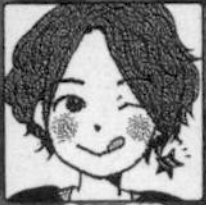
Shojii

Editor Shojii has commented on each one this time!!

Milk (Hokkaido)

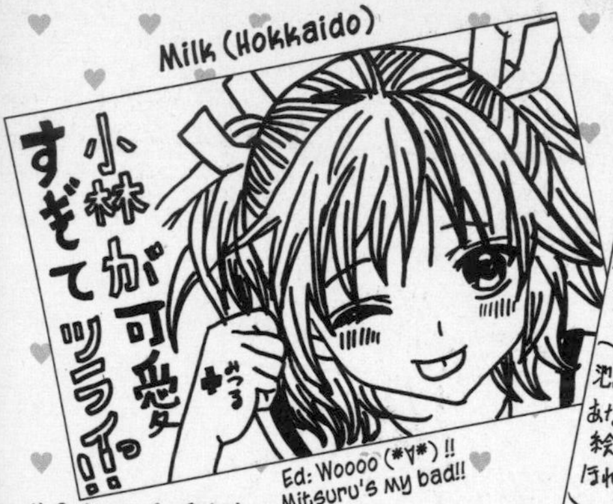
小林が可愛すぎてツライっ!!
みつる

Ed: Woooo (*∀*)!! Mitsuru's my bad!!

Raimu Hiiragi

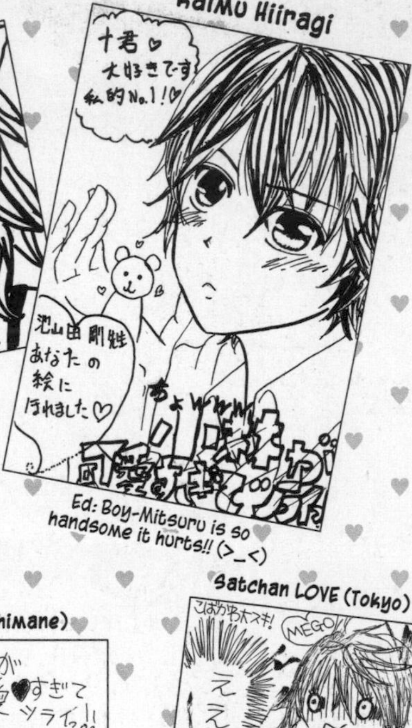
十君♡ 大好きです 私的No.1!♡
池山田剛先生 あなたの絵に惚れました♡

Ed: Boy-Mitsuru is so handsome it hurts!! (>_<)

Y.O. loves So Cute! (Fukushima)

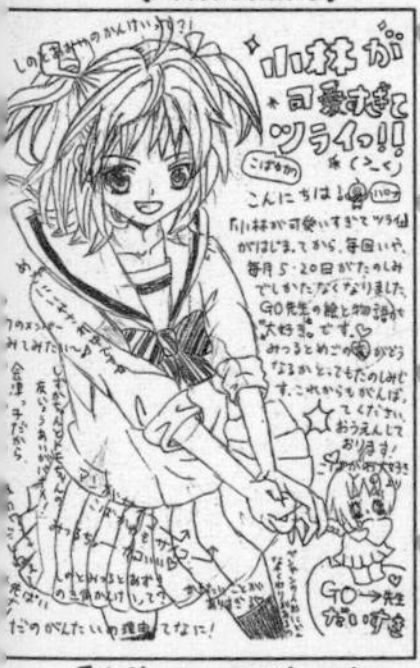
小林が可愛すぎてツライっ!!

Ed: Your passionate comments are hot!!

Kanami Shimogaki (Shimane)

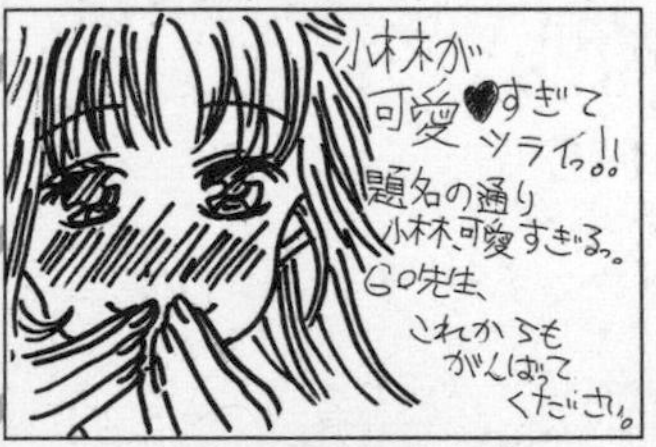
小林が可愛♥すぎてツライっ!!
題名の通り 小林、可愛すぎるっ。
GO先生、
これからも がんばって ください。

Ed: Your drawing is just too cute!!

Satchan LOVE (Tokyo)

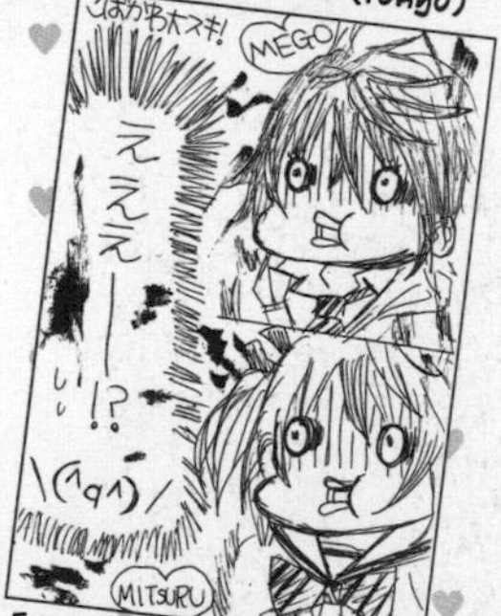
こばかわ大スキ!
MEGO
えええーーい!?
\(^o^)/
MITSURU

Ed: The twins display their shockingly weird faces!!

Send your fan mail to:

Go Ikeyamada
c/o Shojo Beat
VIZ Media, LLC
P.O. Box 77010
San Francisco, CA 94107

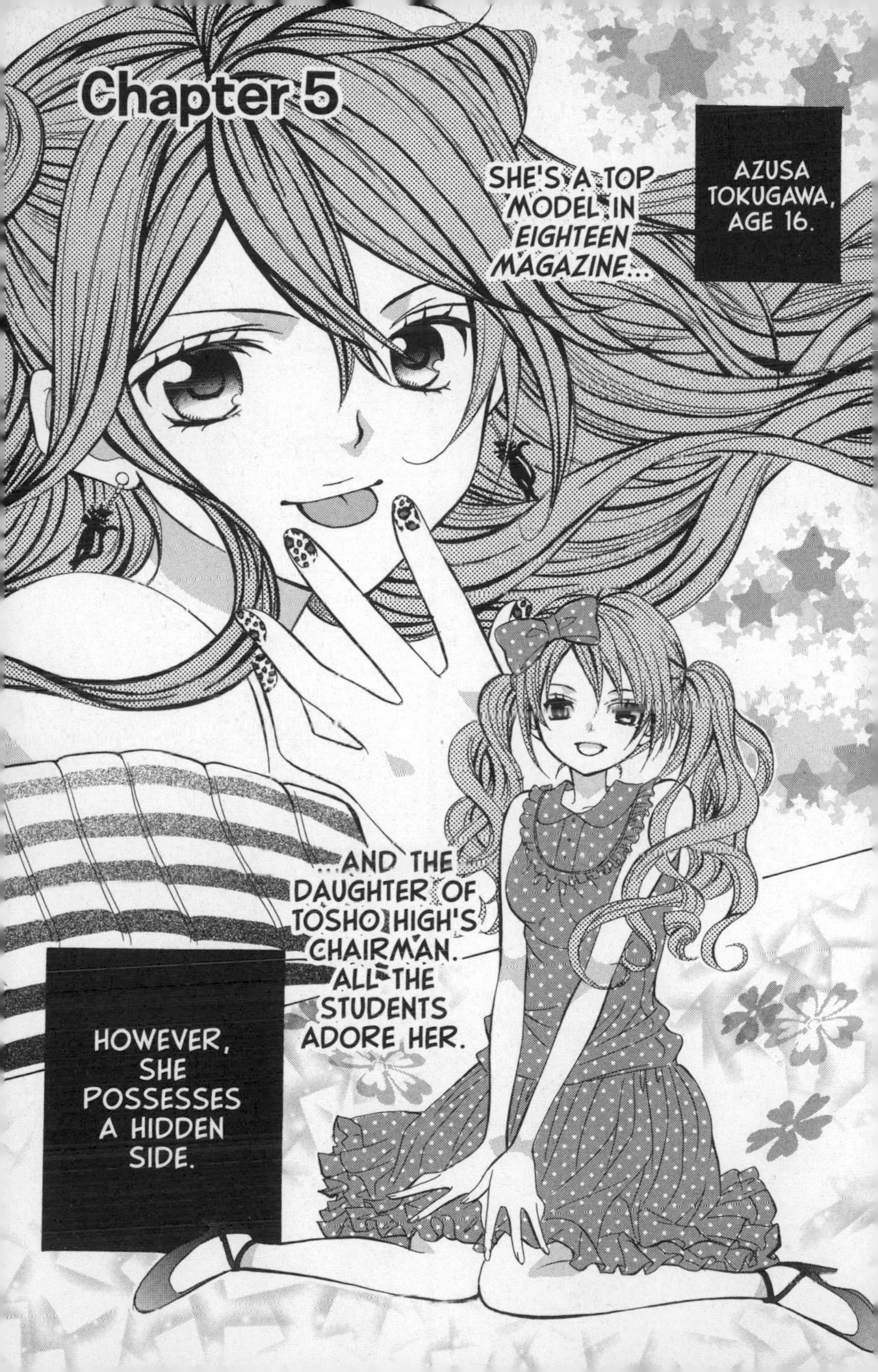
Chapter 5
AZUSA TOKUGAWA, AGE 16.
SHE'S A TOP MODEL IN EIGHTEEN MAGAZINE...
...AND THE DAUGHTER OF TOSHO HIGH'S CHAIRMAN. ALL THE STUDENTS ADORE HER.
HOWEVER, SHE POSSESSES A HIDDEN SIDE.

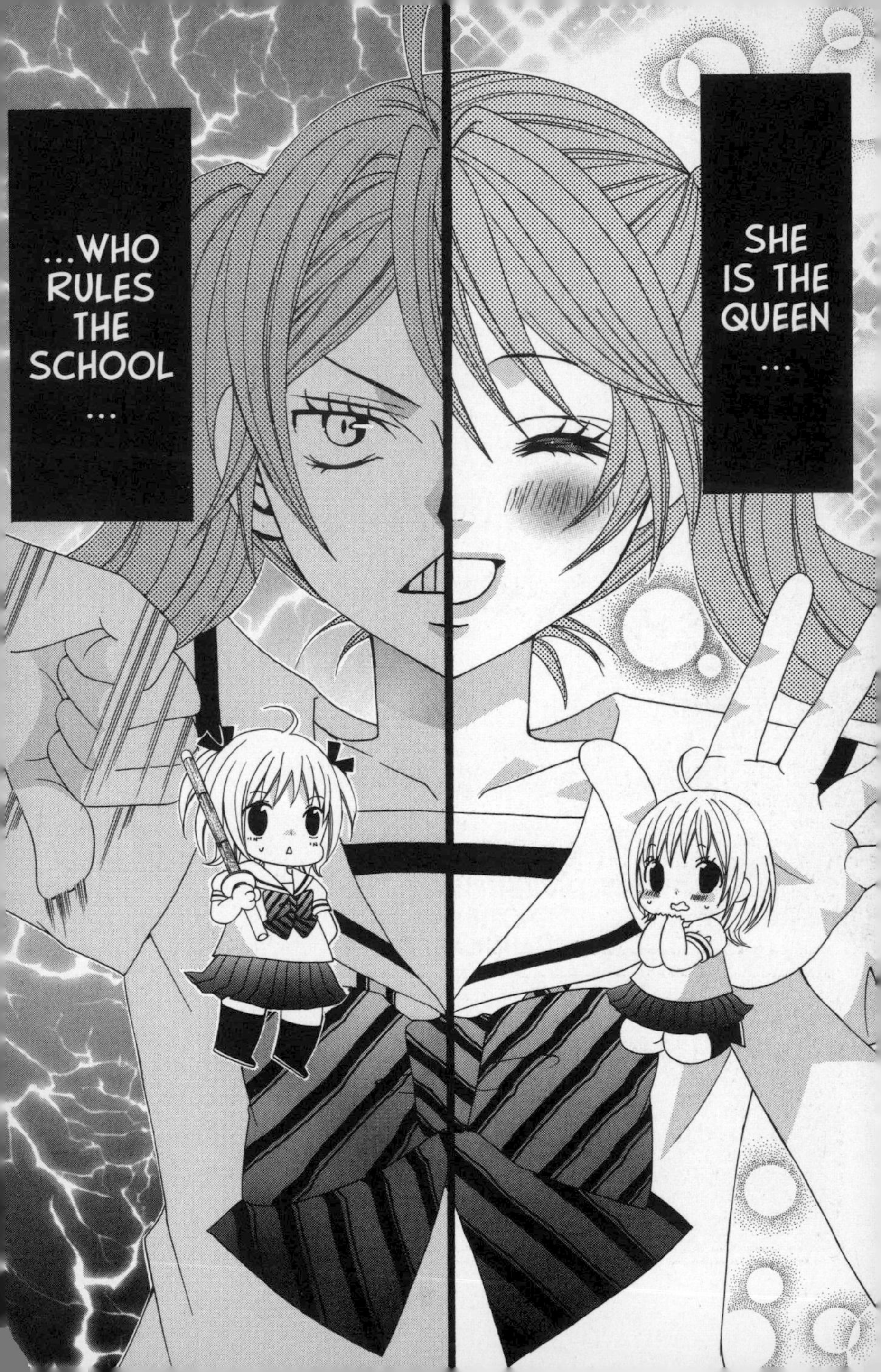
SHE IS THE QUEEN ...
...WHO RULES THE SCHOOL ...

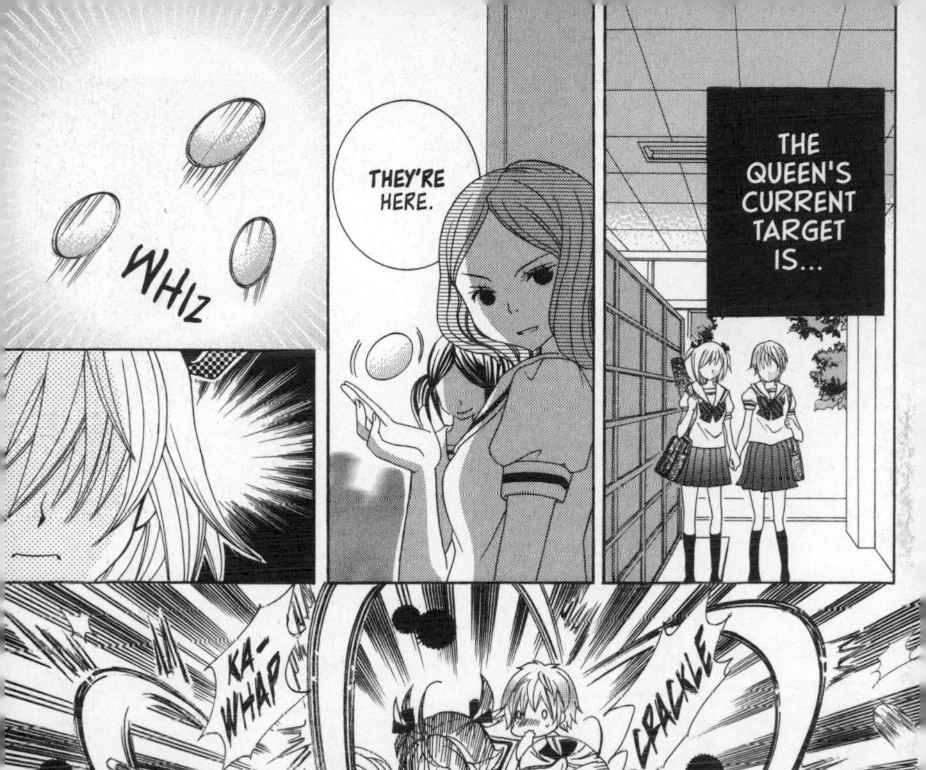
THE QUEEN'S CURRENT TARGET IS...
THEY'RE HERE.
WHIZ
CRACKLE
KA-WHAP
WHAP
SMASH

What's new!

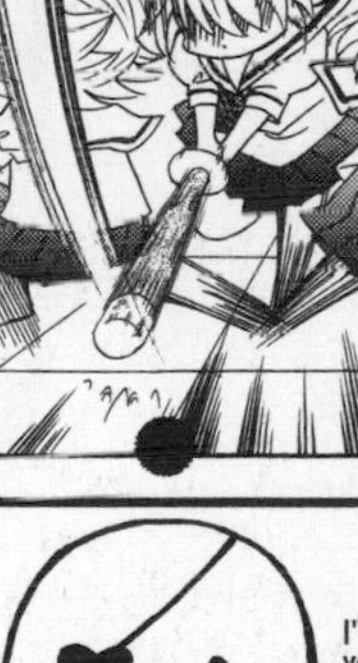

I SAW *EVA Q!* I'M A FAN OF AYANAMI REI-CHAN, BUT I ALSO THOUGHT EYE-PATCH ASUKA WAS UBER CUTE. ♪ I'M LOOKING FORWARD TO THE FINAL EPISODE!

I'VE STARTED DRINKING YOMEISHU (A MEDICINAL LIQUOR) SINCE I'VE RECENTLY BECOME FRAIL. (*BITTER SMILE*).

RIN, MY BELOVED NEPHEW, HAS TURNED 11... TIME REALLY FLIES. (^#^)

I'M NOW INTO THE *JOJO* ANIME, *SENGOKU BASARA, INAZUMA ELEVEN, THE GUNDAM SEED* RERUNS, AND KIS-MY-FT2, AN ALL-MALE JOHNNY'S IDOL GROUP. ♪ ♪
I WANT TO SEE THEM LIVE, BUT THE TICKETS SEEM VERY HARD TO GET.
I'D LIKE TO MAKE A ROUND FAN. ♡

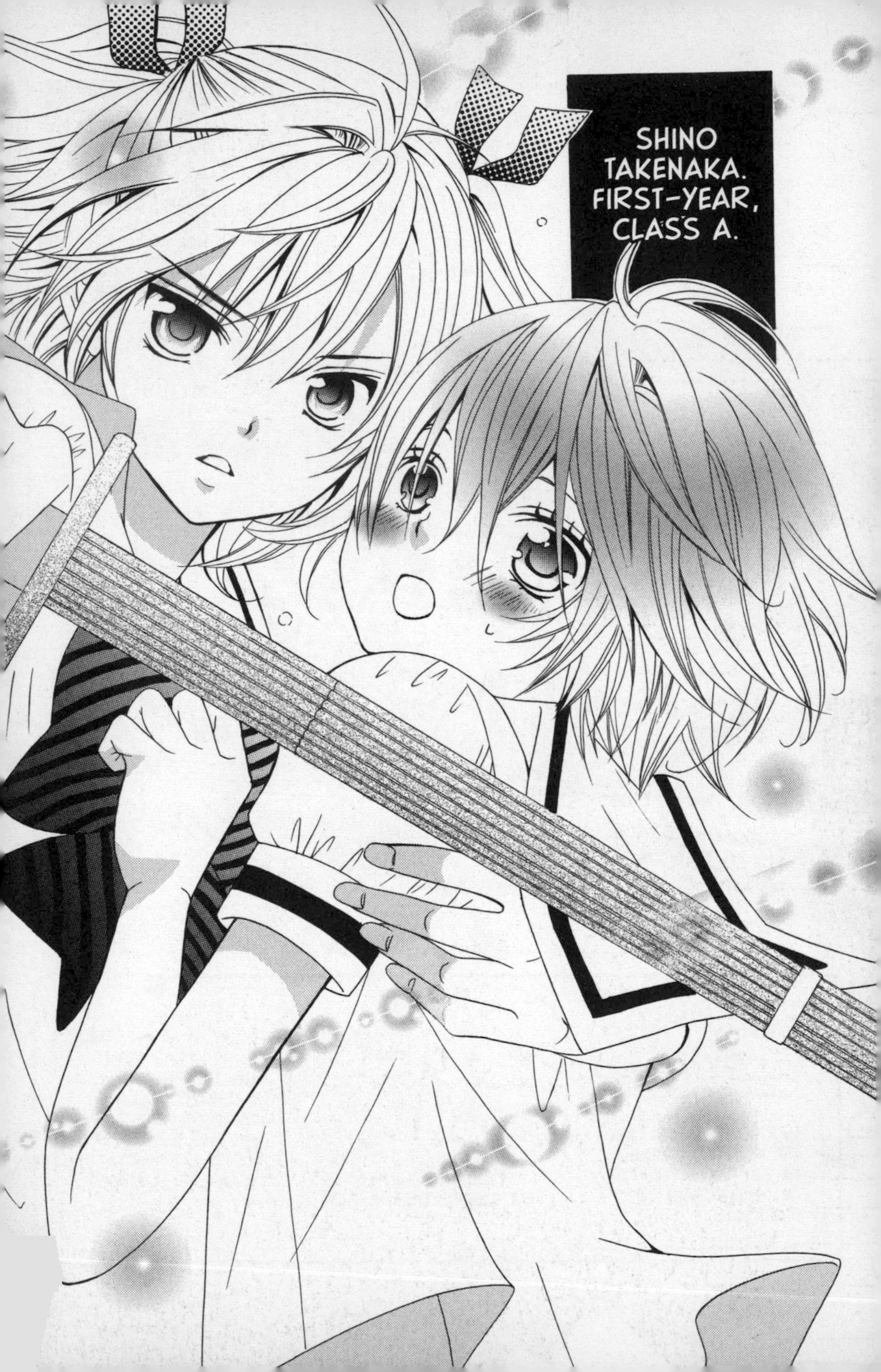
SHINO TAKENAKA. FIRST-YEAR, CLASS A.

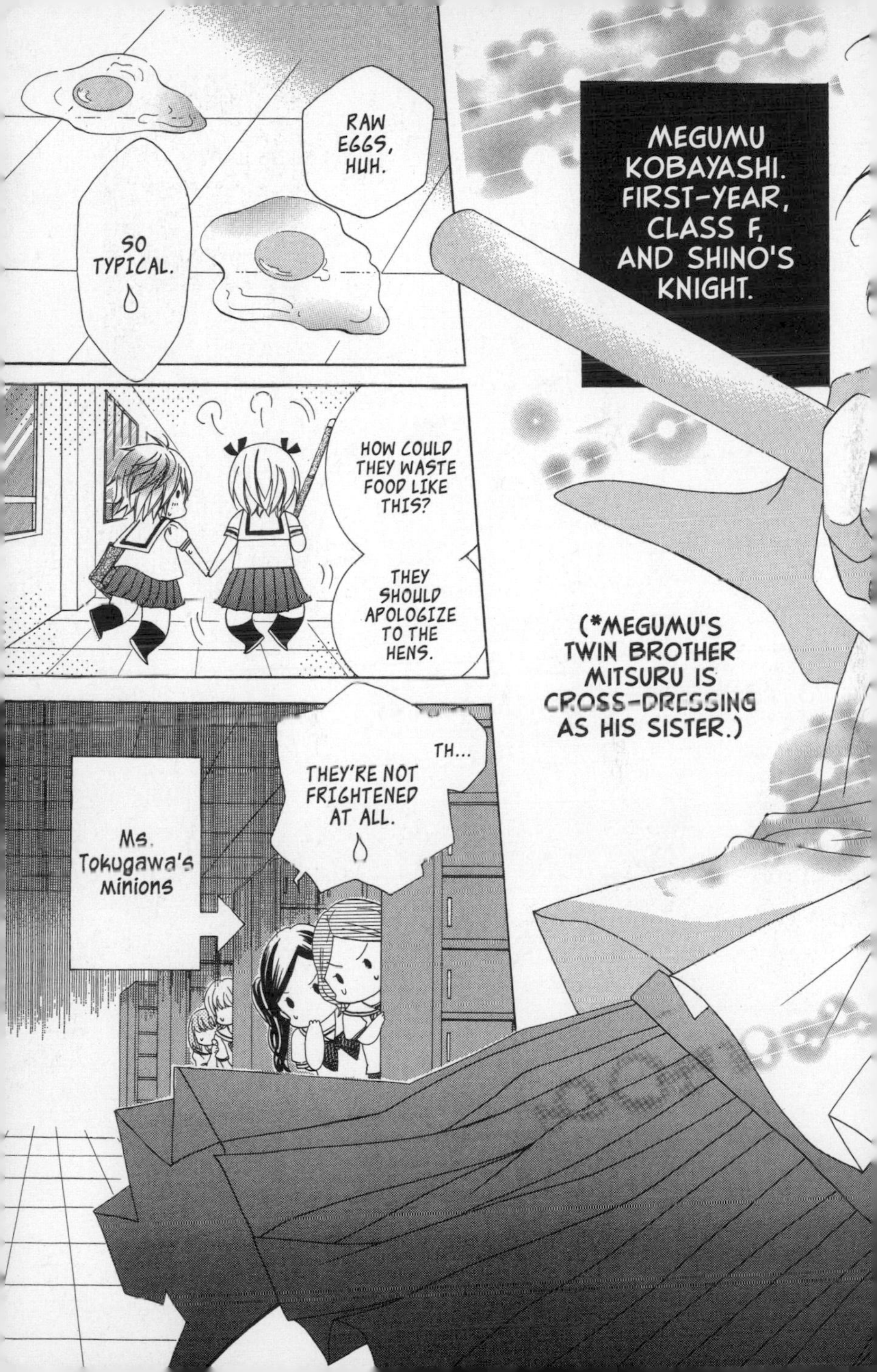
MEGUMU KOBAYASHI. FIRST-YEAR, CLASS F, AND SHINO'S KNIGHT.
(*MEGUMU'S TWIN BROTHER MITSURU IS CROSS-DRESSING AS HIS SISTER.)
RAW EGGS, HUH.
SO TYPICAL.
HOW COULD THEY WASTE FOOD LIKE THIS?
THEY SHOULD APOLOGIZE TO THE HENS.
TH... THEY'RE NOT FRIGHTENED AT ALL.
Ms. Tokugawa's minions

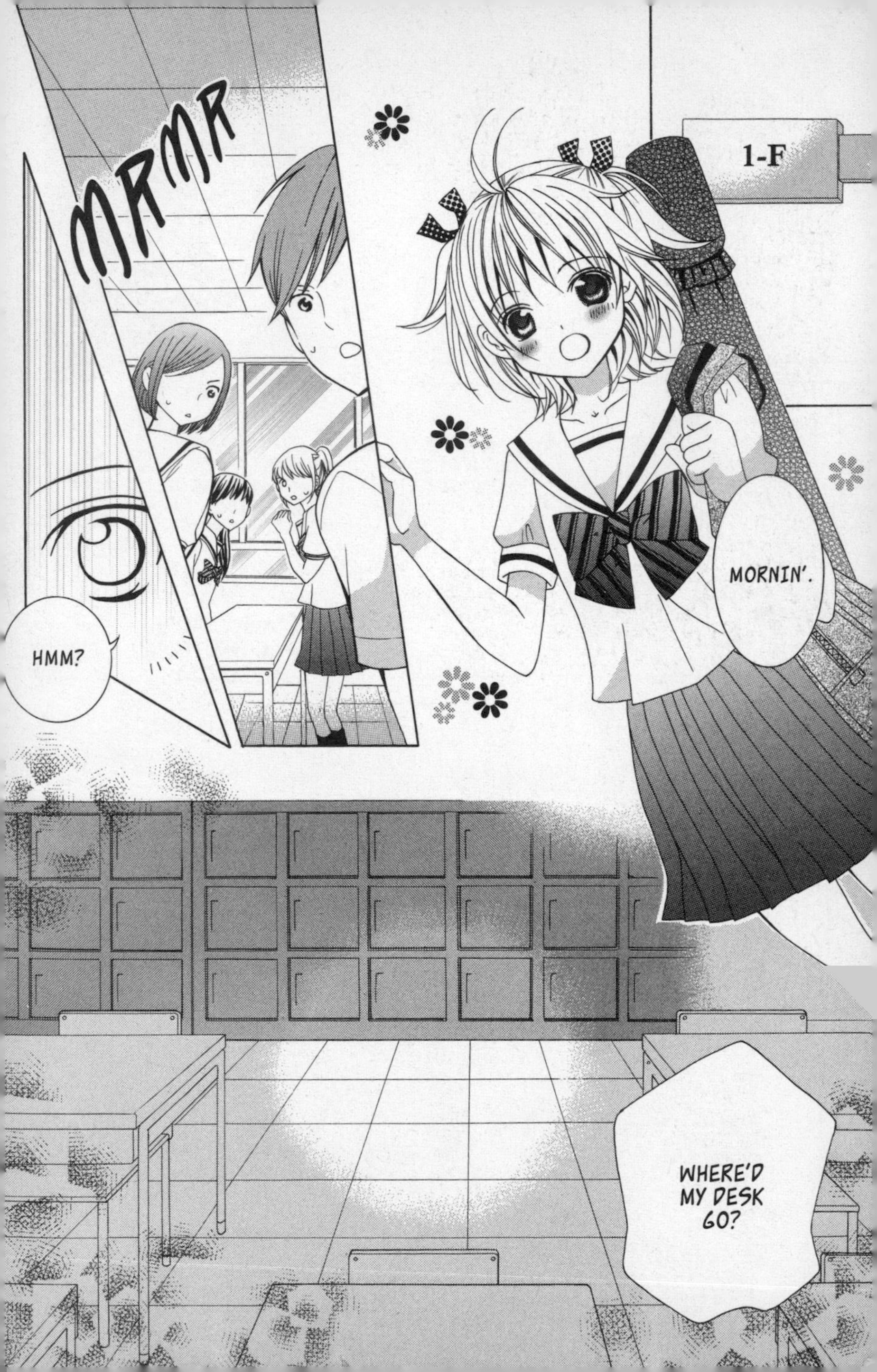
1-F
MORNIN'.
MRMR
HMM?
WHERE'D MY DESK GO?

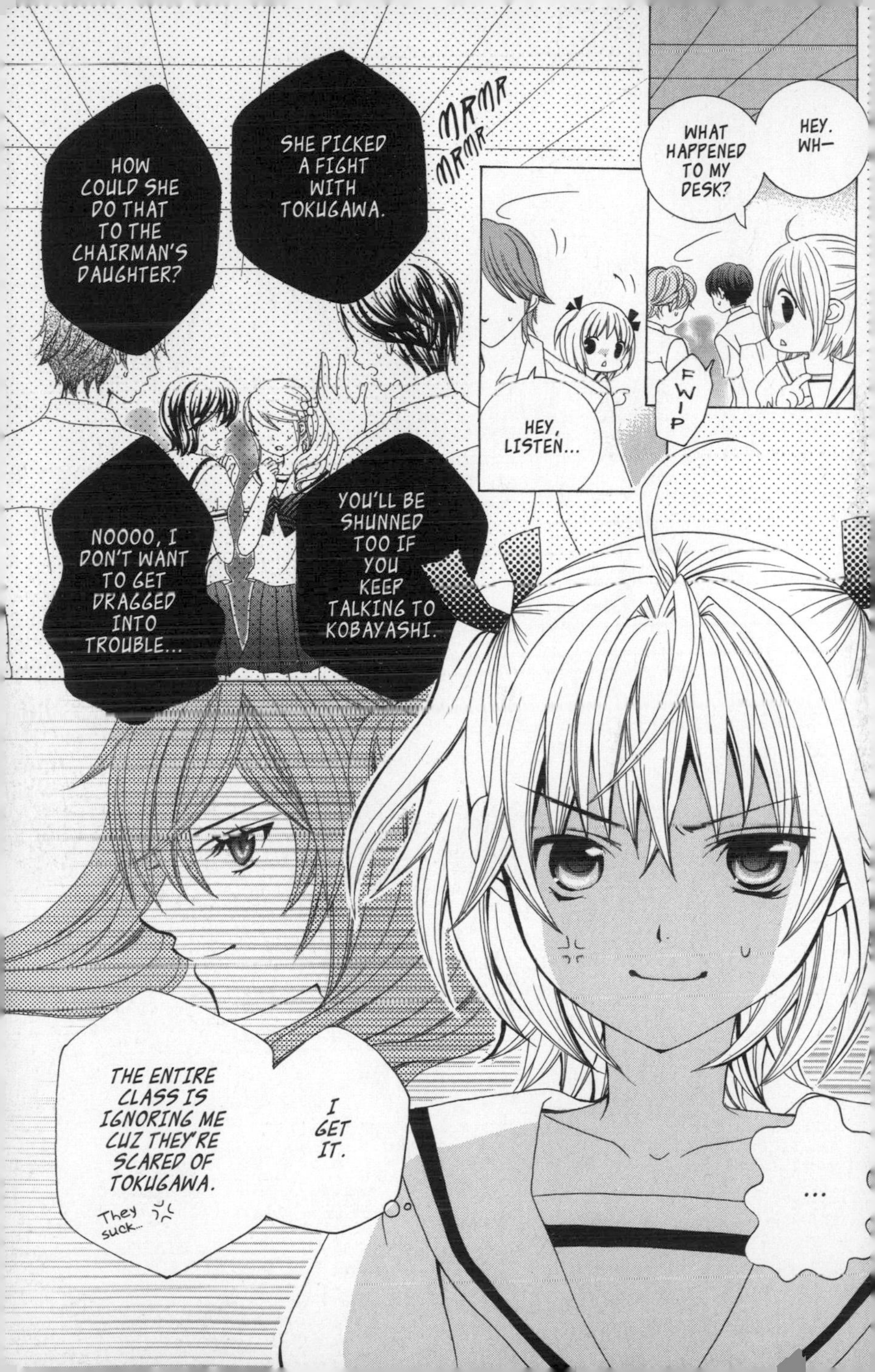
HEY. WH—
WHAT HAPPENED TO MY DESK?
FWIP
HEY, LISTEN...
MRMR MRMR
SHE PICKED A FIGHT WITH TOKUGAWA.
HOW COULD SHE DO THAT TO THE CHAIRMAN'S DAUGHTER?
YOU'LL BE SHUNNED TOO IF YOU KEEP TALKING TO KOBAYASHI.
NOOOO, I DON'T WANT TO GET DRAGGED INTO TROUBLE...
...
I GET IT.
THE ENTIRE CLASS IS IGNORING ME CUZ THEY'RE SCARED OF TOKUGAWA.
They suck...

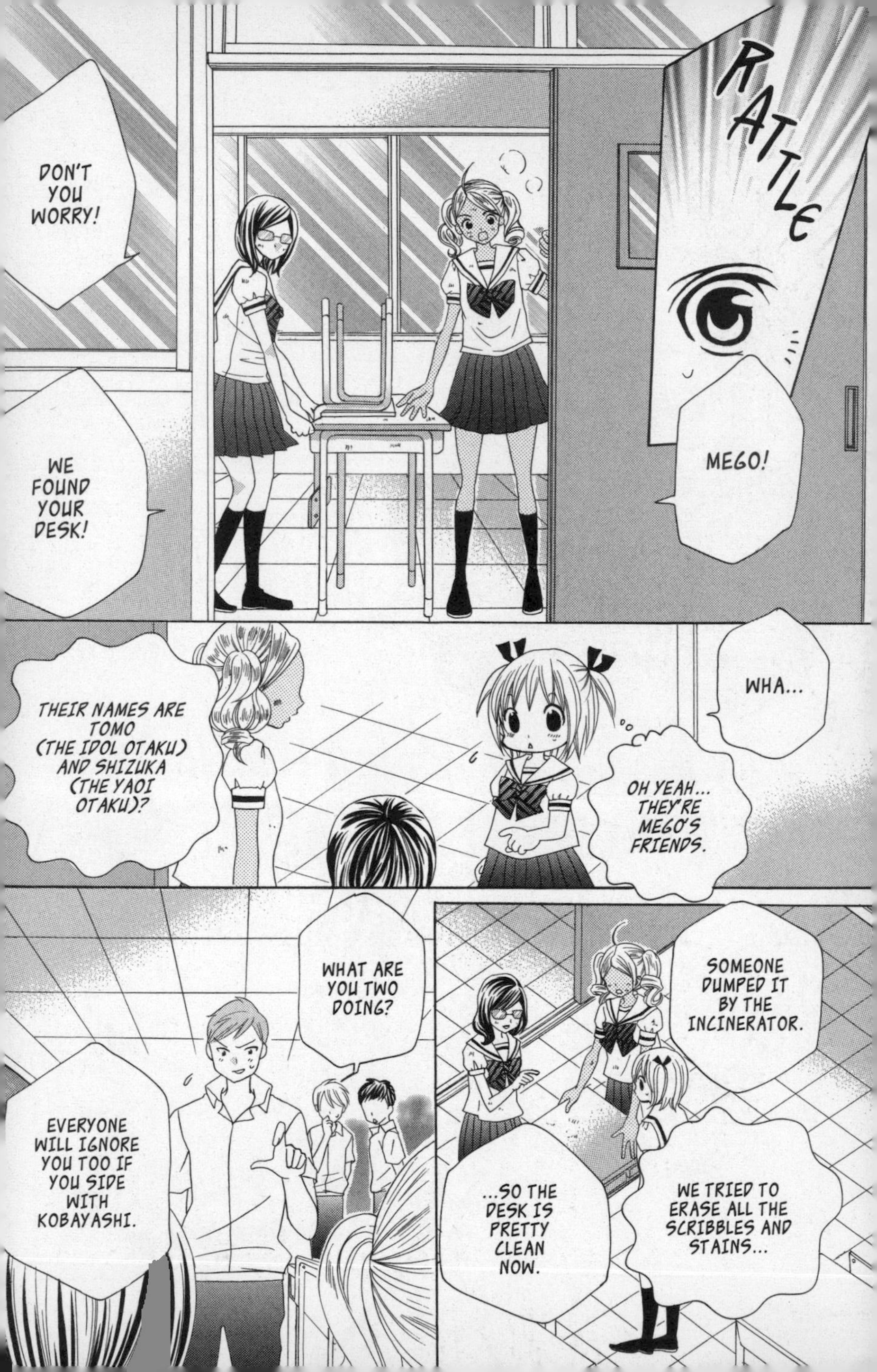
RATTLE
MEGO!
DON'T YOU WORRY!
WE FOUND YOUR DESK!
WHA...
OH YEAH... THEY'RE MEGO'S FRIENDS.
THEIR NAMES ARE TOMO (THE IDOL OTAKU) AND SHIZUKA (THE YAOI OTAKU)?
SOMEONE DUMPED IT BY THE INCINERATOR.
WE TRIED TO ERASE ALL THE SCRIBBLES AND STAINS...
...SO THE DESK IS PRETTY CLEAN NOW.
WHAT ARE YOU TWO DOING?
EVERYONE WILL IGNORE YOU TOO IF YOU SIDE WITH KOBAYASHI.

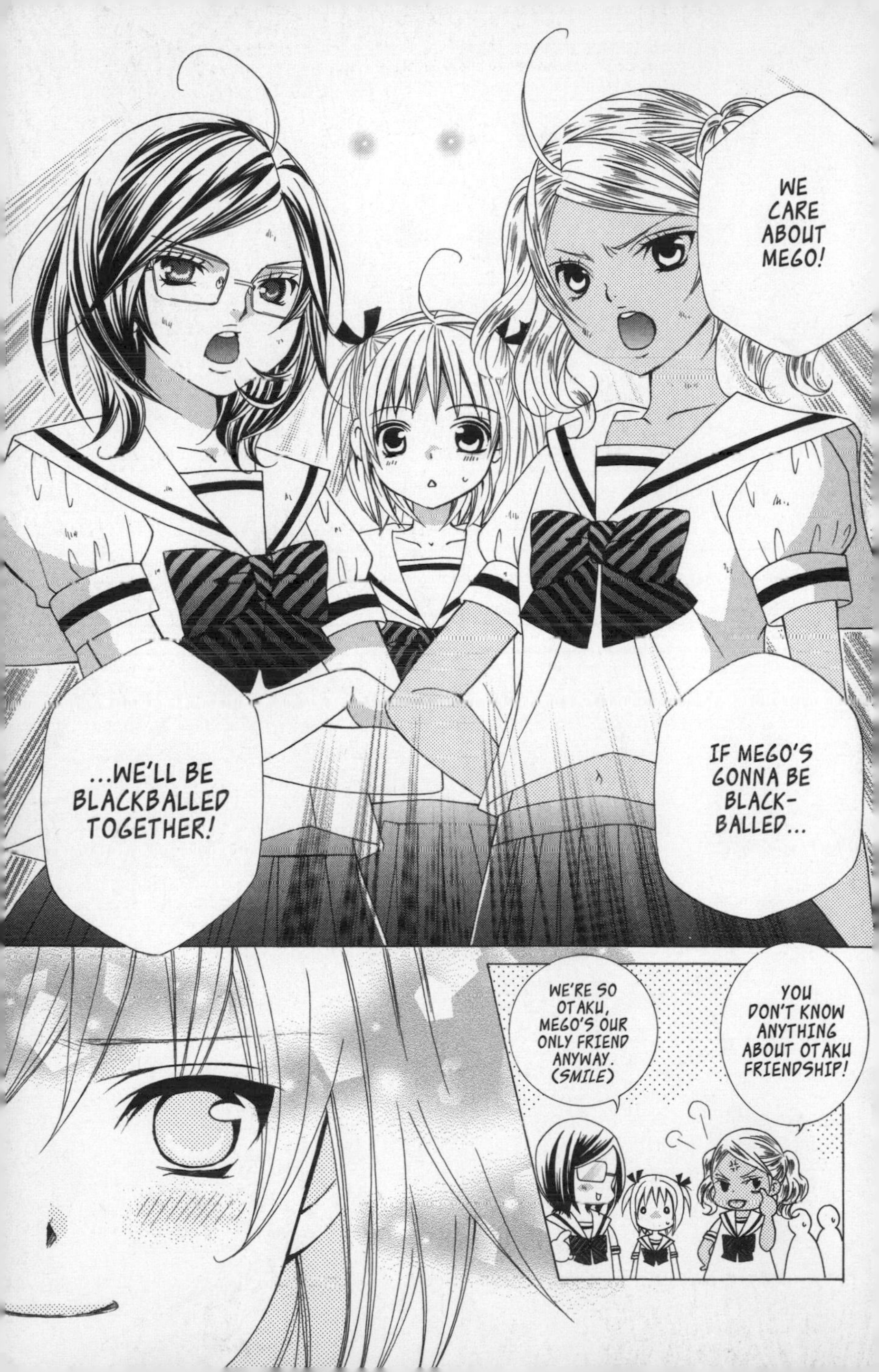
WE CARE ABOUT MEGO!
IF MEGO'S GONNA BE BLACK-BALLED...
...WE'LL BE BLACKBALLED TOGETHER!
YOU DON'T KNOW ANYTHING ABOUT OTAKU FRIENDSHIP!
WE'RE SO OTAKU, MEGO'S OUR ONLY FRIEND ANYWAY. (SMILE)

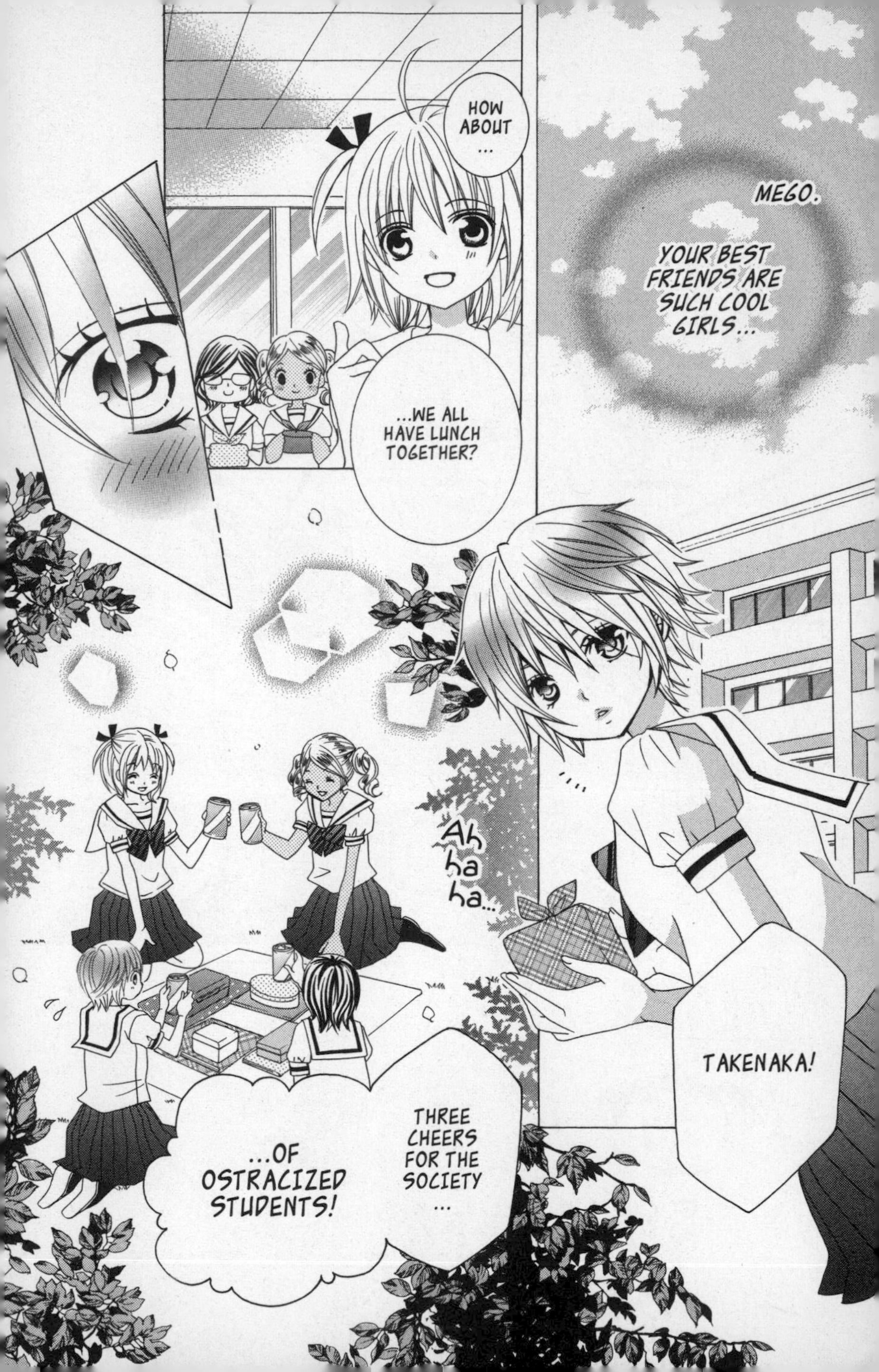
MEGO.
YOUR BEST FRIENDS ARE SUCH COOL GIRLS...
TAKENAKA!
HOW ABOUT ...
...WE ALL HAVE LUNCH TOGETHER?
Ah ha ha...
THREE CHEERS FOR THE SOCIETY ...
...OF OSTRACIZED STUDENTS!

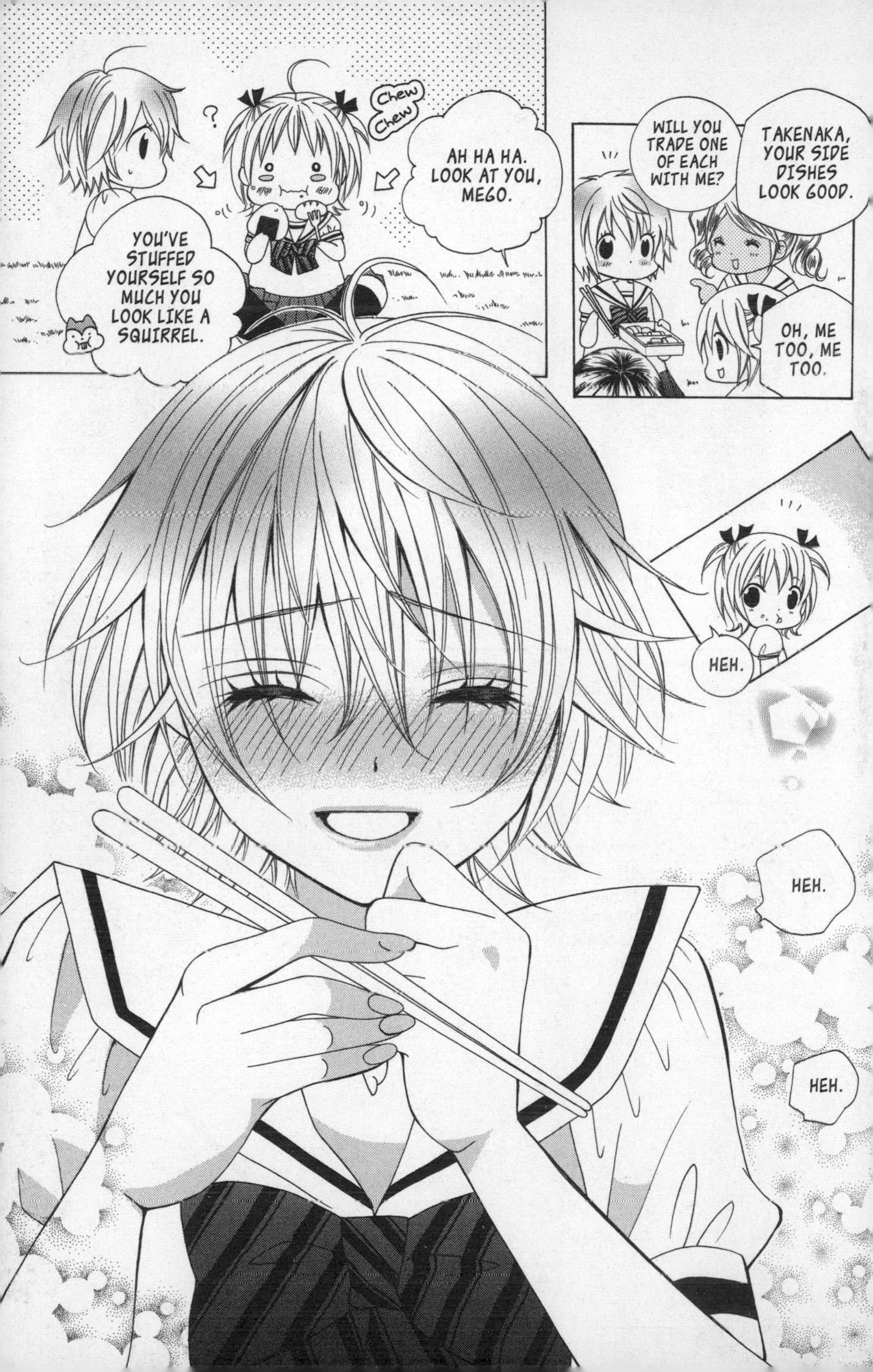
TAKENAKA, YOUR SIDE DISHES LOOK GOOD.
WILL YOU TRADE ONE OF EACH WITH ME?
OH, ME TOO, ME TOO.
Chew Chew
AH HA HA. LOOK AT YOU, MEGO.
YOU'VE STUFFED YOURSELF SO MUCH YOU LOOK LIKE A SQUIRREL.
HEH.
HEH.
HEH.

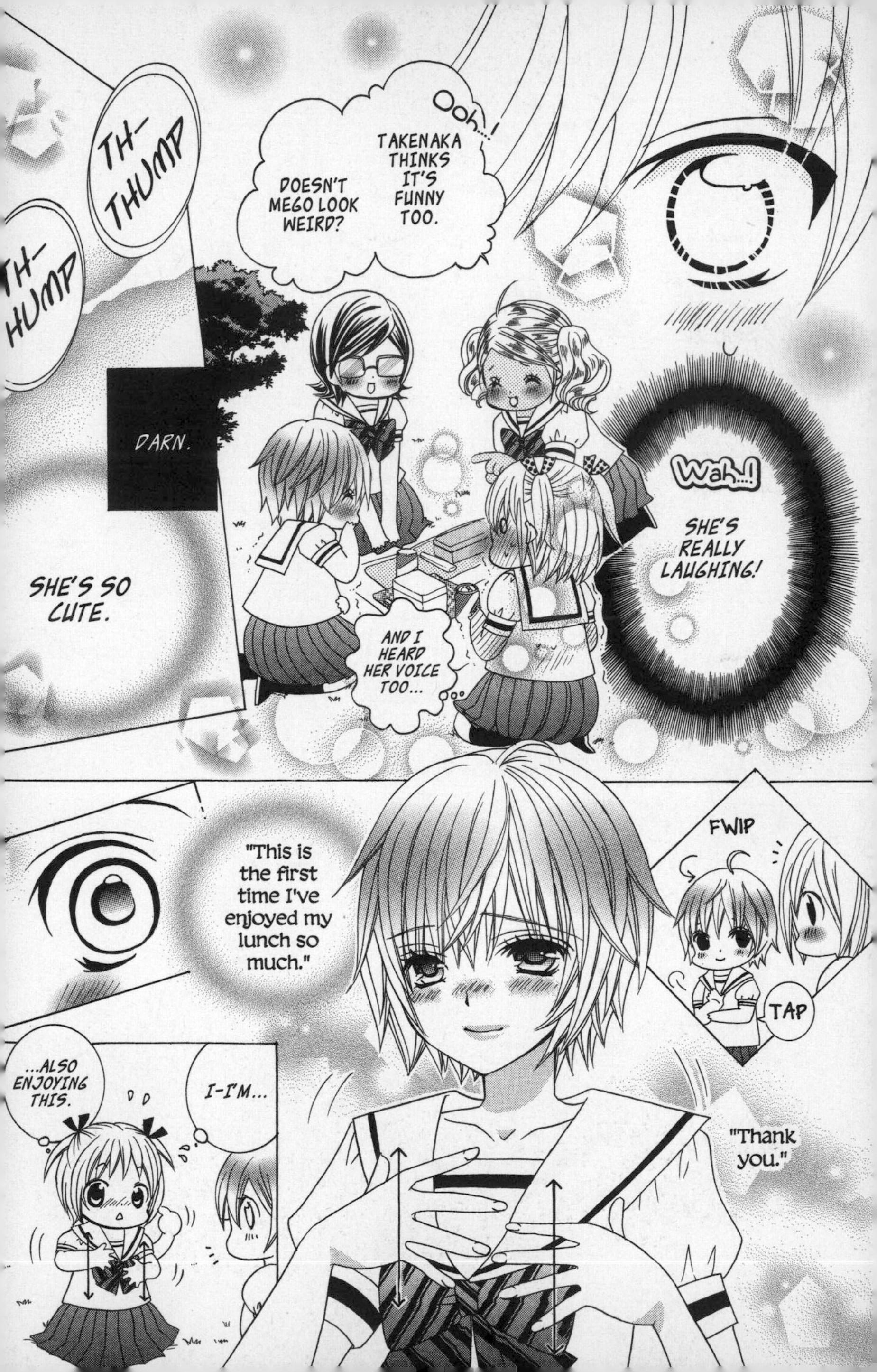
Ooh...!
TAKENAKA THINKS IT'S FUNNY TOO.
DOESN'T MEGO LOOK WEIRD?
Wah...!
SHE'S REALLY LAUGHING!
AND I HEARD HER VOICE TOO...
TH-THUMP
TH-HUMP
DARN.
SHE'S SO CUTE.
FWIP
TAP
"This is the first time I've enjoyed my lunch so much."
"Thank you."
I-I'M...
...ALSO ENJOYING THIS.

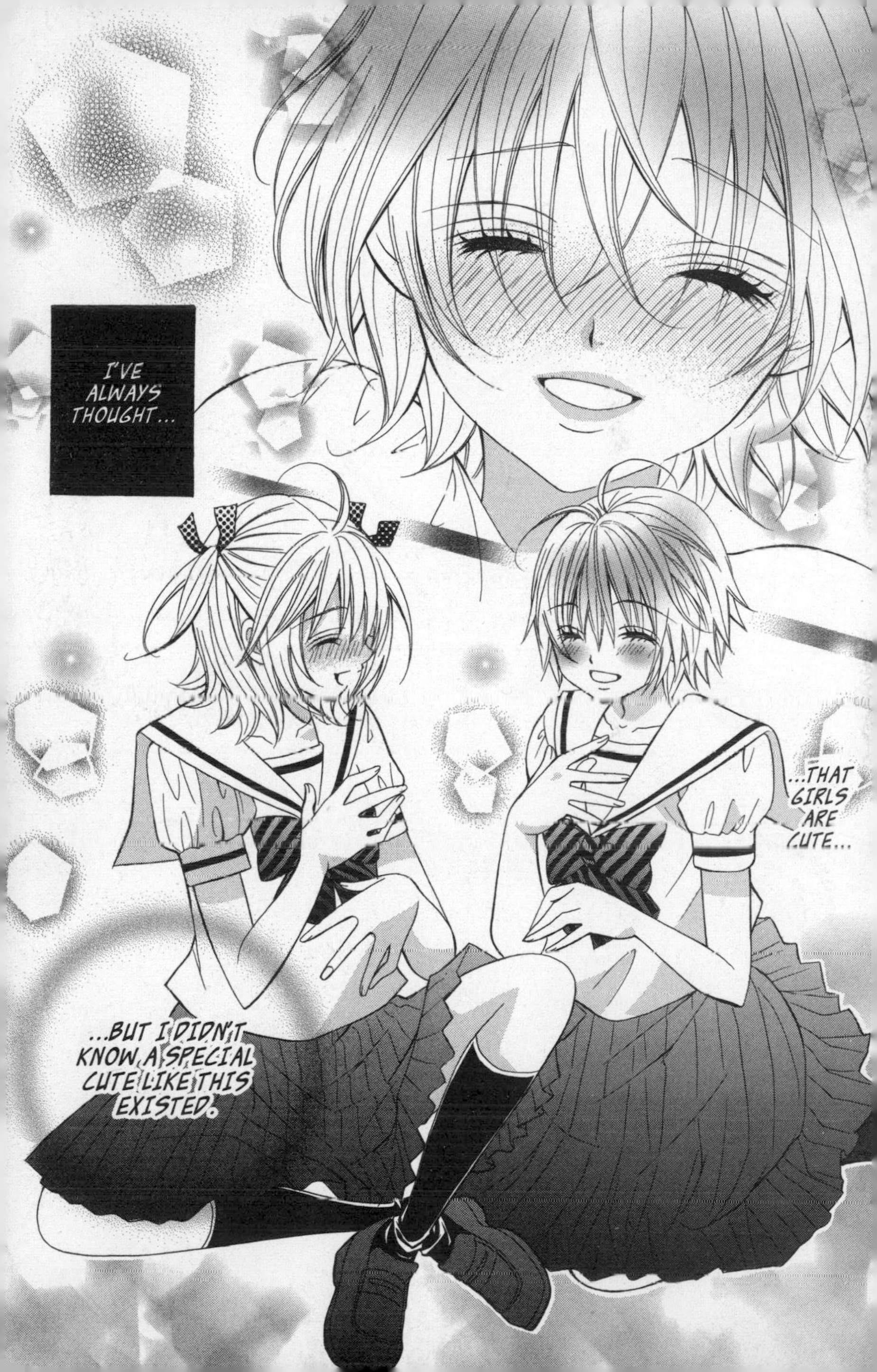
I'VE ALWAYS THOUGHT...
...THAT GIRLS ARE CUTE...
...BUT I DIDN'T KNOW A SPECIAL CUTE LIKE THIS EXISTED.

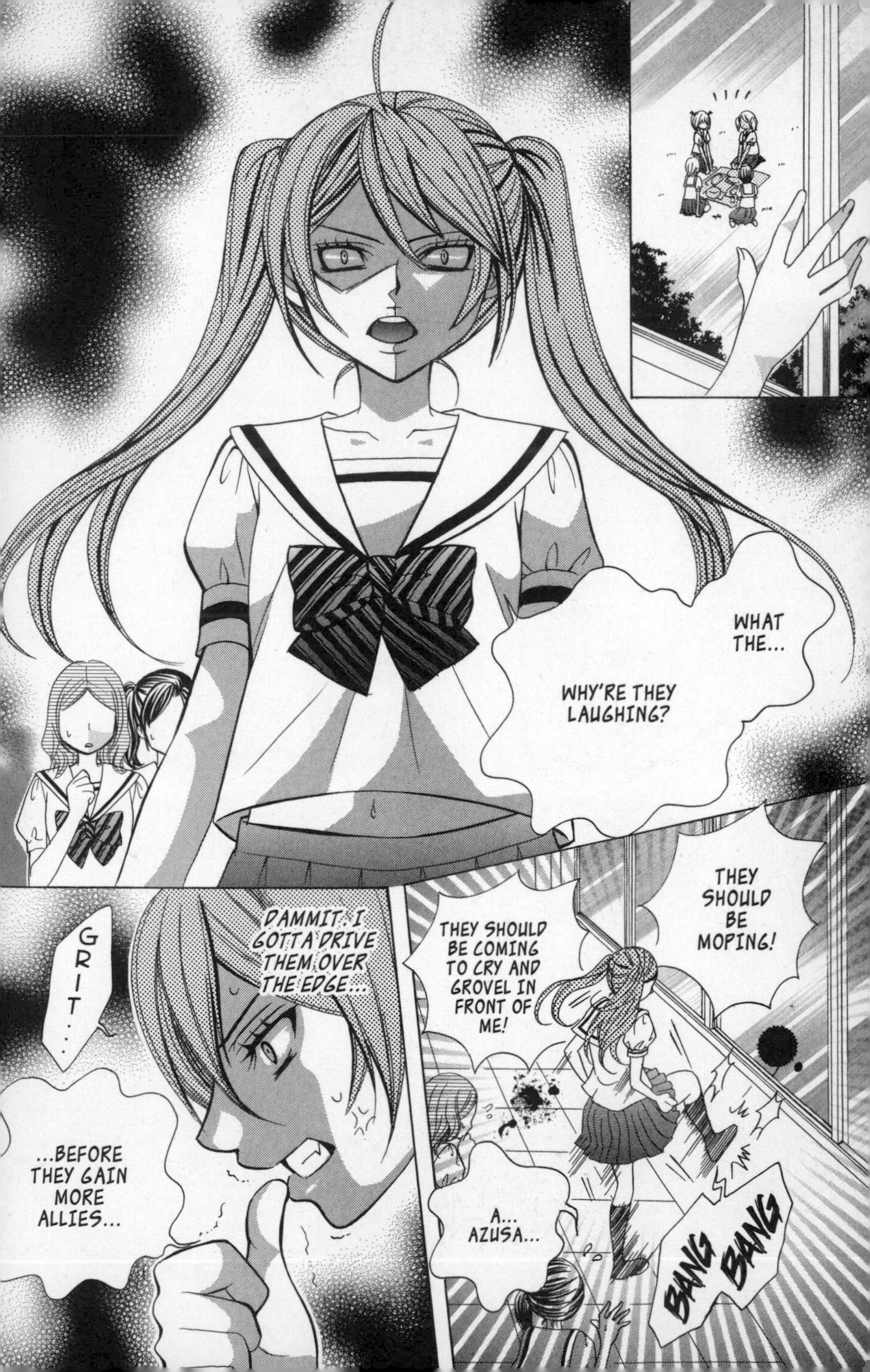
WHAT THE... WHY'RE THEY LAUGHING?
THEY SHOULD BE MOPING!
THEY SHOULD BE COMING TO CRY AND GROVEL IN FRONT OF ME!
BANG BANG
A... AZUSA...
DAMMIT. I GOTTA DRIVE THEM OVER THE EDGE...
GRIT...
...BEFORE THEY GAIN MORE ALLIES...

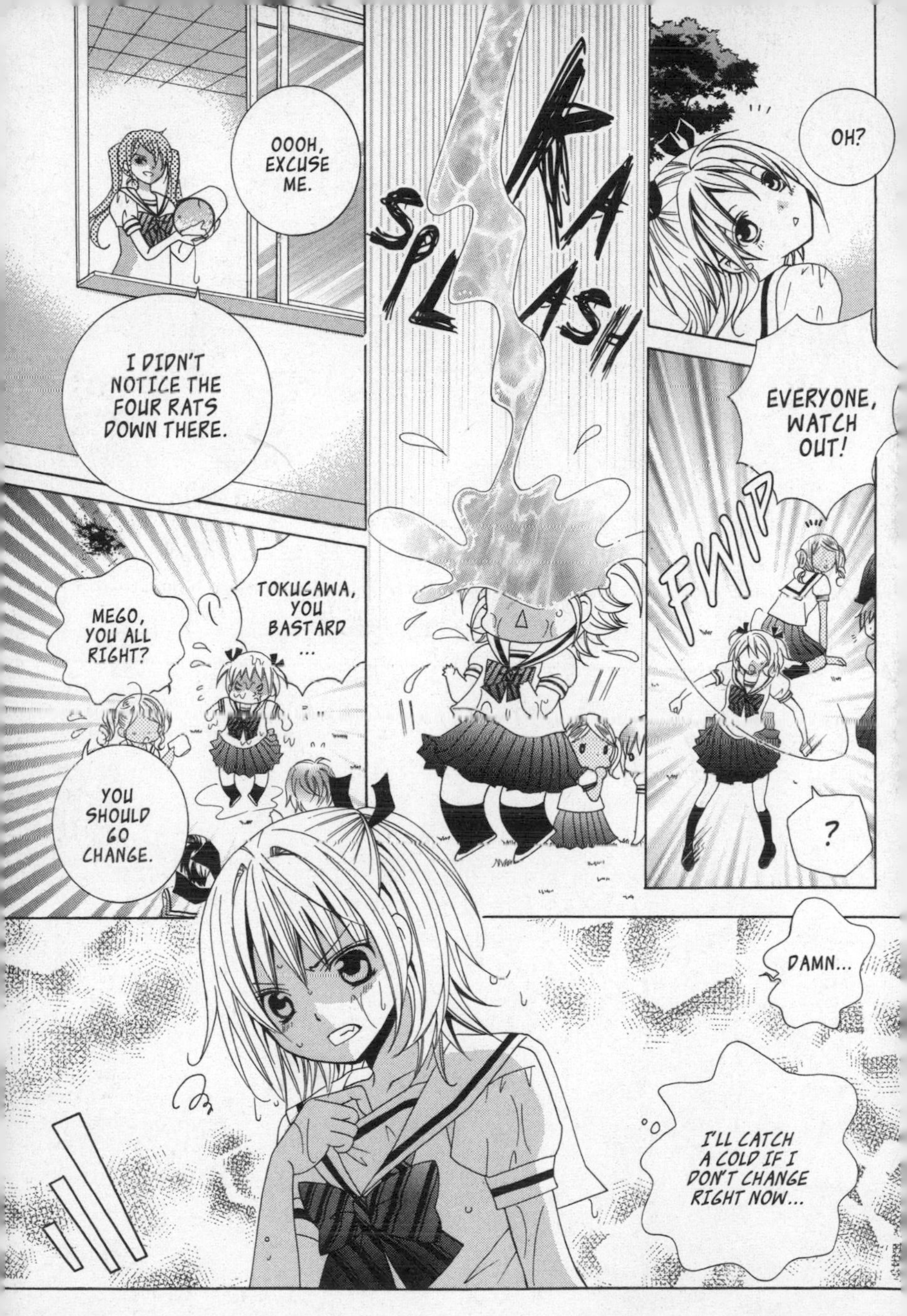
OH?
EVERYONE, WATCH OUT!
FWIP
?
KA SPLASH
OOOH, EXCUSE ME.
I DIDN'T NOTICE THE FOUR RATS DOWN THERE.
TOKUGAWA, YOU BASTARD ...
MEGO, YOU ALL RIGHT?
YOU SHOULD GO CHANGE.
DAMN...
I'LL CATCH A COLD IF I DON'T CHANGE RIGHT NOW...

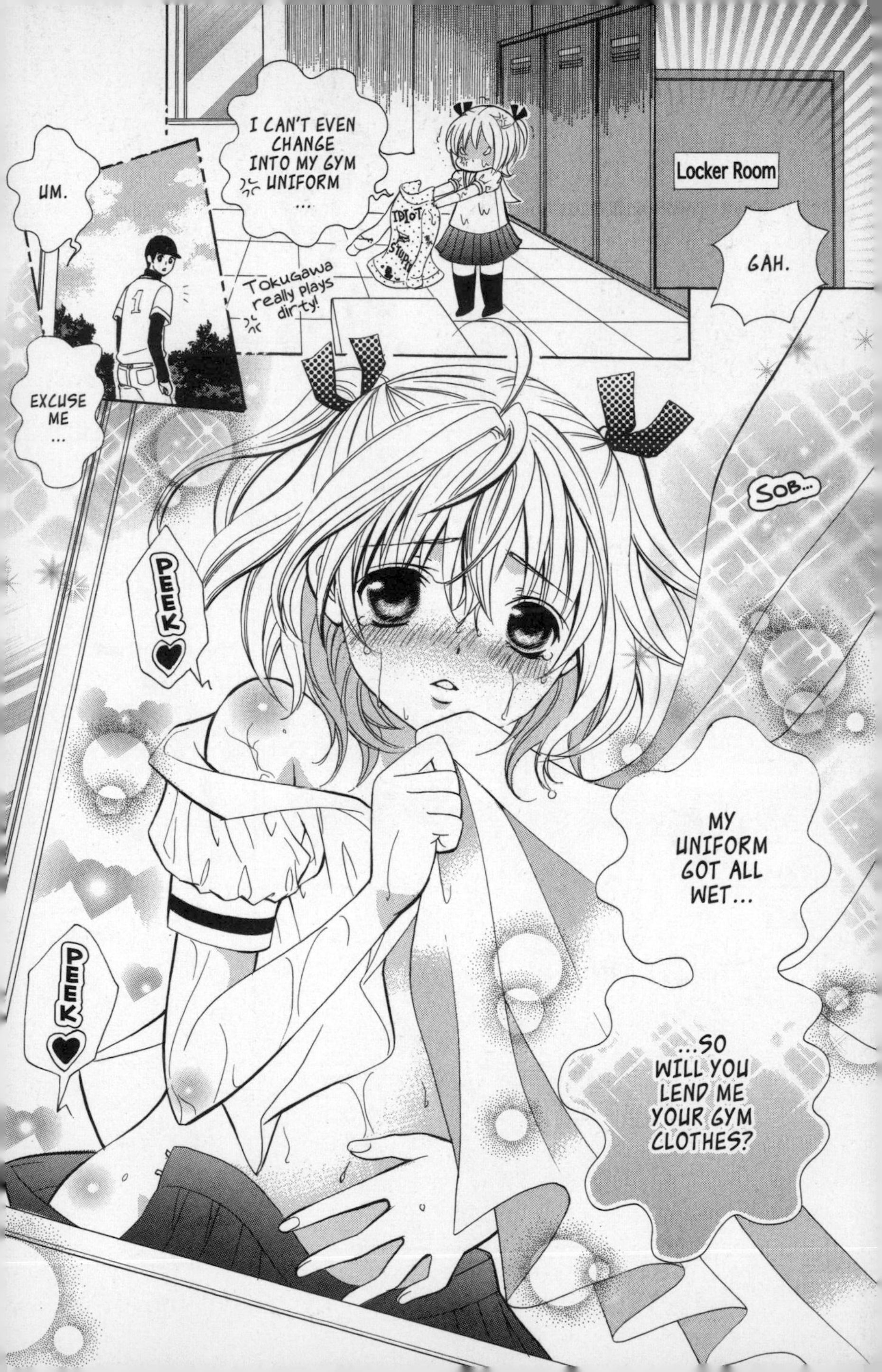
Locker Room
GAH.
I CAN'T EVEN CHANGE INTO MY GYM UNIFORM ...
IDIOT
STUPID
Tokugawa really plays dirty!
UM.
EXCUSE ME ...
SOB...
MY UNIFORM GOT ALL WET...
...SO WILL YOU LEND ME YOUR GYM CLOTHES?
PEEK ♥
PEEK ♥

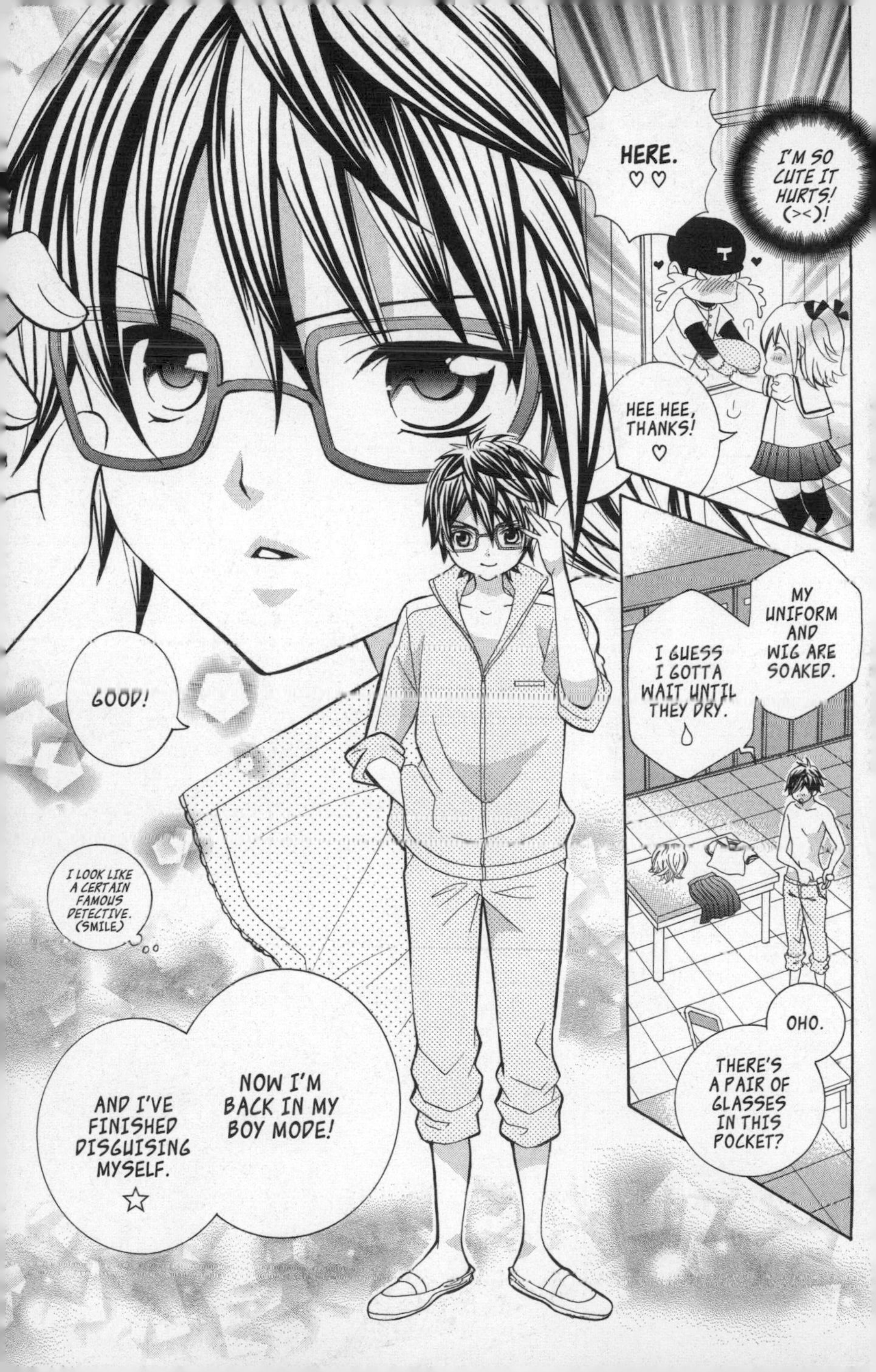
HERE.
I'M SO CUTE IT HURTS! (><)!
HEE HEE, THANKS!
MY UNIFORM AND WIG ARE SOAKED.
I GUESS I GOTTA WAIT UNTIL THEY DRY.
OHO.
THERE'S A PAIR OF GLASSES IN THIS POCKET?
GOOD!
I LOOK LIKE A CERTAIN FAMOUS DETECTIVE. (SMILE)
NOW I'M BACK IN MY BOY MODE!
AND I'VE FINISHED DISGUISING MYSELF. ☆

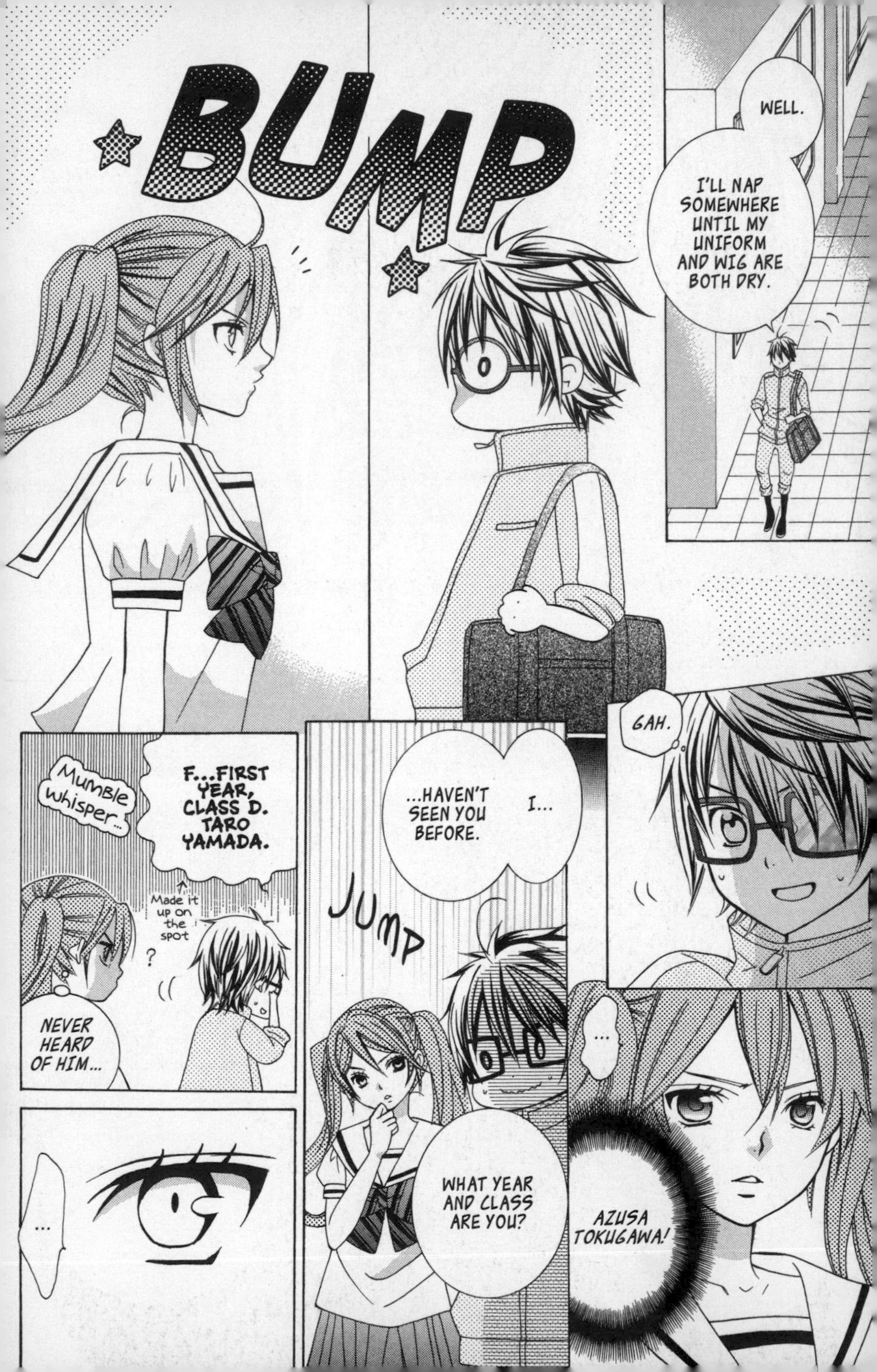
WELL.
I'LL NAP SOMEWHERE UNTIL MY UNIFORM AND WIG ARE BOTH DRY.
BUMP
GAH.
I...
...HAVEN'T SEEN YOU BEFORE.
JUMP
F...FIRST YEAR, CLASS D. TARO YAMADA.
Mumble whisper...
Made it up on the spot
NEVER HEARD OF HIM...
...
AZUSA TOKUGAWA!
WHAT YEAR AND CLASS ARE YOU?
...

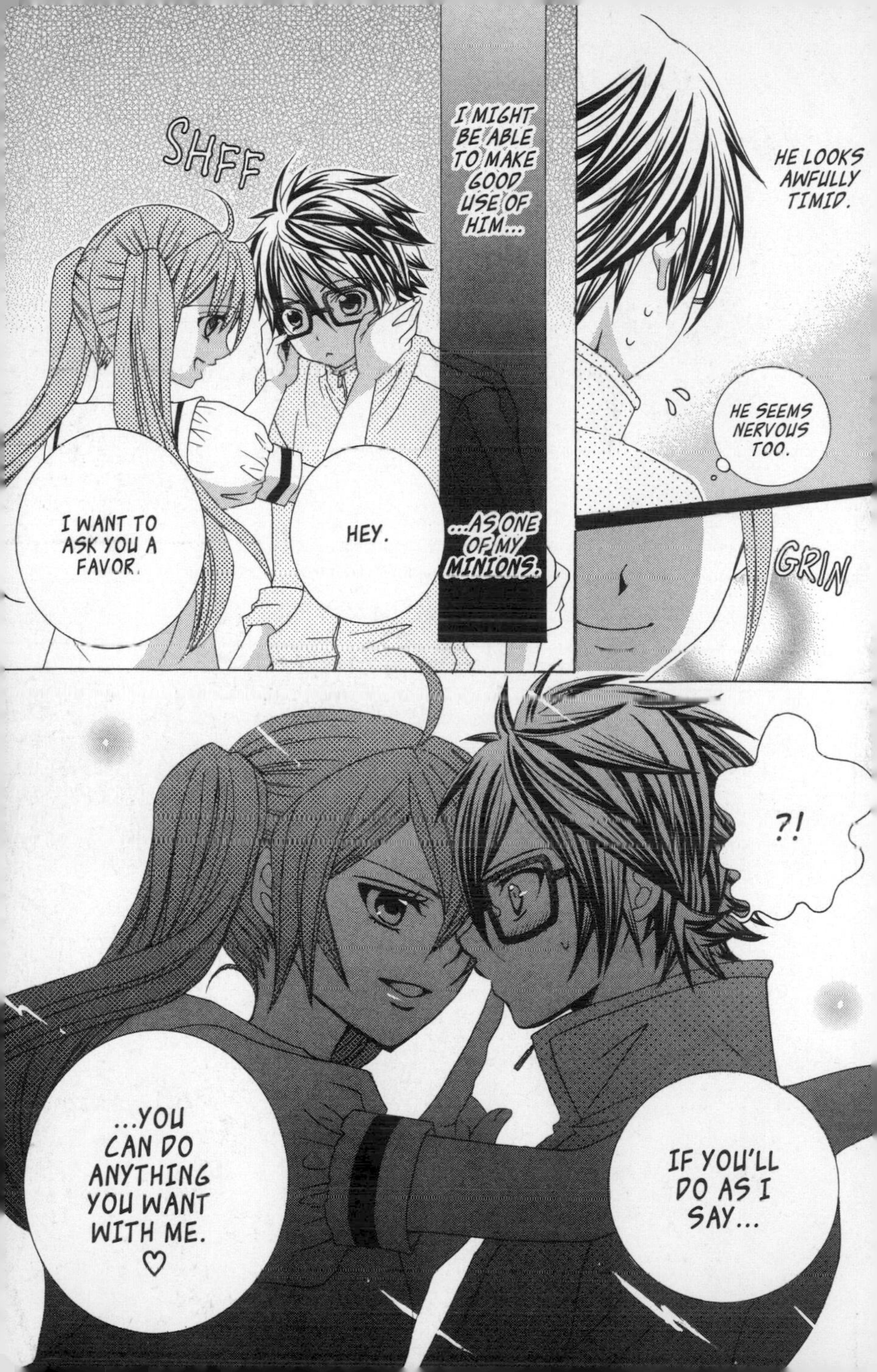
HE LOOKS AWFULLY TIMID.
HE SEEMS NERVOUS TOO.
GRIN
I MIGHT BE ABLE TO MAKE GOOD USE OF HIM...
...AS ONE OF MY MINIONS.
SHFF
HEY.
I WANT TO ASK YOU A FAVOR.
?!
IF YOU'LL DO AS I SAY...
...YOU CAN DO ANYTHING YOU WANT WITH ME. ♡

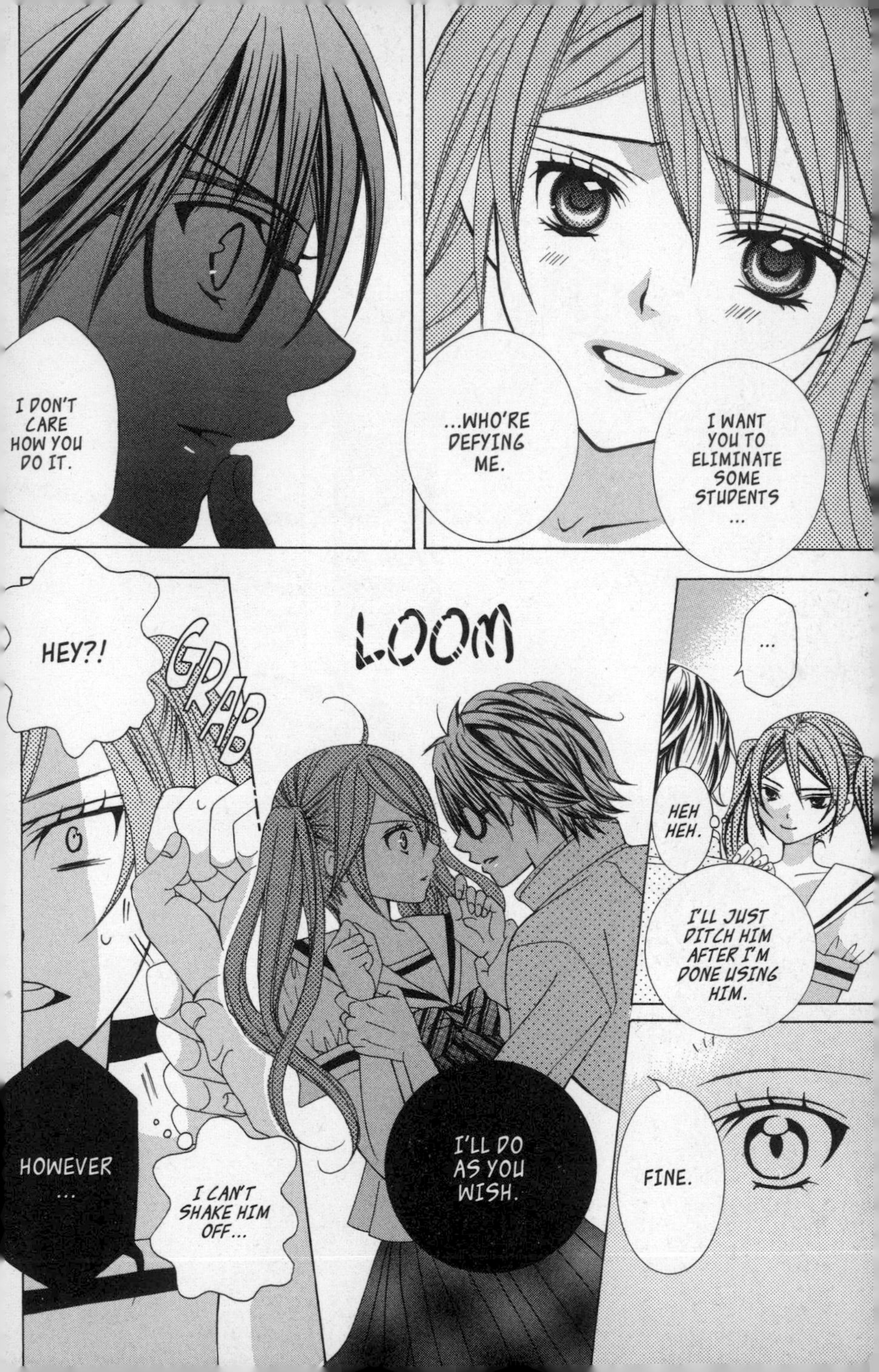
I WANT YOU TO ELIMINATE SOME STUDENTS ...
...WHO'RE DEFYING ME.
I DON'T CARE HOW YOU DO IT.
...
HEH HEH.
I'LL JUST DITCH HIM AFTER I'M DONE USING HIM.
FINE.
LOOM
HEY?!
GRAB
I'LL DO AS YOU WISH.
HOWEVER ...
I CAN'T SHAKE HIM OFF...

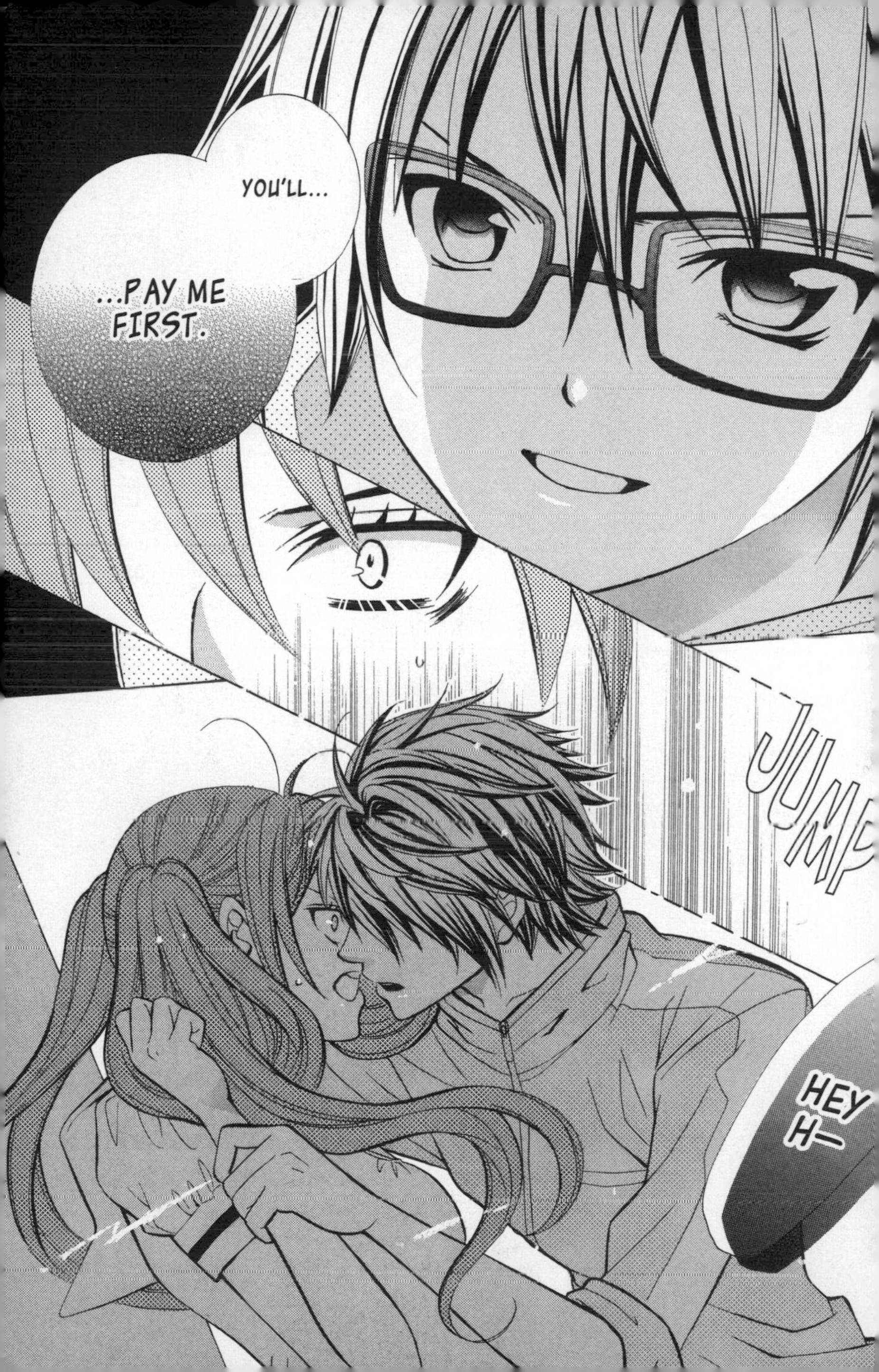
YOU'LL...
...PAY ME FIRST.
JUMP
HEY H—

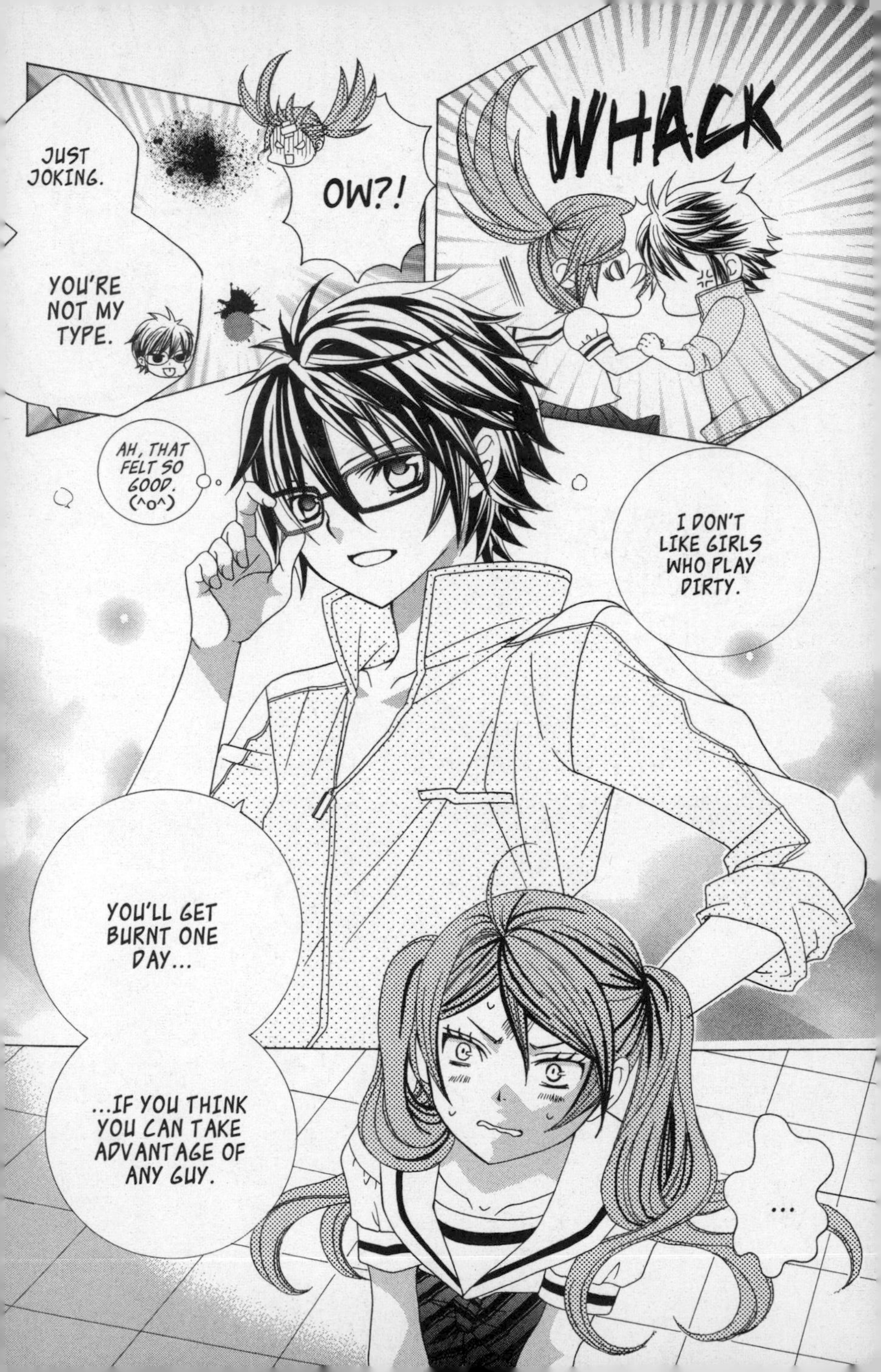
WHACK
JUST JOKING.
YOU'RE NOT MY TYPE.
OW?!
AH, THAT FELT SO GOOD. (^o^)
I DON'T LIKE GIRLS WHO PLAY DIRTY.
YOU'LL GET BURNT ONE DAY...
...IF YOU THINK YOU CAN TAKE ADVANTAGE OF ANY GUY.
...

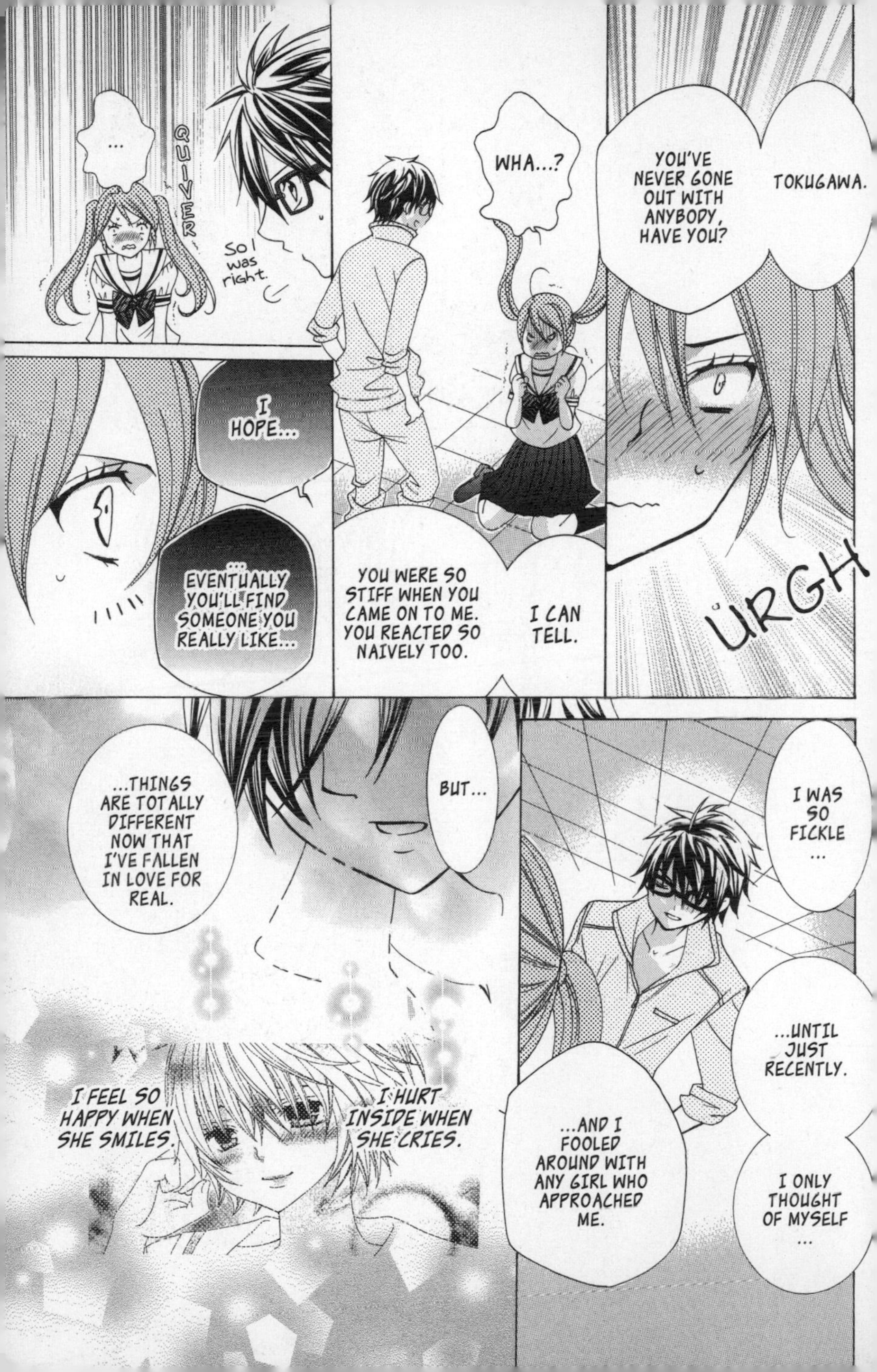
TOKUGAWA.
YOU'VE NEVER GONE OUT WITH ANYBODY, HAVE YOU?
URGH
WHA...?
I CAN TELL.
YOU WERE SO STIFF WHEN YOU CAME ON TO ME. YOU REACTED SO NAIVELY TOO.
...
QUIVER
So I was right.
I HOPE...
...EVENTUALLY YOU'LL FIND SOMEONE YOU REALLY LIKE...
I WAS SO FICKLE ...
...UNTIL JUST RECENTLY.
I ONLY THOUGHT OF MYSELF ...
...AND I FOOLED AROUND WITH ANY GIRL WHO APPROACHED ME.
BUT...
...THINGS ARE TOTALLY DIFFERENT NOW THAT I'VE FALLEN IN LOVE FOR REAL.
I HURT INSIDE WHEN SHE CRIES.
I FEEL SO HAPPY WHEN SHE SMILES.

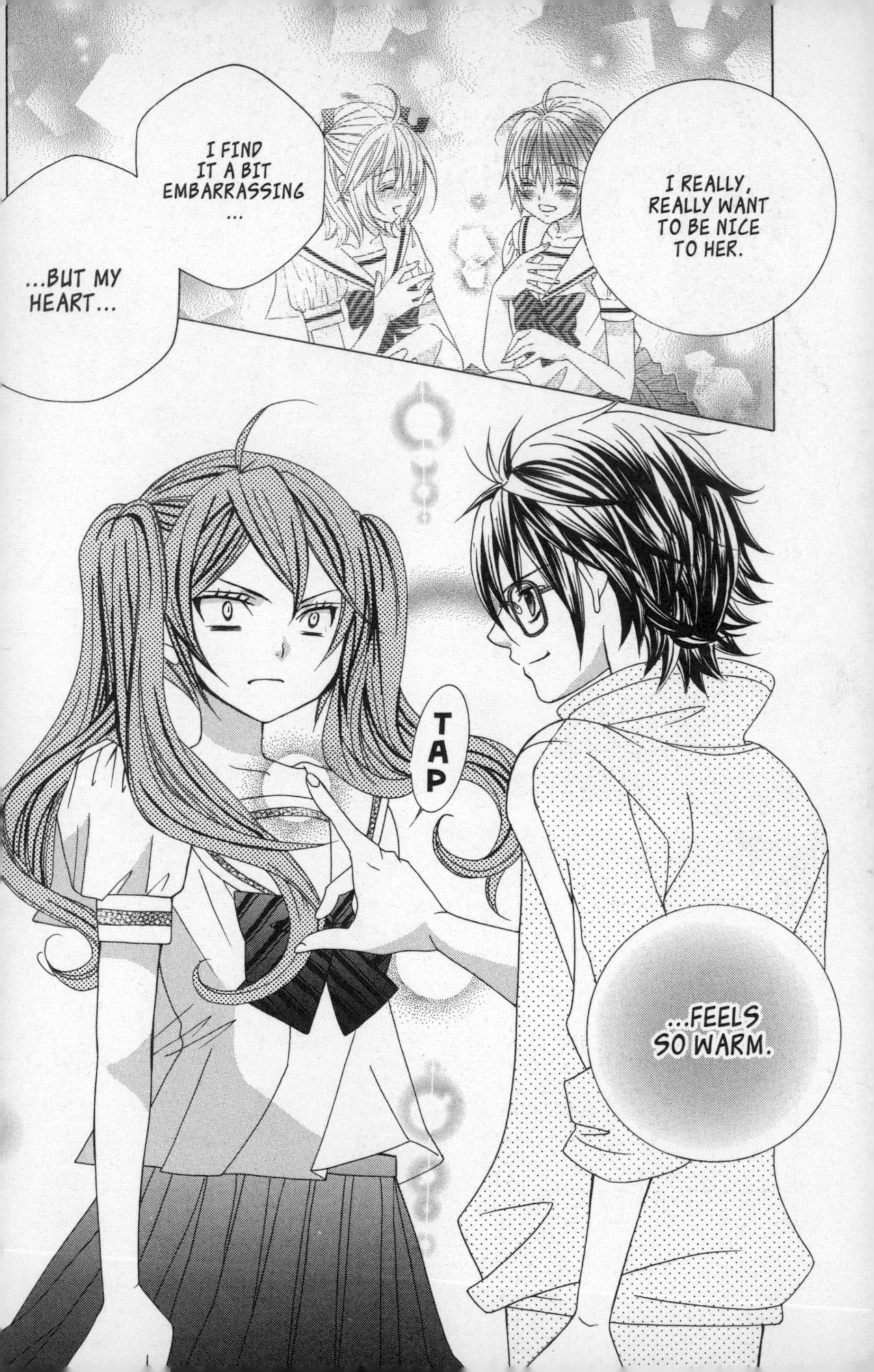

I REALLY, REALLY WANT TO BE NICE TO HER.
I FIND IT A BIT EMBARRASSING ...
...BUT MY HEART...
TAP
...FEELS SO WARM.

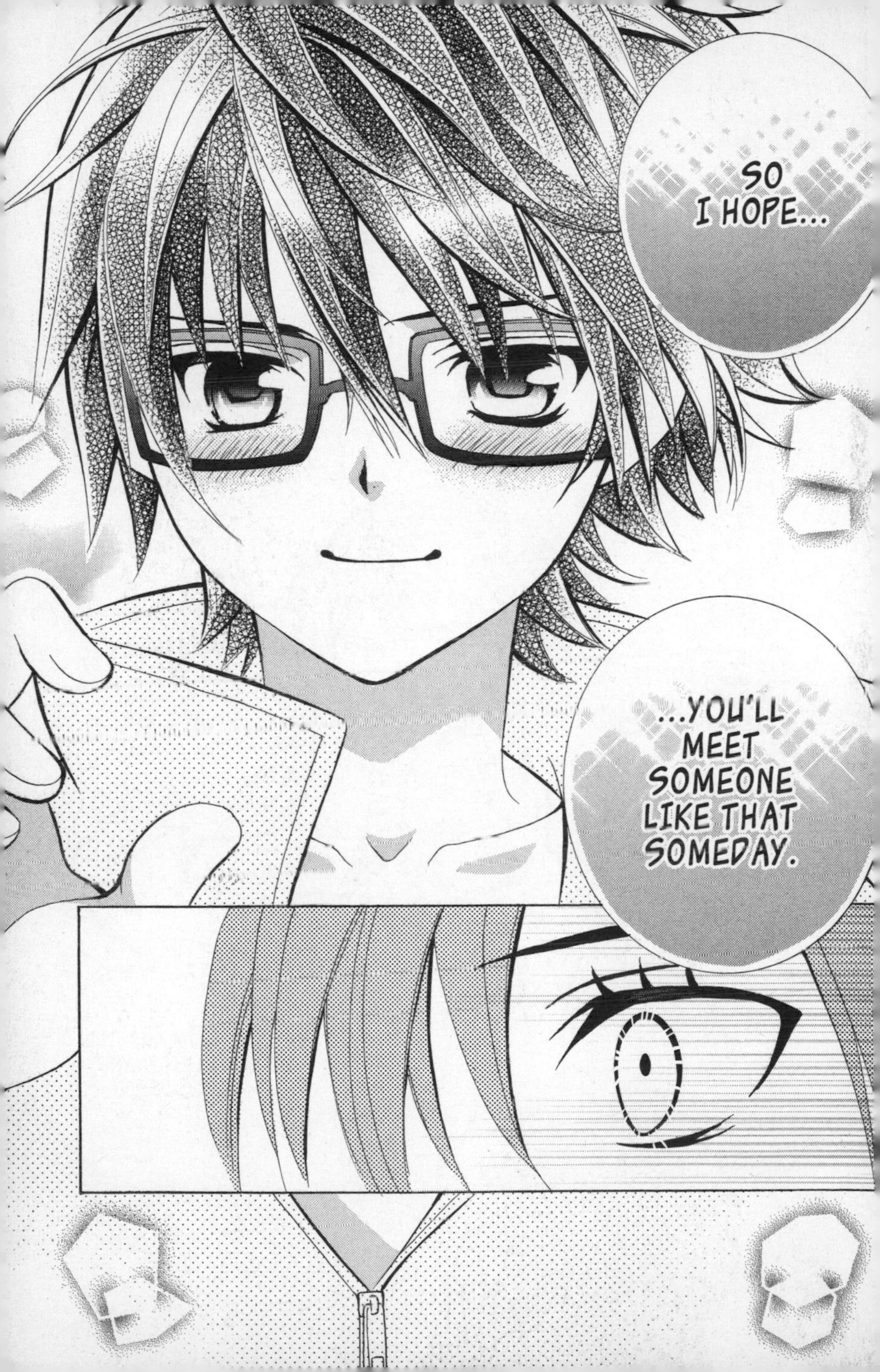
SO I HOPE...
...YOU'LL MEET SOMEONE LIKE THAT SOMEDAY.

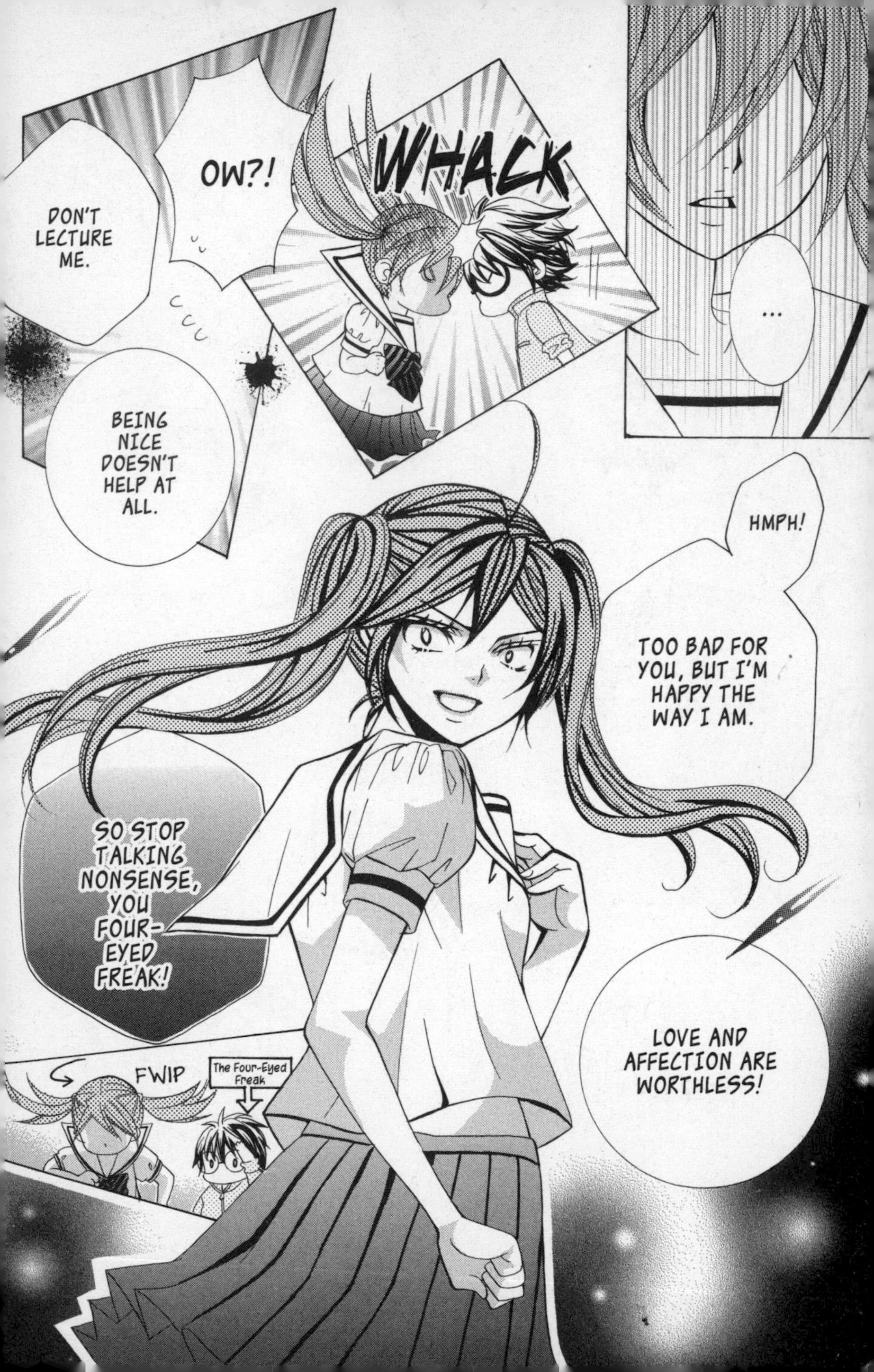
...
WHACK
OW?!
DON'T LECTURE ME.
BEING NICE DOESN'T HELP AT ALL.
HMPH!
TOO BAD FOR YOU, BUT I'M HAPPY THE WAY I AM.
SO STOP TALKING NONSENSE, YOU FOUR-EYED FREAK!
LOVE AND AFFECTION ARE WORTHLESS!
FWIP
The Four-Eyed Freak

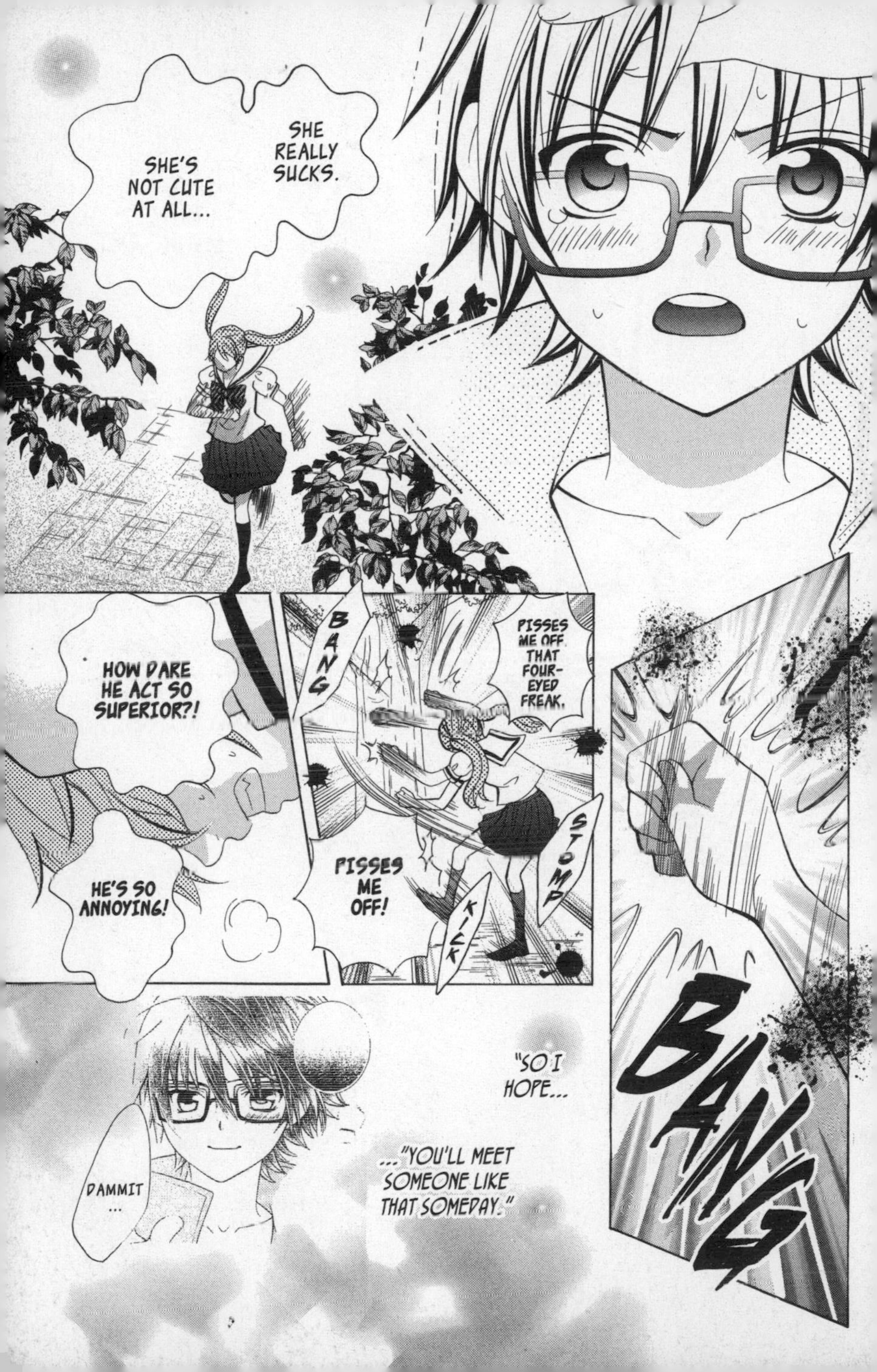
SHE REALLY SUCKS.
SHE'S NOT CUTE AT ALL...
BANG
PISSES ME OFF THAT FOUR-EYED FREAK.
BANG
STOMP
KICK
PISSES ME OFF!
HOW DARE HE ACT SO SUPERIOR?!
HE'S SO ANNOYING!
"SO I HOPE...
..."YOU'LL MEET SOMEONE LIKE THAT SOMEDAY."
DAMMIT ...

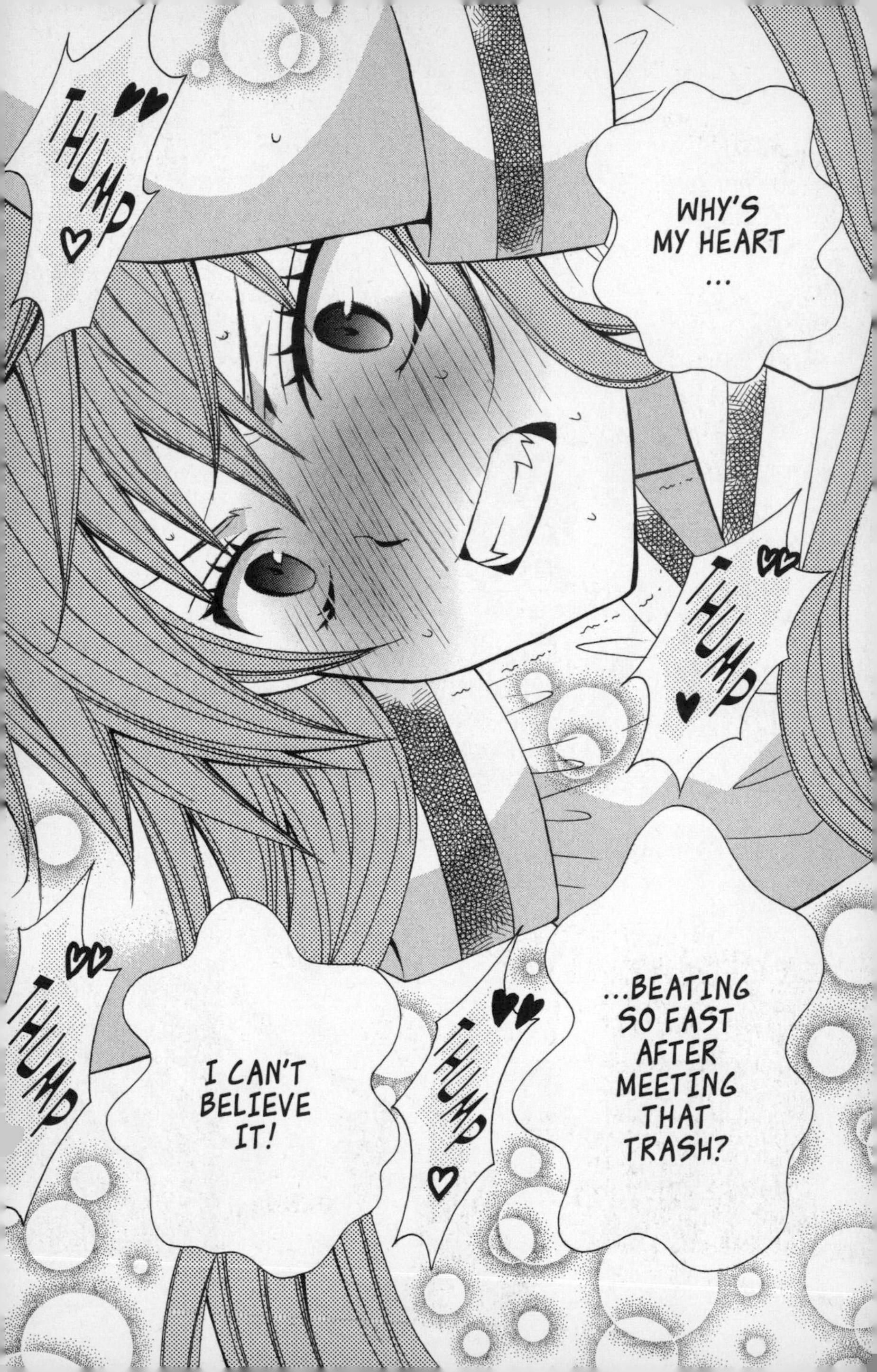
WHY'S MY HEART ...
THUMP
THUMP
...BEATING SO FAST AFTER MEETING THAT TRASH?
THUMP
I CAN'T BELIEVE IT!
THUMP

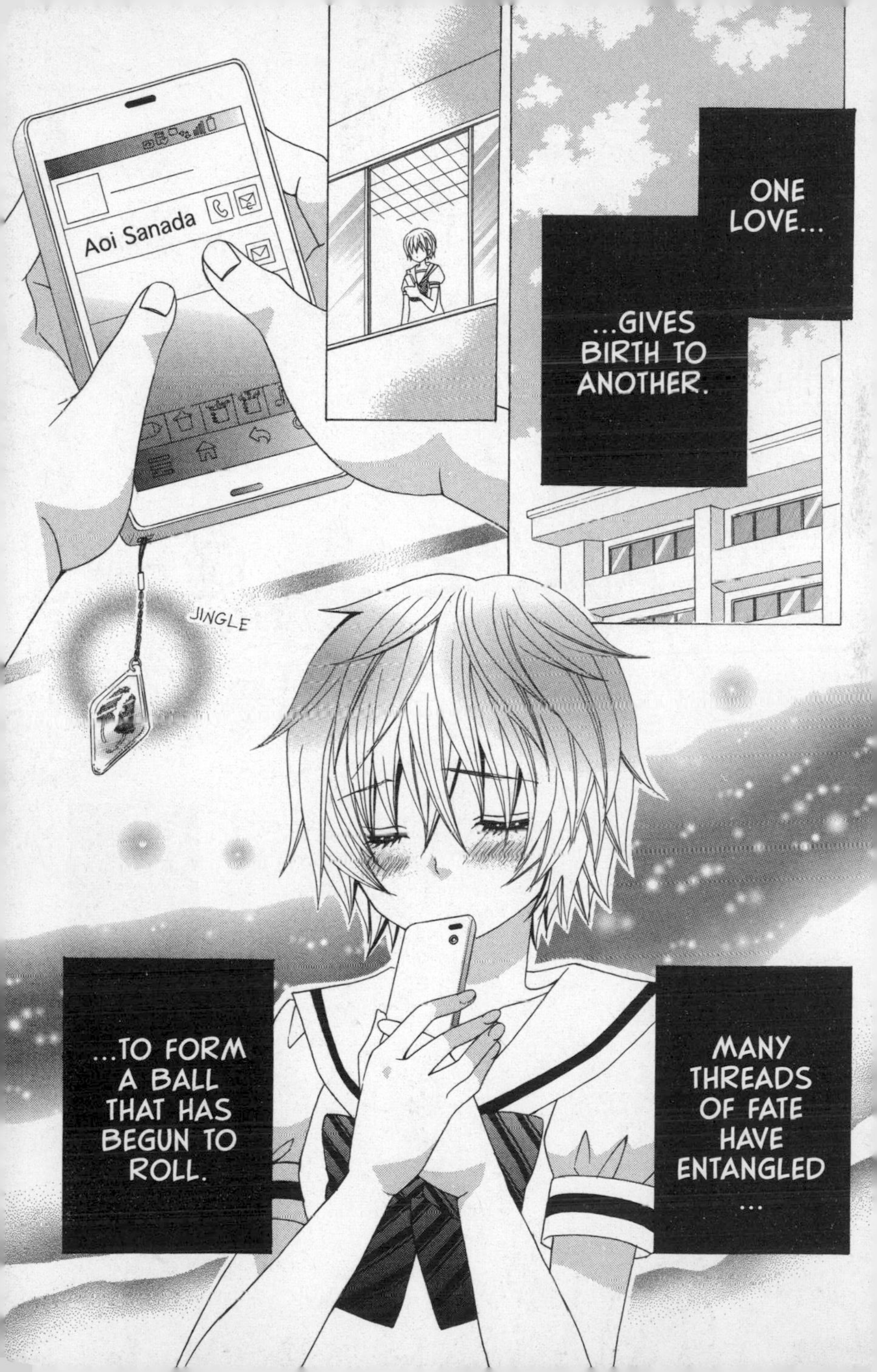
ONE LOVE...
...GIVES BIRTH TO ANOTHER.
Aoi Sanada
JINGLE
MANY THREADS OF FATE HAVE ENTANGLED...
...TO FORM A BALL THAT HAS BEGUN TO ROLL.

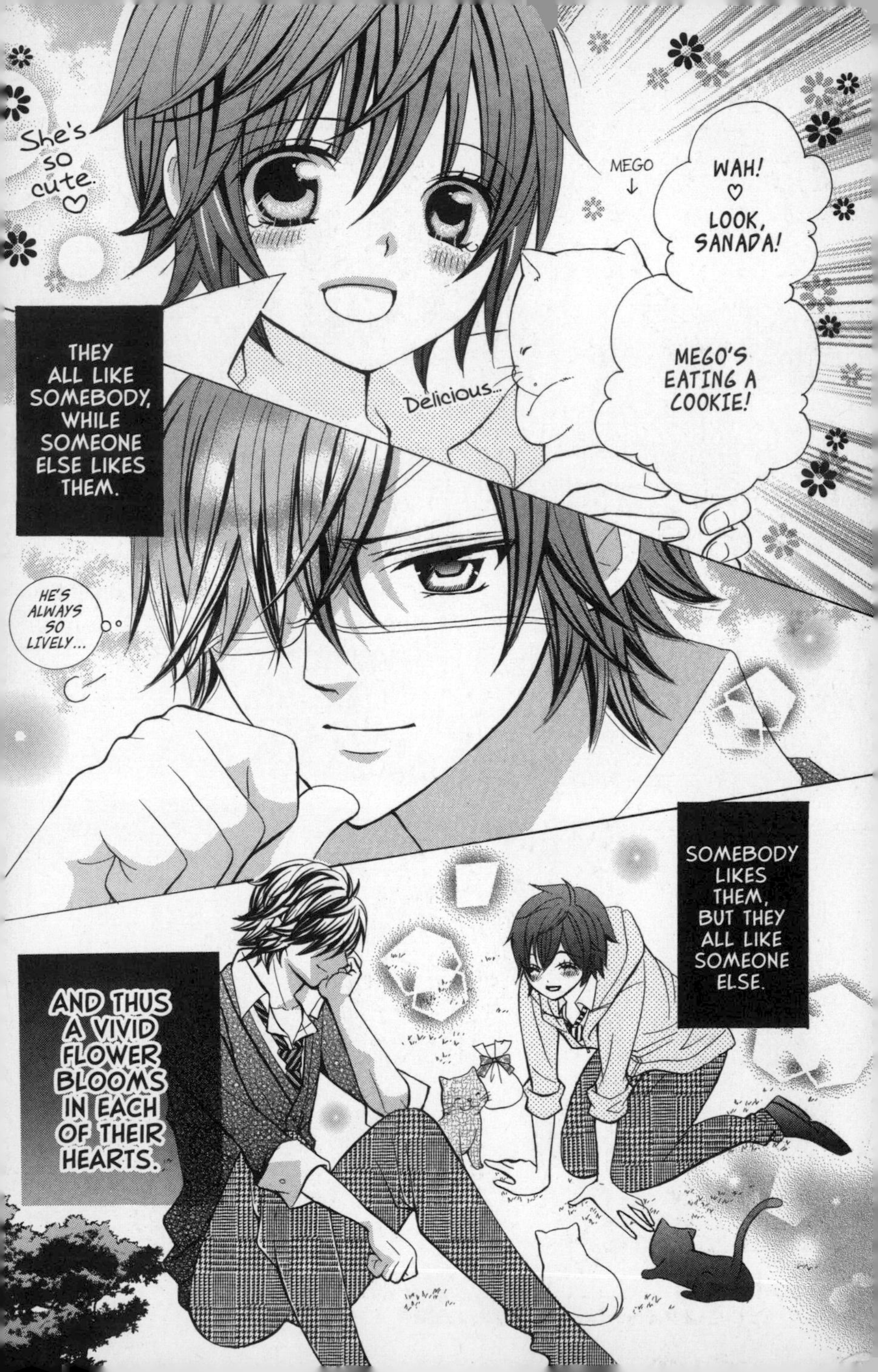
MEGO ↓
WAH! ♡ LOOK, SANADA!
MEGO'S EATING A COOKIE!
Delicious...
She's so cute. ♡
THEY ALL LIKE SOMEBODY, WHILE SOMEONE ELSE LIKES THEM.
HE'S ALWAYS SO LIVELY...
SOMEBODY LIKES THEM, BUT THEY ALL LIKE SOMEONE ELSE.
AND THUS A VIVID FLOWER BLOOMS IN EACH OF THEIR HEARTS.

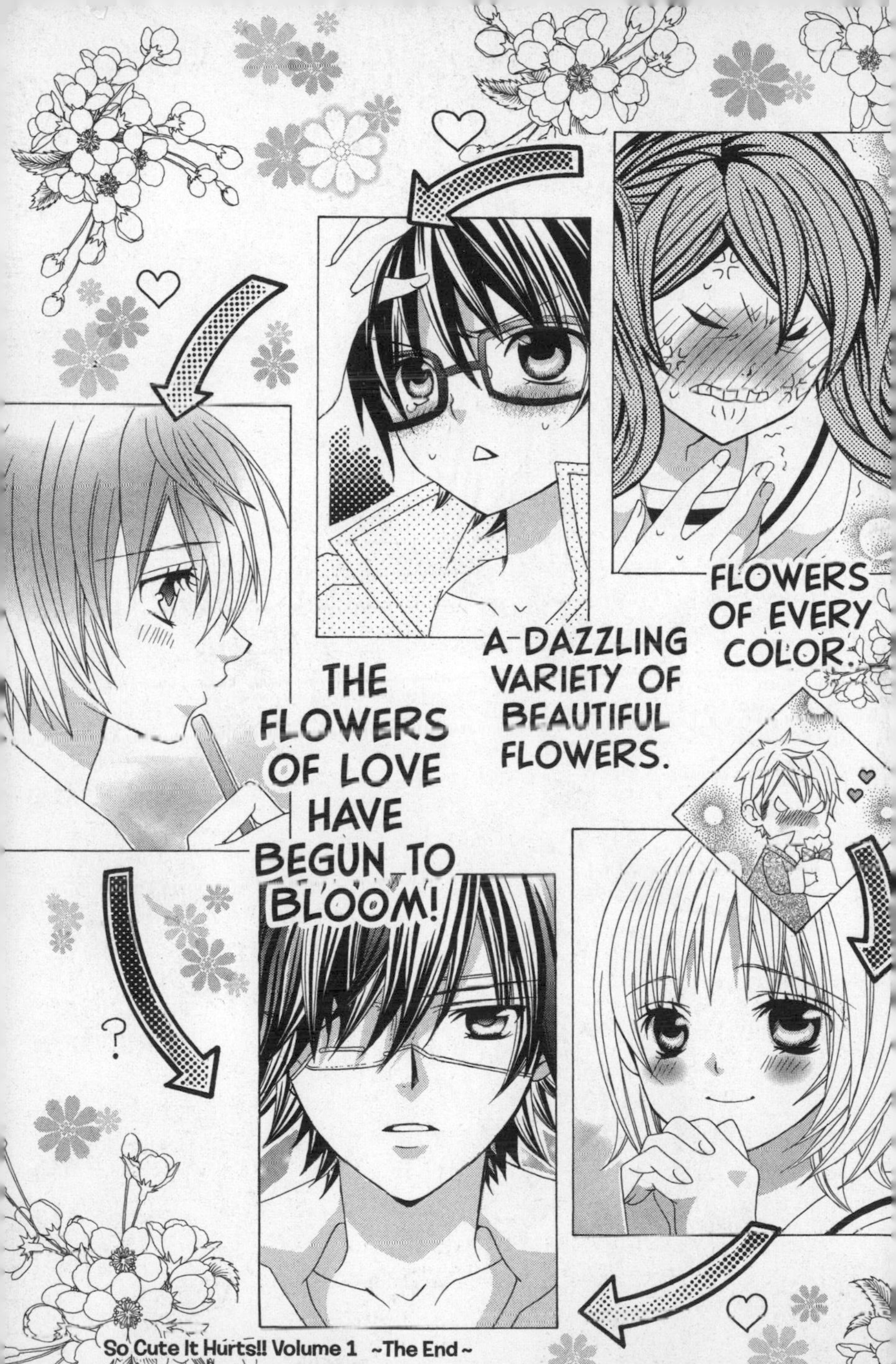
FLOWERS OF EVERY COLOR.
A-DAZZLING VARIETY OF BEAUTIFUL FLOWERS.
THE FLOWERS OF LOVE HAVE BEGUN TO BLOOM!

So Cute It Hurts!! Volume 1 ~The End~

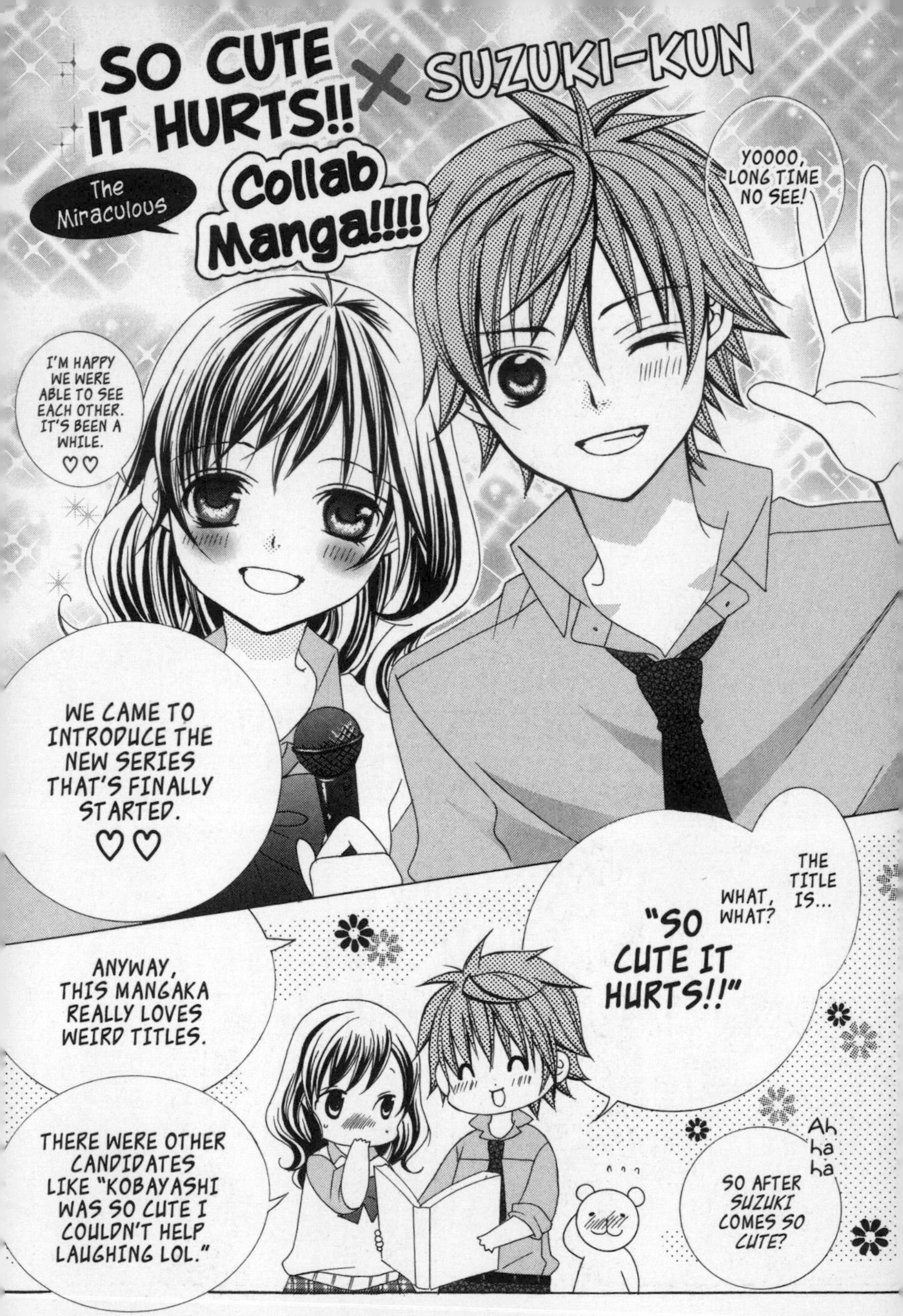
SO CUTE IT HURTS!! × SUZUKI-KUN
The Miraculous Collab Manga!!!!
YOOOO, LONG TIME NO SEE!
I'M HAPPY WE WERE ABLE TO SEE EACH OTHER. IT'S BEEN A WHILE. ♡♡
WE CAME TO INTRODUCE THE NEW SERIES THAT'S FINALLY STARTED. ♡♡
THE TITLE IS...
WHAT, WHAT?
"SO CUTE IT HURTS!!"
ANYWAY, THIS MANGAKA REALLY LOVES WEIRD TITLES.
THERE WERE OTHER CANDIDATES LIKE "KOBAYASHI WAS SO CUTE I COULDN'T HELP LAUGHING LOL."
Ah ha ha
SO AFTER SUZUKI COMES SO CUTE?

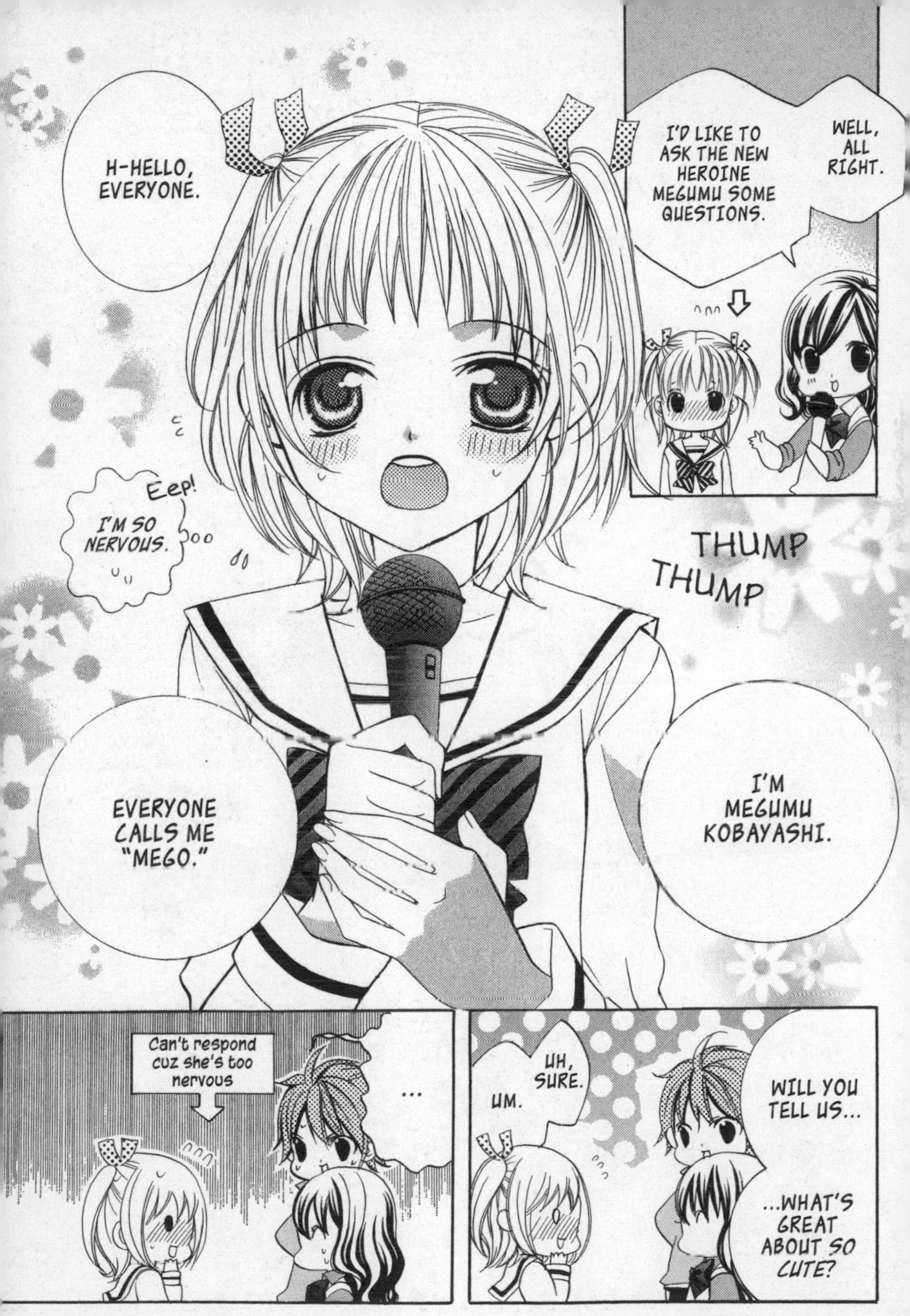
WELL, ALL RIGHT.
I'D LIKE TO ASK THE NEW HEROINE MEGUMU SOME QUESTIONS.
H-HELLO, EVERYONE.
THUMP THUMP
Eep!
I'M SO NERVOUS.
I'M MEGUMU KOBAYASHI.
EVERYONE CALLS ME "MEGO."
WILL YOU TELL US...
...WHAT'S GREAT ABOUT SO CUTE?
UH, SURE.
UM.
...
Can't respond cuz she's too nervous

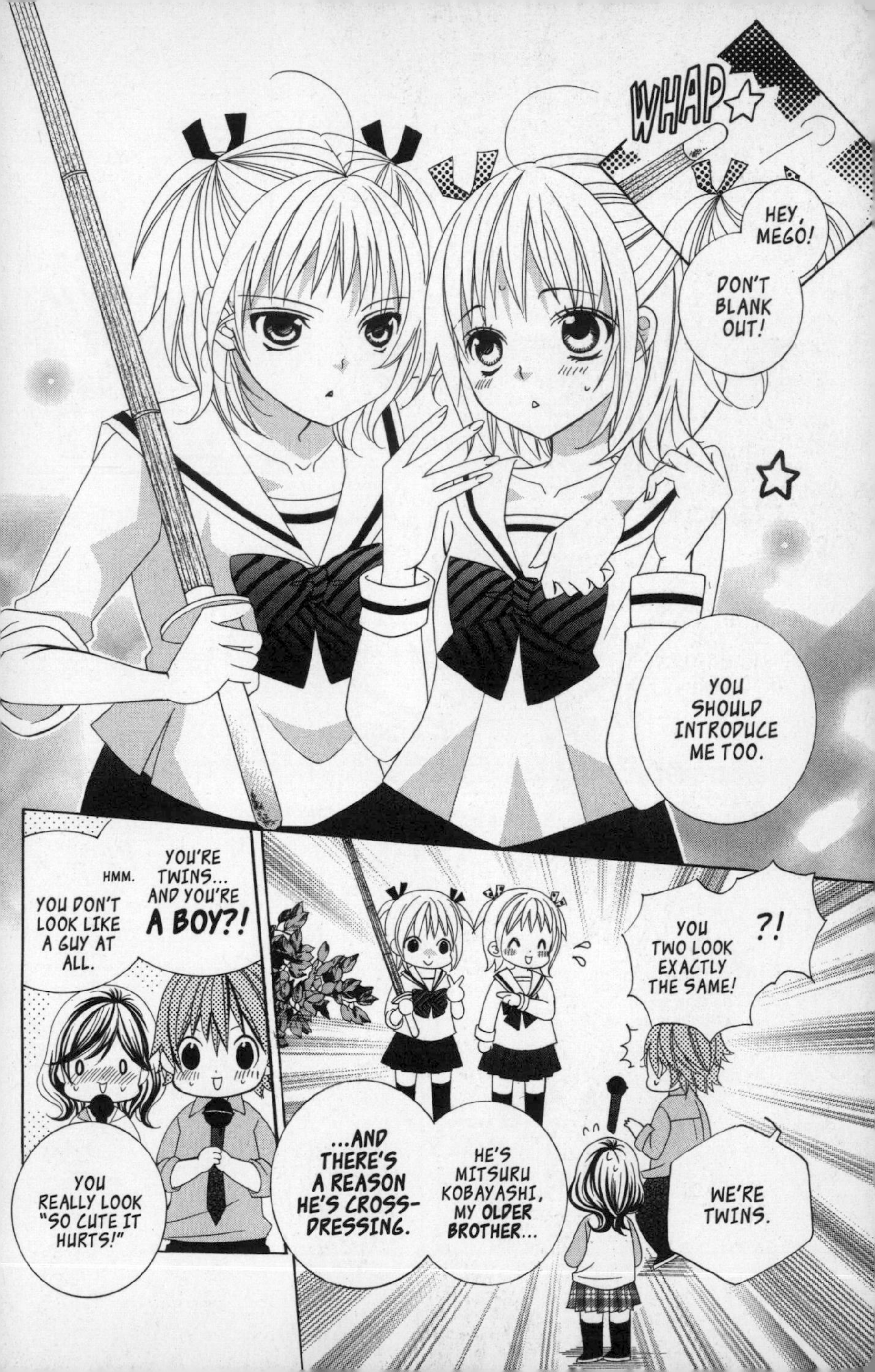
WHAP
HEY, MEGO!
DON'T BLANK OUT!
YOU SHOULD INTRODUCE ME TOO.
YOU TWO LOOK EXACTLY THE SAME!
?!
WE'RE TWINS.
HE'S MITSURU KOBAYASHI, MY OLDER BROTHER...
...AND THERE'S A REASON HE'S CROSS-DRESSING.
YOU'RE TWINS... AND YOU'RE A BOY?!
HMM.
YOU DON'T LOOK LIKE A GUY AT ALL.
YOU REALLY LOOK "SO CUTE IT HURTS!"

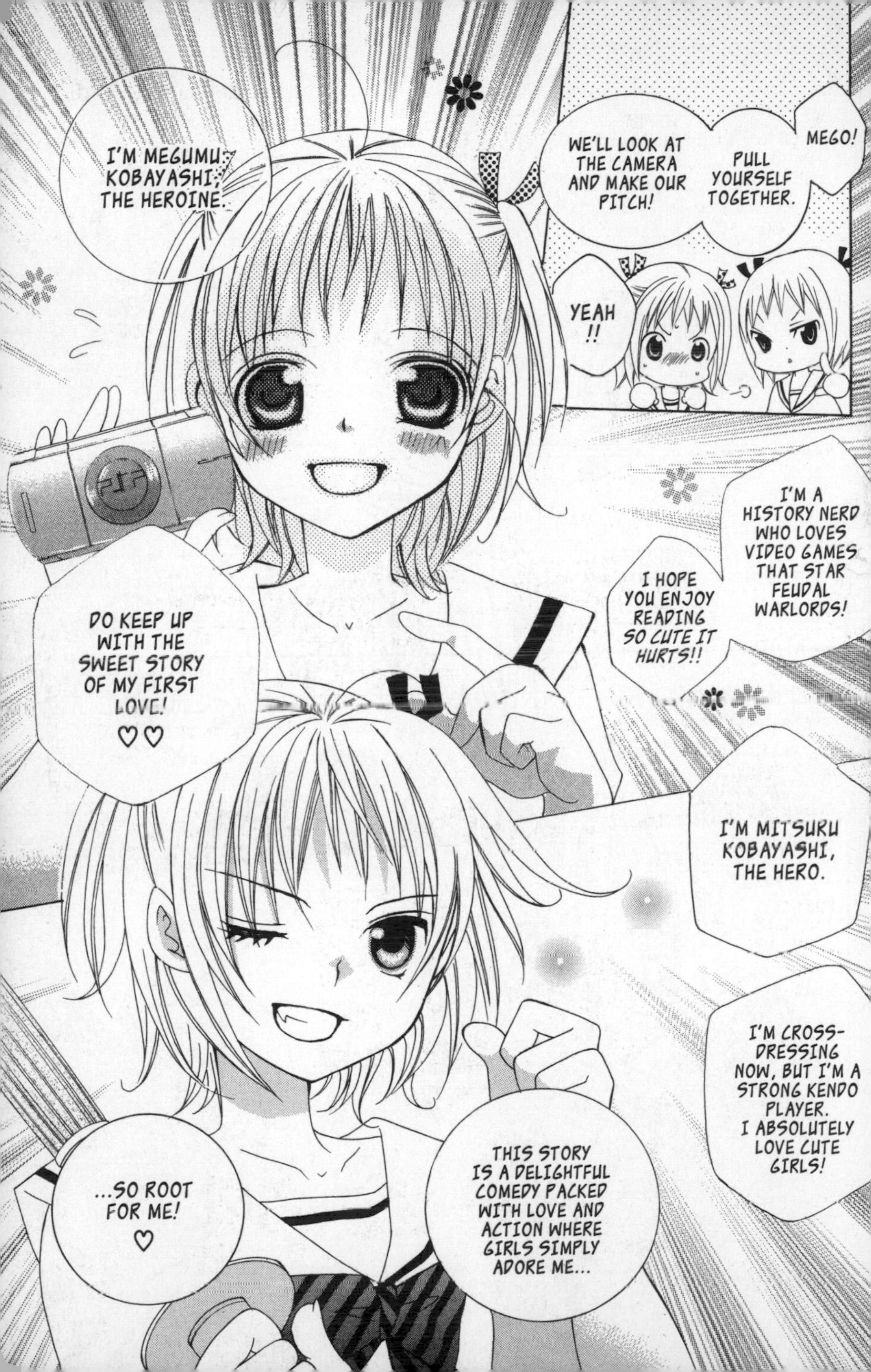
MEGO!
PULL YOURSELF TOGETHER.
WE'LL LOOK AT THE CAMERA AND MAKE OUR PITCH!
YEAH !!
I'M A HISTORY NERD WHO LOVES VIDEO GAMES THAT STAR FEUDAL WARLORDS!
I HOPE YOU ENJOY READING SO CUTE IT HURTS!!
I'M MEGUMU KOBAYASHI, THE HEROINE.
DO KEEP UP WITH THE SWEET STORY OF MY FIRST LOVE! ♡♡
I'M MITSURU KOBAYASHI, THE HERO.
I'M CROSS-DRESSING NOW, BUT I'M A STRONG KENDO PLAYER. I ABSOLUTELY LOVE CUTE GIRLS!
THIS STORY IS A DELIGHTFUL COMEDY PACKED WITH LOVE AND ACTION WHERE GIRLS SIMPLY ADORE ME...
...SO ROOT FOR ME! ♡

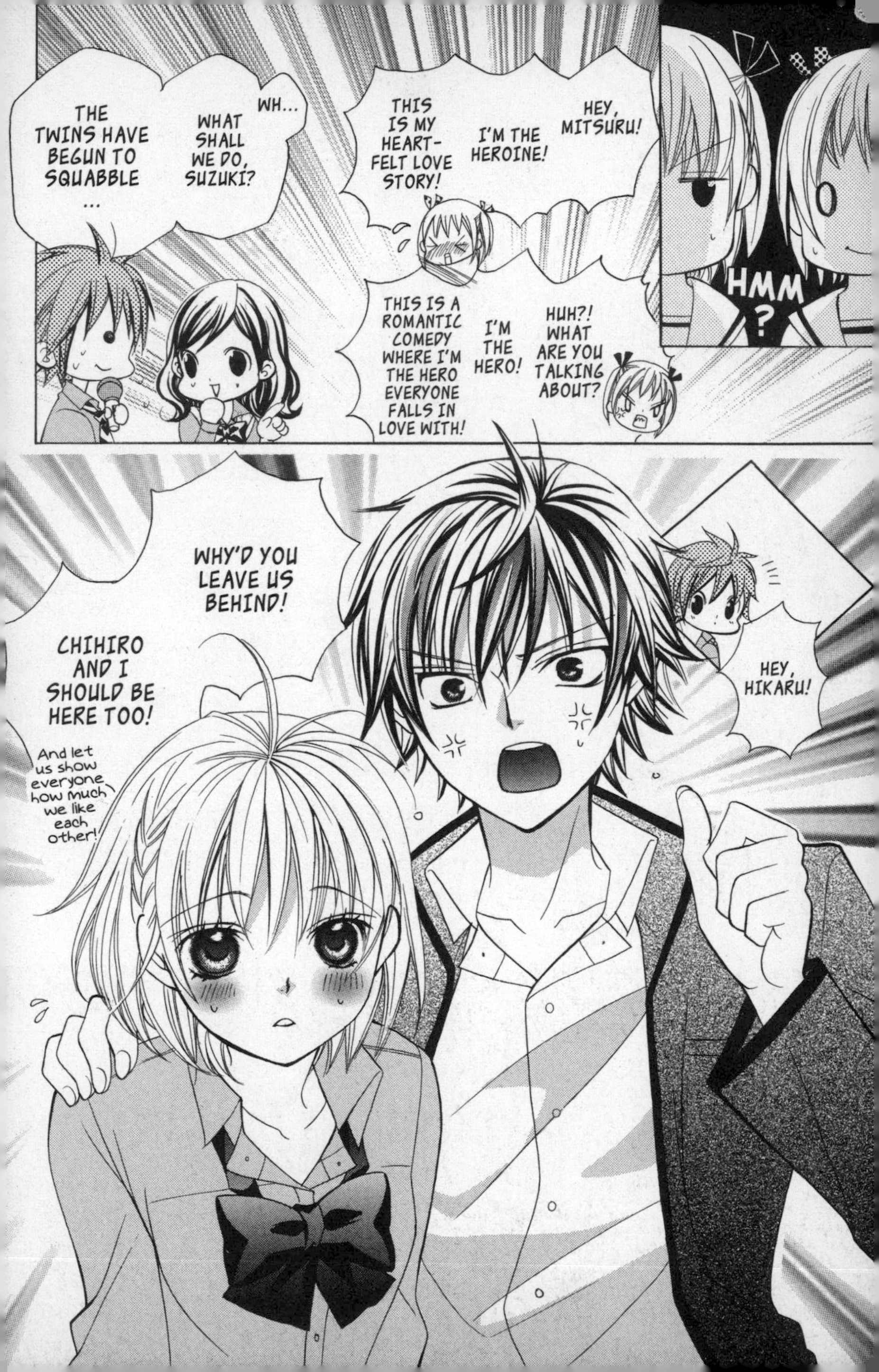
HMM ?
HEY, MITSURU!
I'M THE HEROINE!
THIS IS MY HEART-FELT LOVE STORY!
HUH?! WHAT ARE YOU TALKING ABOUT?
I'M THE HERO!
THIS IS A ROMANTIC COMEDY WHERE I'M THE HERO EVERYONE FALLS IN LOVE WITH!
WH...
WHAT SHALL WE DO, SUZUKI?
THE TWINS HAVE BEGUN TO SQUABBLE ...
HEY, HIKARU!
WHY'D YOU LEAVE US BEHIND!
CHIHIRO AND I SHOULD BE HERE TOO!
And let us show everyone how much we like each other!

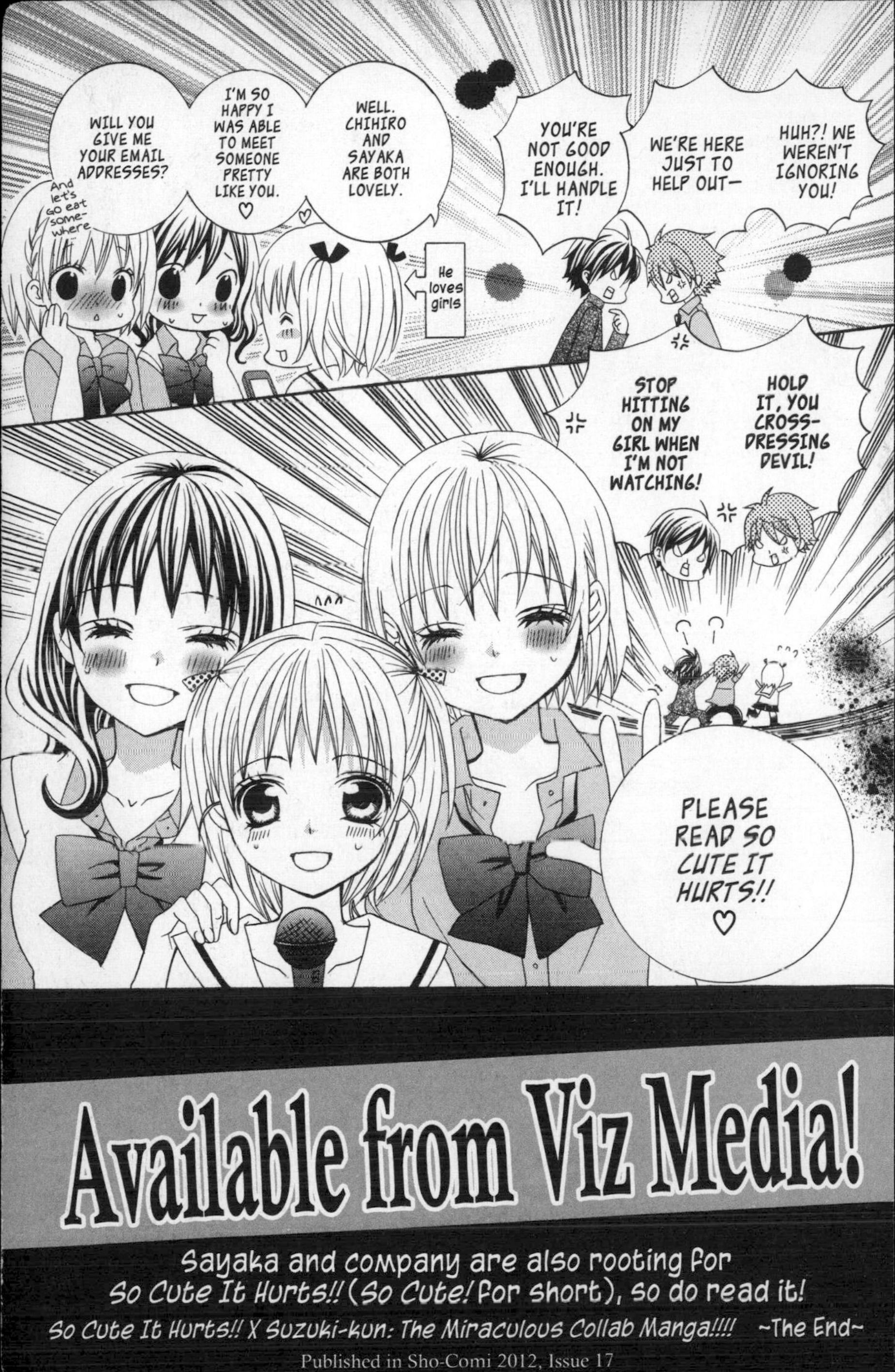
HUH?! WE WEREN'T IGNORING YOU!
WE'RE HERE JUST TO HELP OUT—
YOU'RE NOT GOOD ENOUGH. I'LL HANDLE IT!
WELL. CHIHIRO AND SAYAKA ARE BOTH LOVELY.
He loves girls
I'M SO HAPPY I WAS ABLE TO MEET SOMEONE PRETTY LIKE YOU. ♡
WILL YOU GIVE ME YOUR EMAIL ADDRESSES?
And let's go eat somewhere
HOLD IT, YOU CROSS-DRESSING DEVIL!
STOP HITTING ON MY GIRL WHEN I'M NOT WATCHING!
PLEASE READ SO CUTE IT HURTS!! ♡

Available from Viz Media!

Sayaka and company are also rooting for *So Cute It Hurts!!* (*So Cute!* for short), so do read it!

So Cute It Hurts!! X Suzuki-kun: The Miraculous Collab Manga!!!! ~The End~

Published in Sho-Comi 2012, Issue 17

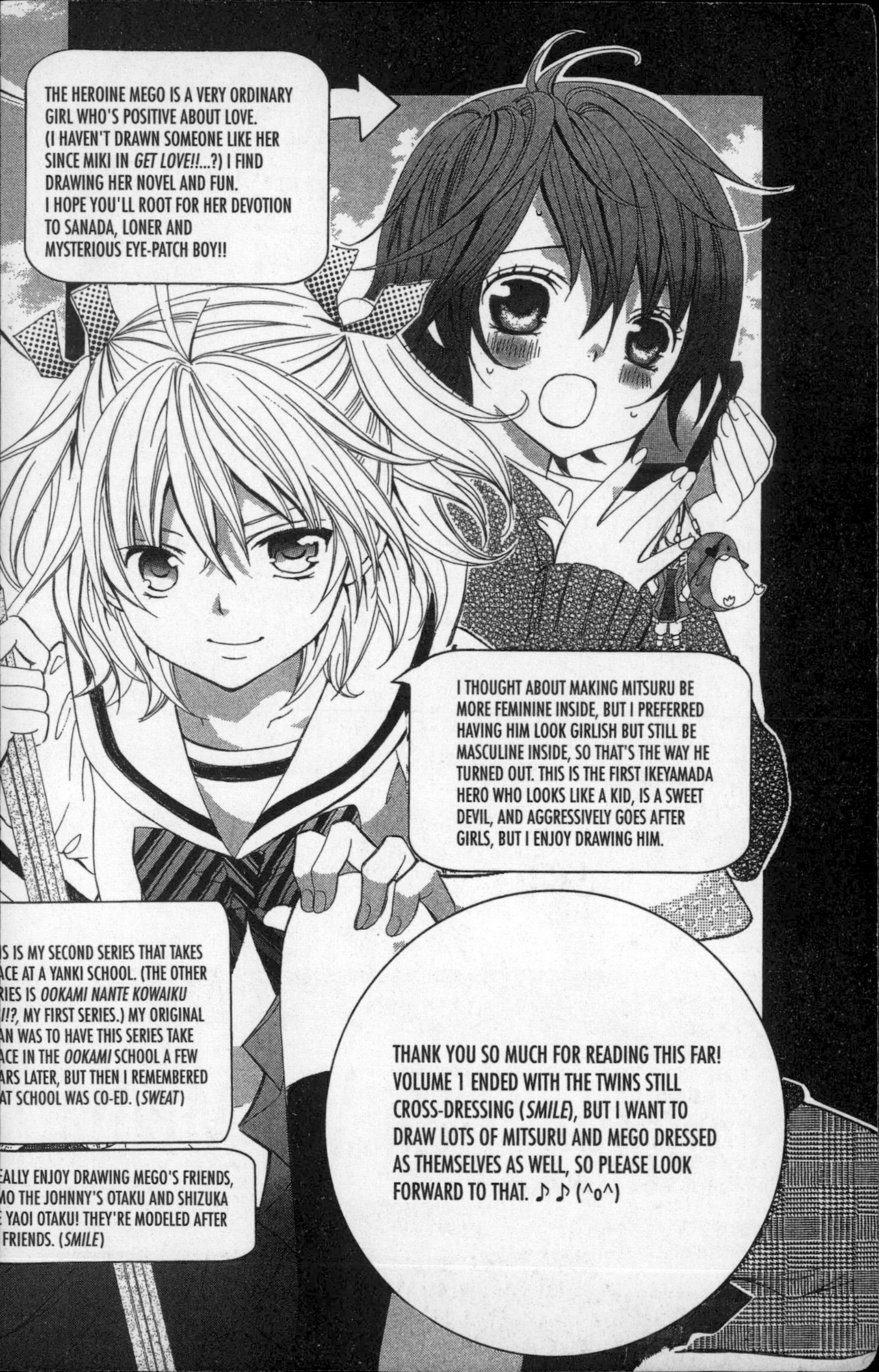
THE HEROINE MEGO IS A VERY ORDINARY GIRL WHO'S POSITIVE ABOUT LOVE. (I HAVEN'T DRAWN SOMEONE LIKE HER SINCE MIKI IN GET LOVE!!...?) I FIND DRAWING HER NOVEL AND FUN. I HOPE YOU'LL ROOT FOR HER DEVOTION TO SANADA, LONER AND MYSTERIOUS EYE-PATCH BOY!!
I THOUGHT ABOUT MAKING MITSURU BE MORE FEMININE INSIDE, BUT I PREFERRED HAVING HIM LOOK GIRLISH BUT STILL BE MASCULINE INSIDE, SO THAT'S THE WAY HE TURNED OUT. THIS IS THE FIRST IKEYAMADA HERO WHO LOOKS LIKE A KID, IS A SWEET DEVIL, AND AGGRESSIVELY GOES AFTER GIRLS, BUT I ENJOY DRAWING HIM.
THANK YOU SO MUCH FOR READING THIS FAR! VOLUME 1 ENDED WITH THE TWINS STILL CROSS-DRESSING (SMILE), BUT I WANT TO DRAW LOTS OF MITSURU AND MEGO DRESSED AS THEMSELVES AS WELL, SO PLEASE LOOK FORWARD TO THAT. ♪♪ (^o^)
S IS MY SECOND SERIES THAT TAKES ACE AT A YANKI SCHOOL. (THE OTHER RIES IS OOKAMI NANTE KOWAIKU I!?, MY FIRST SERIES.) MY ORIGINAL AN WAS TO HAVE THIS SERIES TAKE ACE IN THE OOKAMI SCHOOL A FEW ARS LATER, BUT THEN I REMEMBERED AT SCHOOL WAS CO-ED. (SWEAT)
EALLY ENJOY DRAWING MEGO'S FRIENDS, MO THE JOHNNY'S OTAKU AND SHIZUKA E YAOI OTAKU! THEY'RE MODELED AFTER FRIENDS. (SMILE)

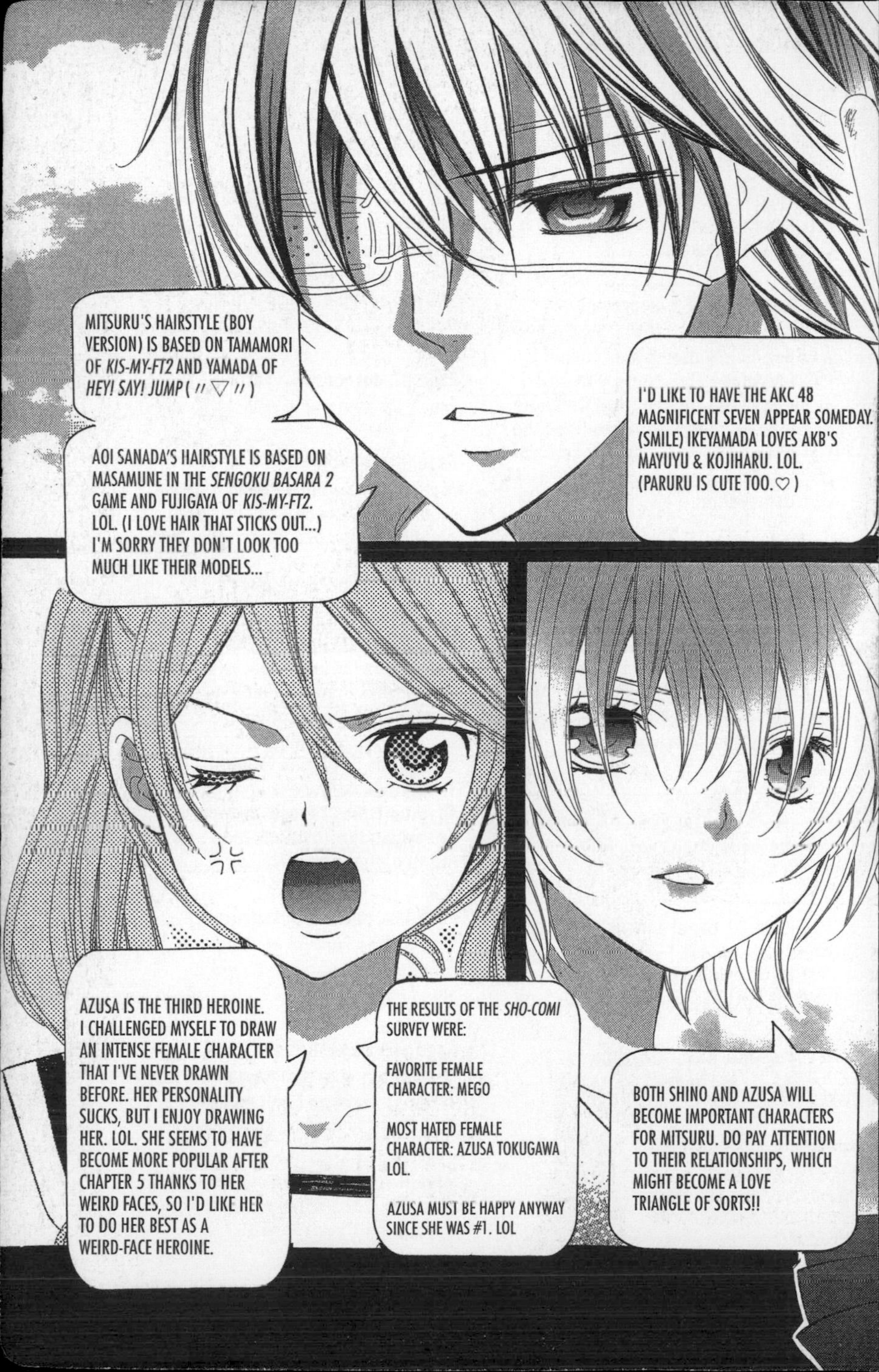
I'D LIKE TO HAVE THE AKC 48 MAGNIFICENT SEVEN APPEAR SOMEDAY. (SMILE) IKEYAMADA LOVES AKB'S MAYUYU & KOJIHARU. LOL. (PARURU IS CUTE TOO. ♡)
MITSURU'S HAIRSTYLE (BOY VERSION) IS BASED ON TAMAMORI OF *KIS-MY-FT2* AND YAMADA OF *HEY! SAY! JUMP* (〃▽〃)
AOI SANADA'S HAIRSTYLE IS BASED ON MASAMUNE IN THE *SENGOKU BASARA 2* GAME AND FUJIGAYA OF *KIS-MY-FT2*. LOL. (I LOVE HAIR THAT STICKS OUT...) I'M SORRY THEY DON'T LOOK TOO MUCH LIKE THEIR MODELS...
BOTH SHINO AND AZUSA WILL BECOME IMPORTANT CHARACTERS FOR MITSURU. DO PAY ATTENTION TO THEIR RELATIONSHIPS, WHICH MIGHT BECOME A LOVE TRIANGLE OF SORTS!!
THE RESULTS OF THE *SHO-COMI* SURVEY WERE:
FAVORITE FEMALE CHARACTER: MEGO
MOST HATED FEMALE CHARACTER: AZUSA TOKUGAWA LOL.
AZUSA MUST BE HAPPY ANYWAY SINCE SHE WAS #1. LOL
AZUSA IS THE THIRD HEROINE. I CHALLENGED MYSELF TO DRAW AN INTENSE FEMALE CHARACTER THAT I'VE NEVER DRAWN BEFORE. HER PERSONALITY SUCKS, BUT I ENJOY DRAWING HER. LOL. SHE SEEMS TO HAVE BECOME MORE POPULAR AFTER CHAPTER 5 THANKS TO HER WEIRD FACES, SO I'D LIKE HER TO DO HER BEST AS A WEIRD-FACE HEROINE.

GLOSSARY

Page 4, author note: Light novel
Light novels are similar to young adult novels in the U.S.

Page 7, panel 2: Sengoku era
The Sengoku (or Warring States) period in Japan lasted from the end of the 15th century to the end of the 16th century. Conflicts between feudal lords defined the era and were finally defused when the Tokugawa shogunate was established.

Page 8, panel 1: Kendo
Japanese fencing.

Page 8, panel 3: Akechi Boys' High
The school shares a name with a 16th century feudal lord named Mitsuhide Akechi who betrayed his overlord Nobunaga Oda.

Page 12, panel 5: Yaoi
Boy's Love, or stories with male-male romance made for a largely female audience.

Page 30, panel 4: Azusa Tokugawa
Azusa shares her last name with Ieyasu Tokugawa, who established the Tokugawa shogunate in 1603.

Page 66, panel 4: 1,250 yen
About $11.70 U.S.

Page 75, panel 3: Sayaka Hoshino, Erika Aoi
Characters in Go Ikeyamada's previous series *Suki desu Suzuki-kun!!*. Sayaka and Erika both become star actresses.

Page 87, author note: Furoku
Free gifts that come with magazines.

Page 99, panel 1: Yanki
A *yanki* is a juvenile delinquent or young gangster. They're young people who smoke, start fights, etc. Some create gangs, and some just wander the streets alone.

Page 99, panel 2: Aoi Sanada
Aoi shares his last name with Yukimura Sanada, a feudal warlord who served the Toyotomi clan. He died at Osaka Castle during the last of a series of battles fought by the Tokugawa shogunate against the Toyotomi clan. Ieyasu Tokugawa destroyed the Toyotomi clan as a result of these battles.

Page 134, panel 1: Dokuganryu
This means "one-eyed dragon." Masamune lost his right eye to smallpox.

Page 146, panel 1: Tosho High
Tosho High shares a name with the Toshogu shrines, Shinto shrines dedicated to Ieyasu Tokugawa.

Page 167, panel 3: Famous detective
This refers to the main character of the manga *Case Closed*.

AUTHOR BIO

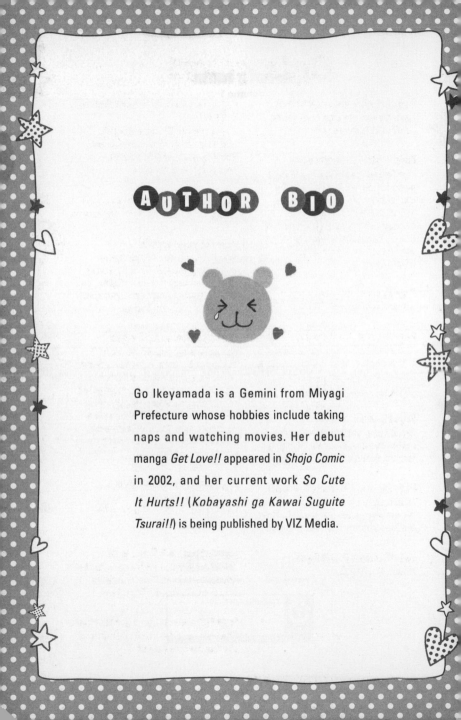

Go Ikeyamada is a Gemini from Miyagi Prefecture whose hobbies include taking naps and watching movies. Her debut manga *Get Love!!* appeared in *Shojo Comic* in 2002, and her current work *So Cute It Hurts!!* (*Kobayashi ga Kawai Suguite Tsurai!!*) is being published by VIZ Media.

SO CUTE I
Volu

Shojo Beat Edition

STORY AND ART BY
GO IKEYAMADA

English Translation & Adaptation/Tomo Kimura
Touch-Up Art & Lettering/Joanna Estep
Design/Izumi Evers
Editor/Pancha Diaz

KOBAYASHI GA KAWAISUGITE TSURAI!! Vol.1
by Go IKEYAMADA
© 2012 Go IKEYAMADA
All rights reserved.
Original Japanese edition published by SHOGAKUKAN.
English translation rights in the United States of America, Canada,
United Kingdom and Ireland arranged with SHOGAKUKAN.

Published by VIZ Media, LLC
P.O. Box 77010
San Francisco, CA 94107

10 9 8 7 6 5 4 3 2 1
First printing, June 2015

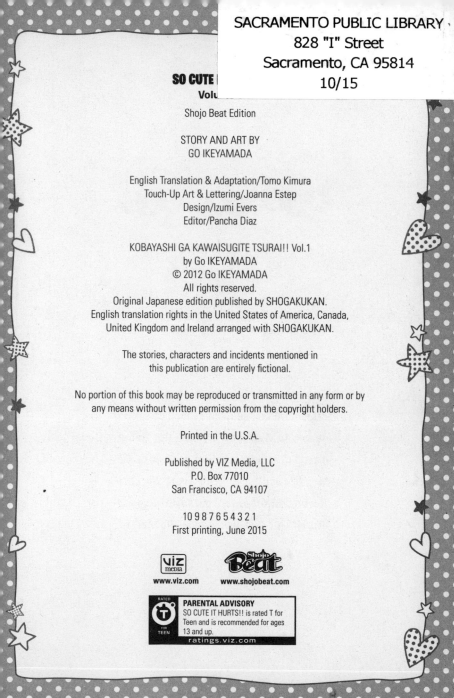

www.viz.com   www.shojobeat.com